'In an ocean of studies on the Grand Epic – The *Mahābhārata* – Brian Black's voice is unique, fresh and compelling. In a careful and detailed dialogic reading of select plots involving central characters like Bhishma, Draupadi, Duryodhana and Sri Krishna, the author points out inherent dialogicality in the epic text. This work is an important contribution to Indological and Dialogic Studies'.

Lakshmi Bandlamudi*, Professor,*
City University of New York.

'This wonderfully rich book by Brian Black emphasizes the often noted subtlety of the *dharma* in the *Mahābhārata*, and brilliantly shows how that subtlety carries different connotations depending on who is speaking, and the circumstances. This insightful work provides depth and specificity to our view of the text's presentation of the *dharma* as subtle, and is a major contribution to our understanding of the *Mahābhārata*'.

Bruce M. Sullivan*, Professor Emeritus,*
Northern Arizona University.

In Dialogue with the *Mahābhārata*

The *Mahābhārata* has been explored extensively as a work of mythology, epic poetry, and religious literature, but the text's philosophical dimensions have largely been under-appreciated by Western scholars. This book explores the philosophical implications of the *Mahābhārata* by paying attention to the centrality of dialogue, both as the text's prevailing literary expression and its organising structure. Focusing on five sets of dialogues about controversial moral problems in the central story, this book shows that philosophical deliberation is an integral part of the narrative. Black argues that by paying attention to how characters make arguments and how dialogues unfold, we can better appreciate the *Mahābhārata*'s philosophical significance and its potential contribution to debates in comparative philosophy today.

This is a fresh perspective on the *Mahābhārata* that will be of great interest to any scholar working in religious studies, Indian/South Asian religions, comparative philosophy, and world literature.

Brian Black received his MA and PhD at SOAS (University of London) and is now a lecturer in the Department of Politics, Philosophy and Religion at Lancaster University. His research interests include Indian religion and philosophy, comparative philosophy, the use of dialogue in Indian religious and philosophical texts, and Hindu and Buddhist ethics. He is the author of the book *The Character of the Self in Ancient India: Priests, Kings, and Women in the Early Upaniṣads*.

Dialogues in South Asian Traditions
Religion, Philosophy, Literature and History
Series Editors:
Laurie Patton, Middlebury College, USA
Brian Black, Lancaster University, UK
Chakravarthi Ram-Prasad, Lancaster University, UK

Face-to-face conversation and dialogue are defining features of South Asian traditional texts, rituals, and practices. Not only has the region of South Asia always consisted of a multiplicity of peoples and cultures in communication with each other, but also performed and written dialogues have been indelible features within the religions of South Asia; Hinduism, Buddhism, Jainism, Sikhism, and Islam are all multi-vocal religions. Their doctrines, practices, and institutions have never had only one voice of authority, and dialogue has been a shared tactic for negotiating contesting interpretations within each tradition.

This series examines the use of the dialogical genre in South Asian religious and cultural traditions. Historical inquiries into the plurality of religious identity in South Asia, particularly when constructed by the dialogical genre, are crucial in an age when, as Amartya Sen has recently observed, singular identities seem to hold more destructive sway than multiple ones. This series approaches dialogue in its widest sense, including discussion, debate, argument, conversation, communication, confrontation, and negotiation. Opening up a dynamic historical and literary mode of analysis, which assumes the plural dimensions of religious identities and communities from the start, this series challenges many outdated assumptions and representations of South Asian religions.

In Dialogue with the *Mahābhārata*
Brian Black

For more information and a full list of titles in the series, please visit: https://www.routledge.com/Dialogues-in-South-Asian-Traditions-Religion-Philosophy-Literature-and-History/book-series/ASTHASIAREL

In Dialogue with the *Mahābhārata*

Brian Black

Routledge
Taylor & Francis Group
LONDON AND NEW YORK

First published 2021
by Routledge
2 Park Square, Milton Park, Abingdon, Oxon OX14 4RN

and by Routledge
52 Vanderbilt Avenue, New York, NY 10017

Routledge is an imprint of the Taylor & Francis Group, an informa business

British Library Cataloguing-in-Publication Data
A catalogue record for this book is available from the British Library

Library of Congress Cataloging-in-Publication Data
Names: Black, Brian, 1970– author.
Title: In dialogue with the Mahābhārata / Brian Black.
Description: Abingdon, Oxon ; New York : Routledge, 2021. | Includes bibliographical references and index.
Identifiers: LCCN 2020026724 (print) | LCCN 2020026725 (ebook) | ISBN 9780367436001 (hardback) | ISBN 9780367438142 (ebook)
Subjects: LCSH: Mahābhārata—Criticism, interpretation, etc. | Dialogue in literature.
Classification: LCC BL1138.27 .B59 2021 (print) | LCC BL1138.27 (ebook) | DDC 294.5/923046—dc23
LC record available at https://lccn.loc.gov/2020026724
LC ebook record available at https://lccn.loc.gov/2020026725

ISBN: 978-0-367-43600-1 (hbk)
ISBN: 978-0-367-43814-2 (ebk)

Typeset in Sabon
by codeMantra

To Yulia, Harrison, and Sonya

Contents

Acknowledgements xi

Introduction 1

1 Bhīṣma's vows 23

2 Draupadī's marriage 57

3 Duryodhana's despair/Yudhiṣṭhira's decision 82

4 Draupadī's questions 115

5 Kṛṣṇa's conversations 148

Conclusion 178

List of characters 191
List of parvans 195
Bibliography 199
Index 209

Acknowledgements

This book is not only about dialogue, but it is also very much the product of the many conversations, discussions, and debates I have had with colleagues, students, and friends about the *Mahābhārata*. There are many dialogue partners I would like to thank for their feedback and insights during the time I have been writing this book. First, I thank my colleague Chakravarthi Ram-Prasad, with whom I have been discussing the *Mahābhārata*, as well as other topics in Indian philosophy and religion, for the past ten years. I also thank the Arts and Humanities Research Council, which provided the financial support and teaching cover for me to write this book.

I offer heartfelt thanks to Naomi Appleton, who has read drafts of every chapter, as well as a draft of the final manuscript. Her feedback, support, and friendship has been invaluable throughout this entire process. I also express my sincere gratitude to Jackie Hirst, who – after hearing me deliver a rather speculative conference paper eight years ago – told me I was writing a book before I realised it myself. She has read drafts of many chapters, offering indispensable feedback each time.

I am also grateful to the following people who have read drafts of chapters and offered constructive comments: Uma Chakravarti, Jonathan Geen, Emily Hudson, Tamar Reich, Bruce Sullivan, Lynn Thomas, and Anand Vaidya. I also thank the following people, with whom I have had conversations about the *Mahābhārata* and dialogue over the past several years: Rajeev Bhargava, Simon Brodbeck, Kunal Chakrabarti, Arti Dhand, Jessica Frazier, James Hegarty, Alf Hiltebeitel, Veena Howard, Monika Kirloskar-Steinbach, James Madaio, Laurie Patton, Kumkum Roy, Chinmay Sharma, David Smith, and Zuzana Špicová. I also thank the anonymous reviewers for their feedback.

I am deeply appreciative of my students at Lancaster over the past ten years, who have not only indulged my interest in the *Mahābhārata*, but have also asked many thought-provoking and sometimes unexpected questions along the way. In particular I thank Sophie Barker, Alex Owens, and Katie Work. I am also grateful to the many GCSE and A-Level teachers across the UK with whom I have had conversations about teaching Indian religions and philosophies.

There are a number colleagues at Lancaster who have been particularly supportive of my research over the past several years: Patrick Bishop, Gavin Hyman, Kim Knott, Shuruq Naguib, and Chris Partridge. I also thank Katherine Young, who has helped me organise academic conferences and numerous activities for teachers, all related to the *Mahābhārata* in one way or another.

I would also like to thank Larry Manzo, a dear friend and creator of the Mahabharata podcast, with whom I have had numerous conversations about themes explored in this book. And I thank my friend Gene Lushtak, one of my most enduring and inspiring dialogue partners. I am immensely grateful for the love and support of my mother Mary, uncle Peter, and aunt Jody. Finally, and most of all, I thank Yulia, Harrison, and Sonya – I dedicate this book to you.

Introduction

In the opening scene of the *Mahābhārata*, the professional storyteller Ugraśravas approaches a group of brahmins in the Naimiṣa Forest. After a brief exchange, Ugraśravas recounts another conversation, this one between the brahmin Vaiśaṃpāyana and King Janamejaya. It is this verbal encounter that then segues into Vaiśaṃpāyana telling the tale of the Pāṇḍavas and Kauravas, the narrative that most readers today would recognise as the central story of the *Mahābhārata*. These two conversations, at the very beginning of the text, bring attention to dialogue as a central literary feature of the *Mahābhārata*. In addition to the two dialogues that frame the text, many of the crucial scenes in the main narrative unfold as verbal exchanges, with the central characters discussing and debating amongst themselves about how they should act in a number of difficult and morally ambiguous circumstances. Moreover, the main narrative contains numerous dialogues embedded within it, all of which reflect back on the central narrative in one way or another, both informing and extending the discussions and debates among the main characters.

Dialogue is a recurring and significant aspect of Indian philosophical and religious literature generally,[1] but nowhere is it explored more profoundly and more elaborately than in the *Mahābhārata*. As Lakshmi Bandlamudi has reflected: 'Dialogue and dialogic relations characterize the *Mahābhārata* in every dimension' (2018: 216). The dialogical framing of the text has been discussed on a number of occasions,[2] and many individual dialogues within the text have been analysed in considerable detail.[3] There have also been some valuable studies that explore the *Mahābhārata* 'dialogically' in one way or another. As we will see later in this Introduction, Tamar Reich (1998) takes a dialogical approach to examine how the *Mahābhārata* includes opposing points of view in contestatory relationships. Meanwhile, Bandlamudi (2011) uses Bakhtin's theory of dialogics to examine the exchanges between the *Mahābhārata* and its readers. Both of these studies, in their different ways, have shown that attention to the dialogical aspects of the *Mahābhārata* opens up far-reaching understandings of the text. Nevertheless, the most fundamental aspect of dialogue in the *Mahābhārata* – the verbal exchanges between characters – remains relatively unexplored.

This book takes these verbal exchanges between characters as its starting point. I will argue that by paying attention to how the literary form of dialogue operates, we can gain new insights into the text's philosophical implications. My primary assumption in examining dialogue in the *Mahābhārata* is that its use as a literary medium is neither accidental nor ornamental. Rather, I maintain that this structure and form was used to communicate particular meanings by the composers of the text. By paying closer attention to the dialogue form, I will demonstrate that philosophical deliberation is an integral part of the *Mahābhārata* – both within the text through the discussions between characters and outside of the text through the ways that it provokes further philosophical reflection from its readers.

Although its self-designation as *itihāsa* ('history') has often been privileged by Western scholars, the *Mahābhārata* invites a philosophical engagement through some its other ways of describing itself. As Alf Hiltebeitel has shown, it is a multi-genre text that refers to itself with a number of different labels (2005: 465). Among them are some self-descriptions that express philosophical concerns, such as *upaniṣad* (1.1.191) and *mahaj-jñāna* ('great-knowledge'; 1.1.25; 1.1.49), as well as *dharma-śāstra* (treatise on *dharma*; 1.56.21) and *mokṣa-śāstra* (treatise on *mokṣa*; 1.56.21).[4] Because of my focus on dialogue, I pay particular attention to the *Mahābhārata*'s self-description as an *upaniṣad*. As I have explored previously, the dialogue form features prominently in the Upaniṣads as a vital medium through which the texts convey their most well-known teachings, such as *karma, yoga, ātman,* and *brahman.*[5] Although there are a number of differences between dialogues in the Upaniṣads and in the *Mahābhārata* – with the latter containing a much wider range of styles and structures – some of the literary and philosophical features of dialogue in the *Mahābhārata* seem to have emerged from the Upaniṣads.

I have explored elsewhere the many prominent characters from the Upaniṣads, such as Yājñavalkya, Uddālaka Āruṇi, Śvetaketu, and Janaka, who make brief appearances in the *Mahābhārata.*[6] Although their instances are comparatively few considering the length of the *Mahābhārata*, the scenes in which these characters appear and their direct and indirect interactions with the main characters connect the narrative worlds of the Upaniṣads and the *Mahābhārata*. Moreover, in the outer frame story of the *Mahābhārata*, the bard Ugraśravas narrates the text to a brahmin called Śaunaka, a name that appears on several occasions in the Upaniṣads.[7] As I have suggested elsewhere, we might see Śaunaka's role as the primary listener of the *Mahābhārata* as contributing towards the text's characterisation of itself as an *upaniṣad* (2017: 197).

In addition to identifying itself as an *upaniṣad*, the *Mahābhārata* uses dialogue in similar ways. Like the Upaniṣads, the *Mahābhārata* contains dialogues between literary characters about some of the central ideas and concepts of Indian philosophical and religious traditions. In addition to many lengthy discussions about *dharma*, the text also includes conversations and debates about truth (*satya*), fate (*daiva*), human agency (*puruṣakāra*), *karma*, liberation (*mokṣa*), *yoga*, non-violence (*ahiṃsā*), ultimate reality (*brahman*), the self (*ātman*), and devotion (*bhakti*). Some of these ideas feature prominently in the dialogues we will consider in this book. Even though the *Mahābhārata* is often described in Western terms as narrative, story, myth, or epic, I take its self-portrayal as an *upaniṣad* as crucial to understanding how it explores its core religious and philosophical ideas.

In the Upaniṣads, teachers often present their teachings as beyond ordinary language and experience, characterising core doctrines such as *ātman* and *brahman* as hidden or concealed, imperceptible or indescribable. Such descriptions portray knowledge as difficult to obtain and just out of reach. As we will see, such depictions of religious and philosophical knowledge also appear in the *Mahābhārata*, particularly in discussions about *dharma*. Characters in the *Mahābhārata* discuss *dharma* extensively, not only providing a number of different understandings, but also commenting on its elusive nature. In a number of the text's most pivotal discussions, characters describe *dharma* as 'subtle' (*sūkṣma*).[8] Adam Bowles has shown that this description of *dharma* has its background in the way that the Upaniṣads portray its highest teachings as beyond understanding.[9] Because of the repeated use of this description in the *Mahābhārata*, A.K. Ramanujan has suggested that not *dharma*, but *dharma-sūkṣmatā* is the text's central theme:

> It is not *dharma* or right conduct that the *Mahābhārata* seems to teach, but the *sūkṣma* or subtle nature of *dharma* – its infinite subtlety, its incalculable calculus of consequences, its endless delicacy. Because *dharma-sūkṣmatā* is one of the central themes that recur in an endless number of ways, the many legal discussions are a necessary part of the action.
>
> (1991: 435)[10]

As we will see, different characters describe *dharma* as subtle for different reasons, so the connotations of *sūkṣma* can change, depending on the context. One of the themes we will follow throughout this book and will return to in the Conclusion is how the *Mahābhārata* develops this Upaniṣadic trope of subtlety.

David Shulman has traced another Upaniṣadic theme that is further developed in the *Mahābhārata* – the posing of enigmatic questions (*praśna*) that provoke further reflection. As Shulman explains, *praśna*s are 'not "riddles" in a strict sense', but point 'to a baffling, ultimately insoluble crystallization of conflict articulated along opposing lines of interpretation' (1996: 153). In posing such questions, Shulman sees the *Mahābhārata* as part of 'the Upaniṣadic speculative tradition' (1996: 153). As we will see throughout this book, the *Mahābhārata* raises a series of moral questions and portrays prolonged discussions between characters about how to address these questions. Repeatedly, moral questions are posed in relation to highly consequential situations in which there are deep uncertainties about how to act in accordance with *dharma*. Bimal Krishna Matilal approached these moral questions in terms of dilemmas. According to Matilal, the moral dilemmas in the *Mahābhārata* are both central to the text and 'illustrations of perennial problems in moral philosophy' (2002: 21). Matilal described 'moral dilemmas' as situations that 'present irreconcilable alternatives' (1989: 6). They are situations in which a choice must be made between two or more courses of actions, where there is no clear answer as to which course of action is more correct, and where the situation remains in some sense unresolved. Indeed, Matilal describes moral dilemmas as 'unresolvable' (1989: xi).

Despite building on many of Matilal's insights, this book focuses more on the text's philosophical questions than on moral dilemmas. Each chapter will begin with a question or set of questions put forward by one of the characters and will then analyse a number of dialogues that, in one way or another, continue the inquiry. As J.A.B. van Buitenen has reflected, the *Mahābhārata* is 'a series of precisely stated problems imprecisely and therefore inconclusively resolved, with every resolution raising a new problem' (1973: 29). This book takes such 'precisely stated problems' as its starting point, focusing on how they are explored in five particular sets of dialogues. All of the episodes I discuss are similar to dilemmas in the sense that they remain unresolved issues among the characters within the text. But I treat them more as philosophical questions rather than dilemmas because many of the dialogues that address these questions take place after decisions have been made or actions have been performed. In several cases, characters act very quickly, even rashly, with little or no deliberation beforehand. Often, the most extensive philosophical discussions take place retrospectively. In this way, the questions we will encounter in this book are sometimes less about what characters should do and more about how characters evaluate, justify, and criticise both their own actions and the actions of others after events have taken place. In each chapter, I will examine both how central philosophical questions are addressed in individual dialogues and how different dialogues addressing the same questions unfold as ongoing debates.

In this book I understand the term 'dialogue' in three main ways: (1) as verbal encounter: the conversations, discussions, and debates between characters within the text; (2) as intra-textuality: the relationship between different dialogues in different sections of the text; and (3) as hermeneutics: my interpretive approach to the text. In most of the remainder of this Introduction, I will prepare the way for the subsequent chapters by discussing each of these three understandings of dialogue and how they are related to the book as a whole. First, however, let me briefly introduce the five sets of moral questions and their contexts within the narrative.

Five moral questions

Each set of questions is posed in relation to a central episode that punctuates the main story. Most of the events in the main story take place in the human realm, as two groups of cousins, the Pāṇḍavas and Kauravas, compete over who is the rightful heir to the throne. The central narrative chronicles their rivalry from their childhoods and early adulthoods, to the fateful dicing match between them, through to a devastating war and its aftermath.[11] All the main human characters are incarnations and/or descendants of divine figures, so their actions and interactions also take on a cosmic importance. Because of their divine identities, the actions of the main human characters are often portrayed as destined or inevitable. Nevertheless, few characters in the main story are aware of their divine identities, and, as such, they exhibit very human concerns throughout – ruminating on their choices, praising and blaming others for their actions and inactions, and experiencing intense emotional reactions to their own situations and the actions of others. As we will see, characters discuss and debate extensively about their own moral responsibilities and the moral responsibilities of others. In each chapter, we will explore a different set of such deliberations in relation to one of five crucial events in the unfolding of the story.

Chapter 1 begins with Satyavatī's question whether Bhīṣma will give up his vows to save the future of his family. As the only child of King Śaṃtanu, Bhīṣma was expected to be the next king. But soon after he is anointed the crown prince, he learns his father has fallen in love with the fisher princess Satyavatī. In order to satisfy the conditions of Satyavatī's father to approve her marriage with his father, Bhīṣma makes two demanding and far-reaching vows: (1) to pass on his claim to the throne to Satyavatī's future son and (2) the 'awesome' or 'terrifying' vow to practice celibacy. It is this second promise that earns him the name Bhīṣma ('Awesome' or 'Terrifying'), the name by which he is known throughout the remainder of the story. The immediate consequence of these two vows is the absence of a straightforward heir to the throne.

This chapter will examine five dialogues that, in one way or another, reflect on Bhīṣma's vows. All the dialogues in this chapter include Bhīṣma, but he discusses or reflects on his vows differently with different interlocutors at different stages in the narrative. His interlocutors in these dialogues include Satyavatī (his stepmother); Śiśupāla (his enemy); Duryodhana (the eldest of the Kaurava brothers); and Yudhiṣṭhira (the eldest of the Pāṇḍava brothers). Some of the tensions we will examine more closely are between the various reasons or justifications that Bhīṣma gives for his vows. In addition to the many defences offered by Bhīṣma, his dialogical encounters with others give voice to those who challenge him, offering a sustained counter-perspective about the dharmic status of his vows. By exploring the many conversations about Bhīṣma's vows as an ongoing deliberation, this chapter shows that the dialogue form puts into play competing perspectives, characterising the moral problem of Bhīṣma's vows as a central question of the text that is never completely resolved. Additionally, this chapter shows how the discussions about Bhīṣma's vows consider different perspectives dialectically through time, thus pointing to the temporal contingency of moral decisions.

Chapter 2 begins with the question of whether it is possible to follow *dharma* while knowingly acting in violation of *dharma*. This question is posed by Drupada, who has serious reservations about allowing his daughter to enter into a polyandrous marriage with the five Pāṇḍavas, despite reassurances from Yudhiṣṭhira, as well as Vyāsa (paternal grandfather of both sets of cousins and author of the *Mahābhārata*). This chapter will address Drupada's question by analysing a series of dialogues about Draupadī's marriage. Draupadī is the central female character in the *Mahābhārata*. Her marriage to all five Pāṇḍava brothers is both one of the most consequential and most controversial episodes in the central story. It is consequential because this marriage sets in motion the Pāṇḍavas establishing their claim to half the kingdom and their subsequent attainment of universal sovereignty. It is controversial because it violates the dominant marriage practices established by the time of the developed text. Indeed, the dharmic ambiguities that persist about one woman being married to five men will haunt Draupadī during most of the remainder of the story.

The dialogues about the polyandrous marriage take place both before and shortly after Draupadī's wedding to the Pāṇḍavas, unfolding as four distinct, yet interconnected, discussions between (1) Vyāsa and the five Pāṇḍava brothers; (2) Yudhiṣṭhira, Arjuna (the third eldest Pāṇḍava), and Kuntī (mother of the three eldest Pāṇḍavas); (3) Yudhiṣṭhira and Drupada; and (4) Vyāsa and Drupada. As we will see, throughout these dialogues, there is a strong connection between the characters' social identities and the types of arguments they make. In particular, different meanings of *dharma* are explored through the distinct ways that different characters make their arguments. In addition to representing a variety of personal perspectives, these dialogues include a range of justifications for the controversial marriage. Rather than try to look for an original explanation or try to identify which explanation is most likely an interpolation, this chapter assesses how these different arguments unfold within the discussions and how they relate to each other. As I will suggest, the plurality of religious and philosophical views that are explored in relation to Draupadī's wedding is an example of a dharmic way of reasoning and represents moral deliberation with others as an important practice of *dharma*.

Chapter 3 begins with Janamejaya's question about the events leading up to the dicing match. As we have seen, Janamejaya is the primary listener in the inner dialogue that frames the text. As the great-grandson of Arjuna, Janamejaya is listening to his own family history when hearing Vaiśaṃpāyana's narration. His request for further information about the events leading up to the dicing match prompts Vaiśaṃpāyana to recite the second of three versions of a dialogue between King Dhṛtarāṣṭra (father of the Kauravas) and Duryodhana (Dhṛtarāṣṭra's eldest son). These dialogues take place in the immediate aftermath of Yudhiṣṭhira performing a royal ritual in which he asserts his position as universal sovereign. Deeply envious of his cousin's extravagant display of superiority, Duryodhana convinces his father to host a dicing match, during which the Kauravas will attempt to win back the entire kingdom. In addition to discussing this dialogue within the unfolding of the narrative, this chapter will reflect upon the implications of the *Mahābhārata* containing three versions of the same scene. Rather than try to see any of these versions as older or more integral to the text as a whole, this chapter looks at how each of these versions depicts the moral responsibility of the characters contributing to the dicing match differently. In addition to giving us different lenses for understanding this particular episode, their juxtaposition within the same text offers a further insight into how the dialectic between fate and human agency plays out in the *Mahābhārata*.

In this chapter, we will also look at a series of dialogues Yudhiṣṭhira has with Vidura (his uncle), Draupadī, and Śakuni (maternal uncle of the Kauravas). In these dialogues, Yudhiṣṭhira offers a number of different reasons for why he accepts the invitation to play dice. Looking at these dialogues featuring Duryodhana and Yudhiṣṭhira alongside each other, we will see that, despite the many appeals to fate and predetermination, not to mention the doctrine of the divine plan and Kṛṣṇa's divinity, the characters in the *Mahābhārata* place an extraordinary amount of emphasis on their own moral decision-making. This chapter will examine how characters treat each other and themselves as morally responsibility agents, while they also confront the limitations of their own agency. As we will see, these dialogues featuring Duryodhana and Yudhiṣṭhira not only address Janamejaya's question about the events leading up to the dicing match, but also offer depth to the moral implications of his question concerning who is responsible for this disastrous occasion.

Chapter 4 begins with Draupadī's question about whether she can be considered free, even if her husbands have been confined to servitude. Draupadī poses this question in the royal assembly hall in the immediate aftermath of the dicing match. During the match, Yudhiṣṭhira had gambled everything away, including his brothers, himself, and Draupadī. But because Yudhiṣṭhira staked her after staking himself, Draupadī disputes the Kauravas' claim that she has lost her freedom along with her husbands. In addition to analysing Draupadī's arguments, this chapter will examine the arguments of two other female characters, Śakuntalā and Sulabhā, both of whom also debate about the status of women in royal assembly halls. As we will see, Draupadī, Śakuntalā, and Sulabhā each make arguments that, in one way or another, address the issue of female agency, as well as the problem of gender biases within *dharma*. But in addition to facing some of the same issues, each of them makes arguments unique to their own specific circumstances. Rather than any one of them speaking on behalf of all women, the actions and arguments of Draupadī, Śakuntalā, and Sulabhā make vital contributions towards a deeper understanding of *dharma* that insists upon female perspectives.

Chapter 5 begins with Arjuna's question about the nature of the divine and how it reveals itself. Arjuna poses this question to Kṛṣṇa, whose multiple and overlapping identities include being Arjuna's cousin, brother-in-law, and friend, as well as being recognised by many characters in the narrative – including Arjuna – as God. Arjuna's question and Kṛṣṇa's reply constitute part of the *Bhagavad Gītā*, which is the most famous dialogue in the *Mahābhārata*. This dialogue takes place on the battlefield, just as the war between the Pāṇḍavas and Kauravas is about to begin. In approaching the *Bhagavad Gītā* as a dialogue, I will pay particular attention to Arjuna's contributions to the conversation, both in how he frames the encounter through the lens of his moral problem and in how his subsequent questions continue to direct the course of their exchange.

In addition to looking at how the *Bhagavad Gītā* characterises Kṛṣṇa's divinity, we will also explore it in relation to several other dialogues with Kṛṣṇa that take place during and after the war. Two of these subsequent dialogues also include Arjuna, but Kṛṣṇa's other interlocutors are Balarāma (Kṛṣṇa's brother), Gāndhārī (wife of Dhṛtarāṣṭra and mother of the Kauravas), and Uttaṅka (a sage and devotee of Kṛṣṇa). By examining the *Bhagavad Gītā* in relation to these other dialogues, this chapter demonstrates how the dialogue form contributes to characterising a dialogical and interactive theology of Kṛṣṇa. While in the *Bhagavad Gītā* Kṛṣṇa gives his most detailed description and most explicit enactment of his status as the all-powerful creator and destroyer of the universe, the five subsequent dialogues with Kṛṣṇa also characterise him as God, but develop his divine status in different ways. Despite his claims to be all-knowing and all-powerful, Kṛṣṇa is characterised through dialogue as a deity that can be questioned, challenged, ridiculed, and even cursed.

From attempts to persuade Bhīṣma to relinquish his vows (Chapter 1), to discussions about the legitimacy of Draupadī's marriage (Chapter 2); from the contrasting accounts of how Duryodhana justifies his envy of his cousin's power, to the multiple explanations Yudhiṣṭhira gives for his decision to play dice (Chapter 3); from the problems posed by Draupadī's questions in the *sabhā* after the dicing match (Chapter 4), to Arjuna's despair over whether or not to fight in the *Bhagavad Gītā* (Chapter 5) – these five episodes drive the plot forward, as each plays a crucial role in the narrative trajectory towards the war and its aftermath.

Dialogue as verbal encounter

What I am referring to when using the term 'dialogue', first and foremost, is the narrative depiction of verbal encounters between two or more characters. There are several Sanskrit words, including *saṃvāda*, *anuvāda*, *upadeśa*, *pradeśa*, *samāgama*, and *saṃbhāṣya*, which are used to describe conversational episodes between characters.[12] The focus of this book is not on the terms, however, but rather on specific episodes in which characters encounter others in a verbal exchange. As we will see, dialogue is a particularly rich and complex literary expression because there are always a range of issues being addressed simultaneously: the interlocutors, their interaction, the content of their conversation, the context of their encounter, its stakes and consequences, and how these and other components relate to each other. The dialogues we will explore in this book are not passive or scripted, but rather dynamic encounters between competing voices in urgent circumstances. Despite the sometimes deterministic arguments put forth by some characters, there remains a spontaneity and unpredictability when they encounter each other in face-to-face discussions.

As Vittorio Hösle has shown, focusing on dialogue can bring attention to a text's philosophical methods. In his book *The Philosophical Dialogue: A Poetics and Hermeneutics*, Hösle describes how different aspects of philosophy are embedded within the dialogue form itself:

> In real conversations, arguments are exchanged, and the connections between the individual propositions that constitute arguments as such belong to the domain of logic. However, propositions are presented through speech acts, and their authors are persons. But relations between persons belong to the domain of ethics. Thus in the philosophical dialogue the two basic disciplines of theoretical and practical philosophy seem to be bound together in an especially close way.
>
> (2012: xvi)

As Hösle describes, not only does philosophical dialogue depict conversations about philosophical topics, but also the form itself demonstrates particular ways of doing philosophy. Like Hösle, I see dialogue as an important medium of philosophy that is found in different traditions around the world. Although Hösle confines his study to Western sources, he specifically mentions the Upaniṣads, *Bhagavad Gītā*, and Pāli Buddhist sources as examples of philosophical dialogue (2012: 72). Hösle's observations about philosophical dialogue are relevant here because the *Mahābhārata* – like many of the dialogues Hösle analyses – also contains dialogues that exhibit logical arguments and explore the ethical relationships between interlocutors.

Although not represented as linear proofs, dialogues in the *Mahābhārata* contain embedded arguments as characters articulate reasons in their attempts to persuade each other to think or act in particular ways. Dmitri Nikulin characterises dialogue, quite straightforwardly, as conversation with others. Nikulin describes how philosophy emerges from dialogue when a conversation becomes a discussion in which reasons are given and arguments are made – when there is an attempt to persuade

(2010: ix–xii).[13] As we will see, characters in the *Mahābhārata* make decisions and act in accordance with specific reasons; characters articulate and make explicit their reasons in the form of arguments when in verbal encounters with others. In each chapter, we will examine the relationship between dialogue and philosophy by paying close attention to how characters make arguments, what types of arguments they make, how they respond to the arguments of others, and how their arguments contribute to the outcome of their debates.

In addition to the specific arguments made by individual characters, we will also explore the philosophical implications of the ways that their discussions unfold. In taking this approach, I follow Hans-Georg Gadamer, who – in his engagement with Plato's work – has perhaps explored the philosophical implications of dialogue as much as anyone. Gadamer was drawn to Plato's dialogues because he saw philosophical dialogue itself – the conversations we have with others about shared concerns – as fundamental to how we experience and develop understandings of the world we live in. In his readings of Plato, Gadamer rejects the search for an overall meaning or hidden doctrine. Rather, Gadamer pays close attention to the 'directions of questioning' between Socrates and his interlocutors (1985: 186).

One of the meanings of 'in dialogue' in the title of this book is that we can find new understandings of the *Mahābhārata* in the dialogues – that we have much to learn from analysing more closely how dialogue works throughout the text. Following Gadamer, I do not attempt to uncover a unifying teaching or hidden meaning. Rather, I see the structures of the dialogues themselves as the guide to appreciating the *Mahābhārata*'s philosophical import. In each chapter, we will examine a particular philosophical question by analysing how it is addressed by characters with distinct perspectives, as they consider different issues at stake in changing circumstances.

One of the ways that Gadamer understands the unfolding of philosophical dialogue is to take seriously the identity of the individual interlocutors and how they interact with each other. As P. Christopher Smith explains, Gadamer approaches each of Plato's dialogues as 'a developing discussion' between specific individuals, with their relationship to each other and the context in which they interact as informing what they say:

> In each case ... we are dealing with a specific situation in which Socrates speaks to individuals who have special concerns and who, being the people they are and having the perspectives they do, define the horizons of what Socrates wants to say and can say.
>
> (1980: ix–x)

Similarly, the dialogues in the *Mahābhārata* root otherwise abstract philosophical doctrines as arguments of specific individuals in concrete situations. In reading the *Mahābhārata* as philosophy, I do not assume that the text teaches a specific doctrine or set of doctrines, but I explore the philosophical value of the questions the text poses and the ways that the text addresses them.

Moreover, like in Plato's dialogue, the *Mahābhārata* portrays characters as having unique points of view and their conversations with others as defined by the horizons of their specific relationships with each other. Indeed, because of its complex dialogical structure, the *Mahābhārata* explores the perspectival dimension of dialogue far more extensively than the works of Plato. The dialogues that we will examine in this book not only contain the different vantage points of the characters involved, but their verbal encounters are filtered through the two dialogues that frame the text as a whole. In addition to the multiple layers of narration, the text contains a number of different authoritative voices within it, such as Vyāsa, Kṛṣṇa, Bhīṣma, and Yudhiṣṭhira. Although these characters are often presented as more knowledgeable than others, their views and arguments are nevertheless rooted within their own subjective perspectives, each of which is doubted and challenged on several occasions. In contrast to the dialogues of Plato, where the various interlocutors tend to revolve around the dominant figure of Socrates, in the *Mahābhārata* there is no central authoritative position. As such, the unfolding of dialogue does not lead towards eternal and universal ideas, but rather maintains a range of interpenetrating voices in tension with each other. By portraying characters disagreeing with each other, responding to each other's arguments, and revising their own arguments as circumstances change, the *Mahābhārata* invites a multi-perspectival exploration into philosophical questions, particularly questions about *dharma*.

Multiple perspectives remain in tension because many of the *Mahābhārata*'s most consequential dialogues remain unresolved. This non-closure has similarities with dialogues in the Upaniṣads, where teachers tend not to disclose the full articulation of their teachings, but rather point their students towards knowledge that is often characterised as beyond sense perception and beyond language. Given that a true understanding remains beyond direct communication, the unresolved and episodic nature of Upaniṣadic dialogues prompts further reflection, both for the students within the text and for audiences outside it. Similarly, many dialogues in the *Mahābhārata* raise questions that remain unanswered. In addition to the type of non-closure portrayed in the Upaniṣads, in which a teaching is never complete, the most pivotal dialogues in the *Mahābhārata* lack closure because of disagreements between characters. As we will see, dialogues do not tend to reach conclusions, but rather to initiate new conversations. Every discussion leads towards or refers back to another one. When we look at the exchanges of arguments between characters in verbal encounters, we can see that the *Mahābhārata* represents inquiry into the nature of *dharma* as an ongoing process.

Dialogue as intra-textuality

In addition to the literary depictions of verbal encounters between characters, I also use the word 'dialogue' to refer to the relationship between different conversational episodes. In this sense, another connotation of 'in dialogue' in the title of this book refers to the ways that the *Mahābhārata* is in dialogue with itself. From a literary perspective, the ways that dialogues from different sections of the text are related to each other can, of course, be explained in terms of inter-textuality – or, in the case of the *Mahābhārata*, intra-textuality.[14] Different dialogues are intra-textual in the sense that they share some of the same structures, motifs, and themes, as well as deeper conceptual assumptions. But by using the word 'dialogue' to describe the relationship between different sections of the text, I am referring to more than the ways in which all literary works are intertextual. Rather, I will highlight how each individual verbal encounter contributes to wider philosophical conversations that are going on across the text. As we will see, individual dialogues often explicitly or obliquely refer to other dialogues, sometimes extending arguments, but often directly contesting claims made in other contexts. As Tamar Reich explains: 'portions of the text can be most fruitfully read as a comment, a response, or an interpretation to other, pre-given portions' (1998: viii). In each chapter, we will examine individual dialogues not only in terms of the arguments and interactions of the interlocutors in that particular episode, but also in terms of the ways each dialogue participates in wider debates going on across the *Mahābhārata*.

Although it might seem obvious that different sections of a single text are in dialogue with each other, much of the early Western scholarship treated the *Mahābhārata* as disjointed and incoherent. Until relatively recently, most Western scholars approached the text diachronically, as composed over a long period of time, perhaps up to 1,000 years (c. 500 BCE–500 CE).[15] Such scholars assumed that, because it consisted of diverse material from different historical periods, the text lacked unity. This view was most influentially articulated by E.W. Hopkins, who proposed that the *Mahābhārata* was originally an oral epic that expanded over time. Hopkins posited that the text's compositional history had three distinct stages: (1) an original epic core, (2) the addition of myths, and (3) its Brahmanisation, with additions of 'didactic' material. One of the recurring assumptions among scholars who have adhered to this view is that much of the devotional and ethical material is new to the *Mahābhārata* and thus less central to it. Indeed, Hopkins thought of the added material as corrupting the text, calling it 'the most vicious masses of didactic fungus' (1898: 10).[16] For Hopkins, it would be fruitless to explore the relationship between different sections of the text because later redactors added material arbitrarily: 'Tale is added to tale, doctrine to doctrine, without much regard to the effect produced by the juxtaposition' [1901] (1993: 370).

Scholars such as Moriz Winternitz had hoped that a critically reconstituted text would excise all or most of the didactic material and get us closer to its presumed epic core.[17] During the middle-third of the 20th century

(1933–1966), V.S. Sukthankar and a team of scholars based in Pune completed a Critical Edition of the *Mahābhārata*, working from more than 800 manuscripts across India.[18] Instead of producing a text resembling an 'epic core', the Critical Edition, which rejects huge masses of material that are embedded in the popular tellings and variations of the *Mahābhārata*, has demonstrated that the so-called didactic material is integral to the text throughout the entire Sanskrit manuscript tradition. In other words, the Critical Edition offers no support to the conjecture that the ethical and devotional materials were later additions to the text.[19]

Part of the problem in much of Western scholarship on the *Mahābhārata* has been the use of the word 'didactic', which conveys the sense of being 'dogmatic', 'moralistic', or 'pedantic'. Its pejorative connotations are abundantly clear in Hopkins' description of almost everything outside the main narrative as 'didactic fungus' (1898: 10). His notorious phrase remains indicative of much of Western scholarship that has criticised ancient Indian traditions for not having a branch of philosophy on ethics comparable to European antiquity, while at the same time weakening the philosophical power of the *Mahābhārata* by reducing its copious discussions of ethics as irrelevant or preachy. As we will see, the so-called 'didactic' sections are not 'moralistic' or 'pedantic' when we read them as part of a dynamic and ongoing dialogue with other sections of the text.

Since the publication of the Critical Edition, more and more scholars have attempted to make sense of the variety, complexity, and ambiguity of the *Mahābhārata*, rather than continue to privilege some parts of it as more fundamental than others. Scholars who continue to accept the theory that the *Mahābhārata* was composed in stages over a long period of time have tended to treat what they consider to be newer material as interpolated according to styles and structures already present in the text.[20] Bowles has summed up this view nicely: 'In my view, there is much evidence to suggest that the "*Mahābhārata*" ... has always included and, therefore, been designed with, both narrative and didactic material' (2007: 34–35).

Meanwhile, many scholars today reject the theory that the *Mahābhārata* was composed in stages over several centuries. The first Western scholar to propose this view was Joseph Dahlmann. As John Brockington summarises:

> Joseph Dahlmann in 1895 ... reject[ed] the view that the *Mahābhārata* consisted of an original saga and several later accretions and ... assert[ed] the essential unity of the text, which he saw as the work of a single author who combined earlier myths, law books and teachings into a single whole – broadly speaking the epic in its present form – as a work of popular instruction.
>
> (1998: 46–47)

As Sukthankar points out, Dahlmann's view showed 'that the relation between the narrative and the didactic matter in our epic was definitely not of a casual character, but was intentional and purposeful' [1957] (2016: 20–21). Although Sukthankar rejected Dahlmann's claim of a single author, he agreed in characterising the narrative and didactic material as inseparable: 'not a single line of the didactic matter is lacking in purpose and in organic connection with the whole' [1957] (2016: 86).

More recently, Hiltebeitel has presented what could be considered an updated version of Dahlmann's view. Hiltebeitel also approaches the *Mahābhārata* as a unified text, but – like Sukthankar – he rejects Dahlmann's claim that it was composed by a single author. Instead, Hiltebeitel proposes that the text is the product of an authorial team working together towards a common purpose.

> I would ... urge that the *Mahābhārata* must have been written over a much shorter period than is usually advanced ... by 'committee' ... or 'team' ... and at most through a couple of generations.
>
> (2001b: 20)

In proposing a unitary composition, Hiltebeitel treats all material as equally integral to any overall interpretation of the text.

Hiltebeitel further imagines that the authorial committee would have incorporated contributors with different fields of expertise, including 'a philosopher and a dharmaśāstra connoisseur among them, and perhaps a retired Brahmin general (a *senāpati*), while a master of the house kept them all to a common purpose' (2001b: 169). Moreover, following the suggestion of Madeleine Biardeau, Hiltebeitel postulates that women, if not part of the committee, would have been just 'beyond earshot, but definitely heard' by its members: 'the poets have listened to their mothers, wives, sisters, and daughters, and probably sometimes listened well ... the epic poets' wives ... are probably one of the reasons that so many of the epic's women, and in particular Draupadī, come to life' (2001b: 167). Although speculative, Hiltebeitel's portrayal of the authorial committee invites us to consider the range of voices that might have contributed to a compositional team. If I were to speculate along with Hiltebeitel, I would include – given the variety of perspectives we find within the text itself – an even greater diversity of voices contributing to such a committee.

In addition to the relationship between the so-called narrative and didactic sections, another issue that has troubled Western scholars is the existence of both obvious repetitions and direct contradictions throughout the manuscript tradition. As Sukthankar explains, it was not the remit of the critical editors to try to harmonise, but rather to reconstitute a base-line text that all available manuscripts had in common.

> To resolve such anomalies ... is beyond the scope of this edition, since the entire manuscript tradition evidence unanimously supports the conflation, which is too old and too deep-rooted to be treated by the

> ordinary principles of textual criticism. If we went about, at this stage of our work, athetizing such passages as were self-contradictory or as contradicted the data of some other part of the epic, there would not be much left the Mahābhārata to edit in the end'.
>
> (1933: lxxxvii)

While some scholars have criticised the Critical Edition for not attempting to smooth out these recurrences and inconsistencies, by rigorously following the methods of textual criticism the editors have revealed such occurrences as part of the very fabric of every known version within the Sanskrit manuscript tradition.

How then, do we make sense of what appear to be repetitions and inconsistencies? Ramanujan has argued that repetition is a recurring literary technique in the *Mahābhārata* that often adds depth to central episodes, such as the dicing match, the disrobing of Draupadī, and the *Bhagavad Gītā*. Tracing a number of occasions where different characters face the same circumstances, or when the same character confronts similar situations on more than one occasion, Ramanujan sees repetition as 'the central structuring principle' of the *Mahābhārata* (1991: 421). Similarly, Hiltebeitel addresses repetitions and contradictions, not as flaws within the text's design, but as instances that can add depth to our understanding of how the text was woven together. According to Hiltebeitel's depiction of the compositional process, the composers had 'a delight in concealment' and were 'not averse to rough joins, repetitions and reiterations, multiple and deepening causalities, overdetermination, and intriguing contradictions' (2001b: 164). In other words, the *Mahābhārata*'s repetitions and contradiction are not blemishes, but puzzles created by a team of poets with 'extraordinarily subtle ... motivations' (2001b: 164).

In addition to the instances where repetitions and contradictions can be explained in terms of the literary design of the text, in some cases the text's ambiguities can be better understood in terms of the *Mahābhārata*'s multi-vocality. While agreeing with Ramanujan and Hiltebeitel – as well as others – who portray the text as artfully and purposefully constructed, I also think the *Mahābhārata* contains genuine disagreements, as well as conflicting philosophical and religious commitments. Throughout the text, opposing doctrines and perspectives are put into sometimes agonistic and unresolved tension with each other. As we will see, many of the repetitions and contradictions can be seen in terms of competing voices that contribute to lively debates going on within the text.

In approaching the *Mahābhārata* as an ongoing debate, I draw on the work of Tamar Reich, who characterises much of the relationship between different sections of *Mahābhārata* as 'contestatory'. In her doctoral thesis, *A Battleground of a Text: Inner Textual Interpretation in the Sanskrit Mahābhārata*, Reich engages with the literary theorist Mikhail Mikhailovich Bakhtin to perform a '*dialogic* reading' that celebrates the

Mahābhārata's heterogeneity and is 'sensitive to the variety of voices found within the textual tradition' (1998: 22). Reich argues that the text was composed 'dialogically', in the sense that authors deliberately juxtapose units that express different, and even contradictory, worldviews. As she explains:

> In this process many types of discourse were brought together dialogically, in the sense that when they were juxtaposed within the same fixed textual entity a dialogical relationship between them could emerge. Well, actually, Bakhtin's term dialogical' is a little too benign – 'contestatory' more precisely describes the quality of the verbal interaction in many cases.
>
> (1998: 31)

Seen in this way, the text itself is a conversation, and sometimes a fierce debate. Instead of singling out certain sections as hypothetically more central than others, a dialogical reading, then, pays attention to tensions and disagreements as integral aspects of controversies going on across the text. As Reich explains:

> If … the multi-vocality of the text is intimately connected with the practice of textual expansion, one cannot try to weed out the later stuff with the hope that the older 'core' will give us the 'real', 'original' meaning. Similarly, one cannot try to rid the main narrative from the huge mass of secondary narratives attached to it, with the hope that the 'main' narrative will give us the 'main' meaning. It is precisely by examining the ways in which the later materials connect with the earlier ones that we will begin to recognize the agency of the anonymous authors and hear their voices.
>
> (1998: 32)

For Reich, the heterogeneity of the text explains not only the tensions between the narrative and the so-called didactic sections, but also the wide range of views that are included in almost every section – such as between Vaiṣṇava and Śaiva theologies, between arguments for war and teachings on non-violence, and between the religious values focused on *dharma* (*pravṛtti*) and those focused on *mokṣa* (*nivṛtti*). With the *Mahābhārata*'s inclusion of these and other tensions in mind, Reich concludes: 'heterogeneity is a deliberate characteristic of the *Mahābhārata*'.[21]

Building on Reich's insights about the dialogical nature of the text, this book will look at the intra-textual relationship between different dialogues in terms of how they often address the same questions in different ways. Rather than view different voices and arguments as contradictions or inconsistencies, I will approach them as contrasting perspectives that are sometimes agonistic and contestatory. Ultimately, then, for my purposes, the question of whether the *Mahābhārata* was composed over centuries or within a generation or two is beside the point. The Critical Edition demonstrates that disagreement and contestation are integral to the *Mahābhārata* across the entire Sanskrit manuscript tradition.

In each chapter, we will read different sections of the text as in dialogue with each other by tracing how a single philosophical question is discussed on distinct occasions by a range of characters in changing circumstances, and sometimes at different narratorial layers. In each case, we will see that philosophical questions generate ongoing conversations, thus exploring the same issue from different perspectives and in relation to different contexts. As I will demonstrate, cases of tensions and disagreements are by no means extraneous or accidental, but rather vital contributions to ongoing explorations into *dharma* and other philosophical issues.

Moreover, each chapter contains at least one example of what might be described as a contradiction or repetition. In Chapter 1, we will juxtapose the narrative account of Bhīṣma's vows with his criticism of a sage known for keeping his vow, despite the harm it causes to others. As we will see, Bhīṣma's diametrically opposing views are not an inconsistency or editorial oversight, but rather part of an ongoing exploration of his vows. In Chapter 2, we will note that Vyāsa tells the story about Draupadī's previous birth on two occasions to justify the polyandrous marriage. Rather than interpreting this as an editorial mistake, we will consider the rhetorical context of each account, as Vyāsa addresses different audiences in distinct situations. In Chapter 3, we will look at three versions of a dialogue between Duryodhana and Dhṛtarāṣṭra. Instead of discounting these three versions as repetitions or contradictions, we will examine them as contesting accounts, each one conveying something different about the meaning of this pivotal conversation and its role in leading to the dicing match. In Chapter 4, we will contrast the text's portrayal of independent and articulate female characters with its misogynist views. Rather than interpreting the vitality of female characters such as Draupadī, Śakuntalā, and Sulabhā as somehow unusual or accidental in a text with an otherwise patriarchal agenda, we will engage with their arguments as contributing to female counter-perspectives that are integral to the text's ongoing deliberation on *dharma*. In Chapter 5, we will contrast Kṛṣṇa's teachings and divine revelations in the *Bhagavad Gītā* with other dialogues where his teachings and divinity are presented differently, sometimes being challenged or rejected.

Dialogue as hermeneutics

In addition to the literary depictions of conversations between characters and the relationships between different sections of the text, I also use the word 'dialogue' to refer to my own engagement with the text. Here I am following Gadamer, who viewed the process of interpretation as a type of conversation. In this sense, another meaning of 'in dialogue' in the title of this book refers to my own encounter with the *Mahābhārata*. To be in dialogue with a text, Gadamer explains, is to open oneself up to the text: '[A] person trying to understand a text is prepared for it to tell him something' [1975: 282]. Gadamer rejects any claims of an objective or scientific way of reading a text, but rather cultivates a hermeneutic that is not so much a method to be imposed, but a mode of reading that allows the text to have a voice.

As discussed earlier, I approach the *Mahābhārata* philosophically because of its self-descriptions, content, and form. Another, equally important, motivation is my attempt to engage with the *Mahābhārata* as a dialogue partner, rather than merely as an object of study. As we have seen, the first Western scholars to research the *Mahābhārata* often treated the text with contempt. Although recent Western scholarship has engaged much more positively with the text – examining themes such as its literary richness, its mythological complexity, or its contribution to the development of Indian religious traditions – there remains a tendency in Western institutions to study the *Mahābhārata* strictly as a historical curiosity, as a remnant of India's past, but with no conceptual value to today's world. I am not suggesting that a historical approach is not worthwhile, or that the text-historical method has not produced important insights into the structure, style, and historical context of the text. However, I am suggesting that Western academic studies have largely treated the *Mahābhārata* as an artefact, rather than as a living conceptual resource.[22]

Similar to the ways that Western philosophers still draw upon the works of Greek and Roman philosophies when discussing issues related to dialectic, ethics, political theory, gender theory, epistemology, ontology, and metaphysics, I engage with the *Mahābhārata* as a living and vibrant dialogue partner that has much to contribute to philosophical debates today. Rather than reading the *Mahābhārata* as merely an object of study, I am interested in the contemporary relevance of its questions, discussions, and arguments. As we will see in each chapter, characters debate about what might be considered perennial philosophical topics, such as truth (Chapter 1), justice (Chapter 2), agency (Chapter 3), gender (Chapter 4), and the divine (Chapter 5). But in addition to the profundity of its intellectual content, the *Mahābhārata* remains philosophically vital because of the ways that it compels its readers to reflect on their engagements with others and their own processes of thinking.

Although approaching the *Mahābhārata* as a dialogue partner has been lacking in much of Western scholarship, this is how it has been interpreted within the Indian commentarial tradition. As Arti Dhand has noted, traditional commentators on the *Mahābhārata* approached the text as a fully integrated whole that offered religious and philosophical teachings: 'That the purpose of a literary work is to foster self-understanding and emotional tranquility (*śānti*), leading to *mokṣa*, is taken for granted by the traditional commentators on the *Mahābhārata*' (2008: 10).[23] Along these lines, Vrinda Dalmiya and Gangeya Mukherji have characterised the *Mahābhārata* as an 'agent of dhārmic instruction' that offers 'moral training' that can transform its audiences: 'As a pedagogical tool, the *Mahābhārata itself* attempts to *initiate change in us*, its listeners/readers' (2018: 16, italics original).[24] In this way – and similar to what we have observed in Gadamer's work on Plato – Dalmiya and Mukherji see the *Mahābhārata*'s pedagogical value, not in any particular doctrine, but in the questions that it poses and the ways in which it discusses these questions. Unlike a Greek or Shakespearean tragedy where a conflict of views can be debilitating for moral judgement, the *Mahābhārata* – Dalmiya and Mukherji suggest – offers a moral training that encourages readers and listeners to 'be creative and adaptive': 'Differences in moral judgments, doubts and confusions, instead of leading to paralysis, actually enable ethical judgment on a case-by-case basis' (2018: 14).

Building on Dalmiya and Mukherji's insights, this book brings attention to the role of dialogue in offering the text's dharmic instructions. Throughout, we will explore the relationship between the medium of dialogue and its philosophical message of provoking further and deeper reflections into *dharma*. As we will discuss in Chapter 2, the term *dharma* is notoriously difficult to translate or even explain. One scholar who has done well to capture its dynamic connotations is Wilhelm Halbfass, who has remarked:

> Dharma... is neither a "natural" order immanent in the subsistence of the world nor an "objective" transcendental order and lawfulness. Instead, it is the continuous maintaining of the social and cosmic order and norm.
>
> (1988: 315)

Halbfass' reference to the cosmic order points to a metaphysical sense of *dharma* as a higher morality. The *Mahābhārata*, however, is deliberately vague about defining any metaphysical understanding of *dharma*. Like the Upaniṣads' portrayal of *ātman* and *brahman*, the *Mahābhārata* characterises *dharma* as always out of reach, as continually something to be learning more about. In this way, we can extend Halbfass' description of *dharma* as something that is continuously maintained as referring not only to the constant performance of our social obligations, but also to the continuous need to reflect on how we perform these obligations.

The *Mahābhārata* compels us into dialogue with others by vividly portraying the ways that characters engage in discussions with each other. Despite the wide range of views expressed and the variety of ways that moral discussions unfold, one recurring feature of dialogue is that it is portrayed as an integral aspect of living dharmically. As we will see, many of the dialogues we will examine in this book express the sense that living according to *dharma* is not merely following family and class obligations as rules or commandments, but rather requires a moral commitment to all interactions that one has with others. Part of *dharma*, then, is entering into dialogue with the uniqueness of each person and the specificity of every situation.

The *Mahābhārata* compels us into dialogue with ourselves by portraying unresolved tensions in *dharma* that require further deliberation. In each chapter, we will explore how dialogue conveys its dharmic instruction by focusing on a different case that the *Mahābhārata* encourages reflection upon. In examining how these five moral cases are presented through dialogue, we can see the text as a series of contested debates, each of which is both a unique situation and part of an ongoing exploration about making moral choices. In addition to moving through, even directing, a sequential narrative, the dialectics of dialogue also invite non-linear readings, as dialogues across the text share some of the same moral questions. As we will see, new meanings open up when we look at how different dialogues relate to similar questions in different ways. Dalmiya and Mukherji suggest that 'the epic asks us to saturate ourselves in these differences – to actively seek them out and to even imaginatively produce them ourselves' (2018: 14).

One of the tensions that the *Mahābhārata* compels us to consider is the relationship between the speeches and actions of its central characters. The greatest authorities on *dharma* sometimes make contradictory arguments, become equivocal, or simply remain silent in the most crucial circumstances; meanwhile, characters who often represent the forces of *adharma* (immorality) can sometimes make compelling cases and exhibit virtuous behaviour. In addition to these inversions and paradoxes in how *dharma* is enacted by the characters, it is repeatedly portrayed as beyond description and explanation. We noted earlier that Ramanujan has described 'the subtle nature of *dharma*' as the central theme of the *Mahābhārata*' (1999: 23). We have also seen that such descriptions seem to draw from the pedagogical rhetoric of the Upaniṣads that provokes further reflection and consideration. In prompting us to ponder the subtlety of *dharma*, the *Mahābhārata* stimulates what we might think of as 'dharmic reasoning'. What I mean by this is the consideration of a range of understandings of *dharma* in relation to a specific situation. As Sukthankar explains:

> Dharma is not simple and unitary, but manifold and complex. There are thus, for instance, rājadharma and prajādharma, jñātidharma and kuladharma, varṇāśramadharma, dānadharma, āpaddharma and mokṣadharma, strīdharma and so on and so forth. They must all be known accurately, if one is to act rightly, that is, according to the dictates of Dharma in all the various situations in life, smooth and rough, pleasant and unpleasant, normal and abnormal.
>
> [1957] (2016: 82)

Here, Sukthankar identifies a number of types of *dharma* that will feature prominently in the dialogues we discuss in this book, such as *rāja-dharma* (the *dharma* of kings), *kula-dharma* (the *dharma* of family obligations), *varṇāśrama-dharma* (the *dharma* of caste and stage of life), *āpad-dharma* (the *dharma* of extenuating circumstances), *mokṣa-dharma* (the *dharma* of renouncers), and *strī-dharma* (the *dharma* of women). In each chapter, we will look at dialogues in which characters talk about these and other types of *dharma* in sometimes conflicting relationships with each other.

As we will see, rather than prioritise one meaning of *dharma* over all others, the *Mahābhārata* indicates that a higher understanding consists of a consideration of its various meanings and how they relate to each other in any given situation. A number of the characters who are most knowledgeable about *dharma* – such as Bhīṣma, Yudhiṣṭhira, Draupadī, and Kṛṣṇa – make arguments by complexly bringing multiple understandings of *dharma* together. While some aspects of *dharma* are clearly emphasised on some occasions, no aspect eclipses all others in all circumstances. This does not mean that *dharma* becomes completely relative, but rather that an essential aspect of striving towards a deeper understanding of *dharma* is understanding its range of meanings, including its ambiguities and tensions. Moreover, it means that *dharma* needs to be reflected upon in relation to the specificity of each situation. By addressing each moral case differently, the *Mahābhārata* does not offer a specific formula for making moral choices, but rather indicates that every decision needs to be explored in its own unique complexity.

Through the centrality of philosophical deliberation within the narrative, the *Mahābhārata* suggests that sustained dialogue and reflection constitute integral aspects of cultivating *dharma*. In this way, the *Mahābhārata* is not merely 'about' *dharma*, but it develops *dharma* for those readers and listeners who engage with the moral questions it raises. In each chapter I will explore a particular moral problem as a case to be deliberated upon, not only by the characters within the text, but also by us, as the text's dialogical partners. Indeed, more than the characters within the story, we have all the available arguments before us. Because of the *Mahābhārata*'s claim to universality, as Dalmiya and Mukherji remind us, this dharmic instruction is available to everyone: 'As a text for all, the *Mahābbhārata*'s message about how to act, even though relayed to kings and warriors, is relevant for ordinary beings like ourselves' (2018: 14).

Notes

1 For further discussion of dialogue across Indian philosophical and religious traditions, see Black and Patton (2015); Black and Ram-Prasad (2019).
2 See, for example, Minkowski (1989), Black (2007b), Bowles (2007), Adluri (2011), Earl (2011), Hegarty, (2012), Hiltebeitel (2015a).
3 See, for example, Bailey (1983), Fitzgerald (2002a), Malinar (2007a), Patton (2007), Ram-Prasad (2018), Hegarty (2019), Sullivan (2019), Thomas (2019).
4 Adluri, who brings attention to these two in particular, notes: 'Hiltebeitel's careful studies of the epic thus open up an alternative way to look at the epic, one that does not privilege a hypothetical core over the epic's literary and philosophical aspects' (2011: 9).
5 See Black (2007a, 2011, and 2015b). See also Ganeri (2007: 13–38).
6 For the relationship between the Upaniṣads and *Mahābhārata*, see Black (2017).
7 For further discussion of the character Śaunaka, see Patton (2011: 113–135), Black and Geen (2011: 19–20), and Black (2017: 187–189; 197).

8 For a survey of the sporadic appearances of this description of *dharma* in the *Mahābhārata*, see Hara (1997).

9 For further discussion, see Bowles (2007: 101–103); see also Hiltebeitel (2011: 99–101) and Adluri (2017: 5).

10 Hudson also recognises the subtle nature of *dharma* as the central theme, indeed the central problem of the *Mahābhārata* (2013: 3). However, Hudson takes this description as 'disorienting' *dharma*, rather than as an Upaniṣadic nudge towards seeking deeper and more complex understandings.

11 For overviews of the main story, see van Buitenen (1973: xiii–xvi), Brockington (1998: 28–34), Fitzgerald (2004a: 61–68), and Smith (2009: xv–xviii). For abridged versions of the entire story, see Narasimhan (1996) and Smith (2009). For a detailed audio introduction to the entire story, see Manzo 2010–2012, the Mahabharata Podcast: https://mahabharatapodcast.blogspot.com.

12 See Black and Patton (2015: 2); and Black and Ram-Prasad (2019: 2–3).

13 According to Nikulin, despite emerging from dialogue, philosophy eventually – at least in a Western context – disassociates itself from dialogue: 'In modern philosophy ... dialogue is ousted by the advent of the Cartesian, self-centered, autonomous, and universal subject, who develops its dialectic of philosophical analysis as the method of correct reasoning' (2010: xii).

14 Julia Kristeva popularised the term intertextuality to refer to the ways that all literary works share literary features with other texts (1980). For discussions of intertextuality in the context of Indian religious and philosophical texts, see Ramanujan (1999), Bailey (1999), and Black and Geen (2011).

15 For an excellent overview of 19th- and early 20th-century scholarship on the *Mahābhārata*, see Sukthankar [1957] (2016: 1–31). For more recent overviews, see Brockington (1998: 129–158), Adluri (2011, 2013b), Hiltebeitel (2012), and Sullivan (2016).

16 Other well-known scholars who were dismissive of the *Mahābhārata*'s size and heterogeneity include Moriz Winternitz and Hermann Oldenberg, who described it as a 'literary unthing' and a 'monstrous chaos' (quoted in Hiletebeitel 2001b: 1; see also Sukthankar [1957] 2016: 1).

17 Winternitz proposed this at the eleventh International Conference of Orientalists in Paris in 1897.

18 According to Mehendale, the editors examined about 1,300 manuscripts, but used about 800 of them (2009: 10).

19 Because it is representative of the manuscript tradition as a whole, I have based my engagement with the *Mahābhārata* on the Critical Edition. All citations of the *Mahābhārata* in this book, unless otherwise noted, are from the Critical Edition. For discussions of the Critical Edition and its critics, see Sullivan (1999: 17–22), Hiltebeitel (2011: 14–20), and Adluri (2011: 9–11). For a guide to and thorough defence of the Critical Edition, see Adluri and Bagchee (2018).

20 See, for example, van Buitenen (1978:19) and Bowles (2007: 189).

21 Personal communication 23 November 2019.

22 As Chakrabarti and Bandyopadhyay observe: 'The *Mahābhārata* is at once an archive and a living text; a museum and a laboratory; and a sourcebook, complete by itself, and an open text, perennially under construction' (2014: xix).

23 For a brief summary of the views of some traditional commentators, see Dhand (2008: 11–12). For an in-depth study of the views of Ānandavardhana, see Tubb (1991: 171–2003). See also Hudson (2013: 56–61). For a list and brief description of all commentaries on the *Mahābhārata*, see Adluri and Bagchee (2018: 397–423).

24 Sukthankar was one of the first modern scholars to claim that the *Mahābhārata* offered a moral teaching about *dharma*: 'the epic aims at impressing upon the reader or rather the listener the paramountcy of moral values' [1957] (2016: 90).

1 Bhīṣma's vows

Introduction

Bhīṣma, whose birth name is Devavrata ('he whose vows are of the gods'), is the son of King Śaṃtanu and the goddess Gaṅgā. His divine identity is Dyaus, the eighth of a group of deities known as the Vasus. According to Vaiśaṃpāyana's narration, two generations before Bhīṣma's birth, the other seven Vasus and his mother Gaṅgā had made an agreement (*samaya*) that Bhīṣma will be born as human, but remain sonless (1.191.20–22). After growing up with his mother in heaven, Bhīṣma returns to his father and is anointed the crown prince. Soon afterwards, he learns that his father has fallen in love with the fisher princess Satyavatī. In order to fulfil the conditions of Satyavatī's father to approve her marriage with his father, Bhīṣma makes two demanding and far-reaching promises: (1) to pass on his claim to the throne to Satyavatī's future son and (2) the 'awesome' or 'terrifying' vow to practice celibacy. It is this second promise that earns him the name Bhīṣma ('Awesome' or 'Terrifying'), the name by which he is known throughout the remainder of the story. J.A.B. van Buitenen has described Bhīṣma's vow of celibacy as one of the most consequential events in the story: Bhīṣma's vow 'introduces all the later complications of succession. His oath, undertaken to aid his father, becomes a curse on his father's posterity' (1981: 2).

One generation later, after her two sons die without having produced any heirs, Satyavatī asks Bhīṣma to give up his two promises and marry her son Vicitravīrya's widowed queens:

> Your brother's queens, the good daughters of the king of the Kāśis, both lovely and in the bloom of their youth, are yearning for sons, Bhārata! Beget children on them, so that our line may continue, beget them at my behest, lord. Pray carry out the *dharma* that applies here. Be consecrated as king of the realm, rule the Bhāratas, take a wife by *dharma*, lest you drown your forbears.
>
> (1.97.9–11)[1]

Here, Satyavatī urges Bhīṣma to renounce his vows to maintain the family line. By citing *dharma*, Satyavatī's question poses a conflict for Bhīṣṃa: to keep his promises or to serve his family. As we will see, Satyavatī's attempt to persuade Bhīṣma is the first of several revisitations of his vows, sometimes through direct challenge by an interlocutor, other times by Bhīṣma offering a different account of events, and finally by an oblique self-criticism.

In this chapter, we will look closely at the circumstances under which Bhīṣma makes his vows, and then we will consider how they are discussed by narrators and characters in a series of five dialogues. We will pay close attention to what Bhīṣma and his interlocutors say about his vows – how they explain, justify, and criticise them. As we will see throughout this book, characters in the *Mahābhārata* – despite their divine identities and contributions towards the divine plan – tend to talk about themselves and others as moral agents who are responsible for their choices and actions. In the dialogues that we will examine in this chapter, both Bhīṣma and his interlocutors portray his vows as the result of actions he had a choice to perform and, in some cases, as promises that could be revoked for the right reasons in the right circumstances. It is notable that neither Bhīṣma nor any of his interlocutors make arguments about his vows by invoking fate, destiny, or the will of Dhātṛ (Ordainer) – all of which play prominent roles in arguments about some of the other moral questions we will discuss in this book. Despite Bhīṣma's divine identity and the curse he is born to fulfil, the moral status of his vows is a topic of repeated debate and reflection.

All the dialogues we will examine in this chapter include Bhīṣma, but he discusses or reflects on his vows differently with different interlocutors. These dialogues are between (1) Bhīṣma and Satyavatī, which takes place a generation after his initial vows; (2) Bhīṣma and Śiśupāla, which takes place just after Yudhiṣṭhira's royal ritual (*rājasūya*); (3) Bhīṣma and Duryodhana, which takes place during the failed peace negotiations before the war; (4) Bhīṣma and Duryodhana, which takes place immediately before the war; and (5) Bhīṣma and Yudhiṣṭhira, which takes place after the war, as the Pāṇḍavas reflect back on their actions during the war and prepare for kingship. By looking at these dialogues together, I will treat them as an ongoing conversation about the moral status of Bhīṣma's vows. As we will see, Bhīṣma gives different justifications for his vows as he responds to different interlocutors, in different circumstances, and at different stages in the narrative. Meanwhile, some of his interlocutors, as well as Bhīṣma himself, offer challenges that characterise his vows as morally problematic.

While looking at these dialogues alongside each other, we will also note that Bhīṣma continues to make further vows. In addition to his most famous vows to renounce the throne and to observe celibacy, Bhīṣma makes five more solemn promises: (1) to be truthful to his vows, (2) never to abandon *kṣatriya-dharma*, (3) not to engage in battle with a woman or someone of ambiguous gender, (4) not to retreat from battle, and (5) to fight against the Pāṇḍavas. Each of these is distinct, yet each is also, to some degree, interconnected with his other promises, particularly the first two. As we will see, the different types of vows he takes, the different reasons for which he takes them, and the different ways that they come into conflict with his interpersonal obligations bring to attention further reasons to question, not only his own vows, but also the practice of vow-taking more generally.

In the final section of the chapter, we will look at the multiple explanations for Bhīṣma's death. As we will see, the causes of his death are explained differently by different characters on different occasions. Rather than seeing the multiple explanations as inconsistencies, we will treat them as contestatory views, each with their own perspectives on Bhīṣma's death and the narrative arc of his life as a whole. As we will see, the multiple explanations for Bhīṣma's death are an illustrative example of a recurring tendency throughout the *Mahābhārata* in which several reasons are given for morally problematic episodes.

The dialectics of taking vows

Throughout the *Mahābhārata*, vows are highly regarded as acts of extreme difficulty. They are also invested with enormous power, as those who carry out their vows shape the world around them. Of all the characters in the main story, Bhīṣma is the most famous vow-taker. His vow of celibacy, in particular, achieves for him the ultimate triumph over fate – control over his mortality, as we shall see later in the chapter. Despite depicting the positive virtues of vows and of those who perform them, the *Mahābhārata* also lays bare the unforeseen and sometimes brutal consequences that even those vows made with the utmost sanctity and sincerity can have on other people. As the story unfolds, Bhīṣma's vows are repeatedly questioned as their wide-ranging repercussions are examined. Each time he is asked to renounce his vows, Bhīṣma adamantly refuses, sometimes adding new understandings of why he took them in the first place. Although Bhīṣma is highly praised for steadfastly living up to his word, his vows are also characterised as morally problematic.

As we noted in the Introduction, philosophical dialogues include not only philosophical content, but also philosophical methods embedded within their structures. In this chapter, I will approach the ongoing discussions about Bhīṣma's vows as a case study on how the *Mahābhārata* explores moral problems through dialogue. Similar to what some Western philosophers have called 'dialectic', many dialogues in the *Mahābhārata* set up contrasts and tensions between different doctrines. Hans-Georg Gadamer, with Hegel in mind, describes dialectic as 'thinking in contradictions' (1980: 93). Similarly, Dmitri Nikulin, when discussing Plato, describes dialectic as proceeding 'in terms of opposites' (2010: 5–6). What both of these philosophers capture is that dialectic can be understood as a philosophical way of thinking that involves juxtaposition and comparison. Whereas both Gadamer and Nikulin emphasise contradiction and opposition, I think dialectic in the *Mahābhārata* would be better characterised in terms of contrast and tension. Moreover, whereas some Western philosophers have seen the oppositions of dialectic resulting in a synthesis, in the *Mahābhārata*, contrasts and tensions tend to remain unresolved. As we will see throughout this book, there are a number of competing ideas that are repeatedly juxtaposed with one another, such as *kula-dharma* and *kṣatriya-dharma*; *pravṛtti* and *nivṛtti*; *karma-yoga* and *mokṣa-dharma*; fate (*daiva*) and human agency (*puruṣakāra*); and violence and non-violence (*ahiṃsā*). These dichotomies are not only represented as distinct doctrines in different sections of the text, but are put into dialogue with each other through the different arguments made by characters when in conversations with each other. In this way, the dialogue form is a crucial way through which the *Mahābhārata* explores its core religious and philosophical ideas in relation to each other and in the context of specific cases.

This might seem obvious, but not all dialogues – either in the *Mahābhārata* or in other contexts – are like this. For example, some dialogues in the *Mahābhārata*, as well as in texts such as the Upaniṣads and Nikāyas, are more pedagogical than dialectical. Although even pedagogical dialogues can include some tensions and ambiguities, speakers tend not to express contrasting points of view, and the verbal exchanges between teacher and student often work together to disclose a single teaching, rather than to put two or more arguments into an oppositional relationship. What I am suggesting, then, is that many dialogues in the *Mahābhārata* are dialectical in the sense that they convey a philosophical method in which opposing arguments are compared and contrasted through juxtaposition. Sometimes dialogue is used to harmonise contrasting views, but, more often, discussions come to a close with tensions remaining. Some views seem to be prioritised more than others, because they are more often repeated, expressed at key moments in the story, or articulated by particularly authoritative characters. Nonetheless, in offering an array of views in a series of moral cases, the *Mahāhārata* is able to hold together multiple views without establishing a fixed hierarchy between them and without completely synthesising them.

In the context of Bhīṣma's vows, there is an ongoing tension between the different justifications for him taking his vows and different reasons for renouncing them. As the narrative unfolds, Bhīṣma defends his vows from a number of different positions, including the importance of maintaining them for their own sake, for being true to his word, for the sake of *kula-dharma,* and for the sake of *kṣatriya-dharma.* Meanwhile, some of the reasons he should give up his vows include maintaining the family lineage, adhering to *kula-dharma,* abiding by the wishes of his mother, protecting a wronged woman, and observing *ahiṃsā.*

While many individual dialogues set up dialectics between different views and perspectives through the arguments of the different characters, dialectical relationships also emerge between dialogues as the narrative unfolds. As we have seen in the Introduction, different sections within the text sometimes have a contestatory relationship with each other. In this way, much of the intra-textuality in the *Mahābhārata* is specifically dialectical because different dialogical episodes will address the same questions in different ways. Thus, an important aspect of dialectic in the *Mahābhārata* is that dialogues from different parts of the text are related to each other by contributing to the same ongoing examination of a central moral question. In other words, by returning to the same questions throughout the narrative, the *Mahābhārata* explores the temporal dimension of dialectic – that the relationships between arguments change as circumstances change.

The narrative context of Bhīṣma's first two vows

Śaṃtanu, Satyavatī, and Satyavatī's father (1.94.41–52)

Vaiśaṃpāyana's narration of the circumstances leading up to Bhīṣma's vows celebrates them as difficult and heroic acts that receive the praise of the gods and of all those who witness him making them. Nevertheless, the way that Vaiśaṃpāyana tells the story emphasises their moral ambiguity. As Vaiśaṃpāyana recounts, when seeking out the source of a sweet fragrance, King Śaṃtanu encounters a lovely maiden and asks her who she is and what she is doing. The maiden, Satyavatī, replies that she is the daughter of the King of the Fishers and that she plies a raft across the river at her father's command. Notably, Śaṃtanu does not ask Satyavatī anything else, but goes to her father to ask for his permission to marry her. The Fisher King shows enthusiasm for the union, but demands that Śaṃtanu make a 'covenant' (*samaya*) that any son born from their marriage will inherit the throne. Unable to agree, King Śaṃtanu despondently returns to his palace.

Here we see that the backstory of Bhīṣma's vows begins with a 'covenant' (*samaya*) his father refuses to make. We might see his father's reluctance to take a vow as the proper course of action that Bhīṣma should follow himself. Before encountering Satyavatī, Śaṃtanu had already anointed Bhīṣma as the crown prince (1.94.38), so presumably he does not want to go back on his word. Another point worth noting is that despite speaking very briefly here, Satyavatī uses the term *dharma* in the sense of a family obligation, saying that she plies the raft across the river because this is what her father had commanded her to do. As we will see, arguments based on *kula-dharma* will be key to her arguments later.

Śaṃtanu, Bhīṣma, and the king's minister (1.94.53–66)

When Śaṃtanu returns to Hāstinapura, he is overcome with sorrow because of his desire for Satyavatī. When Bhīṣma approaches his father, asking why he is sorrowful when his kingdom is secure, Śaṃtanu replies that he is concerned about the future of the lineage. More specifically, he says that he is concerned that he only has one son – Bhīṣma – and should anything happen to him there would be no heir to the throne. He assures Bhīṣma that he is not interested in marriage, but only in the survival of the lineage. He then claims that, according to *dharma*, having only one son is equivalent to having no sons. Śaṃtanu concludes by assuring Bhīṣma that this is the reason (*kāraṇa*) for his suffering (*duḥkha*) (1.94.63). Here, Śaṃtanu does not tell his son about his desire for Satyavatī, but rather masks his infatuation as a concern about the future of the lineage. In addition to attributing his overwhelming distress to family obligations, Śaṃtanu specifically tells Bhīṣma he does not want to marry again, even though he has just asked Satyavatī's father for her hand in marriage.

Perhaps suspecting that his father is lying to him, Bhīṣma seeks out an old councillor to question him about the reason behind his father's grief. The councillor then tells Bhīṣma about the boon (*vara*) that the Fisher King had asked for from Śaṃtanu. Upon hearing this, Bhīṣma – along with a group of old *kṣatriya*s – goes to the Fisher King to ask for Satyavatī's hand on behalf of his father (1.94.67). The fact that Bhīṣma knows the real reason for his father's grief indicates that he deliberately chooses to privilege his loyalty to his father over his duty to be the crown prince. But even though he will later justify this decision as based on loyalty to his father, it is striking that his father never asks him to seek out Satyavatī. Instead, without consulting anyone, Bhīṣma makes a decision that was not his to make and one that will have devastating consequences for his family for generations to come.

Bhīṣma and Satyavatī's father (1.94.67–94)

When Bhīṣma approaches Satyavatī's father, the Fisher King raises his concern about the possibility of rivalry between Bhīṣma and Satyavatī's male offspring. Interestingly, he does not say yes or no to the marriage, but merely presents succession as a problem. Bhīṣma responds by making the first of two vows, declaring that Satyavatī's son will become the king:

> Now hear what is in my mind, and accept it as the truth (*satya*), most truthful king. The man is not born, nor will he be born, who dares say the same. I shall do as you are counselling me. The son who is born from her shall be our king!
>
> (1.94.78–79)

The Fisher King acknowledges Bhīṣma's sacrifice, but points out that any future children of Bhīṣma might still claim the throne. Again, the king does not ask Bhīṣma to make any promises, but merely presents this as a problem, something for which he has great 'doubt' (*saṃśaya*) (1.94.84). In response, Bhīṣma makes a further promise:

> Chief of the fishermen, great king! Hear this word of mine that I speak for my father's sake while these *kṣatriya*s are listening. I have already

> renounced the kingdom, king – now here I make my resolve about my progeny. From this day onward I shall practice celibacy (*brahmacarya*). And though I shall remain sonless, the imperishable world in heaven shall be mine!
>
> (1.94.86–88)

The two words most commonly used to designate Bhīṣma's promises are *pratijñā* (promise) and *vrata* (vow). Here, in his account of Bhīṣma's first two promises, Vaiśaṃpāyana uses the word *pratijñā*, but both are referred to as *vrata* later in the narrative, suggesting that the two terms can be used interchangeably. George Thompson has suggested that vows – along with truth-acts, oaths, confessions, curses, blessings, and charms – can be viewed as speech-acts, in the sense that they are utterances that 'accomplish something' (1998: 126). More specifically, vows are 'promissory', in the sense that they pertain to future events (1998: 142). Another recurring feature of vows, as well as other speech-acts, is that they emphasise the moral character of the person who proclaims them. As Bruce Sullivan has reflected: 'All these speech acts derive their perceived efficacy from a shared ideology according to which words spoken by a person are empowered by that person's qualities: truthfulness and the fulfilment of one's vows enable one to affect the world with words'.[2] With Thompson's observations in mind, both of Bhīṣma's initial promises can be seen as speech-acts in which he attempts to bring about the marriage of his father to Satyavatī. They are also 'promissory' in the sense that they pertain to future events and are taken in front of an audience – in addition to the Fisher King himself, Bhīṣma makes his promise in front of the group of *kṣatriya*s he had brought with him. The audience of *kṣatriya*s is important because, as we will see later, Bhīṣma will closely associate vow-taking with *kṣatriya-dharma*.

In his first promise, we should note, Bhīṣma only states that Satyavatī's son should become the king, not that he should never become king in any circumstances. It is Bhīṣma's second promise – to live a life of a *brahmacārin* – that persuades the king to give his daughter's hand in marriage to Bhīṣma's father. In addition to the king's enthusiastic reply, there is a divine response, as *deva*s, seers, and *apsarā*s proclaim: 'He is Bhīṣma!' (1.94.90). Similarly, when he returns to Hāstinapura, Bhīṣma is praised again, this time by the princes in the court, who, noting his difficult act (*duṣkara karman*), also proclaim: 'He is Bhīṣma!'. His father responds to his difficult act (*duṣkara karman*) by granting him the boon of choosing his own time of death (1.94.94).

As we can see, Vaiśaṃpāyana's narrative portrays Bhīṣma's vow of celibacy very positively, as it not only convinces Satyavatī's father to agree to the marriage, but it is also praised as a heroic act by the gods, the princes in the court, and his father. Indeed, it is through taking this vow that he – who up to this point is known as Devavrata – acquires his name 'Bhīṣma', which is bestowed on him twice, first by the gods and then by the princes of the court. His father clearly endorses his vows when he grants his son the boon to choose his own time of death.

In addition to highlighting the public declarations of praise, Vaiśaṃpāyana's narration also exposes some of the problems with Bhīṣma's vows by laying bare the dubious circumstances under which they were pronounced. As we have seen, Bhīṣma's father lies to him, explaining his sorrowful state in terms of the future of the lineage, rather than because of his infatuation with a young woman. Although Bhīṣma knows the truth when he goes to Satyavatī's father, the fact that he makes his vows without being asked to raises the question whether Bhīṣma should have taken them in the first place. Crucially, despite the enormity of his decision, Bhīṣma acts quickly, perhaps impulsively, without the opportunity for discussion or debate. In this way, Vaiśaṃpāyana does not portray Bhīṣma's vows as dilemmas – as difficult choices he had to make. Instead, his vows only become moral problems in retrospect, as they are re-evaluated from the perspective of different interlocutors, in different situations, as the consequences of his vows lead in disastrously unintended directions.

Bhīṣma and Satyavatī (1.97–99)

Let us turn our attention to an episode one generation later, when Satyavatī asks Bhīṣma to give up his promises. After Śaṃtanu and Satyavatī marry, they have two children, Citrāṅgada and Vicitravīrya. Citrāṅgada dies in a battle, after which Bhīṣma performs the *rākṣasa* type of marriage for Vicitravīrya, for which he abducts three queens from Kāśi: Ambā, Ambikā, and Ambālikā.[3] Soon after being taken to Hāstinapura, Ambā tells Bhīṣma that she was already engaged and hence goes back to her fiancée. We will return to Ambā's story and how it reflects back on Bhīṣma's initial vows later in this chapter.

Meanwhile, Vicitravīrya marries the two princesses, but dies before fathering any children. In an effort to solve this dynastic crisis, Satyavatī asks Bhīṣma to give up his two promises and marry Vicitravīrya's widowed queens:

> You know the *dharma*s, in full and in part, you know the various (*vividha*) traditions (*śruti*), you know the Veda in every way. I see the disposition by *dharma*, the proper custom of family (*kulācāra*), and the procedure in difficult situations (*kṛcchra*) as securely lodged with you as with Śukra or Bṛhaspati.
>
> (1.97.5–6)

By citing a variety of authorities, Satyavatī implies that when Bhīṣma's vows are considered from a wider range of perspectives, there are legitimate grounds for him to give them up. By referring to 'the proper custom of family' (*kulācāra*), she indicates that there is traditional support for marrying the wives of one's step-brother – a practice we find in other instances in the *Mahābhārata*. And by mentioning 'difficult situations' (*kṛcchra*), she is perhaps pointing in the direction of *āpad-dharma*, which she will mention explicitly a bit further on in this dialogue. Finally, by referring to Bṛhaspati and Śukra, the divine teachers of both the *deva*s (gods) and *asura*s (demons), she thus includes both their perspectives. Moreover, Bṛhaspati is named as one of Bhīṣma's teachers in heaven (1.94.34).[4] Notably, in presenting a range of intersecting points, all of them based on *dharma* and tradition, Satyavatī makes an argument similar to those made by Yudhiṣṭhira when he defends the polyandrous marriage (Chapter 2), and by Draupadī when she defends her autonomy after the dicing match (Chapter 4). We might wonder why, then, Satyavatī's arguments are so easily dismissed by Bhīṣma and by Vaiśaṃpāyana who is narrating this scene.

After presenting her case, Satyavatī then specifically asks Bhīṣma to father children with Ambikā and Ambālikā for the sake of continuing the family lineage, again characterising her request in terms of *dharma* (1.97.11). By framing her argument in terms of the continuation of the lineage, Satyavatī's request parallels that of Śaṃtanu's explanation for his sorrow a generation earlier. But whereas Bhīṣma's father used the future of the lineage to disguise the real reasons for his suffering, Satyavatī genuinely has the future of the lineage in mind.

Despite Satyavatī's appeal to a multiplicity of *dharma*s and Vedic authorities, Bhīṣma refuses to marry the princesses, citing the 'highest promise' (*parā pratijñā*) he had taken to renounce offspring. He acknowledges that Satyavatī is quoting the 'highest (*para*) *dharma*', but nevertheless uses this occasion to reinforce his previous promises with another promise:

> Here I promise (*prati* + √*jñā*) my truth (*satya*), again, Satyavatī – I shall forsake the three worlds, and the sovereignty of the Gods, or whatever surpasses both, before I forsake my truth (*satya*)! Earth shall forsake its fragrance, water its taste ... Indra shall renounce his power and the king of the Dharma [shall renounce] *dharma*, but never shall I resolve to forsake my truth (*satya*).
>
> (1.97.14–18)

In making the initial contrast between the 'highest *dharma*' and the 'highest truth', Bhīṣma articulates the emerging dilemmas created by his vows: keeping his own word or maintaining his obligations towards others. Notably, Bhīṣma does not restate his earlier vows to renounce the throne or to live a life of celibacy, but rather makes a new promise to be true to his vow.

Satyavatī responds, assuring Bhīṣma that she regards him as a man of truth. Then she reminds him that his vows were taken for her sake, indicating an authoritative perspective from which to question whether the vows remain relevant. Satyavatī continues her argument by repeating her plea to save the lineage and then suggests Bhīṣma could break his vows by following *āpad-dharma* for the higher purposes of continuing the lineage and supporting his family (1.97.21–22). Throughout the *Mahābhārata*, *āpad-dharma* is often invoked as a justification for acting against *dharma* in exceptional circumstances. Indeed, an entire section of Bhīṣma's post-war teaching to Yudhiṣṭhira is devoted to the topic. As Adam Bowles defines it, *āpad-dharma*

> fundamentally means 'right conduct in times of distress', and refers to the relaxing of normative rules of behaviour when extraordinary social, environmental or other difficulties, have made these normative rules difficult to follow. In short, *āpaddharma* refers to exceptional rules for exceptional circumstances
>
> (2007: 2)

Satyavatī's reference to *āpad-dharma* is the first time in the main narrative when a character mentions the term.[5] Vaiśaṃpāyana and Bhīṣma both respond to her invocation of *āpad-dharma* as if she is making too extreme an argument. Vaiśaṃpāyana describes her as 'straying from *dharma*', while Bhīṣma accuses her of not following *dharma* and, thus, potentially bringing about the destruction of the family (1.97.24–25). Notably, when claiming that she is straying from *dharma*, Vaiśaṃpāyana describes Satyavatī as 'babbling' (√*lap*) and desirous for grandsons (1.97.23). These belittling remarks contrast sharply with his own narration, in which Satyavatī cites traditional authorities and invokes widely recognised teachings on *dharma*. Moreover, she never says anything specifically about grandsons, but rather argues for what is best for the sake of the lineage, which is legitimately under threat in these circumstances.

Bhīṣma then recounts the tale of the seer Utathya, in which the blind brahmin Dīrghatamas fathers eleven sons and then acts as surrogate father for the heir to King Balin. Bhīṣma uses this story to suggest using the practice of *niyoga*. As Arti Dhand explains:

> *Niyoga* is the custom of levirate marriage, a special provision in the sexual ethics of ancient and classical India. It allowed for a woman to obtain children through the instrument of another man, if her husband were diseased, infertile, or otherwise incapacitated.
>
> (2004: 38)[6]

Here, Bhīṣma suggests that *niyoga* can be practised according to *āpad-dharma*, telling Satyavatī to invite a brahmin to father children with the wives of Vicitravīrya. We should recall that it was Satyavatī's idea to invoke *āpad-dharma*, but here Bhīṣma reinterprets how they should do so. Rather than resort to *āpad-dharma* to justify abandoning his promises, Bhīṣma argues that they should invoke *āpad-dharma* to justify the practice of *niyoga*. Satyavatī replies, telling Bhīṣma that he has spoken the truth and represents the *dharma* of the family. She then informs him about her pre-marital son

Vyāsa, suggesting that he could perform *niyoga* with Ambikā and Ambālikā. It is notable that after Bhīṣma approves of this scheme, Vaiśaṃpāyana refers to his approval as a 'promise' (*pratijñā*) (1.99.21), thus connecting his role in co-organising *niyoga* with his previous promises.

At the beginning of this chapter, we discussed how dialectic can be understood as the interplay of contradictory principles or opposing forces. In the conversation between Bhīṣma and Satyavatī, there is a dialectic between the arguments of the two characters. Although both Satyavatī's case for abandoning the vows and Bhīṣma's defences of them are articulated in terms of *dharma*, their arguments emphasise different aspects of *dharma*. Satyavatī – whose two children have died without a male heir – portrays Bhīṣma's promises as violating his *kula-dharma*, while Bhīṣma justifies them in terms of *kṣatriya-dharma*.

The dialectic between the different views on Bhīṣma's vows also plays out over time, as arguments for and against them change as circumstances change. In Vaiśaṃpāyana's narration of the circumstances under which Bhīṣma initially takes his vows, they are explained in terms of his loyalty to his father. Satyavatī's emphasis on *kula-dharma*, then, has particular relevance because it offers a counterargument to Bhīṣma's initial justification. Moreover, Satyavatī brings attention to the new context, indicating that the original reasons for his vows no longer apply. But rather than continue to argue from the perspective of family loyalty, Bhīṣma takes an additional vow, effectively giving himself a new justification for keeping his old ones. In taking the additional vow, Bhīṣma reinterprets his initial promises in terms of his adherence to the vows themselves, rather than in terms of loyalty to his father. The evolving justifications for his vows bring attention to the temporal dimensions of dialectic. In other words, a central aspect of dialectic in the *Mahābhārata* is the consideration of the same question within different contexts.

Another understanding of dialectic, often associated with Hegel, is the juxtaposition of contrary views for the sake of resolving the conflict between them. According to Kenneth Dorter in a study of the *Bhagavad Gītā*, one of dialectic's characteristic features is that 'opposing points of view … progressively come to agreement' (2012: 308). On some level, something similar happens in the encounter between Bhīṣma and Satyavatī. As we have seen, when proposing *niyoga*, Bhīṣma uses the same terminology introduced by Satyavatī, but he uses it to make a different point. Rather than completely rejecting Satyavatī's argument, he redeploys her invocation of *āpad-dharma* to reach what could be considered a synthesis of their positions.[7] In other words, despite making opposing arguments based on *dharma*, Satyavatī and Bhīṣma come to a resolution through *āpad-dharma*. Bringing juxtapositions to a possible resolution illustrates how dialectic can be seen as a philosophical method that can bring about agreement.

Although some dialogues in the *Mahābhārata* offer potential resolutions between opposing views, I think Dorter overemphasises the role of synthesis in dialectic, at least in the *Mahābhārata* and *Bhagavad Gītā*. In the case of the dialogue between Bhīṣma and Satyavatī, their discussion might appear to result in the combination of viewpoints to achieve a mutually desired end – the continuation of the lineage – but their dialogue also presents a number of unresolved tensions, particularly within different understandings of *dharma*. Within *kula-dharma*, by acting out of duty to his father in the short term, Bhīṣma puts his family in danger in the long term; within *kṣatriya-dharma*, by living up to his word, he is unable to fulfil other class-related duties such as having male children and protecting women. In addition to the ongoing tensions within both types of *dharma* at a conceptual level, there is also the ongoing problem of the future of the lineage at a narrative level. Their dialogue might be resolved in the short term as Bhīṣma and Satyavatī work together to continue the dynastic line, but because their plan leads to the breach within the family, Bhīṣma's vows will continue to be questioned.

Bhīṣma and Śiśupāla (2.33–42)

Śiśupāla is the next character to challenge Bhīṣma's vows. In a heated exchange that takes place on the day of the unction during Yudhiṣṭhira's *rājasūya*, Śiśupāla condemns Bhīṣma for advising Yudhiṣṭhira to give the guest gift to Kṛṣṇa. As van Buitenen points out, by bestowing the guest gift to Kṛṣṇa as part of his *rājasūya*, Yudhiṣṭhira is appointing him as the next in line for the position of universal sovereign. As the King of Cedi, Śiśupāla strongly objects to Kṛṣṇa, who is not a king, receiving the honour. Indeed, van Buitenen suggests that Śiśupāla might have had 'such pretensions himself' (1975: 23). Śiśupāla also has other objections to Kṛṣṇa, who he sees as responsible for the assassination of Jarāsaṃdha,[8] his former ally. It is also noteworthy that Śiśupāla had assisted Jarāsaṃdha in attacking Mathurā, Kṛṣṇa's ancestral home.[9] The angry exchange between Śiśupāla and Bhīṣma is particularly dramatic not only because it offers the most scathing criticisms of Bhīṣma's vows and his behaviour more generally, but also because Śiśupāla is killed by Kṛṣṇa immediately afterwards, an act that – as we will see in Chapter 3 – is considered morally problematic by Duryodhana and contributes to him wanting to take revenge on Yudhiṣṭhira.

Before engaging with Bhīṣma directly, Śiśupāla addresses Yudhiṣṭhira, telling him that Kṛṣṇa does not deserve a regal honour. Despite criticising him, Śiśupāla does not blame Yudhiṣṭhira, not only because he knows that Bhīṣma advised him to anoint Kṛṣṇa, but also because he regards him and his brothers as 'children' (*bāla*), who do not yet understand the subtlety of *dharma* (2.34.3). As we discussed in the Introduction, the portrayal of *dharma* as subtle is a recurring theme throughout the *Mahābhārata*. Śiśupāla's invocation of this understanding of *dharma* on this occasion is significant because such an understanding is closely associated with all three characters he opposes here: Yudhiṣṭhira, Bhīṣma, and Kṛṣṇa. Not only do all of them use this phrase (as we will see in subsequent chapters), but also all are regarded by other characters in the text as authorities on *dharma*. It is not clear whether Śiśupāla claims to have a subtle understanding himself, but by talking about *dharma* in this way, he uses the language associated with his interlocutors against them.[10]

Bhīṣma defends his decision by proclaiming the divine status of Kṛṣṇa:

> For Kṛṣṇa alone is the origin of the worlds as well as their dissolution, for Kṛṣṇa's sake is all that exists here offered. He is the Unmanifest Cause and the Sempiternal Doer, higher than all creatures.
>
> (2.35.22–23)

Kṛṣṇa has had a rather mysterious presence in the narrative up to this point, and this is the first public statement in the main narrative about his divine status as creator and destroyer of the universe. Vaiśaṃpāyana prepares his audience for this revelation just before this scene, when he recounts Nārada recollecting that Kṛṣṇa is Nārāyaṇa, and indeed that all the kings assembled at Yudhiṣhtira's *rājasūya* are incarnations of divine beings (2.13.11–21). But Nārada's recollection is to himself and does not inform any of the assembled kings about what he is thinking. Bhīṣma, then, is the first character within the main story to reveal the divine identity of Kṛṣṇa to others.

After the Pāṇḍavas give Kṛṣṇa the guest gift, Bhīṣma reiterates Kṛṣṇa's divinity, praising him as 'the beginning' (*prabhava*) and 'the end' (*nidhana*) (2.37.14). Śiśupāla replies, saying that Bhīṣma should be ashamed of himself, as he is a 'defiler of his family' (*kula-pāṃsana*) (2.38.1). He then characterises Bhīṣma as having an ambiguous sexual identity, saying that he is of a 'third nature' (*tṛtīyā prakṛti*) (2.38.2) who speaks in violation of *dharma*. Here, Śiśupāla's first response to the message of Kṛṣṇa's divine identity is to attack the integrity of its messenger. In addition to accusing Bhīṣma of violating *dharma*, Śiśupāla suggests that he took his vow of celibacy because he is unable to father children.

Śiśupāla then begins to challenge the claims that Bhīṣma had made about Kṛṣṇa, wondering why he extols a mere cattle herder. As we will see in Chapter 5, Śiśupāla's criticisms are the first in an ongoing series of challenges to Kṛṣṇa's divinity and teachings. But unlike the dialogues that involve Kṛṣṇa himself, this exchange includes a stronger denial of his divine identity, as well as a harsher criticism of his character more generally. Śiśupāla then turns his attention back to criticising Bhīṣma's understanding of *dharma*, saying that he does not know *dharma* (2.38.15), that he speaks of *dharma* but does not honour it (2.38.19), and that he ignores *dharma* (2.38.20). Throughout his argument, Śiśupāla challenges Bhīṣma's adherence to both *kula-dharma* and *kṣatriya-dharma*: *kula-dharma* because he has not held up his duty to the lineage and has put its future in jeopardy; *kṣatriya-dharma* because he does not have sons. Śiśupāla also appeals to a more general sense of *dharma*, of knowing the right thing to do. In this case, he questions how Bhīṣma could have abducted Ambā if he knows *dharma* (2.38.21). Śiśupāla then criticises Bhīṣma for allowing his brother's wives to sleep with another man, repeating that he has 'no *dharma*' (2.38.24). Keeping Sullivan's comments in mind – that the efficacy of a vow is 'empowered by that person's qualities' – we can see that by questioning his qualities, Śiśupāla is arguing that Bhīṣma's words cannot be taken as true because he habitually violates *dharma*.

Śiśupāla then returns to criticising Bhīṣma's vow of celibacy, calling it a lie that he preserves because of either ignorance or impotence (2.38.24). Here, for the second time, Śiśupāla indicates that Bhīṣma's vow disguises a sexual flaw. Śiśupāla then further accuses Bhīṣma of not fulfilling his *dharma*, arguing that his 'vows and fasts' (*vratopavāsa*) are worthless without progeny and that he will die at the hands of his own family (2.38.27–28). It is difficult to determine if there is any veracity to Śiśupāla's accusations. Considering his status as an historic enemy of Kṛṣṇa, we might doubt whether his allegations can be believed. However, it is noteworthy that Bhīṣma does not deny any of the charges. Also, because Vaiśaṃpāyana's narration leaves Bhīṣma's motivations for making his vows unclear, Śiśupāla's accusations offer a plausible explanation for why Bhīṣma might make such extreme vows, despite knowing that his father was lying to him and despite no one asking him to make them.

A bit further on, Bhīṣma argues that Śiśupāla is only criticising him because it is part of Kṛṣṇa's will, reasoning that because no king would dare challenge him, Śiśupāla must be acting according to fate (*daiva*) (2.41.2). Here, Bhīṣma uses the word *daiva*, which literally means 'of the gods'. In the dialogues leading up to the dicing match (see Chapter 3), both Dhṛtarāṣṭra and Yudhiṣṭhira will speak of *daiva* to refer to a situation that they consider to be beyond their control and in some sense destined. Here, however, Bhīṣma characterises *daiva* in terms of acting according to the 'intention' (*buddhi*) of Kṛṣṇa. In making this claim, Bhīṣma undermines the credibility of Śiśupāla's arguments by denying him any agency in making them. Crucially, however, Bhīṣma does not actually defend himself against any of the charges Śiśupāla makes against him. Rather than engage with any of Śiśupāla's criticisms, he again resorts to personal attacks.

Śiśupāla then criticises Bhīṣma's loyalty to Kṛṣṇa, accusing him of not listening to traditional teachers of *dharma* (2.41.14). Here, he tells the story of a *bhūliṅga* bird who instructs others to avoid danger, but who acts recklessly. Like this bird, Śiśupāla concludes, Bhīṣma speaks 'words without knowing the right *dharma*' (2.41.22). After this, Bhīṣma invites the angry kings to challenge Kṛṣṇa to a duel – an invitation that Śiśupāla accepts, only to be killed by Kṛṣṇa.

In his exchange with Śiśupāla, we see much harsher criticisms of Bhīṣma's vow than anywhere before or after. Although Śiśupāla's real target is Kṛṣṇa, his attacks on Bhīṣma are an attempt to undermine the integrity of the person who first articulates Kṛṣṇa's divinity. Van Buitenen has suggested that Śiśupāla's challenge can be seen as a trace of the original *rājasūya* ritual, as depicted in the Vedic ritual texts (1975: 23). Tamar Reich has also taken Śiśupāla as serving the ritual function as the challenger or reviler of the ritual:

> The Rājasūya episode, in which the rival king, Śiśupāla, challenges Yudhiṣṭhira's consecration as regional overlord and ends up losing his head, combines the two agonistic motifs [described in ritual texts], namely, the outsider who breaks into the sacrificial arena and disrupts the sacrifice, and the verbal contest.
>
> (1998: 277)[11]

As Reich explains, agonistic rituals such as the *rājasūya* and *aśvamedha* included dramatic verbal exchanges between a 'praiser', who extols the glory of the main deity of the ritual, and a 'reviler', who 'insults and censures the same god' (1998: 277). Reich argues that according to the logic of the *rājasūya*, any evil that emerges from the practice of the ritual is 'shifted to the opponents' (1998: 278). According to Reich, even though Kṛṣṇa is criticised, the role of the reviler 'ultimately enhances Kṛṣṇa's credentials' (1998: 277).

While it may be the case that the inclusion of Śiśupāla as a reviler is further evidence of the ritual structure of the *Sabhā Parvan* (see Chapter 3), it should also be noted that there are some key differences between the narrative depiction of the debate in the *Mahābhārata* and the way verbal exchanges are presented in ritual sources. Although Śiśupāla reviles Kṛṣṇa, he criticises him as the king's anointed successor, not as the main deity of the ritual. Moreover, Śiśupāla does not challenge the ritual itself, nor does he challenge Yudhiṣṭhira, who is sponsoring the ritual. With this in mind, we might wonder if Śiśupāla's criticisms ultimately enhance Kṛṣṇa's credentials in the way that they might in a more traditional ritualistic setting. By focusing on the dialogue within the unfolding of the narrative, I think we can see Śiśupāla's criticisms – rather than being absolved through ritual – as adding a voice to ongoing challenges to both Kṛṣṇa and Bhīṣma. Śiśupāla himself is silenced when he is beheaded, but his accusations are never countered. Indeed, we might keep Śiśupāla's suspicion of an ulterior motive in mind as we reflect on how subsequent dialogues characterise Bhīṣma's vows.

Bhīṣma and Duryodhana (5.145)

The next dialogue to discuss Bhīṣma's promises is between Bhīṣma and Duryodhana. Unlike the debates Bhīṣma has with Satyavatī and Śiśupāla, this exchange does not include explicit arguments for giving up or challenging his promises. Nevertheless, it contributes to the ongoing deliberation on his vows because Bhīṣma once again describes them in new ways, this time contradicting Vaiśaṃpāyana's narration of them. Appearing in the *Udyoga*

Parvan, this dialogue takes place after the Pāṇḍavas have returned from thirteen years of exile and their rivalry with the Kauravas has intensified. In one of the *Udyoga Parvan*'s many dialogues that attempt to negotiate peace, on this occasion Bhīṣma urges Duryodhana not to go to war with the Pāṇḍavas. In making this case, Bhīṣma tries to persuade Duryodhana to consider his responsibly towards his family above his personal ambitions. Bhīṣma implicitly compares Duryodhana's situation now with a situation from his own past, when – he claims – his actions saved his family from destruction. The details of his narration, however, elicit further questions about his vows, as they expose both his complicity in maintaining his father's lie about the reasons for his marriage to Satyavatī and the degree of suffering he is willing to ignore in others to maintain the truth of his word.

In his recollection, Bhīṣma conceals his father's lie by claiming that his concern was about having a second son. As Bhiṣma explains, when he learned of his father's desire, he brought him Satyavatī, 'who was to be my mother' (5.145.18). He then describes his 'difficult promise' (*pratijñā duṣkarā*) to Duryodhana:

> For the sake of my father and family I swore a difficult promise, as you well know, to be neither king nor father. And here I live confidently, keeping my promise.
>
> (5.145.19)

Bhīṣma goes on to explain that after Śaṃtanu died, he installed Vicitravīrya as king. Notably, Bhīṣma does not mention Śaṃtanu's initial encounter with Satyavatī, only that he brought her to fulfil his father's desire for another son. By omitting the details about the Fisher King's conditions for the marriage, Bhīṣma fails to provide any context or explanation for why he would make such difficult promises. Nevertheless, he describes his vows as for the benefit of his father and family.[12]

He then mentions a duel with the famous brahmin warrior Rāma Jāmadagnya – an armed confrontation that was not part of Vaiśaṃpāyana's narration in the *Ādi Parvan*, but one that Bhīṣma will describe to Duryodhana as part of the *Ambā Upākhyāna* later in the *Udyoga Parvan* (5.170–193). In the *Ambā Upākhyāna*, it is Ambā asking Rāma Jāmadagnya for help in taking revenge on Bhīṣma that prompts Bhīṣma's duel with him. It is striking, then, that Bhīṣma does not even mention Ambā in this account. Rather than fighting over whether Bhīṣma should give up his vow and take Ambā back, as portrayed in the Ambā story, here Bhīṣma gives no explanation for why he fights him, only mentioning that Rāma Jāmadagnya had been banished because the townspeople feared him.

Bhīṣma continues with his account of his past, telling Duryodhana that his 'subjects' (*prajā*) asked him to give up his promises by imploring him to become their king during a time of plague. Despite their concerns of a dwindling population, complaints of widespread suffering, and pleas for him to rescue them by becoming their king, Bhīṣma keeps his promise. He then adds that his mother, ministers, house priests, and brahmins also implored him to be the king (5.145.29–30). Bhīṣma reiterates that, despite these pleas, he reminded them about the 'promise' (*pratijñā*) he had made to renounce the throne and remain celibate, repeating that it was made out of respect for his father and for the sake of the family (*kula*) (5.145.31). He then recounts addressing Satyavatī once more, when he reinforced his commitment to his promise (*pratijñā*).

Compared to the *Ādi Parvan*, this is a vastly different rendition of the circumstances under which he is asked to give up his vows. According to Vaiśaṃpāyana's narration, Satyavatī asks Bhīṣma to become king because there is no longer an heir, but in this account, Bhīṣma is asked to save the kingdom from disease. Although not stated explicitly, this account strongly indicates that Bhīṣma is responsible for the plague by not ascending the throne. Indeed, Satyavatī had already warned about similar possibilities when she said that a kingdom without a king is in danger of drought (1.99.40–41). While it is not clear how Bhīṣma has caused the plague, the *Mahābhārata* contains many examples that portray natural disasters as a reflection of an incompetent or truant king. As Lynn Thomas explains: 'when the king is bad or absent, society and nature fall apart: there is no rain and people are tormented by plague and disasters' (2007: 192). In this case, Bhīṣma portrays his own decision to uphold his vows and refuse the role of king as directly responsible for his kingdom suffering from plague.

Whether Bhīṣma is exaggerating his role or merely remembering different details than Vaiśaṃpāyana, his own testimony gives his promises and their consequences a different character. It is not just his mother and family members, but the entire kingdom who wants him to give up his promises and become king. Moreover, by recalling his subjects' appeal to rescue them, Bhīṣma makes the circumstances under which he is asked to give up his promises more dramatic – in Vaiśaṃpāyana's account, he is asked to save the future of his family, but here he is asked to save all his subjects from imminent death. Whereas Satyavatī used arguments to try to persuade Bhīṣma, his subjects make a more urgent and emotional plea for him to save their lives. With the stakes even higher, Bhīṣma's persistence is both more extraordinary and more tragic. Even with an entire population dying of plague, Bhīṣma refuses to give up his promises.

Crucially, Bhīṣma ends his account by mentioning the three sons that were born from the *niyoga* episodes, explaining to Duryodhana that his father was born blind, and therefore not qualified to be king. He further clarifies that because Pāṇḍu became king, the Pāṇḍavas are the heirs. He concludes by urging Duryodhana to obey his words and give the Pāṇḍavas half the kingdom. By explaining how his father was disqualified, Bhīṣma uses his account of the family's history to discredit Duryodhana's own claims to the throne. Moreover, by describing his vows as for the benefit of his family and *niyoga* as saving his family,[13] Bhīṣma makes a parallel between what he is asking Duryodhana to do now and what he claims to have done two generations earlier. In addition to offering Bhīṣma's own perspective on his vows, this dialogue offers a poignant contrast between Bhīṣma taking credit for saving the family as a young man and his current situation where he is helpless to influence Duryodhana without the authority of holding the position of king that he had renounced. Moreover, in its deviation from Vaiśaṃpāyana's narration in the *Ādi Parvan*, Bhīṣma's rendition raises the question of whether he is being truthful to Duryodhana. Does Bhīṣma lie to protect his vows? If so, we might wonder if mischaracterising them undermines his claim to adhere to truth.

It is noteworthy that this dialogue is one of several between Bhīṣma and Duryodhana. As we will see in the following section, the story of Ambā is narrated by Bhīṣma to Duryodhana, and the two of them have several dialogues in the *Bhīṣma Parvan*, some of which mirror and deepen the frame dialogue between Saṃjaya and Dhṛtarāṣṭra. Moreover, both of the Bhīṣma/Duryodhana dialogues that we are analysing in this chapter are embedded within other dialogues. The one we have just discussed is narrated by Kṛṣṇa to Yudhiṣṭhira, while the one we will examine in the following section is embedded within a dialogue between Saṃjaya and Dhṛtarāṣṭra. We might see the multiple lenses through which both these Bhīṣma/Duryodhana dialogues are conveyed as deepening the perspectival dimension of juxtaposing Bhīṣma's accounts of his own biography with Vaiśaṃpāyana's version of events. Not only does this juxtaposition challenge us to consider the unique perspective of each narrator, but in particular it elicits the question as to whether Bhīṣma is a reliable narrator.

Bhīṣma and Duryodhana: the *Ambā Upākhyāna* (5.170–197)

One of the episodes that raises the most questions about Bhīṣma's vows is the *Ambā Upākhyāna*. As we have noted, this is another account told by Bhīṣma himself, again in a conversation with Duryodhana. This episode, which tells the story of Ambā and Śikhaṇḍin, appears in the *Udyoga Parvan* on the eve of the war. Although Bhīṣma does not indulge in explicit self-reflection, his narration explores the negative effects of his vows by bringing attention to the suffering they caused one woman in particular. His portrayal of Ambā's circumstances after the *rākṣasa* marriage offers an oblique, but scathing, critique of his vows. It also points to larger injustices suffered by women when men neglect to consider the negative effects of their actions (see also Chapter 4). Additionally, Bhīṣma's account of Ambā's story puts his vows into a karmic narrative that not only explores their damaging consequences for others, but also places them in a larger web of vows taken by others – one of which contributes to his own death.

Bhīṣma's narration begins with him taking yet another vow. When Duryodhana asks him about the strengths and weaknesses of the warriors in the Pāṇḍava army, Bhīṣma describes Śikhaṇḍin as a great warrior who will earn fame through his exploits in battle (5.168.1–2). After his assessment of the Pāṇḍava warriors, Bhīṣma returns to the topic of Śikhaṇḍin, declaring:

> I shall not kill a woman, or one who was a woman before. For you may have heard that Śikhaṇḍin was once a woman, king. Born a girl, he later became a man. I shall not fight him.
>
> (5.169.19–20)

Although other characters refer to Śikhaṇḍin in passing before this scene, this is the first occasion where Bhīṣma says he will not fight him and the first mention of any vow not to fight a woman. Significantly, just before declaring this vow, Bhīṣma reminds Duryodhana of his first two vows, saying that the world knows he relinquished the kingship and maintained his vow (*vrata*) of celibacy (*brahmacarya*) to please his father (5.169.17). Bhīṣma does not explain the relationship between his two initial vows and this one, but we might see his first two vows as the basis on which he makes this one.

As a further explanation, Bhīṣma narrates the story of Ambā and Śikhaṇḍin, beginning his account with his abduction of the three princesses: Ambā, Ambikā, and Ambālikā. Bhīṣma tells Duryodhana that after bringing her back to the palace, Ambā asked him to let her return to Śālva, who she had already promised to marry. Bhīṣma allows her to return, but then Śālva rejects her, saying that she now belongs to Bhīṣma and should go back to him. Rather than returning, Ambā departs the city, reflecting that she is the most miserable young woman on earth and wonders who is to be blamed for her predicament. After considering the culpability of Śālva, her father, herself, and Dhātṛ (5.173.6), Ambā finally decides that Bhīṣma is to blame:

> Bhīṣma Śāṃtanava was the beginning of my misfortune, I see now that I have to revenge myself on Bhīṣma, by austerities (*tapas*) or battle (*yudha*), for I consider him the cause of my misery (*duḥkha*)
>
> (5.173.8)

Although she does not identify this as a vow or promise, Ambā's declaration clearly follows the formula of a vow, in that it is a statement of intention to perform certain actions for the sake of achieving specific results. An important aspect of her story as it unfolds is Ambā's persistent effort and discipline in following the vows she takes, despite the many obstacles she faces along the way. The beginning of her story emphasises how she, despite her best efforts, is prevented from following her *dharma* as a woman because she is abducted by Bhīṣma and then rejected by Śālva.

Her misery continues when she approaches a group of ascetics, sharing with them her intention to practise severe asceticism. They advise her to return to her father's house, warning her that it is not appropriate for a woman to renounce. Here, we see a further exploration of the gendered consequences of Bhīṣma's vows. After the abduction, she was prevented by Bhīṣma from fulfilling her *dharma* as a householder, but here she faces obstacles to living as a renunciate. The *Mahābhārata* includes countless examples of men who either choose between or straddle the competing lifestyles of the householder and the renunciate. In Ambā's case, however, rather than having the options of either or both of them, she is caught between them without any choices. Nevertheless, she ignores the ascetics' advice, explaining that she can no longer live in her father's house and that it is her wish to practise austerities.

Bhīṣma and Rāma Jāmadagnya

After her brief discussion with the ascetics, Ambā follows their advice by approaching Rāma Jāmadagnya. As we have seen in his previous dialogue with Duryodhana, Bhīṣma's battle with Rāma Jāmadagnya seems to be a core part of his personal narrative. The most extended portrayal of their battle, however, is in the *Ambā Upākhyāna*. What is particularly intriguing about their duel is the complex relationship between the two of them. Rāma Jāmadagnya is one of Bhīṣma's celestial teachers, as named by Vaiśaṃpāyana in the *Ādi Parvan* (1.94.35), while in this story too he is depicted as his *guru*. Their character portraits are also inversions of each other: Bhīṣma is a *kṣatriya* who lives as a brahmin, while Rāma Jāmadagnya – who is known for slaying the entire *kṣatriya* race twenty-one times – is a brahmin who lives as a *kṣatriya*.[14] Additionally, both Bhīṣma and Rāma Jāmadagnya are known for making great vows. As we will see, in this story they each take an additional vow and break it.

In the *Ambā Upākhyāna*, Ambā convinces Rāma Jāmadagnya to take her case to Bhīṣma. After talking to Ambā, Rāma Jāmadagnya confronts Bhīṣma on the banks of the Sarasvatī River, where he instructs him to take Ambā back. Bhīṣma, however, refuses, saying that it is now too late and reminding him that Ambā had requested to be allowed to return to Śālva. Bhīṣma then declares another vow:

> I will not abandon *kṣạtra-dharma* for either fear or compassion, greed or self-interest: that is the vow (*vrata*) by which I live.
>
> (5.178.11)

Although he claims that he already lives by this vow, he has not made this exact declaration before. The closest of his previous vows to this one is what he declared to Satyavatī: to always live by the truth of his word. On that occasion, he also linked keeping his word with the *dharma* of *kṣatriyas*, but here it is the focus of the vow.

Rāma Jāmadagnya responds by threatening to kill Bhīṣma if he does not do as he says. I will not discuss in detail the long duel that ensues between

Bhīṣma and Rāma Jāmadagnya (5.180–183). However, a notable episode during this battle is when both Bhīṣma and Rāma Jāmadagnya make further vows. When the celestial spectators beg Bhīṣma and Rāma Jāmadagnya to retreat from battle, both refuse. At this point, Rāma Jāmadagnya vows not to retreat from battle (5.186.21–22). Then, Bhīṣma proclaims:

> My vow (*vrata*) in this world is that I would never turn away and retreat from battle and be hit in the back by arrows! Neither greed nor cowardice, fear not self-interest can make me abandon the perpetual (*śāśvata*) *dharma*: my mind is set!
>
> (5.186.25–26)

Here, while fighting against each other with weapons, Bhīṣma and Rāma Jāmadagnya extend their duel to vows, with both declaring the same intended action: not to retreat from battle. Also, both portray their vows as everlasting, while Bhīṣma adds an appeal to a celestial audience, saying that he took his vow 'before the world'. Without going into detail about Rāma Jāmadagnya's vows, we can see that Bhīṣma's promise here is yet again a different declaration than any he has made previously. While he has already vowed to renounce the throne, to be celibate, to uphold his word, and to follow his *kṣatriya-dharma*, this is first time that he specifically refers to a vow never to turn away from battle.

Despite vowing to keep fighting, both Bhīṣma and Rāma Jāmadagnya eventually give in to the celestial spectators, when Nārada and Gaṅgā intervene by obstructing the duel. After the battle ends, Rāma Jāmadagnya apologises to Ambā for not being able to defeat Bhīṣma. Ambā says she understands, but then declares that she will never go to back to Bhīṣma and that she will go wherever needed to bring him down in battle.

Ambā's vow

Bhīṣma then recounts the remainder of Ambā's life story, telling Duryodhana about her fourteen years of extreme asceticism. As her story unfolds, Ambā's predicament continues to demonstrate the harsh consequences of Bhīṣma's vows, inviting us to explore the circumstances of her own vows and their role in bringing about the death of Bhīṣma. Ambā's story includes a number of occasions in which she declares her intention to seek revenge on Bhīṣma. When she first heads off to the forest, she declares to herself that either through austerities (*tapas*) or through battle (*yudha*), she will exact revenge on Bhīṣma (5.173.8). She then beseeches Rāma Jāmadagnya to kill Bhīṣma (5.176.38).

During her renunciate wanderings, Ambā again declares her intention to seek revenge on Bhīṣma, this time in a short encounter with Gaṅgā, who, we should remember, is Bhīṣma's mother. Gaṅgā asks her why she is inflicting so much pain onto herself, to which Ambā replies that because Bhīṣma could not be defeated she has undertaken self-mortification for the sake of killing him: 'May this be the fruit (*phala*) of my vow (*vrata*) in another body' (5.187.32).

Then, Ambā again vows to take revenge on Bhīṣma in a brief encounter with some ascetics who ask her what she seeks to achieve through her severe austerities. She replies:

> I have resolved (*niścaya*) that only by killing Bhīṣma shall I find peace (*śānti*). I shall not desist, brahmins, until I have slain Gaṅgā's son in battle, him because of whom I have found this everlasting life of misery (*duḥkha*), deprived of the world of a husband, neither a woman nor a man! This [resolve] is lodged in my heart, for that I have undertaken this vow (*saṃkalpa*). I am totally disgusted with being a woman and I have resolved (*kṛtaniścaya*) to become a man: I want to pay Bhīṣma back, and I am not to be diverted.
>
> (5.188.3–6)

As with Bhīṣma, Ambā takes several vows, but hers are far more similar to each other than his. Here she reiterates her desire to kill Bhīṣma, but on this occasion she is more specific about her own role in doing the killing. She also further characterises her own suffering as a consequence of Bhīṣma's vow, explaining that without a husband she was neither a woman nor or man. But while claiming that her lack of role in society has left her without a gender, she also explains that it was only because she was a woman that she was prone to being left without a gendered status. She thus resolves to become a man. Although Ambā had previously vowed to take revenge upon Bhīṣma either through austerities or through combat, she did not specify that she could not exact the revenge as a woman. Thus, this is the first and only time that becoming a man becomes part of Ambā's vows.

After this, Śiva appears in his divine form to promise that her vow will be fulfilled. When Ambā wonders how she – as a woman – can slay Bhīṣma, Śiva replies that she will be reborn as the son of Drupada and then kill him. After Śiva disappears, Ambā builds a funeral pyre and makes one final vow while entering the flames: 'For Bhīṣma's death' (5.188.18). Taken together, her vows demonstrate her extraordinary efforts to overcome the many obstacles that confront her. Despite being abducted, then abandoned, then rejected as an ascetic, Ambā nevertheless practices enough austerities to support her vows to kill Bhīṣma. That Bhīṣma has vowed not to kill Śikhaṇḍin seems to be his indirect acknowledgement that he is responsible for Ambā's suffering. Yet Ambā's vow also remains in some ways unfulfilled. Not only does she need Śiva's intervention, but even with his involvement the vow only partially comes true, as Ambā is initially reborn as the female Śikhaṇḍinī (5.189) and then, according to some characters, only plays a supporting role in killing Bhīṣma.

At the end of his narration of Ambā's story, Bhīṣma restates his vow not to kill a woman:

> This my vow (*vrata*) has always been renowned in the whole world: that I shall shoot no arrows at a woman, a former woman, one with the name of a woman, and an apparent woman, joy of the Kauravas, and for this reason I shall not kill him when he ambushes me in battle.
> (5.193.62–65)

As we have seen, the story of Ambā begins with Bhīṣma describing the vow that prevents him from fighting Śikhaṇḍin, and here he concludes his account by restating the same vow. But whereas in its first articulation he connects the vow to his own vow of celibacy, here he describes his vow not to fight Śikhaṇḍin as already 'renowned' (*viśruta*) in the 'whole world' (*pṛthivī*). Also, whereas in the first account of this vow he declares that he will not fight a woman or someone who once was a woman, here he adds both someone with the same name as a woman and an apparent woman.

Compared to the other discussions about Bhīṣma's vows, the *Ambā Upākhyāna* presents them differently again. While his other encounters consider the negative effects of his vows in terms of the future of the lineage and the lives of his subjects, the *Ambā Upākhyāna* demonstrates in detail the negative effects of his vows on one woman. Although his initial vows are not themselves criticised, the sages who discuss Ambā's circumstances make it absolutely clear that Bhīṣma is responsible for her predicament. As they see it, because Bhīṣma had carried out the abduction of Ambā and her two sisters, he is the one who should protect her now. Although they do not explicitly ask him to renounce his vows, they imply that Bhīṣma's responsibility towards Ambā is greater than his responsibility to keep his vows.

In addition to offering a critical perspective on his vows, Bhīṣma's account of the *Ambā Upākhyāna* also depicts the first time that he breaks one of his vows. Indeed, Bhīṣma's broken vow gets further amplified, but also perhaps justified, as it happens in unison with Rāma Jāmadagnya – the other well-known vow-taker – breaking his vow. Interestingly, no character or narrator ever reflects on the implications of Bhīṣma breaking this vow. But considering the ways that his vows are interlinked with each other, we might wonder if him breaking this vow has any effect on the truth of his other vows.

In addition to Bhīṣma's vows, this story also depicts Ambā and Rāma Jāmadagnya as making vows; and in both cases, their vows conflict with one of Bhīṣma's. With Rāma Jāmadagnya, his vow balances Bhīṣma's so equally that they both have to give them up. In the case of Ambā, Bhīṣma not only has to live by his own vow, but his death will be caused – at least partly – by the vow of another. But if this story demonstrates the importance of vows, it also indicates the many problems of a strict expectation that vows must be kept under all circumstances. Ambā's entire tragic story is presented as the consequences of Bhīṣma's actions. And while no one in Bhīṣma's account ever asks him directly to renounce his vow of celibacy, this seems to be implied when Rāma Jāmadagnya asks him repeatedly to take Ambā back.

Assuming that this is what Rāma Jāmadagnya is asking, the implications are different from when Satyavatī asked him to do the same. When Satyavatī asked Bhīṣma to give up his vow, there were no living heirs because both her sons had already died and the surviving queens were not yet pregnant. Crucially, she asked Bhīṣma to give up his vows in circumstances where they were clearly not relevant anymore. Here, however, it is implied that Vicitravīrya is still alive, so if Bhīṣma were to marry Ambā at this particular stage in the story, then he would clearly be violating the terms of his vows, as he did not yet know that Vicitravīrya would die without any heirs. One interpretation, then, would be that Rāma Jāmadagnya confronts Bhīṣma with the dilemma of whether to keep his vow or to save a woman's life. But the story remains vague, never indicating explicitly where these episodes would fit into Vaiśaṃpāyaṇa's narrative in the *Ādi Parvan*. As such, it is not clear whether Bhīṣma really has to make a choice in this way. Whereas Satyavatī emphasises that Bhīṣma's duty is to continue the dynasty, Rāma Jāmadagnya emphasises that his duty is to protect the woman he abducted. In the *Ambā Upākhyāna*, then, the main criticism against Bhīṣma is not that he has disrupted the lineage, but that he has not taken responsibility for the suffering he has caused to one woman in particular.

Like his previous dialogue with Duryodhana, in the *Ambā Upākhyāna*, Bhīṣma narrates events from his own past that offer a critical perspective on his own vows. Interestingly, while Bhīṣma makes it clear how he knows what he is narrating to Duryodhana, it is not clear how Saṃjaya – who recounts the dialogue between Bhīṣma and Duryodhana to Dhṛtarāṣṭra – knows about their conversation.[15] In the beginning of the *Bhīṣma Parvan*, Vyāsa will grant Saṃjaya the divine eye, but this is a power he does not yet have. Nonetheless, this story is connected to the war books by sharing the same narrator and listener. Moreover, it is significant that the *Ambā Upākhyāna* – the last story recited before the beginning of the battle books – links Bhīṣma's vows directly to the war itself.

Bhīṣma and Yudhiṣṭhira: the story of Kauśika (12.110)

When the war is finally over and the Pāṇḍavas have won, Yudhiṣṭhira – who has now established himself as the undisputed heir to the throne – is so overcome with remorse that he wants to become a religious renouncer. Along with his brothers and his wife Draupadī, he approaches Bhīṣma, who lays dying on a bed of arrows, having been mortally wounded during the war. Bhīṣma's instruction, which comprises most of the *Śānti* and *Anuśāsana Parvans*, has the rhetorical objective of trying to convince Yudhiṣṭhira to become king. At one point during Bhīṣma's long teaching, Yudhiṣṭhira asks his paternal grandfather about how to be a virtuous person:

> Bhārata, how can a man who desires to be steadfast in *dharma* go on? Learned man, bull of the Bharatas, tell me this as I make this inquiry. Truth (*satya*) and falsehood (*anṛta*) both pervade all realms. What might a man who is resolved to follow *dharma* do with regard to these two? What is truth, anyway? And what is falsehood? And what is everlasting (*sanātana*) *dharma*? At what times should one speak what is true (*satya*)? And when might he speak what is false (*anṛta*)?
>
> (12.110.1–3)

In the way he poses his questions, Yudhiṣṭhira indicates that he understands there is conflict between speaking the truth and following *dharma*. In response to Yudhiṣṭhira's question, Bhīṣma refers to the story of Kauśika – a sage whose vow always to tell the truth leads to the death of innocent people. Bhīṣma's response is intriguing, not only because it offers a critical perspective on the general practice of adhering to vows, but also because it resonates specifically with his own vows to renounce the throne and practice celibacy.

We should note that Bhīṣma's long discourse in the *Śānti* and *Anuśāsana Parvan*s takes place while he has the 'divine eye' (*divya cakṣus*), granted to him by Kṛṣṇa, but while Vyāsa is 'authoritatively present' (Hiltebeitel 2001a: 265). As we will see in subsequent chapters, other characters will be granted the divine eye in other episodes – always granted to them by either Vyāsa or Kṛṣṇa. Although the divine eye can bestow slightly different powers to different characters depending on the context, here Bhīṣma is promised by Kṛṣṇa: 'Anything you conceptualize pertaining to *dharma*, to anything pertaining to *artha*, you shall have your very best mind with regard to that' (12.52.19). When he responds to Yudhiṣṭhira's question about how to live a virtuous live, Bhīṣma draws on the knowledge accessible to him through his divine vision and does not include an explicit reflection on his own actions. Nevertheless, the story of Kauśika – a sage known for his vow always to tell the truth – offers a critical perspective from which to consider Bhīṣma's own promises.

Bhīṣma begins his response to Yudhiṣṭhira by explaining that truth (*satya*) is 'difficult to establish' (*aniṣṭhita*), because sometimes telling a lie is the truth, while speaking the truth is a falsehood. To illustrate his point, Bhīṣma brings up the examples of Balāka and Kauśika, both of whom Kṛṣṇa had discussed earlier in the narrative to make some of the same points to Arjuna during the *Karṇa Parvan* (8.49; see Chapter 5).[16] Bhīṣma describes Balāka as 'vulgar' (*anārya*) and of 'limited understanding' (*akṛtaprajña*), but as someone who gained 'tremendous merit' (*sumahat puṇya*) after killing a blind beast (12.110.7).[17]

Bhīṣma then contrasts Balāka with Kauśika, whom he describes as 'foolish' (*muḍha*) – one who desires *dharma* (*dharma-kāma*) but does not know *dharma* (12.110.8). As a consequence, Kauśika acquires 'tremendous evil' (*sumahat pāpa*). Bhīṣma concludes that *dharma* can be determined through 'reasoning' (*tarka*), adding that *dharma* is ultimately measured according to the criterion of non-violence (*ahiṃsā*). Notably, Bhīṣma criticises Kauśika's actions, yet without specifying what the sage had done wrong. In contrast, when Kṛṣṇa tells this story to Arjuna in the *Karṇa Parvan*, he explains that on one occasion Kauśika had told some bandits the whereabouts of people who were hiding from them, causing all the people to be killed.[18] Despite not providing the whole story, Bhīṣma nevertheless concludes that because the truth led to the death of innocent people, Kauśika should have told a lie.

This short exchange has fascinating implications for how we might interpret Bhīṣma's own vows earlier in the narrative. Bhīṣma's account of Kauśika – a man who thought he was following *dharma*, but acted in a way that led to the harm of others – has obvious resonances with his own situation. In particular, the Kauśika story includes the doctrine of *ahiṃsā*, portraying non-harm to others as a higher value than truth. Although none of his previous dialogues about his vows mention the term *ahiṃsā*, we can see that Bhīṣma's own truth-telling has been repeatedly considered in relation to its harm to others. When Satyavatī urges Bhīṣma to give up his vows, she argues that the future of the family is at stake. Similarly, when Bhīṣma tells Duryodhana about keeping his vows despite his subjects' appeal to him to save them, he specifies the suffering they endure from plague. The psychological depth of the harmful consequences of his vows are most fully explored in the account of Ambā. Although Bhīṣma does not mention his own vows in his teaching to Yudhiṣṭhira, the message he communicates from the Kauśika story reaffirms a repeated criticism.

However, what is most striking about Bhīṣma's version of this story is a detail he omits. When Kṛṣṇa tells Arjuna about Balāka and Kauśika, he provides far more information about both of their situations. According to Kṛṣṇa, Kauśika discloses the whereabouts of the people because he has taken a vow (*vrata*) always to tell the truth (8.49.41–42). In other words, Kṛṣṇa portrays this vow as causing the death of innocent people – a point that he uses to draw parallels with Arjuna's vow to kill anyone who insults his Gāṇḍīva bow (see Chapter 5). In Kṛṣṇa's version, this detail makes the lessons gained from the story more specifically about vows. We might take Kauśika's vow-taking as implied in Bhīṣma's version as well. But in not including the vow in his account to Yudhiṣṭhira, Bhīṣma casts Kauśika's truth-telling as a more general intention to follow *dharma*, rather than resulting from a specific promise. Is it possible that Bhīṣma omits this detail to distance his own situation from that of Kauśika's? If so, then Bhīṣma's omission might convince himself that he is not like Kauśika, but it is less likely to fool Yudhiṣṭhira, who is present when Kṛṣṇa tells this story to Arjuna in the *Karṇa Parvan*.

We should recall that in both his dialogues with Duryodhana, Bhīṣma is the narrator of his own story. In both cases, despite including details that betray the harmful consequences of his vows, he characterises them in a positive light. But when talking to Yudhiṣṭhira in the *Śānti Parvan* – although not reflecting on his vows directly – he delivers a teaching that offers a much more critical perspective on his own actions. The tension between Bhīṣma's teachings and actions raises the question of how he knows what he says to Yudhiṣṭhira during his post-war instruction. Characteristically, the narrative gives conflicting accounts. One of the reasons why Vyāsa tells Yudhiṣṭhira to seek instruction from Bhīṣma is because he knows all things and all *dharma* (12.38.7). Cast in this light, Bhīṣma's teachings are one last heroic effort to save his family by educating a reluctant king on how to rule according to *dharma*. But if that is the case, then at what point in the story did he learn what he teaches? If Hiltebeitel (2001b) is correct that Bhīṣma learned much of this during his time in heaven (1.94.31–36), then we might wonder where all his knowledge of the *Śānti* and *Anuśāsana Parvan*s was when he impulsively took his vow of celibacy, when he ignored Satyavatī's proposal for saving the lineage, when he could not answer Draupadī's questions after the dicing match (see Chapter 4), when he could not convince Duryodhana to compromise with the Pāṇḍavas, or when he would not agree to protect Ambā.

However, if we follow the implications of the divine vision granted to him by Kṛṣṇa (12.52.20), then we do not have to attribute Bhīṣma's sources to lessons he had already learned when visiting his mother in heaven, but rather to what knowledge he has access to through the divine eye itself. Taken this way, it might be possible to see his lengthy teachings as a meditation on his own past actions, as much as they are advice to Yudhiṣṭhira as the future king. That Bhīṣma might be learning from his own teachings perhaps makes sense of the fact that the person who is among the most responsible for the war and who kills ruthlessly in battle can instruct never to harm any living being; that one of the most misogynistic characters in the *Mahābhārata* can offer some of the most progressive views on gender from the ancient world;[19] and that the one whose vows have led to devastating consequences can offer a teaching implicitly instructing that one should give up one's vows if they lead to the harm of others. In other words, perhaps it is not only that Bhīṣma has already proven his credentials for being able to give the teachings of the *Śānti* and *Anuśāsana Parvan*s, but also that these are the teachings he needs to learn to take responsibility for his own actions, as he prepares himself for death.

The multiple causes of Bhīṣma's death

As we have seen, the dialogues about Bhīṣma's vows explore the moral implications of his actions from a number of perspectives. Throughout Vaiśampāyana's narrative, Bhīṣma is lauded as a man of great vows. Yet his vows are repeatedly questioned, with a number of episodes revealing the harsh consequences they have on other people. In addition to the dialogues discussing his promises, another important aspect of understanding their implications is how they relate to Bhīṣma's death. As we will see, there are a number of distinct explanations for his death, almost all of them directly related to vows – both his own and other people's.

The first explanation to unfold in the main story is that Bhīṣma has the ability to choose his own time of death. As we have seen, Bhīṣma earns this boon from his father immediately after taking his vow of celibacy. According to this understanding, Bhīṣma is the sole agent in bringing about his death; other characters might deliver the killer blow, but ultimately Bhīṣma is responsible. Bhīṣma reiterates this understanding in the *Bhīṣma Parvan*, when he refers back to his vow of celibacy, saying that in recognition of his difficult promise, his father had granted him (1) the ability to choose his time of death and (2) inviolability (*avadhya*) in battle (6.114.33). Interestingly, Bhīṣma mentions two boons here, when, in the *Ādi Parvan*, Vaiśaṃpāyana had mentioned only the first one. As we have seen in his two previous dialogues with Duryodhana, Bhīṣma's own descriptions of the circumstances surrounding his initial vows often differ from Vaiśaṃpāyana's accounts. Here, the mention of a second boon is an added detail, but does not really change the character of what his father had bestowed on him, as much as it reiterates the first boon – that only Bhīṣma will decide when it is time for his death.

Immediately after recalling his father's boons, Bhīṣma decides that it is indeed time for him to die, a decision supported by the gods watching from above (6.114.34–35). Yet shortly after, Bhīṣma tells sages – sent by his mother in the form of geese – that it is an inauspicious time to die and he should wait, on his bed of arrows, until the sun is heading north rather than south (6.114.96–97). As he says to the geese:

> May the boon of dying at will, that was granted to me by my great-spirited father, hold true. Since the time of my departure is totally up to me, I will hold my life-breath till then.
>
> (6.114.98–99)

That Bhīṣma can even change his mind demonstrates that he is indeed in control of his time of death. He then postpones his demise by fifty-eight days (13.153.27), during which he lies on his bed of arrows through the remainder of the war before giving his long instruction to Yudhiṣṭhira.

A distinct, yet overlapping, explanation of Bhīṣma's death is that it is the result of Ambā's vow to kill him. As we have seen in the *Ambā Upākhyāna*, Ambā's circuitous reincarnation into the male warrior Śikhaṇḍin is the fulfilment of her vow to kill Bhīṣma. Saṃjaya confirms this portrayal of events at the beginning of the *Bhīṣma Parvan*, when he announces to Dhṛtarāṣṭra that Bhīṣma has been killed by Śikhaṇḍin (6.14.7). Although Saṃjaya will later describe Arjuna as the one who kills Bhīṣma, with Śikhaṇḍin playing a supporting role, here and on other occasions, he presents Śikhaṇḍin as the sole culprit. For example, in the *Udyoga Parvan,* Saṃjaya tells Dhṛtarāṣṭra that Dhṛṣṭadyumna – the general of the Pāṇḍava army – assigned Śikhaṇḍin to line up against Bhīṣma (5.161.7). And when he reports Arjuna's speech to the Kaurava court, Saṃjaya quotes Arjuna as declaring that Śikhaṇḍin will slay Bhīṣma (5.47.35–36). Notably, here Arjuna does not even mention his own involvement in slaying Bhīṣma, despite later making a vow to kill him and being credited for doing so by Saṃjaya in his narration. Similarly, when Saṃjaya outlines the key match-ups for the upcoming war, he declares that Śikhaṇḍin will kill Bhīṣma – again not mentioning Arjuna (5.56.12). The claim that Śikhaṇḍin kills Bhīṣma is also made by other characters, such as Bhīmasena, who says that Śikhaṇḍin was born to kill Bhīṣma (5.149.29–32), and Yudhiṣṭhira, who reminds Śikhaṇḍin of his vow to kill Bhīṣma (6.81.18). Here, Yudhiṣṭhira is not referring to Ambā's vow, but rather to one made by Śikhaṇḍin to Yudhiṣṭhira in the presence of Drupada. Also, in the Vaiśaṃpāyana frame at the beginning of the *Droṇa Parvan*, Janamejaya credits Śikhaṇḍin with overcoming Bhīṣma (7.1.1).

While these examples show that several characters attribute Bhīṣma's death to Śikhaṇḍin, others credit Arjuna. As with Ambā and Śikhaṇḍin, Arjuna also takes a vow to kill Bhīṣma. In the *Bhīṣma Parvan*, when Kṛṣṇa attempts to race after Bhīṣma, Arjuna stops him, fearing that Kṛṣṇa will break his vow not to fight. Arjuna then vows that he will kill Bhīṣma:

> All this burden is on me. I will slay the observer of rigid vows (*yata-vrata*). I swear by my weapons, by truth and by my good deeds, that I will exterminate the enemies, enemy-slayer.
>
> (6.102.67–68)

Further on, Kṛṣṇa tells Yudhiṣṭhira that Arjuna had previously taken a vow (*pratijñā*) to kill Bhīṣma (6.103.35). Although it is not clear how widely Arjuna's vow to kill Bhīṣma is known, a number of characters credit Arjuna with delivering the killer blow. In Saṃjaya's narration of the episode as it unfolds in the *Bhīṣma Parvan* (6.114.13), he describes Arjuna shooting the arrows while taking shelter behind Śikhaṇḍin. This is also how Bhīṣma's death is depicted by Ugraśravas, when summarising the *Mahābhārata* to the *ṛṣi*s of the Naimiṣa Forest (1.2.157). Similarly, in his summarising lament in the *Ādi Parvan*, Dhṛtarāṣṭra tells Saṃjaya that Bhīṣma was felled by Arjuna, with Śikhaṇḍin standing in front of him (1.1.126). Moreover, Bhīṣma himself sees Arjuna as the one who will mortally wound him when he tells Yudhiṣṭhira how he can be killed (6.103.74–78). Meanwhile, later during the war, Arjuna claims he killed Bhīṣma, explaining that he did so while protected by Śikhaṇḍin (8.49.84). The tension between these two explanations for Bhīṣma's death is most vivid at the end of the *Anuśāsana Parvan*, when Gaṅgā, lamenting the death of her son, says that he was killed by Śikhaṇḍin (13.154.21). Kṛṣṇa, however, corrects her, explaining that Bhīṣma was killed by Arjuna according to *kṣatriya-dharma* (13.154.29).

As we can see, the *Mahābhārata* remains ambiguous about how Bhīṣma dies. The most common explanation is that both Arjuna and Śikhaṇḍin played a role. Nevertheless, on some occasions, Śikhaṇḍin is named without any mention of Arjuna, while on others Arjuna is given all the credit. Although both of them had made vows, the ambiguity of who claims responsibility remains unresolved. Crucially, though, these different accounts of the way he dies characterise his death differently. By dying at the hands of Śikhaṇḍin – fulfiling Ambā's vow – Bhīṣma's death is portrayed as tragically karmic: he is slain by the vow of the person whose life he ruined because of his refusal to give up his own vows. According to this narrative, Bhīṣma both lives by his vows and dies by his vows. That perhaps Bhīṣma does not want to be remembered in this way is suggested by his strong objection that a single arrow piercing his body could be traced back to Śikhaṇḍin (6.114.62–67).

Alternatively, his death by Arjuna gives Bhīṣma a much more heroic demise. Rather than being slain by a lesser-known warrior of ambiguous gender, in Arjuna, Bhīṣma is killed by the greatest archer in the world. In this account again, Bhīṣma is slain by someone who took a vow to kill him, but here that vow is far less personal. Arjuna vows to kill Bhīṣma to prevent Kṛṣṇa from breaking his own vow not to fight, not because of any vengeance against Bhīṣma. So, while Bhīṣma also dies by a vow in this narrative, his death is not cast as the karmic consequences of his own actions. Meanwhile, the narrative that Bhīṣma can choose his own time of death casts his vow of celibacy as an exceptional deed that is rewarded by the ultimate boon – control over his own mortality.

Conclusion

In this chapter, we have taken the question of Bhīṣma's vows as our first case study for examining how the *Mahābhārata* explores moral questions through dialogue. As we have seen, Bhīṣma's vows are discussed, evaluated, and criticised as he and his interlocutors offer a number of perspectives from which to reflect on them. The different points in the narrative from which his vows are questioned shed light on the temporal contingency of moral decisions. By repeatedly returning to the changing circumstances and consequences of his vows – particularly his first two – the text takes seemingly virtuous deeds as a starting point for an ongoing ethical exploration.

In Vaiśaṃpāyana's narration, Bhīṣma is shown to be misled by his father and as being aware of his infatuation with Satyavatī before going to meet the Fisher King. Although no narrator or character ever points this out explicitly, Vaiśaṃpāyana's account lays bare the fact that Bhīṣma's vows were ones that he was not compelled to make. Nonetheless, Vaiśaṃpāyana's narration also portrays Bhīṣma's vows to renounce the kingdom and to live a life of celibacy as virtuous and heroic acts. Similarly, Satyavatī praises Bhīṣma, but characterises his vows as situational and contextual, thus questioning their relevance as circumstances change. Their dialogue explores the vows through different types of *dharma* and tensions within these types of *dharma*. By placing emphasis on the original aim of the vows, Satyavatī suggests that they are no longer necessary. It is during his dialogue with Satyavatī that Bhīṣma doubles down on his initial vows, declaring that he will always live by their truth. Meanwhile, Śiśupāla characterises Bhīṣma's vows as hiding a sexual deficiency, suggesting that despite what he claims, there is an unspoken reason for his promises. By calling him a liar and questioning his real motivations, Śiśupāla not only portrays the vows as duplicitous, but also offers a counter-argument to the very points Bhīṣma had used to justify his vows in his dialogue with Satyavatī.

Bhīṣma's dialogue with Duryodhana returns to the issue of the implications of his vows for the future of the family. Bhīṣma tells Duryodhana that he took his vow of celibacy out of loyalty to his father. The context of their dialogue, however, with war imminent, reminds us that the very situation they find themselves in can be traced back to Bhīṣma's vow of celibacy. Even on the eve of destruction, Bhīṣma defends his past actions as saving the family. There is an interesting contrast, then, between seeing Bhīṣma as the cause of his family's problems or as the one who once saved them. This dialogue also sets up a contrast between Vaiśaṃpāyana's and Bhīṣma's narrations. Although Vaiśaṃpāyana's version is clearly portrayed as the more authoritative of the two, the discrepancy between them invites reflection upon the reliability of the text's narrators. We are reminded that any moral question is represented from a subjective and situated perspective. In the *Ambā Upākhyāna*, Bhīṣma again describes his vows positively in terms of his adherence to truth and *dharma*, but also gives a detailed account of the harmful consequences of his actions and as sowing the seeds of his own destruction. In both his dialogues with Duryodhana, Bhīṣma is confronted with the personification of the negative consequences of his actions.

In the *Śānti Parvan*, Bhīṣma's account of Kauśika obliquely offers a critical lens through which to interpret his own circumstances. Here, Bhīṣma instructs Yudhiṣṭhira that there is a difference between literal truth and a higher truth, that sometimes lying is the right thing to do if truth leads to harming others. Although Bhīṣma does not explicitly tell Yudhiṣṭhira that vows can be broken, this might be implied because Kauśika's truth-telling is linked to a solemn vow in another version of this story. The fact that Bhīṣma himself is the narrator invites us to consider the tensions between his teachings and actions. Indeed, the relationship between Bhīṣma's actions in the main story and his teachings in the *Śānti* and *Anuśāsana Parvan*s is perhaps the most vivid illustration of the types of textual contrasts that previous scholars explained away in terms of a lack of cohesion between the main story and the so-called didactic sections. In this chapter, we have seen that rather than these sections having little regard 'to the effect produced by their juxtaposition', dialogues in all sections of the text are connected through ongoing deliberations about moral issues. More specifically, the dialogues in this chapter are connected by the fact that they all include Bhīṣma and all offer reflections upon his vows in one way or another. Instead of somehow being marginal or extraneous, we have seen that Bhīṣma's reflections upon his vows in the *Śānti Parvan* are the culmination of repeated reflections upon the moral consequences of his vows and on his own responsibility for taking them. After years of defending them, as he looks back on his life when his death approaches, he indicates indirectly that the suffering caused to others might indeed outweigh any virtue of living by his vows.

Finally, when Bhīṣma is mortally wounded, the topic of his vows emerges yet again, this time as he invokes the boon granted to him by his father for his vow of celibacy. The complex, ambiguous circumstances of his death also set up the interactions and potential conflict between different vows made by different people. As we have seen, the many different and, to some extent, incompatible explanations for his death are illustrative examples of the *Mahābhārata*'s tendency to offer multiple interpretations for some of the text's most significant episodes. In this case, as we are offered different explanations for his death, we are also offered different lenses from which to look back on his life and to reflect on the moral status of his vows.

As we discussed in the Introduction, dialogue in the *Mahābhārata* often explicitly includes contestatory points of views. In the case of Bhīṣma, although his vows are clearly characterised as both heroic and virtuous, the many challenges to them offer a sustained counter-perspective. By reading these dialogues dialectically – paying attention to the contrasts and tensions set up within dialogues and between them – we have seen that Bhīṣma's vows are an ongoing topic of moral questioning. Compared to how dialectic is understood in other philosophical contexts, the *Mahābhārata* contributes to this way of thinking because of its complex and multilayered textual structure. In the *Mahābhārata*, dialectic is never merely a sequence of binary contradictions, but rather a continuous play of multidimensional juxtapositions: different concepts, different temporal contexts, different personal perspectives, and differences within the same subjective perspective. In exploring all these contrasts in relation to the same issue – in this case Bhīṣma's vows – the *Mahābhārata* offers a complex and multiperspectival exploration of dialectical reasoning.

By paying attention to the dialectical features of dialogue in the *Mahābhārata*, we not only see that philosophical deliberation is an integral part of the narrative itself, but that through dialogue the text provokes further deliberation from its readers. In addition to the many individual dialogues that remain unresolved, the intra-textual relationships between dialogues show that the same question can be addressed on multiple occasions, even after decisions have been made and actions have been taken. It is never too late to revisit a decision or scenario long since past, as there is always the possibility of another argument to be made or a new perspective to consider. As the *Mahābhārata* sets up a series of tensions between contrasting ideas, contexts, and perspectives, it leaves it open to us to explore the relationship between them.

Notes

1 Throughout this book, translations from the *Mahābhārata* are from the Chicago edition (Books 1–5; 11, & 12) and the Clay Sanskrit Library (Books 6–9). In some cases, I have slightly modified translations to leave key words, such as *dharma*, untranslated, or to convey a more literal rendering.

2 I quote from an unpublished paper that Bruce Sullivan kindly shared with me. The provisional title of the paper is 'The Poetics of Performative Speech Acts: Literary Expressions of Truth, Power, and Virtue'.

3 For a discussion of this type of marriage, see Jamison (1996: 218–235).

4 For a discussion of Bhīṣma's sources, see Hiltebeitel (2001a).

5 The only previous occasions of this term in the *Mahābhārata* are when Ugraśravas names the *Āpad-dharma* section of the *Śānti Parvan* in his two summaries at the very beginning of the text (1.2.64; 1.2.198).

6 See the following examples for other occasions of *niyoga* (1.111.33–35; 1.168; 1.173). For discussion of *niyoga*, see Dhand (2004: 38–47) and Brodbeck (2009: 63–69). Although *niyoga* is referred to widely in ancient Indian literature, it seems to have been controversial. As Dhand points out, following Kane: 'Some *Dharmasūtra* theorists (such as Guatama) approved the practice as a compassionate and pragmatic allowance. Others (e.g., Āpastambha) condemned it as immoral. Yet others, such as Manu and Nārada, approved it with caution' (2004: 38–39). It is not surprising, then, that Bhīṣma suggests it as *āpad-dharma*, rather than as standard practice.

7 For a discussion of other dialogues that reach agreement in similar ways, see Black (2015a).

8 Earlier in the *Sabhā Parvan*, Bhīmasena kills Jarāsaṃdha, accompanied by Kṛṣṇa and Arjuna. Although Kṛṣṇa did not kill Jarāsaṃdha himself, it was his idea to carry out the attack (2.18–22).

9 Van Buitenen speculates that, as Jarāsaṃdha's army commander, Śiśupāla was likely the one who carried out the attack on Mathurā (1975: 25).

10 We should keep in mind that neither Bhīṣma nor Kṛṣṇa has described *dharma* as subtle at this point in the narrative. And although Yudhiṣṭhira describes *dharma* as subtle when defending the polyandrous marriage to Drupada (See Chapter 2), Śiśupāla is not present. Nevertheless, considering that all three of these characters are known as authorities on *dharma*, it is possible that Śiśupāla already associates this understanding with them. In any case, Śiśupāla's use of this description here is different to how other characters describe the subtlety of *dharma*.

11 See also Reich (1998: 282–283, 2001: 151).

12 It is interesting that Bhīṣma here refers to Satyavatī as Kālī, hinting at a divine identity for her. Vaiśaṃpāyana once refers to Satyavatī as Kālī in his narration of her dialogue with Bhīṣma in the *Ādi Parvan* (1.99.21). See Hiltebeitel (2011: 367–373) for some possible implications of this epithet.

13 In this same discussion in the Kaurava court, Vidura seems to agree with Bhīṣma's portrayal of himself as saving the family, as he asks him to save it again (5.146.18).

14 For more on Rāma Jāmadagnya, see Fitzgerald (2002b).

15 On two occasions, Bhīṣma refers to the spies he has sent out to report back to him on Ambā's activities (5.187.13; 5.189.18).
16 For further discussion of the parables of Balāka and Kauśika, see Matilal (1989, 2002: 26–35), Ganeri (2007: 89–92), and Hiltebeitel (2011: 21–25).
17 Kṛṣṇa will portray Balāka more favourably, saying that he was 'curious' or 'astonishing' (*āścarya*) (8.49.31), but acted cruelly. Bhīṣma, however, depicts him as 'vulgar'.
18 For further comment on the differences between these versions, see Fitzgerald's note (2004b: 750).
19 Here I am thinking in particular of the arguments put forward by Sulabhā (12.308). As Ram-Prasad has noted: 'It does not seem by accident that it is the strange warrior [Bhīṣma] in whose mouth is put the most strikingly supportive and unambiguous narrative of a woman's autonomy in the *Mahābhārata*' (2018: 61). Importantly, Bhīṣma also narrates other episodes that support female autonomy and challenge traditional gender hierarchies, such as the stories of King Bhaṅgāśvana (13.12) and Aṣṭāvakra and Dīśā (13.19–22).

2 Draupadī's marriage

Introduction

While Bhīṣma's vows are presented as controversial, Draupadī's polyandrous marriage to the five Pāṇḍavas is regarded as scandalous. As her father makes clear, one woman marrying four men violates all accepted marriage practices. When Yudhiṣṭhira announces his intentions for his brothers and him to share Draupadī as their common wife, Drupada asks Vyāsa:

> How can one woman be the wife of many men ... and yet *dharma* not be broken? Declare it all to us, good sir, how this can be'
>
> (1.188.5)

This question about the dharmic status of the polyandrous marriage is one of the central moral problems in the *Mahābhārata* – not only because the marriage is a pivotal episode as the narrative unfolds, but also because it raises a number of ongoing tensions throughout the narrative, such as between different types of *dharma*, and between human and divine agency. This chapter will pay particular attention to the question of whether the marriage can be justified in terms of *dharma*. Throughout, we will closely examine the dialogues between the characters who discuss the marriage, the arguments presented, the consequences of their discussions, and the dharmic implications of the dialogue form.

The dialogues about the polyandrous marriage take place both before and shortly after Draupadī's *svayaṃvara*. Literally translated as 'bride-choice ceremony', Draupadī's *svayaṃvara* is a contest in which interested suitors were challenged to string a hard bow and shoot arrows through a contraption at a target.[1] Draupadī's father had set this difficult task in the hope that Arjuna, the third-eldest of the Pāṇḍavas, would win his daughter's hand. The dialogues that discuss the polyandrous marriage unfold as four distinct, yet interconnected, discussions between (1) Vyāsa and the Pāṇḍavas, which takes place before the *svayaṃvara*; (2) Yudhiṣṭhira, Kuntī, and Arjuna, which takes place just after Draupadī has been brought back from the *svayaṃvara*; (3) Yudhiṣṭhira and Drupada, which takes place in Drupada's court; and (4) Vyāsa and Drupada, which takes place in private in Drupada's court. With the participation of Vyāsa, Yudhiṣṭhira, Kuntī, and Drupada, as well as Arjuna and Dhṛṣṭadyumna, these four dialogues include speakers with a wide range of social identities, from brahmin to king, from mother to father-in-law. They are arranged symmetrically, as each main interlocutor speaks with every other, with an additional discussion in which the Pāṇḍavas deliberate amongst themselves. They take place among three generations of family members, with the grandfather Vyāsa setting arguments about the marriage in motion, followed by discussions the Pāṇḍavas have with their mother, and then with their father-in-law. In the final dialogue, the grandfather returns to close the argument. Throughout, there is a strong connection between the characters' social identities and the types of argument they make. As we will see, different meanings of *dharma* are explored through the distinct ways that Vyāsa and Yudhiṣṭhira make their cases. Meanwhile, the prominent words of Kuntī, as well as the silence of Draupadī, offer female perspectives on the dharmic status of the polyandrous marriage.

In addition to representing different personal viewpoints, one of the characteristic features of these dialogues is that they include numerous distinct justifications for the marriage. In this way, these dialogues are an excellent example of the *Mahābhārata*'s tendency to explore moral questions through a plurality of religious and philosophical views. In this case, the reasons given for justifying Draupadī's marriage include (1) karmic retribution; (2) the binding power of words; (3) birth order; (4) abiding by a former promise; (5) following ancient traditions; (6) virtuous behaviour; (7) the authority of the king; and (8) divine intervention. Crucially, all these reasons, in one way or another, are articulated in terms of *dharma*, thus offering a variety of ways to understand this 'ever-elusive' concept (Matilal 2002: 69). Much more than merely enumerating different understandings of *dharma*, however, the dialogues about Draupadī's marriage explore the relationships between them. As we will see, by bringing together many of these understandings into one comprehensive argument, Yudhiṣṭhira both recognises *dharma*'s complexity and offers an implicit method of moral reasoning that takes into consideration a range of factors, without reducing his arguments to one criterion. Similarly, Vyāsa offers human and divine agency as two distinct explanations for Draupadī's marriage, yet invites exploration into how they might overlap or reinforce each other.

Another crucial theme that emerges in these dialogues is that the problem of Draupadī's marriage remains unresolved. Despite hearing a number of arguments defending the dharmic status of the marriage, Drupada is unconvinced at the end of the discussion. The dialogue itself privileges some views over others, either through repetition or by the authority of a particular speaker, but after the marriage takes place, there is never another discussion about it – although the status of the marriage is questioned and criticised in subsequent sections of the text. This non-closure invites further consideration, particularly as the elusive nature of *dharma* is debated in the lead-up to the dicing match, the aftermath of the dicing match, the discussions leading up to the war, Bhīṣma's long instruction after the war, and in other episodes. As with other moral deliberations in the *Mahābhārata*, the discussions about Draupadī's marriage put a number of doctrines in creative tension with one aznother, while never being fully reconciled.

Dharma

As James Fitzgerald notes: 'The word *dharma* signifies a concept that is one of the most central and important topics of thought and debate in the *Mahābhārata*' (2009: 249). As we will see in this chapter, Draupadī's marriage provides the opportunity for some of the text's most complex discussions about *dharma*. Although not all the arguments for Draupadī's marriage specifically mention *dharma*, the topic of the marriage is articulated in terms of *dharma* by all major interlocutors in these discussions. Just before giving his first explanation, Vyāsa asks the Pāṇḍavas if they 'abide by *dharma*' (1.157.4), and he later assures Drupada that there is 'no doubt' (*na saṃśaya*) that the marriage adheres to *dharma* (1.188.19). Kuntī is concerned whether Draupadi will violate *dharma* by participating in the marriage (1.182.5), Yudhiṣṭhira offers several different, yet overlapping justifications – all articulated in terms of *dharma* – and both Drupada and Dhṛṣṭadyumna articulate their objections to the marriage in terms of *dharma*. At the end of the conversation, Drupada is still considering whether the marriage is *dharma* or *adharma*.

The word *dharma*, which first appears in the *Ṛgveda*, is derived from the verbal root √*dhṛ*, which means 'to uphold, support, nourish'. As with the Vedic concept of *ṛta*, which can be considered a cosmic order or natural law, *dharma* is sometimes conceptualised as a cosmological or metaphysical concept that signifies a universal moral order. As Sukthankar explains, this understanding of *dharma* 'presupposes an eternal moral order which is based on cosmic archetypal ideation, which persists immutably and which is utterly independent of and indifferent to merely human preferences, conveniences or manipulation' [1957] (2016: 80). This aspect of *dharma* is manifested through the god Dharma, as well as through both Vyāsa and Kṛṣṇa who sometimes speak of *dharma* in this way. Although this cosmological aspect of *dharma* is the backdrop for the actions of the characters throughout the main story, most of the debates about *dharma* in the *Mahābhārata* are more focused on the actions and choices of individual characters, particularly when they examine their decisions and justify their actions in situations where there are conflicting understandings.

One of the reasons why such *dharma*-conflicts take place with such frequency is because the term is used on so many occasions and in different ways. As Fitzgerald has reflected:

> The single biggest problem in coming to terms with *dharma* in the *Mahābhārata* is the tremendous abundance of instances of it, and then

> the many different modes of variation within and among those different instances of the word.
>
> (2009: 250)

As we will see, the dialogues about Draupadī's marriage demonstrate this point perhaps more than any other episode – with at least seven distinct understandings of *dharma* articulated as the dialogue unfolds. In addition to the different uses of the term, it is invoked by different characters, each of whom offers a different perspective and set of priorities.

Moreover, twice in these dialogues, *dharma* is described as 'subtle' (*sūkṣma*). As we have seen in the Introduction, this portrayal of *dharma* has Upaniṣadic resonances, indicating that a true understanding is beyond description or explanation. Minoru Hara has noted, however, that this description sometimes offers a critical perspective on *dharma*: 'this concept is unique, because its contextual atmosphere occasionally suggests the weakness of *dharma*, and consequently its unreliability, despite a general Hindu belief in the sublime concept of *dharma*' (1997: 516). As we will see in this chapter – and reflect upon further in the Conclusion – there is also a rhetorical dimension of *dharma-sūkṣmatā*, as characters refer to *dharma*'s subtlety to make different types of points. In the dialogues about Draupadī's marriage, for example, the two characters who describe *dharma* as subtle – Yudhiṣṭhira and Dhṛṣṭadyumna – deploy this description for different reasons. In other words, and as we saw in the previous chapter – the subtlety of *dharma* is understood differently by different characters.

Despite such disagreements about *dharma* – both generally and in its more subtle understandings – one of the arguments I will make in this chapter is that the different meanings of *dharma* coalesce around shared practices of moral deliberation through dialogue. In other words, I will argue that the dialogue form conveys something crucial about *dharma* that is not represented in any of its distinct meanings in isolation. Through dialogue, *dharma* is upheld through how characters both make arguments and engage with each other. As we saw in the Introduction, a higher understanding of *dharma* is an understanding of the various types of *dharma* and how they relate to each other in any given situation. As we will see in this chapter, Yudhiṣṭhira's argument in supporting the marriage is an example of dharmic reasoning that explores the moral question of the polyandrous marriage through a wide range of understandings.

In addition to how characters make arguments, the dialogues about Draupadī's marriage also point towards an understanding of *dharma* as an enactment of collective decision-making. Despite strong disagreements about the dharmic status of the marriage, interlocutors engage with each other's views and attempt to achieve a consensus. In this way, we might see engaging in dialogue with others as an important practice of following *dharma* in the *Mahābhārata*. This aspect of *dharma* is captured by Wendy Doniger O'Flaherty and J. Duncan M. Derrett: 'Since *dharma* is hidden, it must be found and activated by a dialectic process, by a context, by each new situation' (1978: xiv–xv). In other words, if *dharma* is activated though dialogue, then the dialogues between characters not only explore its meaning, but also rehearse ways of practising *dharma* in terms of thinking, speaking, and behaving.

Draupadī's marriage in the frame dialogues

The first references to Draupadī's marriage are in the summaries that appear in the frame dialogues. The first summary is told from the perspective of Dhṛtarāṣṭra, who recounts to Saṃjaya each episode in the narrative that made him lose hope of victory in the war. When he mentions the *svayaṃvara*, he only says that Draupadī had been taken as 'all the kings looked on' (1.1.102). It is notable that despite its centrality in the narrative trajectory towards the war, Dhṛtarāṣṭra barely says anything about the marriage here, and certainly does not indicate that there might be something unusual or controversial about it.

The next one to speak about the marriage is Ugraśravas, who, when listing the hundred books to the Naimiṣa *ṛṣis*, describes the marriage as following *kṣatriya-dharma* (1.2.37). In this list, in which most books are merely named, the *svayaṃvara* is one of the few episodes that contains any description. Nevertheless, Ugraśravas gives no indication here that the marriage will later be characterised as dharmically dubious. In his summary of the books, however, he indicates some tensions associated with the marriage by mentioning Drupada's 'examination' (*vimarṣa*) of the proposed marriage (1.2.88). Moreover, he describes the marriage as 'not human' (*amānuṣa*) and 'ordained by the Gods' (*devavihita*) (1.2.88), while specifically associating the marriage episode with the 'wondrous' (*adbhuta*) story of the five Indras (1.2.87). This story will be one of the two explanations for the marriage offered by Vyāsa. Although the dialogues during the main story are more likely to emphasise other reasons – in particular, Kuntī's words and the story of Draupadī's previous birth – here Ugraśravas offers the story of the five Indras as the main reason to explain the marriage.

In Vaiśaṃpāyana's summary, he merely mentions that the Pāṇḍavas won Draupadī (1.55.22), without indicating that it is only Arjuna who participates in the contest. He also neglects to allude to any controversy. Considering that Draupadī's marriage is one of the most blatant and consequential moral problems in the narrative, it is notable that two narrators who appear in the frame dialogues – Dhṛtarāṣṭra and Vaiśaṃpāyana – do not prepare their listeners for the controversy that will surround it in the main story.

Vyāsa and the Pāṇḍavas (1.157): *Karma* and Rebirth

The first dialogue about Draupadī's marriage in the main story is between Vyāsa and the Pāṇḍavas. When thinking about Vyāsa's contribution to these discussions, we should recall that, as the grandfather of the Pāṇḍavas, he has his own interest in continuing the family line; while, as author of the narrative, his appearances within it often move the story along, as well as offer lenses through which to understand its cosmic implications.[2] Additionally, as Bruce Sullivan reminds us, Vyāsa has the power of omniscience, which allows him to 'predict the future, reveal the past, and affect the present conflict in the Bhārata dynasty' (1999: 36). In the account he tells the Pāṇḍavas here, Vyāsa draws on his omniscience to provide an explanation of the marriage that transcends the knowledge of ordinary humans.

Vyāsa visits the Pāṇḍavas when they are in hiding as brahmins, soon after their escape from the burning house of lacquer (1.135–137), and recounts a story about a sage's daughter who had repeatedly asked Śiva for a husband (1.157). As a punishment for her impatience, Śiva granted her five husbands in her next birth. At the end of this story, Vyāsa reveals that Draupadī was this young woman in a previous life and that she will be their wife in this life (1.157.14).

Although not asked to provide a justification, Vyāsa's account offers *karma* and rebirth as the first explanation for the polyandrous marriage. *Karma*, which literally means 'action', is a doctrine of cause and effect that operates both within and across lifetimes. In Vyāsa's story, *karma* operates within the single lifetime of the maiden, as she is able to get Śiva's attention because she satisfied him with her 'austerities' (*tapas*) (1.157.8). *Karma* also operates across lifetimes, both through the maiden's previous 'acts' (1.157.7), which account for her unmarried status, and through the maiden repeatedly asking for a husband, which affects Draupadī. From her actions in a previous life, to the maiden's actions in her own life, to the polyandrous marriage in her future life, Vyāsa's story gives a glimpse of how *karma* works across three different lifetimes.

A number of scholars have commented on the relatively few instances in the *Mahābhārata* of detailed explanations of *karma*.[3] Despite containing few passages of 'substantial discussions on karma and transmigration' (Hill 2001: 29), the *Mahābhārata* nevertheless incorporates understandings of *karma* throughout the narrative in a number of ways. One way, as Emily Hudson points out, is where 'characters invoke the concept in order to explain why they (or others) suffer sudden and unexpected misfortune' (2013: 190). Another way, I would add, is through the unfolding of the narrative itself, where a past action is linked to a present or future episode in the story. As we saw in the previous chapter, Bhīṣma's mistreatment of Ambā motivates her to vow to take revenge. Although there are multiple explanations for Bhīṣma's death, one of them is the karmic explanation that he suffered the consequences of the harm he caused Ambā. Similarly, in the case of Draupadī's marriage, Vyāsa's account portrays Draupadī's present circumstances as the result of her own past actions.

Even if *karma* makes humans accountable for their own circumstances, Vyāsa's story also describes *karma* as working through the divine figure of

Śiva. It is because of Śiva's curse that the maiden will have five husbands in a subsequent birth. The prominent role of Śiva in bringing about the marriage will be highlighted again later, when Vyāsa recounts the story of the five Indras. In this case, however, Śiva's intervention is not described as causing the marriage instead of *karma*, but rather along with it. Although Śiva could be seen to be acting arbitrarily, there is still a sense that he is acting in response to the maiden's actions themselves. Moreover, the previous acts of the maiden seem to have happened outside of Śiva's direct control.

Although there are deterministic aspects of *karma* and rebirth, – particularly when a deity directs the course of events – there is also an implicit notion of human agency. We see this, for example, as the maiden earns her boons from Śiva through her austerities. Despite portraying Draupadī suffering the consequence of actions determined in a former life, this story also shows how the maiden influenced her own circumstances in her own lifetime. Indeed, Vyāsa's account gives Draupadī – as the maiden – a voice in arranging her own marriage, even if she does not speak at all in the discussions about it in her own lifetime. Despite her implied agency, the fact that her own words are used against her adds to the sense that the maiden, although an active participant, has limited control over the outcome of her actions. As Jonathan Geen explains: 'it is made very clear that the noble sage's daughter at no time wanted or intended for Lord Śiva to grant her five husbands, let alone five husbands in a future birth' (2006: 594). Seen in this way, the story of Draupadī's former life only gives her limited agency, thus highlighting the tension between divine intervention and human endeavour that is explored throughout the *Mahābhārata*.

Despite the wide acceptance of the doctrine of *karma* in the *Mahābhārata*, there are very few stories – as Geen points out – about the former lives of individual characters. Whereas such stories are abundant in both Jaina and Buddhist narratives (see Appleton 2014), Draupadī is the only major character whom the narrative depicts as experiencing a full cycle of life, death, and rebirth, and subsequent life – with Vyāsa's first account of Draupadī's previous births representing her through three life cycles. In addition to Draupadī, one of the few other characters whose story is narrated through more than one lifetime is Ambā, whose actions in this life are explicitly related to her situation in her next life, even if she is not reborn exactly how she had wanted to be (see Chapter 1). The examples of Draupadī and Ambā also indicate a potential gender component of *karma* and rebirth in the *Mahābhārata*, as rarely does the narrative recount the past lives of men, instead tending to describe the main male characters as descending from the gods. Relevant to this point is Geen's observation that, whereas Jaina and Buddhist narratives emphasise reincarnation, the *Mahābhārata* is more likely to emphasise incarnation (2006: 596). We will return to the issue of incarnation later in this chapter when we look at the story of the five Indras.

Intriguingly, Geen further argues that this account of Draupadī's former lives might have originally been a Jaina story (2006). Given that multi-life narratives are rare in the *Mahābhārata* but common on Jaina sources, Geen tentatively suggests:

> The presence of such a past-life story in the Hindu version, taken together with the existence of a strikingly similar ancient Jaina version of the story from which to draw, points to the possibility that the Hindu version of Draupadī's marriage has been influenced by the Jaina tradition.
>
> (2006: 600)

Moreover, the Jaina version includes more details about Draupadī's previous lives, thus making her previous acts more explicit and more understandable as to why they would deserve punishment in the future. As Geen points out, in the Jaina version, the maiden does not ask for five husbands by accident, but 'unambiguously desired five men' (2006: 595). Geen speculates that the *Mahābhārata* might have retained the Jaina-inspired account of multiple lifetimes, but removed any details that would implicate Draupadī: 'the modifications made by the Hindu story of Śiva's Boon removed this sinful intentionality and thus relieved Draupadī of the shame that her polyandrous situation arose as a consequence of her own wanton desires' (2006: 595). Although Geen admits that the evidence is not conclusive, his argument compellingly points to the possibility that a Jaina voice contributes to the discussions about Draupadī's marriage as it appears in the Sanskrit manuscript traditions of the *Mahābhārata*. If this were the case, then it would add a Jaina perspective to the wide range of perspectives addressing Draupadī's marriage as a moral problem.

Despite the fact that there are very few multi-life narratives in the *Mahābhārata*, the story of Draupadī's previous birth is given considerable weight in providing an explanation for her polyandrous marriage. Not only is it the first explanation given, it is also the last, as Vyāsa tells this story again, this time to Drupada after the *svayaṃvara* (1.189.41–49). Moreover, when Drupada finally gives in, this is the explanation that he mentions. It is interesting, then, that despite being de-emphasised on other occasions, *karma* across multiple lifetimes is portrayed as one of the most significant explanations for Draupadī's marriage.

Kuntī, Yudhiṣṭhira, and his brothers (1.182): Kuntī's words

The next justification offered for the marriage is Kuntī's inadvertent instruction to her sons to share Draupadī. Kuntī's words are not only the most repeated justification for the marriage within the main story, but they are also the most well-known explanation among modern retellings.[4] In this section, we will reflect on the circumstances under which Kuntī utters her words, the gendered implications of her and others' responses to them, and the active role she plays in making them binding.

After Arjuna wins the archery context during the *svayaṃvara*, he and Bhīmasena return with Draupadī to the potter's house, where all five Pāṇḍavas had been staying in disguise with their mother. As they are approaching the house, they call out to Kuntī to look at the alms (*bhikṣā*) they had collected (1.182.1). Inside the house and without seeing her sons, she tells them to 'enjoy' (*buṅkta*) equally (1.182.2). Kuntī immediately questions her response (1.182.2) and, afraid of violating *dharma*, takes Draupadī by the hand to ask Yudhiṣṭhira to decide on the matter, explaining that because she merely repeated what she often says, her words were spoken 'carelessly' (*pramāda*) (1.182.4). Here, Kuntī describes her words as spoken out of habit, rather than from conviction. Why would what she said in such informal circumstances carry so much weight?

This question returns us to the story of Draupadī's previous life, which, in addition to highlighting the role of *karma* and rebirth, also emphasises the power of speech. Like Kuntī's offhand comment, Draupadī's words in a former lifetime are also considered binding, even though they are the result of a misunderstanding. As Geen observes:

> The fact that the girl obtains five husbands because she has asked for a single husband five times may well reflect the pan-Indian belief in the power of *mantra*, or efficacious speech. The notion that speech, once spoken, has certain and unavoidable consequences is a theme that runs throughout the Hindu *Mahābhārata*.
>
> (2006: 595)

As we saw in the case of Bhīṣma's vows, the power of speech is a central and recurring theme throughout the *Mahābhārata*, particularly as expressed through speech acts such as curses, boons, vows, and acts of truth. But whereas all of these verbal actions are deliberate attempts to affect change on the world, the words of the maiden and Kuntī affect changes neither one of them intends. In the case of the maiden, her words seem to be wilfully misconstrued by Śiva to punish her for her impatience; for Kunti, her words are an offhand remark that is made in response to a misunderstanding. Both cases highlight the imbalanced consequences women suffer from their words compared to men. Whereas in other episodes, Arjuna, Bhīṣma, and others are offered the opportunity to qualify previous speech acts when circumstances change,[5] neither the maiden nor Kuntī is given the chance to take back what they said.

In Kuntī's case, it's worth reflecting on the fact that only she second-guesses her words, despite the fact that they are the result of a miscommunication between herself and two of her sons. Kuntī has very good reason to tell her sons to share, considering the fact that she and they are living at the potter's house, disguised as brahmins, and living off alms they collect from the village (1.176.7). When Arjuna and Bhīmasena are late coming back from the *svayaṃvara*, Kuntī worries because she knows that it is past the time for collecting alms (1.181.37).[6] Not only is it understandable that Kuntī would think that her sons are returning with alms, but it is reasonable to think that Arjuna and Bhīmasena would be expecting their mother to be thinking in those terms when they ask her to look at the alms they had collected. With this in mind, we might wonder why Arjuna and Bhīmasena should not reflect on their own contribution to this situation by misleading their mother about what they were talking about. Indeed, we might see the irresponsible words of Arjuna and Bhīmasena, rather than Kuntī's response, as the real catalyst for setting the polyandrous marriage in motion.[7]

Both Kuntī and the maiden, then, demonstrate the double standards in how the *Mahābhārata* represents the power of women's words. As we saw in Chapter 1, when Satyavatī asks Bhīṣma to give up his vow of celibacy, he does not follow his mother's advice, even though she is fully conscious of what she is saying and backing up her arguments with traditional sources. Or, as we will see in Chapter 4, when Śakuntalā wants Duḥṣanta to recognise her and her son, she is ignored even though she speaks the truth. In contrast, in two of the cases where the words of women are depicted as most binding, either her words are wilfully misinterpreted or she was responding to a misrepresentation of circumstances.

In addition to reflecting on the gender imbalance regarding the binding consequences of speech, it is also important to keep in mind that Kuntī actively lobbies to make her words obligatory. After recounting to Yudhiṣṭhira what has happened, Kuntī asks him to decide on how the words she uttered can avoid being false (1.182.5). Although Kuntī initially characterised her words as careless, here she insists on making them true. Yudhiṣṭhira does not offer an immediate response to her question, but later, when speaking to Drupada, he will present his mother's words as the first justification for the marriage, and then repeat their importance on two subsequent occasions. Considering the emphasis placed on her words in this and the subsequent dialogues, it is worth noting that they become binding not merely because she said them, but because she draws attention to them and demands for Yudhiṣṭhira to make a decision that will render them true. It is also worth noting that despite offering a further explanation for Draupadī's polyandrous marriage, Kuntī's words do not endorse polyandry as in accordance with *dharma*.

In the meantime, Yudhiṣṭhira responds by offering a procedural explanation, arguing that Arjuna should be the husband because he won Draupadī according to the rules of the contest (1.182). Arjuna responds, however, that he should not get married before Yudhiṣṭhira, who is his eldest brother, because it would be against the *dharma* of birth order (1.182.8). After making this intervention, Arjuna reiterates what Kuntī had said before, that it is for Yudhiṣṭhira to decide how to uphold *dharma* (1.182.10). As we will see, Yudhiṣṭhira will present the *dharma* of birth order as his second argument for the marriage when trying to convince Draupadī's father.

When Yudhiṣṭhira finally does make a decision, it is not on the basis of his mother's words or on the basis of birth order, but because of his feelings of love. As Vaiśaṃpāyana narrates the scene to Janamejaya, when the Pāṇḍavas gazed at Draupadī, their 'love' (*manobhava*) became evident (1.182.12). This is not the first time that Vaiśaṃpāyana emphasises the strong feelings that the sight of Draupadī arouses in the Pāṇḍava brothers; during the *svayaṃvara,* he describes them as 'struck by the arrows of love' (1.178.12). As we will see on other occasions, the *Mahābhārata* repeatedly emphasises the role of emotions when exploring how and why characters make the choices that they do. In this case, Yudhiṣṭhira's emotions prompt him to declare that Draupadī will be the wife of all of them (1.182.15). As soon as he says this, he refers to Vyāsa's words. The way this scene unfolds, Yudhiṣṭhira seems to recall Vyāsa's justification only after he has already made up his mind. It is also notable that in his first explanation for the marriage immediately after making his decision, he invokes Vyāsa's words, but not his mother's. As we will see, Yudhiṣṭhira will strongly emphasise the words of his mother when speaking to Drupada later, but here he does not mention them in the crucial moment when he declares that he and his brothers will all marry Draupadī.

In contrast to Kuntī, whose voice is prominent throughout these discussions, we never hear Draupadī speak directly about the marriage. Nevertheless, Vaiśaṃpāyana's narration indicates that she goes along with the unconventional arrangement willingly. After discussing the marriage with Yudhiṣṭhira, Kuntī has a brief word with Draupadī, telling her how to make offerings and how to divide up the food among the Pāṇḍavas. Although Draupadī does not speak, Vaiśaṃpāyana recounts that she 'cheerfully' (*hṛṣṭarūpa*) followed the 'virtuous' (*sādhu*) words of Kuntī (1.184.7). Vaiśaṃpāyana also reports that on her first night with the Pāṇḍavas, she sleeps at their feet on the floor without 'sorrow' (*duḥkha*) (1.184.10). Although there is no indication that the marriage is consummated at this point, the fact that Draupadī has already taken the advice of Kuntī, fed the Pāṇḍavas, and slept alongside them suggests that – although the official wedding has not yet taken place – she has already taken on her role as wife of the Pāṇḍavas and daughter-in-law of Kuntī. Throughout Yudhiṣṭhira's subsequent conversations with Drupada, there will be an ongoing tension between whether the marriage has already been decided or if Drupada needs to be persuaded to accept it.

Yudhiṣṭhira and Drupada (1.187): *Dharma*

As we have seen so far, Vyāsa offers an explanation for Draupadī's marriage before the *svayaṃvara*; then, afterwards, Kuntī discusses with Yudhiṣṭhira the implications of her words. Despite the prominence of these two explanations, Vyāsa and Yudhiṣṭhira make more explicit arguments to defend the marriage when trying to convince Draupadī's father to accept it.

As we will see, both of their arguments are articulated explicitly in terms of *dharma*, but in different ways. Yudhiṣṭhira offers an array of meanings of *dharma* by making at least six distinct, yet overlapping, points. Within this range of meanings, Yudhiṣṭhira focuses on what we might see as the secular domain of *dharma*, appealing to notions of family obligation, ancient tradition, virtuous action, and political power.[8] Vyāsa also frames his case in terms of *dharma*, but his explanations are more cosmological and metaphysical, justifying the marriage in terms of karmic retribution and divine intervention.

Before his dialogue with Drupada, Yudhiṣṭhira offers a justification for the marriage to Drupada's family priest, who approaches the potter's house to confirm the Pāṇḍavas' true identity. Although the family priest describes Drupada as delighted to accept Arjuna as his son-in-law, Yudhiṣṭhira responds defensively, insisting that Arjuna won her fairly according to the rules of the contest (1.185.23). He then describes in detail the feat that Arjuna performed, as if the family priest needed reminding. What is interesting about this short exchange is that the family priest does not know anything about the plan for all five brothers to marry Draupadī, so he only conveys Drupada's enthusiasm about accepting Arjuna into his family. Yudhiṣṭhira, however, is already defending the polyandry, emphasising that the rules of the *svayaṃvara* set out by Drupada had been followed. Although Yudhiṣṭhira does not repeat this line of argument in his dialogue with Drupada, it is interesting that his first defence of the marriage to Drupada – via his family priest – is on procedural grounds. As we will see in Chapter 4, Draupadī's first challenge to the result of the dicing match questions whether the rules of the game had been properly followed. Although characters rarely persuade their interlocutors with rule-based arguments on their own, both Yudhiṣṭhira and Draupadī incorporate procedural understandings into their wider cases about following *dharma*.

Yudhiṣṭhira then discusses the status of the marriage with Drupada when the Pāṇḍavas arrive at his court for the wedding. After Yudhiṣṭhira reveals the Pāṇḍavas' identity, he announces that Draupadī will be the common queen of all five brothers (1.187.22). The first reason Yudhiṣṭhira gives for the polyandrous marriage is Kuntī's words (1.187.22). Notably, Yudhiṣṭhira's reasons for following the words of his mother are different from how Kuntī presented her own argument back at the potter's house. Whereas she was concerned about their veracity, Yudhiṣṭhira instead treats them in terms of his own dharmic obligation to obey his mother. Yudhiṣṭhira will refer to his mother's words again when he sums up his reasons to Drupada before the arrival of Vyāsa (1.187.29) and when he gives his final summation the following day (1.188.15).

The next reason Yudhiṣṭhira gives is that he and his brothers are all still unmarried. Implicitly addressing the fact that Arjuna had won the archery contest at the *svayaṃvara*, Yudhiṣṭhira invokes the *dharma* of birth order to justify his own claim to marry Draupadī. As we have seen, Arjuna had already made this argument at the potter's house when he suggested that Yudhiṣṭhira, as the eldest brother, should marry Draupadī. In addition to the *dharma* of birth order, Yudhiṣṭhira is also concerned with the issue of unity among his brothers. As Arti Dhand explains, there would be 'a very real danger to the family in allowing only one of the brothers to have a wife, while the others remain unmarried' (2008: 118). Despite the significance of this argument – both in making the case for the dharmic status of the marriage and in explaining why Yudhiṣṭhira made his decision for all of them to marry Draupadī – Drupada does not respond to this point, nor will Yudhiṣṭhira raise it again.

Yudhiṣṭhira's next justification is that he and his brothers follow a previous agreement (1.187.24). It is not clear when the Pāṇḍavas made such an agreement, but it is notable that Yudhiṣṭhira uses the word *samaya*, a term that is sometimes used interchangeably with vows (*vrata*) and promises (*pratijñā*). As we saw in the previous chapter, Satyavatī's father uses this word when asking Śaṃtanu to agree to make any son of Satyavatī the heir to the throne (1.94.48), while Rāma Jāmadagnya employs this term to describe a vow he had taken not to fight unless asked by brahmins (5.177.4).[9] In this case, Yudhiṣṭhira offers his previous agreement with his brothers as the third of his initial justifications for the marriage, before concluding that Draupadī becoming a common wife of the Pāṇḍavas is in accordance with *dharma* (1.187.25).

Drupada responds, declaring that it is unacceptable for a woman to have more than one husband, although it is 'ordained' (*vihita*) that one man may have many wives (1.187.26). Whereas Yudhiṣṭhira tried to convince Drupada that the marriage could be considered dharmic based on contingent factors – his obligations to his mother and brothers – Drupada implicitly rejects these reasons, maintaining that the practice of polyandry itself is a breach of *dharma*. Claiming that polyandry 'runs counter to Veda and world' (1.187.27), Drupada rejects the marriage proposal on the basis that polyandry is supported neither by traditional sources nor by common practice.[10]

Yudhiṣṭhira replies with the well-known description of *dharma* as 'subtle' (*sūkṣma*) (1.187.28). As we saw in the Introduction, this description is often invoked to point towards a deeper understanding of *dharma*. Yudhiṣṭhira might be indicating that the marriage abides by such an understanding – one that is rooted in something beyond traditional sources and practices. However, Yudhiṣṭhira then responds to Drupada's argument about precedent by claiming to follow the 'path travelled by the ancient (*pūrva*)' (1.187.28), suggesting that there is indeed traditional support for polyandry. Yudhiṣṭhira then argues for the dharmic status of the marriage based on his own adherence to *dharma*, saying: 'My voice does not tell a lie, nor does my mind dwell on *adharma*'(1.187.30). As we will see with Draupadī in Chapter 4, appealing to one's own virtuous conduct is a recurring and valued line of argument in the *Mahābhārata*'s moral debates. Here, his argument implies that as one who practices *dharma*, he has the authority to speak for *dharma*. He concludes his argument by stating that it is his wish for the marriage to take place and that the dharmic status of the marriage is 'certain' (*dhruva*) (1.187.30). Although he is not yet a king, throughout the encounter Yudhiṣṭhira speaks as if he already has the authority to make pronouncements about *dharma* – implicitly invoking his status as son of Dharma and as the *dharma-rāja*. With this in mind, then, it seems that at least part of the reason why Yudhiṣṭhira refers to *dharma*'s elusive nature is to profess his own authority to speak on its behalf.

Despite Yudhiṣṭhira's certainty, Drupada is not convinced. Then, after a brief hiatus in the conversation, Vyāsa appears and asks to hear everyone's 'views' (*mata*) (1.188.6). This invitation gives Drupada, Dhṛṣṭadyumna, Yudhiṣṭhira, and Kuntī each a chance to defend their views one more time, before Vyāsa will take Drupada aside to make his own case for the marriage in private. Although he does not elaborate, we might take Vyāsa's soliciting the views of others before making his own argument as an example of collective moral reasoning. Despite strong disagreements about the dharmic status of the marriage, Vyāsa engages with other's views and attempts to achieve a consensus.

Drupada, the first to reply, reiterates his previous point by asking how one woman can be the wife of many men without violating *dharma* (1.188.5). Then, countering Yudhiṣṭhira's earlier argument, Drupada says that polyandry has not been practised by the ancients (*pūrva*) (1.188.8). By offering a rebuttal to one of Yudhiṣṭhira's main points, Drupada challenges Yudhiṣṭhira's claim to ground the dharmic status of the marriage in an ancient practice. He concludes by saying that its dharmic status is doubtful (1.188.9). It is not clear why Drupada does not engage directly with Yudhiṣṭhira's other arguments, but by continuing to cast doubt on the dharmic status of the marriage, he clearly rejects Yudhiṣṭhira's claim to speak for *dharma*.

Dhṛṣṭadyumna's first response is to question how an older brother can have sex with the wife of his younger brother and still remain 'strict in virtue' (*tapodhana*) (1.188.10). Although Dhṛṣṭadyumna does not directly refer to any of Yudhiṣṭhira's arguments here, we might see this point as a response to Yudhiṣṭhira's earlier attempt to ground the dharmic status of the marriage in terms of his own virtuous behaviour. Then Dhṛṣṭadyumna repeats Yudhiṣṭhira's description of *dharma* as 'subtle' (*sūkṣma*), but makes a very different point. As we have seen, Yudhiṣṭhira appears to bring attention to the elusive nature of *dharma* to claim his own authority. In contrast, Dhṛṣṭadyumna seems to make the point that *dharma* is too complicated for any of them to understand (1.188.11). Dhṛṣṭadyumna concludes by saying that he cannot decide whether or not the marriage could be supported by *dharma*. Implicitly, Dhṛṣṭadyumna seems to be arguing that as long as he can cast doubt on the dharmic status of the marriage, then he can prevent it from taking place. In other words, rather than arguing, like his father does, that polyandry is definitely not dharmic, he puts the burden of proof on Yudhiṣṭhira.

Yudhiṣṭhira responds by reiterating his earlier appeal to his own virtuous behaviour, repeating verbatim his claim: 'My voice does not tell a lie, nor does my mind dwell on *adharma*' (1.188.13). He then returns to his assertion that polyandry is an ancient practice, this time citing the 'old' (*purāṇa*) story of Jaṭilā who lay with the seven seers. By countering Drupada's rebuttal, Yudhiṣṭhira doubles down on his position that there is a dharmic precedent for polyandry.

A.N. Jaini interprets Yudhiṣṭhira's invocation of the Jaṭilā story as indicating that the Pāṇḍavas have marriage practices different from the Pāñcālas. As Jaini argues: 'The custom of polyandry was prevalent in ancient times ... In Tibet and the Himalayan region, it was an accepted custom' (1989: 72). Jaini further notes that the Pāṇḍavas 'were also brought from the Himalayas' and that other members of the Pāṇḍava family followed practices similar to polyandry 'as can be seen by Kuntī's having three sons from three different persons and Mādrī having two sons from two others persons' (1989: 72–73). Jaini concludes that the 'ethnological fact' of polyandry is the 'real solution' to the moral dilemma of Draupadī's marriage. Although Jaini makes an interesting point about other women from the Pāṇḍava family bearing children from more than one partner, I disagree with his suggestion that this 'ethnological fact' could be the 'solution' to the question of Draupadī's marriage. Firstly, the dialogues about the marriage highlight other justifications far more than this one, particularly Kuntī's words and Draupadī's former birth. Moreover, as we will see, Drupada's unconvinced response at the end of these discussions indicates that there is no 'solution' to justify Draupadī's marriage. As with the *Mahābhārata*'s other moral questions, there are numerous reasons, multiple perspectives, and no definitive answers.

After citing the story of Jaṭilā, Yudhiṣṭhira adds further weight to his mother's words by referring to her as his *guru* (1.188.15). Here we see that Yudhiṣṭhira mentions Kuntī's words on all three occasions he defends the marriage in Drupada's court, thus making them the most emphasised reason in his case for the dharmic status of the marriage. We also see that it is Yudhiṣṭhira, not Kuntī, who insists that her words are binding. Yudhiṣṭhira concludes – again asserting his authority to speak for *dharma* – by stating emphatically: 'I hold it is *dharma*' (1.188.16).

When it is Kuntī's turn to offer her views on the marriage, she gives the shortest response, but perhaps the most influential one. First, she reiterates her son's pronouncement, saying that it is as the '*dharma*-abiding' Yudhiṣṭhira has said (1.188.17). Then, echoing the question she asked Yudhiṣṭhira back at the potter's house, she asks Vyāsa how she can escape speaking a lie (*anṛta*) (1.188.17). Again we see that at no point does Kuntī argue that her words are binding, nor does she defend the marriage as following *dharma*. Rather, she persistently asks how her words can avoid being untrue.

Vyāsa responds, reassuring her that escaping the lie is the 'eternal' (*sanātana*) *dharma* (1.188.18). It is not clear exactly why Vyāsa appeals to *sanātana dharma* here, especially when Kuntī's situation is unique to her and not presented as part of a wider question about abiding by one's words. Nevertheless, describing her adherence to truth in this way shows that Vyāsa takes Kuntī's dilemma very seriously. Despite the fact that other sections of the text will characterise women as liars and speakers of untruth, Vyāsa considers maintaining the truthfulness of Kuntī's words as extremely important. Indeed, as these are his last words before taking Drupada aside in private to give him higher-order justifications for the marriage, Vaiśaṃpāyana's narration suggests that a major motivation throughout this discussion for trying to convince Drupada is to maintain the truth of Kuntī's words. As we can see, Kuntī plays a prominent role, not only because of her initial words themselves, but also because she demands that they be properly considered by her interlocutors.

Before we move on to examine the private dialogue between Vyāsa and Drupada, it is worth taking stock of the main issues of the dialogues in Drupada's court so far. Perhaps the most notable feature is the sheer number of different points put forth in support of the marriage, with Yudhiṣṭhira giving at least six distinct justifications – all of which are framed in terms of *dharma*: (1) his obligation to follow Kuntī's words; (2) the *dharma* of birth order; (3) his previous agreement with his brothers; (4) his following a traditional precedent; (5) his own virtuous behaviour; and (6) his own authority to make pronouncements on *dharma*. As noted in the Introduction and as seen in the many explanations for the death of Bhīṣma, the *Mahābhārata* has a tendency to offer multiple reasons for the text's most controversial episodes. Yudhiṣṭhira's arguments here are one of the best demonstrations of the text's pluralistic approach to moral questions.

In contrasting Yudhiṣṭhira's arguments with those of Drupada, we can also see how this debate reveals different understandings of *dharma*. For Drupada, as we have seen, polyandry cannot be considered *dharma* because there is no traditional source or established practice defending it. In this way, Drupada indicates an understanding of *dharma* that is both unchanging and universal, implying that a woman having more than one husband can never be justified regardless of the circumstances. Yudhiṣṭhira attempts to convince Drupada on his own terms by appealing to a traditional precedent to support polyandry, citing the example of Jaṭilā. Nevertheless, none of Yudhiṣṭhira's other arguments defend polyandry as a dharmic practice in itself, but rather argue that this particular instance of polyandry can be justified because it adheres to other practices of *dharma*, such as following his mother's words, abiding by a past agreement with his brothers, or acting in accordance with his own virtuous behaviour. In this way, Yudhiṣṭhira's description of *dharma* as 'subtle' is a criticism aimed at Drupada for not taking into consideration the various contingencies of this particular case.

Moreover, Yudhiṣṭhira's case demonstrates an implicit method of moral reasoning that takes into consideration a range of factors, without reducing his arguments to one criterion. As Yudhiṣṭhira's arguments unfold, he emphasises different aspects of *dharma* in different ways. The one point that he brings up each time is his mother's words, emphasising this as his central argument. The second point he brings up, the *dharma* of birth order and the avoidance of rivalries between the brothers, is clearly also central to his argument. It is interesting, though, that he does not return to this point again. Neither does he appeal again to the previous agreement he made with his brothers. An argument that he does not begin with, but adopts in response to Drupada's first rebuttal, is that there is a traditional precedent. The other points that he introduces after his first opening statement are his own virtuous behaviour and his own authority to speak for *dharma*. In other words, as his case develops, he puts less emphasis on his *kula-dharma* obligations to his brothers and more on his own actions and authority. The way that Yudhiṣṭhira's argument unfolds here is illustrative of the situational and contextual nature of discussions about *dharma* throughout the *Mahābhārata*. All of Yudhiṣṭhira's points are grounded in *dharma*, but his argument also adapts according to the points of his interlocutor.

In addition to providing an example of dharmic reasoning, we might also see Yudhiṣṭhira's approach as an inclusive method of argumentation that offers his interlocutor a number of possibilities for agreement. By providing various distinct justifications, Yudhiṣṭhira presents Drupada with the opportunity to agree from a number of different starting points. Although Drupada does not ultimately accept the dharmic status of the marriage and only goes along with it after Vyāsa's intervention, we still might see Yudhiṣṭhira's arguments as effective in bringing together the weight of multiple explanations.

Vyāsa and Drupada: incarnations of the gods (1.189.1–40)

After hearing the views of Drupada, Dhṛṣṭadyumna, Yudhiṣṭhira, and Kuntī, Vyāsa reiterates Yudhiṣṭhira's pronouncement, saying that there is 'no doubt' (*na saṃśaya*) that it is *dharma* (1.188.19). Despite framing his justifications as a continuation of Yudhiṣṭhira's position, Vyāsa goes on to give very different explanations for the marriage. In contrast with Yudhiṣṭhira, who tends to speak of *dharma* in terms of procedure, obligation, custom, virtuous practice, and royal authority, Vyāsa – who also uses the term *dharma*, but not as often – makes what could be considered cosmological and metaphysical arguments in the two major justifications he puts forward. First, Vyāsa tells the story of the five Indras, in which he justifies the marriage as part of a divine drama in which the gods have incarnated themselves as humans. Vyāsa then repeats his account of Draupadī's previous life, in an argument that explains her marriage as part of the mechanisms of *karma* and rebirth.

One of the most significant aspects of Vyāsa's arguments is that they are made to Drupada privately, rather than in the wider assembly that included Yudhiṣṭhira, Kuntī, and Dhṛṣṭadyumna, as well as the four other Pāṇḍavas and Draupadī. It is not clear why Vyāsa will not disclose his teaching in front of the others, especially when the Pāṇḍavas and Kuntī have already heard the story of Draupadī's previous life. However, they have not yet heard about their own divine identities, so perhaps Vyāsa does not want to reveal this to them. In any case, the private setting of this dialogue between Vyāsa and Drupada characterises his justifications as more esoteric, compared to the social and political arguments made by Yudhiṣṭhira.

Once they are in private (1.189.1–39), Vyāsa tells Drupada the intricate story of the five Indras (*Pañcendra Upākhyāna*). In his abridged translation, John Smith has summarised the story as follows:

> The gods once performed a sacrifice in the Naimiṣa forest. Yama was busy in his sacrificial duties, with the result that creatures no longer died. The gods complained to Brahmā that nothing now distinguished them from men; Brahmā reassured them that once their rite was completed men would start to die again. As the gods returned to their sacrifice, Indra saw a woman weeping into the Gaṅgā: each of her tears became a golden lotus. When he asked her who she was and why she was weeping, she told him to follow her; he did so, and saw a youth playing dice with some young women. The youth ignored him; Indra began to bluster angrily, but at a glance from the youth he found himself paralyzed. Next the youth, who was Śiva, told the woman to bring him close so that he could be divested of his pride, and at her touch he collapsed to the ground. Now he commanded to remove the summit of the mountain and enter, and when he did so he found four other Indras imprisoned there. When Indra begged for his freedom, Śiva told him that all five Indras would return to their own world only after being born as men. However, he agreed to their stipulation that in their human form they must be begotten by deities: Dharma, Wind, Indra and the Aśvins. He also promised that the goddess Śrī would take human form as their wife. Nārāyaṇa agreed to this arrangement, and plucked from his head one white and one black hair: these entered the wombs of Rohiṇī and Devakī, and from them were born Balarāma and Kṛṣṇa. (2009: 74)

After recounting this story, Vyāsa gives Drupada the divine sight to see the five Pāṇḍavas as the five Indras and his own daughter as Śrī.

This complex tale offers the divine drama of the gods as an explanation for Draupadī's marriage. Importantly, this story contains echoes of the divine plan, which first features in the frame dialogue between Vaiśaṃpāyana and Janamejaya. According to the divine plan, Earth tells Brahmā that she feels she can no longer support all the demons who have taken over the earth (1.58.34); Brahmā orders all the gods to be born on earth to stop the demons; and after gaining approval from Nārāyaṇa, the gods then descend to earth, where they are born into the lineages of brahmin and *kṣatriya* seers (1.59.5).

The story of the five Indras shares with the divine plan a crisis with the earth, the god Brahmā as the deity called upon to solve the crisis, the gods incarnating as humans, and the ultimate endorsement of Nārāyaṇa. More specifically, in both cases, the incarnation of gods as humans directly explains the divine identities of the five Pāṇḍavas. Both stories, then, characterise the circumstances of the Pāṇḍavas as being pre-ordained, as part of cosmic events played out by the gods that are beyond the understanding and control of humans.

By echoing the divine plan, the story of the five Indras portrays Draupadī's marriage as an integral part of a cosmic drama in which the gods save the earth from the demons. According to Hiltebeitel: 'The Story of the Former Indras "authorizes" the polyandry fully and provides a first glimpse ... of Vyāsa's Vedic groundplan' (2001b: 49; see also 2011: 492). Considering that Ugraśravas, the narrator in the text's outer dialogues, strongly associates the *Pañcendra Upākhyāna* with the episode of Draupadī's marriage certainly adds weight to this characterisation. Despite its importance from Ugraśravas' point of view, however, Drupada offers no response, nor does he refer to it at the end of the discussion. Drupada's silence is conspicuous considering that he is given the divine eye to see the Pāṇḍavas as the five Indras and his own daughter as Śrī. Keeping in mind that other characters who are granted the divine eye seem to gain new knowledge or a more complete perspective, we might expect that the sight of his daughter and the Pāṇḍavas as divine incarnations would convince Drupada to accept the marriage. Instead, he remains silent, prompting Vyāsa to offer another explanation.

Vyāsa and Drupada: *Karma* (1.189.41–49)

Perhaps sensing that Drupada remains unconvinced, Vyāsa repeats the account of Draupadī's former life that he had told the Pāṇḍavas before the *svayaṃvara*. On this occasion, he does not include the detail that the maiden's previous actions were responsible for her being without a husband. Nevertheless, with the remainder of the story almost exactly the same, he still communicates the message that actions in a past life are responsible for Draupadī's marriage in this life.[11]

We have looked at this story as explaining the marriage in terms of *karma* and rebirth earlier in this chapter. Here, I would like to reflect on the implications of Vyāsa juxtaposing the story of the five Indras and of Draupadī's previous birth, telling them one after another. According to Hiltebeitel, following Madeleine Biardeau, the two stories are brought together through the figure of Śiva:

> In the legend of the overanxious maiden, it is Śiva's insistence on the polyandric marriage that introduces the adharmic note; and in the myth of the five Indras, it is his intoxication with dice that ... sets up the conditions for the marriage'.
>
> (1976: 81)

The prominent role of Śiva in both stories, together with the fact that they are both narrated by Vyāsa, who is an incarnation of Nārāyaṇa, suggests that they not only reinforce each other, but also contribute to a 'vaster theological drama' (1976: 85).

But in addition to considering the ways that the stories reinforce each other, it is also important to note they are narrated as self-contained episodes that are not directly woven together. In this way, they also provide different accounts for the causes of the marriage that are not necessarily related to each other. Whereas the *Pañcendra Upākhyāna* suggests that the marriage has been brought about by the gods, the story of the maiden presents it as at least partly the consequences of human actions. If we see them as separate stories, then we might see Vyāsa – as author – as offering two different lenses through which to understand the polyandrous marriage within the wider context of the *Mahābhārata*. If the story of the five Indras suggests that the actions of Draupadī and the Pāṇḍavas are manipulated by the gods and are beyond their control, then the story of Draupadī's previous birth invites reading the *Mahābhārata* as a karmic narrative in which the actions and decisions of characters create the conditions for subsequent events in the central story.

As a karmic narrative, Draupadī's marriage plays a major role in setting up future episodes in the story. In the short term, the marriage creates the conditions for the dicing match unfolding as it does. As Geen summarises:

> The polyandrous marriage between Draupadī and the Pāṇḍavas is absolutely central to the Hindu *Mahābhārata*. At the first dicing match between the Pāṇḍavas and Kauravas, Karṇa justifies the humiliation of Draupadī, which occurred at the hands of the Kauravas, by stating that her condition of having more than one husband means that she was already a public woman (II.61.34–36). It was as a result of this humiliation of Draupadī that Bhīma[sena] predicted he would drink Duḥśāsana's blood (II.61.45) and smash Duryodhana's thigh (II.63.11–15), both of which he later carries out.
>
> (Geen 2005: 444, ft. 2)

As Geen points out, the most significant reference to Draupadī's marriage after the *Ādi Parvan* is in the assembly hall after the dicing match, when Karṇa – referring directly to the polyandrous marriage – calls her a whore in front of the entire court:

> The Gods have 'ordained' (*vihita*) that a woman shall have one husband, scion of Kuru. She submits to many men and assuredly is a whore (*bandhakī*). Thus there is, I think, nothing strange about taking her into the hall, or to have her in one piece of clothing, or for that matter naked!
>
> (2.61.35–36)

Here, Karṇa describing the practice of a woman having only one husband as 'ordained' (*vihita*), uses the same term as Drupada had in his dialogue with Yudhiṣṭhira. The similarity in their phrasings suggests that Drupada's earlier concerns are now manifested in the actions of the Kauravas. Moreover, in addition to the notorious disrobing scene in the assembly hall, Draupadī is the victim of sexual assault on two other occasions: the first by King Jayadratha (3.248–256), while she and the Pāṇḍavas are in exile in the forest; and the second by Kīcaka, during the thirteenth year of their exile, when she and the Pāṇḍavas are undercover in the Matsya kingdom (4.14–15).[12] Although neither of these events includes further discussions about the marriage, each one retrospectively adds credibility to Drupada's initial concerns. In looking at the consequences of Draupadī's polyandrous marriage, then, we see that it plays a key role in bringing about the dicing match, the war, and even the future of the Bhārata lineage. Seen as one episode in a chain of causal events, there is a sense that the tragic events of the dicing match, the war, and even the snake sacrifice all happen because of one contingent action after another.

In narrating the stories of the five Indras and of Draupadī's former birth together, Vyāsa, I would argue, invites his listeners to see them as either interconnected windows into the divine plan or as two distinct lenses through which to understand Draupadī's marriage and its relationship with other sections of the narrative. As the author of the text, Vyāsa's contribution to the discussion about Draupadī's marriage is particularly weighty. But rather than resolve the debate, he contributes to its complexity and ambiguity.

Drupada's inconclusive response (1.190.1–4)

When Drupada finally concedes, he gives considerable weight to the story of Draupadī's previous birth, which he refers to specifically by mentioning the words of the maiden and placing responsibility on Śiva (1.190.3–4). The fact that this is the only explanation he mentions suggests that of all the justifications, this is the one that Drupada takes most seriously. But after acknowledging this explanation, Drupada again casts doubt on the marriage, saying that he is still not convinced whether it is *dharma* or *adharma* (1.190.4).

Drupada's uncertainty is perhaps also indicated by his use of the term '*diṣṭa*'(1.190.2), which can mean 'fixed' or 'divinely appointed'. Along with the term *daiva*, *diṣṭa* is often understood in terms of impersonal fate. As Hill has pointed out:

> Impersonal fate is generally called upon to explain the more extreme and inexplicable changes of circumstance … [fate] may be called upon to explain violent swings of fortune … and to account for seemingly incomprehensible or totally unpredictable behaviour or happenings.
>
> (2001: 198–199)

Seen in this light, Drupada's use of the term *diṣṭa* is likely an indication of resignation, rather than an acceptance of any of Vyāsa's or Yudhiṣṭhira's arguments. His uncertainty about the dharmic status of the marriage suggests that he considers the marriage beyond explanation, as well as a personal tragedy. In other words, rather than accepting the marriage, he has simply given up trying to resist it. Moreover, by not explicitly endorsing the marriage, Drupada absolves himself from the moral responsibility of its consequences. As we will see in the following chapters, characters place great importance on the moral implications of their own decisions, despite sometimes viewing their actions as preordained.

At the end of the discussion, it remains unclear whether Drupada has the freedom to choose not to go along with the marriage. This tension is captured in Vyāsa's closing words after recounting Draupadī's previous birth. While concluding from his account of Draupadī's previous life that the marriage is 'ordained' (*vihita*) (1.189.47), Vyāsa at the same time instructs Drupada to act as he 'wishes' (√*iṣ*) (1.189.49). This discrepancy between how Vyāsa describes the marriage and the advice he gives Drupada can be tracked throughout the entire conversation. As we have seen, Yudhiṣṭhira had already made a decision before he even approached Drupada, while Draupadī herself seemed to have begun her married life when she took the advice of Kuntī, fed the Pāṇḍavas, and slept at their feet. Meanwhile, Vyāsa portrays the marriage as following a preordained divine plan. Nevertheless, Vyāsa's instruction for Drupada to do as he wishes, combined with the fact that both Yudhiṣṭhira and Vyāsa go to such lengths to try to convince Drupada, suggests that, despite all the other reasons and justification, his support is indeed necessary and that he has the freedom to make a choice. As we will explore in more detail in the following chapter, throughout the *Mahābhārata,* characters cannot help having reactive attitudes towards each other, expressing resentment and praise in response to each other's actions and behaviours. Despite expressing worldviews that portray their actions as beyond their control, characters interact with each other as though they have moral agency.

Unlike the dialogues about other moral questions we will explore in this book, the dialogues about Draupadī's marriage do not continue in other sections of the text. The marriage is referred to on several occasions, but there is never again a prolonged debate about its moral status. Nevertheless, the controversy is by no means settled after the four dialogues we have looked at here. As Draupadī continues to suffer the consequences of her adharmic marriage throughout the story, we are left to wonder whether one of the justifications is more of a cause than others, or if it takes place as the result of the combination of all of them. In this sense, the dialogues about Draupadī's marriage leave the debate without a resolution, while inviting further deliberation and reflection.

Conclusion

As we have seen throughout this chapter, the dialogues about Draupadī's marriage highlight a number of ways that the *Mahābhārata* addresses moral questions. By shifting interlocutors, these discussions not only present multiple perspectives – from those of the grandfather, to the mother, to the father-in-law, to the brothers – but also offer several possible authoritative voices for ultimately sanctioning the marriage. The marriage is presented as Yudhiṣṭhira's decision in alignment with *dharma*, as the binding consequence of Kuntī's words, and accepted, albeit reluctantly, by Drupada. All the while, it is explicitly endorsed by the sage Vyāsa, who is not only a brahmin and grandfather of the Pāṇḍavas, but also the author of the *Mahābhārata*. Additionally, the silence of Draupadī, the person most directly affected by the marriage, is conspicuous, yet her words and actions in a former life are part of the most repeated explanation. Considering all these voices as making important contributions to the overall discussions, we see that these dialogues do not place authority in a single individual. Even if the words of Vyāsa and Yudhiṣṭhira claim more authority than others, the decision is somehow reached collectively, with different interlocutors defending it for different reasons.

In addition to offering a range of perspectives, the differences between the interlocutors highlight contrasts in their arguments. As we have seen, the distinctive ways that Vyāsa and Yudhiṣṭhira speak about *dharma* indicate a differentiation between secular and religious understandings, but also invite listeners to think of ways these understandings might overlap or reinforce each other. Similarly, the contrast between the representation of Kuntī's words in the discussions about Draupadī's marriage compared to vows and promises made by male characters in other episodes highlights the gendered imbalance concerning the power of speech.

In addition to the range of personal perspectives, the dialogues offer at least eight different explanations for Draupadī's marriage: (1) karmic retribution; (2) the binding power of words; (3) birth order; (4) abiding by a former promise; (5) following ancient traditions; (6) virtuous behaviour; (7) the authority of the king; and (8) divine intervention. Much more than including multiple views, however, the dialogue form explores the relationships between them. As we have seen, the relationship between different types of *dharma* is explored by being presented as one inclusive case. Yudhiṣṭhira's defence of the marriage, I have suggested, is an example of dharmic reasoning that explores the same issue from a number of different aspects of *dharma*, without reducing his arguments to one criterion.

The dialogues about Draupadī's marriage also represent *dharma* as a shared practice of engaging with others in moral deliberation. Vyāsa demonstrates this collaborative approach, for example, when he asks to hear everyone else's 'views' (*mata*) (1.188.6) before giving his own perspective. Although he does not elaborate, we might see his canvassing of opinions as an enactment of collective decision-making. Despite strong disagreements about the dharmic status of the marriage, interlocutors engage with each other's views and attempt to achieve a consensus. In this way, the discussions about Draupadī's marriage portray *dharma* as enacted through dialogue with others. In other words, perhaps what makes the marriage acceptable is not any individual argument put forth, but rather the process of considering a range of views while in deliberative conversation with others.

When we look at Draupadī's marriage in the context of other moral problems in the *Mahābhārata*, we can see that while some views clearly seem to be prioritised, no view eclipses all others in all circumstances. B.K. Matilal has observed that this aspect of moral deliberation in the *Mahābhārata* reflects the non-linear ways of making arguments of everyday situations.

> *Dharma*-conflicts show that the practical resolution of such conflict does not always fix priorities according to the same pattern. It appears to me that this respect for the difficulties encountered in real life is not a mark of irrationality or inconsistency, but emphasizes that we sometimes face moral predicaments for which we cannot find a simply rational solution.
>
> (2002: 60)

In other words, by addressing each moral case differently, the *Mahābhārata* does not offer a specific formula for making moral choices, but rather repeatedly explores how every decision needs to be explored through multiple views. Although the moral status of Draupadī's marriage is never resolved, we might see the dharmic instruction of this moral question as conveying both a pluralistic method of reasoning and an interactive way of deliberating with others.

Notes

1 For a discussion on the *svayaṃvara* and other form of marriage in classical India, see Jamison (1996: 207–257).
2 For further discussions of Vyāsa, see Sullivan (1999), Hiltebeitel (2001b: 32–91).
3 See Hill (2001: 29), Hudson (2013: 189), and Framarin (2018: 65).
4 For how the marriage is interpreted in subsequent literature, see Bhattacharya (2004: 21–22) and Geen (2005).
5 In the *Karṇa Parvan* (8.49), Arjuna, with the help of Kṛṣṇa, qualifies his vow to kill whoever insults his bow (see Chapter 5), while in the *Udyoga Parvan* (5.186), both Bhīṣma and Rāma Jāmadagnya vow not to retreat from battle, yet they both do (see Chapter 1).
6 As she wonders whether her sons might have been recognised or killed, she also wonders if Vyāsa's prediction might have been wrong (1.181.39). Vaiśaṃpāyana does not elaborate here, but it seems that, remembering Vyāsa's story of Draupadī's former birth, she wonders how something could have happened to her sons when their destiny to marry Draupadī has not yet transpired. It is interesting that she remembers Vyāsa's prediction when reflecting on her own, but

when discussing the marriage with her sons, she never refers to his words to add weight to why they should follow her words.

7 Hiltebeitel has also commented on the culpability of Arjuna and Bhīma: 'The announcement of Druapadī as "alms" suggests that Arjuna or Bhīmasena are complicit or have a chancy sense of humor' (2011: 491).

8 For a discussion on 'secular' and 'religious' distinctions of *dharma*, see Black (2019). For discussion of the semantic range of *dharma* in Vedic literature and its particular association with royal authority, see Olivelle (2004: 491–511) and Brereton (2004: 449–489).

9 Śakuntalā also uses this term when referring to Duḥsanta's promise to instal their son as heir to the throne (1.68.16) (see Chapter 4).

10 His argument also brings attention to the gendered imbalance regarding the dharmic status of marrying more than one person at the same time – that the practice is only considered to be a breach of *dharma* when the person with multiple spouses is a woman.

11 When considering the emphasis on *karma*, it is also worth noting that in the Southern Recension of the *Mahābhārata*, Vyāsa gives Drupada yet another justification for the marriage that is a different account of a previous life of Draupadī (see Sukthankar 1933, vol. 1: xxxix and appendix no. 100).

12 For further discussion of these and other episodes featuring Draupadī, see Black (2013).

3 Duryodhana's despair/ Yudhiṣṭhira's decision

Introduction

After the Pāṇḍavas marry Draupadī, they return to the Kuru capital of Hāstinapura. In an effort to settle the Pāṇḍavas' intensifying rivalry with the Kauravas over the throne, Dhṛtarāṣṭra and Bhīṣma offer them half the kingdom. After building a grand assembly hall in their new capital, Yudhiṣṭhira – on the advice of Nārada – hosts a *rājasūya* ritual, through which he claims universal sovereignty. It is in the aftermath of witnessing this opulent display of power, prestige, and wealth, that Duryodhana is persuaded by Śakuni (his material uncle) to take revenge by challenging Yudhiṣṭhira to a dicing match. At one point during Vaiśaṃpāyana's narration of the events leading up to the match, Janamejaya interrupts, asking to hear the account of a dialogue between Duryodhana and Dhṛtarāṣṭra in further detail:

> How came about (*sambhava*) that catastrophic (*mahātyaya*) dicing match among the brothers, where my grandfathers the Pāṇḍavas incurred that calamity (*vyasana*)? … I wish to hear you tell this in detail, brahmin, for this was the root of the destruction of the world.
>
> (2.46.1)

Here, Janamejaya identifies the dicing match as the cause of the apocalyptic war between his ancestors, the Pāṇḍavas, and the Kauravas. On a narrative level, Janamejaya wishes to hear in more depth about the sequence of events that led to this disastrous episode. But we might also detect an ethical dimension to his question, a desire to understand the moral responsibilities of those whose words and actions contributed to bringing about the momentous game. Indeed, playing dice was widely regarded as being morally problematic. Kṛṣṇa, for example, lists dicing among the four vices (3.14.7), Yudhiṣṭhira characterises the game as evil (*pāpa*) and bad practice (*na parākrama*) (2.53.2), and other characters, as we will see, portray gambling with dice as harmful and deceitful. This chapter will explore the ethical implications of Janamejaya's question by looking at the most consequential dialogues leading up to the dicing match, the key characters who contribute to creating the conditions for the game, and the arguments they make both for and against it. We will focus on two sets of dialogues in particular:

- The first set of dialogues revolves around Duryodhana and Dhṛtarāṣṭra, who discuss the game not only with each other, but also with Śakuni and Vidura, in a series of interlinked discussions in the Kaurava court. These conversations detail the events leading up to Dhṛtarāṣṭra sending Vidura to invite Yudhiṣṭhira to play dice. As we will see, both Duryodhana and Dhṛtarāṣṭra bemoan fate for their sense of powerlessness, yet also make claims that assume a certain degree of control over their circumstances. In addition to analysing the content of these dialogues, we will explore the implications of a textual issue – that the *Mahābhārata* includes three different versions of the dialogue between Duryodhana and Dhṛtarāṣṭra. Despite covering some of the same details, each version depicts their arguments for and against the game differently, thus offering three different lenses through which to understand one of the most pivotal scenes in the build-up to the dicing match.
- The second set of dialogues revolves around Yudhiṣṭhira, who explains his decision to play dice to Vidura, Draupadī, and Śakuni. In addition to analysing the different explanations he gives for accepting the invitation, we will explore the degree to which Yudhiṣṭhira had agency in deciding to play, or if events were beyond his control.

By looking at these dialogues together, we will see that Duryodhana, Dhṛtarāṣṭra, Śakuni, Yudhiṣṭhira, and Vidura all contribute to bringing about the game, but that the moral responsibility of each character – particularly of Duryodhana, Dhṛtarāṣṭra, and Yudhiṣṭhira – depends not just on what they do, but on how they understand their circumstances and how they make arguments defending their actions.

Fate and human agency

Although tensions between fate and human agency appear throughout the entire text, in this chapter we will focus on the episodes that lead up to the dicing match. I do this because the dicing match itself is perhaps the central episode through which the dialectic between fate and human agency is explored. With the names of the throws of the dice – *kṛta*, *tretā*, *dvāpara*, and *kali* – corresponding with the names of the four *yuga*s (cosmic epochs), the dicing match is an allegory for the intricate relationship between divine forces and human endeavours. In reflecting on the dicing match as portrayed in the Nala story, David Shulman captures the complex tension between skill and luck as represented in the game of dice:

> It is undoubtedly wrong to imagine that this game is either one of pure chance or entirely an artful exercise of skill; rather, what comes into

> play is some combination of knowledge, of a specialized kind, and the externalization of those powerful and structured forces operating within the player and affecting his every move.
>
> (1994: 22)

One of the challenges for anyone examining the relationship between fate and human agency in the *Mahābhārata*, however, is that at first glance, this relationship appears to be one-sided. Repeatedly, characters express relentlessly fatalistic views about the human condition. In the introduction to his abridged translation, John Smith has characterised the *Mahābhārata* as offering a pessimistic outlook: 'one thing that is said, and is said repeatedly and by different characters, is that fate is supreme and human effort vain. From the humanistic standpoint, the *Mahābhārata* is not an optimistic narrative' (2009: xlii–xliii). Indeed, the *Mahābhārata* includes several concepts and doctrines that characterise the circumstances of humans as beyond their control. In the dialogues in this chapter, the concept most used to invoke a sense of human powerlessness is *daiva*. Literally meaning 'of the gods', *daiva* is often invoked when characters attempt to make sense of perplexing circumstances. As Peter Hill explains, *daiva* often evokes a notion of 'impersonal fate' that is 'generally called upon to explain the more extreme and inexplicable changes of circumstance within the triple-world' (2001: 198). Another way characters explain the human condition is as the plan or design of Dhātṛ (Ordainer). Variously translated as the 'Placer' (van Buitenen) and 'Creator' (Wilmot), Dhātṛ has a number of different connotations in the *Mahābhārata*. Hill describes Dhātṛ as 'an all-powerful personal "force" that predetermines events from motives which are inscrutable, capricious and arbitrary' (2001: 165). Hill has further suggested that Dhātṛ is sometimes invoked in situations where a character is reluctant to blame a specific god for their misfortune (2001: 70).

Another term that is sometimes used in similar situations is *kāla*, usually translated as time. As Luis González-Reimann explains:

> The *Mahābhārata* views time as an oppressive, overpowering force that relentlessly pushes all beings towards their eventual death, and is inextricably intertwined with the uncontrollable force of destiny. So intense is the concern with its destructive nature, that time virtually becomes synonym of death and destruction.
>
> (2010: 20)

Throughout the text, characters routinely speak of *kāla* as compelling them to act the way they do. In addition to the fatalistic ideas that are explicitly discussed in the dialogues leading up to the dicing match, elsewhere the *Mahābhārata* also includes mythological and theological doctrines that explain human action in terms of divine agency. As we have seen in Chapter 2, the divine plan presents the war between the Pāṇḍavas and Kauravas as the unfolding of a cosmic drama between the gods and demons (1.58.34). Moreover, in the *Bhagavad Gītā*, Kṛṣṇa proclaims that only his divine actions have agency and that the actions of Arjuna and other warriors during the war are only instruments acting out his will (11.33).

When we consider the prominence of these doctrines emphasising the powerlessness of human action on a cosmic scale, we might wonder whether there is any room at all for human agency. Julian Woods reflects on the attention the *Mahābhārata* nevertheless pays to the capacity of humans to have a choice between different possible courses of actions:

> Given the countless occasions for frustration or impotence before the weight of circumstance, it may seem remarkable how much credit is given in the epic to our human ability to pursue not only our own ends but the means to achieve them.
>
> (2001: 58)

Woods discusses terms such as *puruṣakāra* and *pauruṣa* that express 'a sense of self-determination and initiative' (2001: 60), a sense of 'freedom of doing', which is 'the power to decide and accomplish what has been decided' (2001: 58).

Considering the genuine deliberation given to 'its ethical intent', Vrinda Dalmiya and Gangeya Mukherji see the dialectic between fate and human agency in the *Mahābhārata* as similar to how the tensions between determinism and freedom have been explored in Western philosophy:

> Philosophically speaking, the tension between human initiative on the one hand and external forces, which include but are not restricted to Time/Fate/Divine purpose/*prārabdha* on the other – in short the *puruṣakāra/daiva* debates scattered throughout the *Mahābhārata* – seem to echo the freedom/determinism debates in Western philosophical literature. In response, compatabilist solutions probing the possibility of action in a deterministic world are available in both contexts.
>
> (2018: 2)

Different scholars have explained the *Mahābhārata*'s 'compatabilist solutions' in different ways. Nicholas Sutton observes that there 'can be no simple solution to the problem of destiny and free-will' (2000: 384), but has proposed that these tensions can be partially explained through 'the doctrinal axis of *pravṛtti* and *nivṛtti*'. Whereas *pravṛtti* refers to the teachings that focus on *dharma*, *nivṛtti* refers to those teachings that focus on *mokṣa*.[1] According to Sutton, *pravṛtti* teachings are more likely to stress that 'an individual's nature is predetermined', whereas the doctrines of *nivṛtti* 'cannot accept such a rigid imposition, for they urge that any individual can renounce his or her *sva-dharma* in order to transcend this world and seek salvation' (2000: 373).

Although Sutton is correct to point out the importance of human agency in *nivṛtti* teachings, he perhaps underestimates the degree to which *pravṛtti* teachings also assume a considerable amount of freedom of action. Teachings such as *sva-dharma*, *varṇāśrama-dharma*, and *strī-dharma*, for example, hinge on the notion that we have some degree of agency in carrying out our responsibilities towards ourselves and others. As Hill points out:

> adherence to *dharma* made more sense if it was believed that human choices and actions were meaningful and could influence the course of events. Without this belief, an attitude of fatalistic resignation or outright hedonism made as much sense as the fulfilment of social duties.
>
> (2001: 360)

In this chapter, I will examine the dialogues leading up to the dicing match to explore how characters negotiate the relationship between fate and human agency through dialogue, as they discuss their decisions and actions with their interlocutors. As we will see, the ways that individual characters make sense of their own situations are rarely either deterministic or libertarian, but resemble what Dalmiya and Mukherji refer to as 'compatabilist solutions'. Dhṛtarāṣṭra and Yudhiṣṭhira, for example, at times describe their situations as completely determined, while they both also make claims about their own abilities to control their circumstances. In other words, characters in the *Mahābhārata* behave as if they have choices to make and as if they can perform actions according to their own volition, despite sometimes characterising their predicaments as determined by outside forces. In this chapter, I will trace two compatabilist solutions in the *Mahābhārata*, both of which are attempts to understand the possibility of human action in a world that is often portrayed as fatalistic.

The first is the way that characters interact with each other when reflecting on their circumstances and making moral decisions. What I have in mind is something similar to Peter Strawson's notion of 'reactive attitudes'. In an attempt to reframe the freedom/determinism debate in Western philosophy, Strawson argued that moral responsibility should be understood in terms of the 'human commitment to participation in ordinary interpersonal relationships' (2008: 12). Strawson uses the term 'reactive attitudes' to describe the ways that we react to each other morally in everyday situations. Through this notion, Strawson emphasises

> the very great importance that we attach to the attitudes and intentions towards us of other human beings, and the great extent to which our personal feelings and reactions depend upon, or involve, our beliefs about these attitudes and intentions.
>
> (2008: 5)

Strawson claims that philosophers often forget 'what it is actually like to be involved in ordinary interpersonal relationships, ranging from the most intimate to the most casual' (2008: 7). In other words, according to Strawson, although the debate about determinism and free will may be important for philosophers, it does not capture how people relate to each other morally in everyday situations. Despite their metaphysical commitments, humans tend to interact with each other as morally responsibly agents.

Similarly, I think we could say that the characters in the *Mahābhārata* exhibit attitudes about themselves and each other that are comparable to what Strawson calls reactive attitudes. Although there are many occasions where characters explain their own actions or inactions as compelled by fate, rarely do they treat others as if they do not have moral responsibility for their actions.[2] Indeed, despite frequently espousing fatalistic views, characters make strong assumptions about their own agency and the agency of others. The expectations that characters have about themselves and others to abide by rules and procedures, fulfil vows, uphold caste obligations, and respect family members are taken far too seriously to suggest that individuals do not have any agency in creating their own circumstances. In previous chapters we have seen Ambā hold Bhīṣma responsible for her tragic circumstances (Chapter 1), while Drupada only goes along with Vyāsa's and Yudhiṣṭhira's insistence on the polyandrous marriage after absolving himself of any responsibility (Chapter 2). In this chapter, we will see Duryodhana blame his strong feelings of resentment on Yudhiṣṭhira's provocations, while Yudhiṣṭhira will claim that he lost his judgement when agreeing to play dice. In these cases and others, despite sometimes invoking the doctrines of *daiva*, Dhātṛ, and *kāla*, characters do not react to each other as if their actions were completely predetermined, but rather behave towards each other as if they are morally responsible for their actions. Rather than offering a metaphysical solution to the freedom/determinism debate, the *Mahābhārata* explores their relationship through dialogues, as characters attempt to understand their circumstances and make decisions about their actions.

In addition to developing ways of understanding moral responsibility in terms of social relationships, characters nevertheless confront the limitations of their agency. The second compatibilist approach I will trace in this chapter is the way that characters explore the possibility of human freedom even when they do not feel they have a choice between different courses of action. What I have in mind here is similar to the way Woods describes how fate and determinism are resolved through *karma-yoga*. As Woods explains, according to *karma-yoga*, '*puruṣakāra* becomes the hallmark of a successful endeavor that is no longer judged for its outwards form or function but for the inner spirit that animates it' (2001: 143). In other words, through the doctrine of *karma-yoga*, some characters in the *Mahābhārata* suggest that humans can gain control over their circumstances by achieving more control over themselves. Perhaps surprisingly, we will see Dhṛtarāṣṭra instruct Duryodhana to control his circumstances by restraining his emotions. Meanwhile, Yudhiṣṭhira approaches the question about moral responsibility, not by asking whether or not he has the power to decide on his own actions, but rather by reflecting on how he can act morally despite the fact that he has limited control over his circumstances. Rather than deliberate on which choice he can make, he explores ways of taking moral responsibility for the choices he feels he has to make.

By looking closely at the dialogues leading up to the dicing match, we will see that the *Mahābhārata* offers detailed and nuanced accounts of the explanations characters give to understand their circumstances and the reasons they offer to defend their choices. Rather than providing a solution to the dialectic between fate and human agency, the *Mahābhārata* confronts its readers with competing arguments that encourage us to reflect upon our own circumstances, choices, and understandings of the world.

Duryodhana's despair

The conversation between Duryodhana and Dhṛtarāṣṭra is presented three times within the reconstituted text of the Critical Edition – twice in the *Sabhā Parvan* and once in the *Śānti Parvan*. The two versions in the *Sabhā Parvan* have been noted by several scholars. In his introduction to the Critical Edition of the *Sabhā Parvan*, Franklin Edgerton was the first to point out that what appears to be one extended exchange between Duryodhana and Dhṛtarāṣṭra is actually two versions of the same encounter. Edgerton describes these dialogues as 'different and inconsistent accounts of the same events' that appear in the text 'side by side' (1944: xxxii). While Edgerton notes 'inconsistencies' between the two versions, van Buitenen sees them as essentially the same account, with the second version bringing 'more color and drama to the story, but ... otherwise completely parallel' (1975: 815). As I will show, despite some overlapping material, these two versions have a number of important differences. Moreover, in addition to these two versions in the *Sabhā Parvan*, the dialogue between Duryodhana and Dhṛtarāṣṭra also appears as part of Bhīṣma's long instructions to Yudhiṣṭhira in the *Śānti Parvan*. Although widely considered to be an interpolation because of its inclusion in a 'didactic' section of the text, this version offers an intriguingly different portrayal of the Duryodhana/Dhṛtarāṣṭra dialogue.

As we have seen in the Introduction, the appearance of different versions of the same episode is a recurring characteristic of the *Mahābhārata*.[3] While A.K. Ramanujan calls repetition a central structuring principle (1991: 421), Alf Hiltebeitel has described heterogeneity as the *Mahābhārata*'s 'trademark', explaining that the 'poets felt no need to harmonize or eliminate what critics call contradictions and doubled passages' (2015b: 155). Rather than treating any of the Duryodhana/Dhṛtarāṣṭra dialogues as more original or authoritative than the others, then, my starting point is that their mutual inclusion within the same text highlights the significance of this episode. I will approach each version as providing a different lens through which to reflect on the moral responsibility of each of the characters who, in one way or another, influence the events leading up to the dicing match.

Duryodhana and Dhṛtarāṣṭra: version 1 (2.43–45)

What I am referring to as the first version of the Duryodhana/Dhṛtarāṣṭra dialogue includes a series of four conversations: Duryodhana and Śakuni; Śakuni and Dhṛtarāṣṭra; Duryodhana and Dhṛtarāṣṭra; and Dhṛtarāṣṭra and Vidura.[4] The first of these conversations begins when Duryodhana and Śakuni are returning to Hāstinapura after Yudhiṣṭhira's *rājasūya*. Observing Duryodhana's gloomy demeanour, Śakuni asks him why he is feeling so upset. Duryodhana gives the following reasons: (1) the entire earth is obedient to Yudhiṣṭhira, (2) the *rājasūya* matched even Indra's sacrifice; (3) the killing of Śiśupāla was an 'offence' (*aparādha*); and (4) the Pāṇḍavas have amassed a huge fortune. He then declares that he can no longer live and that he will enter fire, swallow poison, or drown himself. He adds that he is powerless to gain his own fortune by himself and that he has no allies. He concludes by deciding that fate (*daiva*) is supreme and human effort (*pauruṣa*) useless (2.43.32), a view he repeats (2.43.34) when he explains that he had tried to destroy the Pāṇḍavas before, but to no avail.

Although we might see his moral objection to the killing of Śiśupāla as his most objective reason for opposing the imperial claims of the Pāṇḍavas, this is the only time Duryodhana mentions this either to Śakuni or his father. Instead, he makes it clear that he is most upset by Yudhiṣṭhira's display of wealth, prestige, and power at the *rājasūya*. By referring to *daiva* and *pauruṣa*, Duryodhana presents his situation through the lens of the relationship between fate and human agency. At this particular moment, however, Duryodhana feels completely powerless, thus claiming not to have any control over his circumstances. As Woods explains:

> His references to *daiva* in the days of the Pāṇḍava ascendency are clear expressions of despondency and frustration at the growing fortunes of his cousins, who have not only thumbed their noses at all his evil schemes, but married the Pāñcāla princess, gained half the kingdom, and made themselves masters of the world to boot.
>
> (2001: 57)

As we will see, Duryodhana connects his feelings of misery and resentment to Yudhiṣṭhira's wealth and power in the two other versions of this dialogue, but this is the only occasion where he blames his own sorry state on powers beyond his control.

Despite Duryodhana's claims that human effort is in vain, Śakuni's position offers an interesting contrast to this view. Not only does he incite

Duryodhana to act, but he also plays his own role in bringing about the game. Śakuni tells Duryodhana not to be angry with Yudhiṣṭhira, but his words seem to be dripping in sarcasm. Rather than consoling his nephew, Śakuni reminds him of the Pāṇḍavas' advantages, including their powerful allies, enormous wealth, and military strength (2.44.5–8). Rather than try to calm Duryodhana down, as his father will try to do later, Śakuni is winding him up, giving him even more incentive to seek revenge.

This short exchange portrays Śakuni as manipulating the course of the conversation towards his own ends. In addition to encouraging Duryodhana to seek revenge, he also warns that the Pāṇḍavas cannot be defeated in battle, so they must be defeated by other means. When asked to explain, Śakuni proposes challenging the Pāṇḍavas to a dicing match, supplying the following reasons: (1) Yudhiṣṭhira is fond of playing dice; (2) Yudhiṣṭhira does not know how to play; (3) Yudhiṣṭhira will not refuse a challenge; (4) he (Śakuni) is the best dice player in the three worlds; and therefore (5) Duryodhana should challenge Yudhiṣṭhira to a match. Śakuni concludes that if he is allowed to play dice against him, he will win Yudhiṣṭhira's entire kingdom and all his wealth (2.44.18–21). He then instructs Duryodhana to ask for Dhṛtarāṣṭra's permission.

In this well-ordered argument, Śakuni gives two explanations for why Yudhiṣṭhira will agree to play dice: (1) he loves dice, and (2) he will not reject a challenge. As we will see later in this chapter, Śakuni is proven right that he will not reject a challenge, but Yudhiṣṭhira himself never cites a fondness for dice as a reason explaining why he accepts the invitation to play. Although other characters will associate Yudhiṣṭhira with dicing after the fact, we might wonder how credible Śakuni's explanation is at this point in the story.[5] Does he know something that other characters – perhaps even Yudhiṣṭhira – do not know? Or is he saying whatever he can to convince Duryodhana and just taking a punt on the outcome? Perhaps the famous gambler is taking a gamble here as well.

Duryodhana is convinced, but does not want to propose the idea to his father himself, so he asks Śakuni to go to Dhṛtarāṣṭra to present the plan. When Śakuni approaches Dhṛtarāṣṭra, he encourages the king to check on his son to see what is wrong, describing Duryodhana as 'pale' (*vivarṇa*), 'yellowish' (*hariṇa*), 'weak' (*kṛśa*), 'depressed' (*dīna*), and 'lost in thought' (*cintāpara*) (2.45.4). Here, Śakuni fulfils Duryodhana's request to speak to Dhṛtarāṣṭra, but he does not quite complete the task, as he stops short of revealing his plan to invite the Pāṇḍavas to a dicing match. Instead, Śakuni engineers the subsequent encounter between Duryodhana and Dhṛtarāṣṭra.

After Śakuni's intervention, Dhṛtarāṣṭra approaches Duryodhana to ask why he is 'depressed' (*dīna*) and 'suffering' (*śoka*) when he is the heir, has good relations with his family and allies, and has fine clothes and eats well. Duryodhana explains that is he consumed by 'wrathful anger' (*amarṣa*) (2.45.12), which he attributes to seeing the prestigious guests who attended the *rājasūya* and the lavish gifts that they brought as tribute. He says that his own wealth no longer pleases him now that he has seen Yudhiṣṭhira's fortune (*śrī*), and he cannot stand seeing the Pāṇḍavas prosper while he fails. Duryodhana also briefly justifies his emotional response, arguing that contentment, pride, compassion, and fear destroy good fortune. Duryodhana then begins to list Yudhiṣṭhira's specific winnings at the *rājasūya*, exclaiming: 'Nowhere have I seen or heard of such an inflow of wealth' (2.45.22). After listing more gifts and further describing the opulence of the ritual, Duryodhana then concludes that Yudhiṣṭhira's wealth surpasses the wealth of even the gods (2.45.35). As with his dialogue with Śakuni, Duryodhana explains his grief as directly brought about by witnessing Yudhiṣṭhira's newfound fortune – on this occasion going into more detail describing the wealth, but neglecting to mention the slaying of Śiśupāla.

After Duryodhana's response to his father, Śakuni enters the conversation, offering a solution to Duryodhana's plight by acquiring Yudhiṣṭhira's fortune. He argues: (1) he (Śakuni) is famous throughout the world as a skilled dice player; (2) Yudhiṣṭhira is fond of playing dice; (3) Yudhiṣṭhira does not know how to play; (4) Yudhiṣṭhira will not refuse a challenge; and (5) therefore, Duryodhana should challenge him to gamble (2.45.36–38). Here, Śakuni makes exactly the same points that he did to Duryodhana, but in a different order. We might see this slightly different presentation of his argument as addressing the interests of his different interlocutors. For Duryodhana, who seeks revenge, Śakuni begins his argument with Yudhiṣṭhira's weakness, but for Dhṛtarāṣṭra, he begins with Yudhiṣṭhira's fortune itself, which Duryodhana has explained to his father as the source of his grief. Śakuni also offers the same two reasons for challenging Yudhiṣṭhira that he had offered to Duryodhana: (1) Yudhiṣṭhira is fond of dice, and (2) he will not reject a challenge.

After Śakuni's argument, Duryodhana begs his father to allow the dice match to take place. Dhṛtarāṣṭra replies that he cannot give an answer before consulting Vidura, who he describes as putting *dharma* first and as being impartial to both parties (2.45.42). Duryodhana protests, arguing that Vidura will try to stop the game. Duryodhana then announces that he will die if Dhṛtarāṣṭra does not consent. Ramping up the emotional blackmail, he says: 'When I'm dead, be happy with your Vidura, king. Surely, you shall have the pleasure of all earth: why bother about me?' (2.45.44). After hearing this, Dhṛtarāṣṭra immediately orders for an assembly hall to be built. Revealingly, Vaiśaṃpāyana explains Dhṛtarāṣṭra's motivations: 'though he knew the evils of dicing, he was drawn to it because of the love he bore his son' (2.45.49). According to Vaiśaṃpāyana's narration, Dhṛtarāṣṭra understands the dangers involved in the dicing match and has the good sense to know that he should consult Vidura. Nonetheless, he ultimately decides not to seek his counsel in order to placate his son. Only after ordering the hall to be built does Dhṛtarāṣṭra send for Vidura to tell him about what has happened. Although Dhṛtarāṣṭra's love for his son will be cited on other occasions in the narrative, the first version of this dialogue is the only one of the three that explicitly cites this as a reason for Dhṛtarāṣṭra allowing the game to take place.

Meanwhile, Vidura hears about this plan before approaching the king and immediately understands that it will lead to destruction, saying that 'the Gate of Kali (*kālidvāra*) was upon them' (2.45.50).[6] When he approaches Dhṛtarāṣṭra, Vidura strongly opposes the king's decision and advises him to avoid any conflict. Dhṛtarāṣṭra, however, is unwilling to budge and assures Vidura that his sons will not quarrel with each other, arguing that the game is destined to happen: 'Auspicious or inauspicious, beneficial or otherwise, this friendly (*suhṛd*) game of dice will proceed, for certainly it is so designed (*diṣṭa*)' (2.45.54). Dhṛtarāṣṭra then assures Vidura that because he, along with Bhīṣma, will be present, 'no misfortune (*anaya*) ordained by fate (*daiva*) can possibly occur' (2.45.55). Dhṛtarāṣṭra concludes his remark by reiterating the role of *daiva*: 'I deem it supreme fate (*para daiva*) that brings this about' (2.45.57).

Notably, Dhṛtarāṣṭra gives Vidura two assurances: (1) the game is ordained by fate, and (2) his presence will prevent misfortune from happening. Dhṛtarāṣṭra's invocation of fate is typical of his outlook throughout the *Mahābhārata*. As Woods argues – following Georges Dumézil – there is a strong connection between Dhṛtarāṣṭra and a worldview based on fate:

> Many other characters in the epic speak in the same vein in their troubled moments or when they feel powerless against overwhelming odds. However, Dhṛtarāṣṭra not only expresses these sentiments; he is overwhelmed by them to the point of actually becoming the chosen instrument of *Daiva*
>
> (2001: 4–5)

Dhṛtarāṣṭra's submission to fate comes across most vividly and poignantly during the war, as he listens to Saṃjaya report his army's losses and the deaths of his sons. But while Dhṛtarāṣṭra repeatedly bemoans his unfortunate circumstances, Saṃjaya tells him that he only blames fate because he does not want to take responsibility for his own actions. In his conversation with Vidura, however, Dhṛtarāṣṭra is not complaining about his tragic circumstances, but rather trying to defend his actions as part of a cosmic design. Nevertheless, Vidura voices a strong objection to the king's decision, urging him to take action to prevent the conflict, before walking away in disagreement (2.45.58). Although Dhṛtarāṣṭra routinely blames fate for what he considers to be his tragic circumstances, neither of his main advisors in the story – Vidura here and Saṃjaya during the war – accepts this fatalist outlook as an excuse for the king not doing more to take control of his situation.

Dhṛtarāṣṭra also assures Vidura that the game will not cause divisions, promising that the presence of himself and Bhīṣma will keep things in control. This reason offers an interesting contrast with the previous one.

Whereas his characterisation of the game as destined might be seen as a way for Dhṛtarāṣṭra to dodge personal responsibility, in promising that his presence at the game will protect it from disaster, he claims he can influence fate. By speaking both in terms of destiny and of taking control, Dhṛtarāṣṭra shows that he does not completely operate according to a deterministic framework. Rather, he sees his own actions as having some capacity to shape his circumstances. Tragically, neither he nor Bhīṣma is able to keep order once the dicing match gets started, but we might see his intervention to grant boons to Draupadī as a late attempt to fulfil his assurance to Vidura. The exchange between Dhṛtarāṣṭra and Vidura ends ambiguously. When Dhṛtarāṣṭra sends him to invite Yudhiṣṭhira to the match, Vidura instead heads off towards Bhīṣma (2.45.58).[7] It is at this point that the narrative zooms out to Janamejaya's question.

Summing up, the series of conversations between Duryodhana, Dhṛtarāṣṭra, Vidura, and Śakuni characterises the events leading up to the dicing match in a number of key ways, all of which influence, in one way or another, how Yudhiṣṭhira will respond to Dhṛtarāṣṭra's invitation. Both Duryodhana and Dhṛtarāṣṭra invoke fate, yet they do so differently, and neither of them let their fateful outlook prevent them from taking action. Duryodhana only mentions fate once, after describing to Śakuni his feelings of deep sorrow after the *rājasūya*. As soon as Śakuni presents his plan to challenge the Pāṇḍavas at dice, Duryodhana no longer reflects on feeling powerless, but does whatever he can to convince his father to support the game. Dhṛtarāṣṭra invokes fate when justifying his decision to support the game. Not only does he agree to the plan, but he uses his own authority as king to ensure the game takes place by ordering for a new assembly hall to be built, telling Vidura that his decision is not up for discussion, and then sending Vidura to invite Yudhiṣṭhira. Although he might have agreed reluctantly, once he makes up his mind, Dhṛtarāṣṭra plays an active part in bringing the game to fruition. Dhṛtarāṣṭra does not even try to defend his son's wish to take revenge or to suggest that Yudhiṣṭhira might have overstepped his position in holding the *rājasūya*. Rather, the only explanations he offers to Vidura are that the game is ordained by fate and that it will not be as bad as Vidura thinks.

Duryodhana and Dhṛtarāṣṭra: version 2 (2.46–51)

It is at this point in the narrative that Janamejaya asks to hear the story again in greater detail. As mentioned at the beginning of the chapter, Janamejaya's query provides an opportunity for exploring the question of who holds moral responsibility for the dicing match. After Janamejaya's intervention, the text says: 'Sūta said' (*sūta uvāca*) and then recounts a brief description of Vaiśaṃpāyana: 'Thus addressed by the king, Vyāsa's majestic student, who knew everything, narrated it all as it had happened'(2.46.4). Although he is not named, the *sūta* is clearly Ugraśravas, whose appearance here van Buitenen calls 'unexpected' and 'interesting' (1975: 815). This is one of only three times in the critically reconstituted texts when, after the opening frame story, the narrative zooms out to Ugraśravas' conversation with Śaunaka and the Naimiṣa *ṛṣis*.[8] Emily Hudson sees this occasion, which brings three levels of narration together, as creating 'the effect of the collapsing of time' (2013: 170). As she explains, the collapsing of time is an important frame of reference for the dicing match:

> The word '*kāla*' ... appears in places where the text seems to explicitly suggest that the characters make the disastrous decisions that they do, decisions that lead to the game and ultimately to war, because they are being impelled to do so by time.
>
> (2013: 170)

Although I agree with Hudson in taking this disjuncture in the narrative as an invitation to reflect on the decisions that lead to the dicing match, I do not think that Ugraśravas' unexpected appearance emphasises the concept of *kāla* in particular. The term *kāla* is mentioned by Śakuni in a short dialogue with Yudhiṣṭhira just before the match begins, but it does not appear in the dialogue between Duryodhana and Dhṛtarāṣṭra that immediately follows Ugraśravas' intervention. It seems to me that one of the implications of the zoom out to the Ugraśravas/Śaunaka dialogue here is to remind listeners and readers of the narrative inevitability of the dicing match. Although the characters in the story face their circumstances without the knowledge of what will happen to them, both the Ugraśravas/Śaunaka and Vaiśaṃpāyana/Janamejaya dialogues take place several generations after the events in the main story. In this way, as Smith describes it, the two framing dialogues are a narrative device that conveys a sense of fate: 'The possibility of surprise is lost, but in its place a feeling of grinding inevitability can be established' (2009: xliv).

However, in addition to reiterating the inevitability of the narrative, I think we can also take Ugraśravas' intervention here as bringing attention to the differences between these two accounts of the Duryodhana/Dhṛtarāṣṭra dialogue. Ugraśravas' brief appearance does this by coming just before an alternative account of the Duryodhana/Dhṛtarāṣṭra dialogue, one that confronts us with overlapping, but ultimately different, arguments and explanations for how the dicing match came about. Through Ugraśravas' intervention, as well as Janamejaya's question, the text invites us to explore the relationship between these two accounts. One of the crucial differences between these two versions, as we will see, is the contrasting portrayals of the relative moral responsibility of the characters involved, particularly Duryodhana, Dhṛtarāṣṭra, and Yudhiṣṭhira. With this in mind, Ugraśravas' intervention could be seen as a reminder that no matter how much the dicing match was always going to happen from a narrative perspective, our understanding of moral responsibility depends not just on what characters do, but on why they do what they do. As we will see, the second version portrays Duryodhana and Dhṛtarāṣṭra more sympathetically, while also detailing far more vividly the ways that Duryodhana's emotional response was provoked by the Pāṇḍavas. As such, the second version complicates our understanding of who is morally responsible for bringing about the game.

Vaiśaṃpāyana's second version begins with Dhṛtarāṣṭra thinking to himself about what Vidura would say about the plan to play dice. Whereas in the first account, the plan was introduced by Śakuni at the end of the dialogue, here it is the starting point of the discussion, with no mention of Śakuni or how Dhṛtarāṣṭra has come to know about this plan. Consequently, this account does not highlight Śakuni's role in suggesting the dicing plan to Duryodhana or his part in orchestrating the encounter between Duryodhana and his father. Moreover, Vidura is mentioned right at the beginning of the conversation, rather than at the end. After 'knowing' (*jñā*) Vidura's thoughts, Dhṛtarāṣṭra then tells Duryodhana that because Vidura would not approve and because it is divisive, he should not go ahead with the match (2.46.12).

Unlike in the previous account, where Dhṛtarāṣṭra never actually tries to persuade Duryodhana not to play, here he begins the conversation by urging his son not to go ahead with the game, arguing that dicing will cause conflict and will lead to the destruction of the kingdom. It is notable that when Dhṛtarāṣṭra 'knows' the thoughts of Vidura, he makes the same arguments Vidura made in the previous version. Dhṛtarāṣṭra also argues that Duryodhana should be happy with what he has. Asking about the cause of his 'sorrow' (*śoka*) and his 'suffering' (*duḥkha*), Dhṛtarāṣṭra mentions Duryodhana's position as inheritor of the throne, his good relations with his family, and his fine food and clothing (2.46.14–15). Despite these similarities, there are some notable differences between the two versions. In particular, Dhṛtarāṣṭra appeals to Duryodhana's reason, referring to his 'good education' (*kṛta śāstra*) and his wisdom (*prajña*) – seemingly attempting to elicit a more reflective approach from him.

Like in the first version, Duryodhana explains that he is suffering as a result of witnessing Yudhiṣṭhira's wealth, power, and prestige on display at the *rājasūya*. Duryodhana's explanation here, however, is significantly longer, as he speaks continually for 105 verses, rather than only twenty three verses. During this more extended discourse, Duryodhana not only goes into more detail about the eminent guests, lavish riches, and overall opulence of the ritual, but he also adds other reasons for his suffering that are not mentioned in his previous account. In the process, he gives his feelings of resentment and sorrow more texture and substance. As Edgerton describes it: 'Duryodhana tells in much greater detail of the glories of the *rājasūya*, and this time also of the personal humiliation which he suffered' (1944: xxxii).

One of Duryodhana's main points is that he was insulted when Yudhiṣṭhira asked him to collect the tributes at the *rājasūya* (2.46.24). This is briefly mentioned in Vaiśaṃpāyana's description of the *rājasūya*, where he says that Yudhiṣṭhira gave each of the Kauravas an appropriate duty (2.32.4), with Duryodhana given the task of receiving the gifts (2.32.8). In the first version of the Duryodhana/Dhṛtarāṣṭra dialogue, Duryodhana's role of collecting the gifts is implied, but it is never stated.[9] Here, however, Duryodhana adds more force to his argument by explicitly connecting his present feelings to the *rājasūya*, not only by mentioning his role in receiving the gifts, but also by naming Yudhiṣṭhira as the one who assigned him this task. We do not get any explanation as to why Yudhiṣṭhira specifically asked Duryodhana to register the gifts – perhaps it was unintentional, or maybe it was to rub salt into Duryodhana's wounds. But for whatever reason, Duryodhana's response makes it clear that Yudhiṣṭhira is culpable for provoking Duryodhana's despair.

Duryodhana also tells his father of another provocation: Yudhiṣṭhira addressing him as 'elder'. This is an extraordinary and inflammatory remark, because, if taken literally, it implies that Yudhiṣṭhira acknowledges Duryodhana as the true heir on the very occasion he claims universal sovereignty for himself. Hiltebeitel is probably correct in characterising this remark as said 'mockingly' (2001b: 52). Taken this way, it exposes a cruel side to Yudhiṣṭhira that is rarely seen. Assuming that Duryodhana is offering an accurate account to his father, then his inclusion of this detail further highlights Yudhiṣṭhira's role in inducing his sorrow and jealously. By offering both his task as receiving the gifts and Yudhiṣṭhira's mocking remark as reasons for his despair, Duryodhana portrays his feelings as a response to personal insults, rather than only because of resentment for Yudhiṣṭhira's riches and prestige.

Duryodhana then tells his father about the humiliation he suffers after the *rājasūya*, when he is tricked by the optical illusions of Yudhiṣṭhira's elaborate palace. It is striking that Duryodhana does not mention this in the earlier version. Of course, his humiliation is implied throughout, as his emotional response overcomes him while he is returning from the Pāṇḍavas' palace immediately after this incident. Nevertheless, in the first version, he never tells his father about the humiliations he suffers.[10] In the second version, however, he describes how Bhīmasena laughed at him when he pulled up his trousers only for the floor to be dry, and how Kṛṣṇa and Arjuna laughed at him when he fell into the water, thinking it was the floor. He also points out that Sahadeva, in particular, goaded him after he bumped into the door. In describing this scene to his father – who was not present when it happened – Duryodhana makes his emotional reaction after the *rājasūya* more personal and more sympathetic.

Crucially, Duryodhana's account of this episode is slightly different from how Vaiśaṃpāyana described it earlier in the *parvan*. When identifying who laughed at him, Duryodhana mentions all the same people, but also adds Kṛṣṇa, Draupadī, and the women of the court (2.46.30).[11] Hiltebeitel points out that in the Southern Recension, Draupadī is mentioned in both

Vaiśaṃpāyana's and Duryodhana's accounts, arguing that this is the result of the Southern redactors' general tendency to systematise the more heterogeneous Northern Recension:

> Thus, whereas [the Northern Recension] has Duryodhana add Draupadī's mockery to convince Dhṛtarāṣṭra to host the fateful dice match, [the Southern Recension] generalizes it to both tellings and turns it into the story "everybody knows". The baseline text thus leaves an opening that actually raises the question of what happened. If there is blame at all attached to Draupadī's laughter, the emphasis is on Duryodhana's construal of it in enlisting and obtaining the complicity of this father. Unlike [the Southern Recension], which made it possible to conclude that Draupadī's mockery caused the war, [the Northern Recension], our older and better text, had made that conclusion impossible.
>
> (2015b: 162)

Hiltebeitel adds that the 'mocking laughter of Draupadī' is what 'Indian popular culture' and texts such as the Tamil *Villipāratam* find most memorable about the scene in the Pāṇḍava assembly hall (2015a: 52–53).

Here we see that the causes of the dicing match are presented differently in different recensions of the text. In the Southern Recension, Draupadī's laughter is portrayed as one of the major factors in the build-up to the dicing match; but in the Northern Recension, Draupadī's laughter remains ambiguous. We are left to wonder whether Vaiśaṃpāyana neglected to mention Draupadī and Kṛṣṇa, or if Duryodhana is embellishing his story for the sake of convincing his father. Moreover, even within the Northern Recension, there is a tension between our two Duryodhana/Dhṛtarāṣṭra dialogues: in the first version, as we have seen, Duryodhana's humiliation – regardless of who was laughing – is not even stated as a reason for his despair; while the second version makes his humiliation a major factor for him wanting to take revenge.

Dhṛtarāṣṭra responds by telling his son not to hate the Pāṇḍavas and to be happy with what he has – as he did earlier in this version and in the previous one. Here he again appeals to Duryodhana's reason, telling him to seek 'peace' (*śāmya*) (2.50.3) and to abide by his own *dharma* (2.50.6). Although Duryodhana does not ultimately follow his advice, the dialogue portrays Dhṛtarāṣṭra as actively trying to stop the dicing match and as interacting with his son as if he had the good sense to listen to arguments based on cultivating self-control and following *dharma*.

Duryodhana completely rejects his father's advice, but continues to engage in an argument-based discussion. He praises his father for his mature wisdom (*parigataprajña*) and self-control (*jitendriya*), but says that his advice is confused (2.50.13). He quotes Bṛhaspati as teaching that kings should always look after their own profit. He then appeals to *kṣatriya-dharma*, saying that whether by *dharma* or *adharma*, the duty of a *kṣatriya* is to prevail (2.50.15). Finally, Duryodhana argues that discontent (*asaṃtoṣa*) will lead to greater fortune, saying that he wants to be discontented because it will keep him reaching for more (2.50.18). To illustrate this point, he cites the example of Indra, who made a covenant (*samaya*) not to fight, but then cut off Namuci's head (2.50.20). He concludes that by not acting, he gives his enemy an advantage. In contrast to the first version of this dialogue, where he reverts to emotional blackmail, here Duryodhana defends his emotional response and articulates an argument for seeking revenge. Not only does he appeal to his *dharma* as a *kṣatriya*, but he also draws on his good education by invoking the myth of Indra and Namuci and quoting the teachings of Bṛhaspati.

At this point Śakuni intervenes, declaring that he will take Yudhiṣṭhira's fortune away by challenging him to play dice. Significantly, Śakuni does not explicitly mention his status as a great dice player, nor does he mention that Yudhiṣṭhira loves to play or cannot refuse a challenge. In other words, unlike the other version, in which Śakuni anticipates the question of why dicing would be a particularly advantageous contest to which to challenge Yudhiṣṭhira, this version emphasises Duryodhana's justifications for revenge. Instead of mentioning his own skill at dicing, Śakuni compares the game to a military encounter, calling the dice his bows and arrows, the heart of the dice his string, and the dicing rug his chariot (2.51.2–3).[12] As in the first version, Dhṛtarāṣṭra responds by saying that he will consult with Vidura, and again Duryodhana urges his father not to. This time, however, Duryodhana offers a potentially good explanation not to listen to Vidura, accusing his uncle of being partial to the Pāṇḍavas. He then tells his father to make his own decision, rather than consult others.

After Dhṛtarāṣṭra responds to Śakuni, saying that the game will lead to disaster, Duryodhana re-enters the discussion, now defending the game itself: 'The Ancients bequeathed to us the rules of the game. There is no evil in it, nor blows' (2.51.12). Significantly, this is the only time in any of our three versions of this dialogue where any character defends playing dice as an honourable pastime. Also, rather than portraying it as a form of war, Duryodhana characterises dicing as a preferable alternative because it does not involve violence.

After this argument, Dhṛtarāṣṭra finally agrees, but warns his son that he will suffer as a consequence. He also credits Vidura for seeing what consequences will come, before ordering the hall to be built (2.51.16–19). It is at this point when Dhṛtarāṣṭra instructs Vidura to invite Yudhiṣṭhira to 'a friendly dicing match' (2.51.20–21). Vidura at first refuses, warning that he fears the lineage will come to an end (2.51.24), but Dhṛtarāṣṭra assures him that there will be no quarrels and argues that the game is ordained by fate (*daiva*) and is part of Dhātṛ's design (2.51.25). Compared to the first version, where Dhṛtarāṣṭra describes the game in terms of destiny (*diṣṭa*), here he specifically describes it as a part of Dhātṛ's design, offering a stronger sense of its inevitability. Moreover, despite assuring Vidura that the game will not cause divisions, here he does not claim that his presence will prevent misfortune.

As we can see, there are some similarities between the two versions of the Duryodhana/Dhṛtarāṣṭra dialogue, particularly in relating Duryodhana's emotional state to his reaction to the power and prestige on display at Yudhiṣṭhira's *rājasūya*. But more significant than the similarities are the variations between these two versions, as each dialogue characterises the lead-up to the dicing match differently. Whereas in the first version Duryodhana makes more of an emotional appeal to his father, in the second version he gives a richer description of why he is upset and then makes a reasoned case for why he should take revenge. Rather than merely acting like a spoiled brat, Duryodhana both justifies his emotions as a response to cruel provocations by the Pāṇḍavas and articulates his attempt to seek revenge as a fulfilment of his *kṣatriya-dharma*.

Meanwhile, in the second version, Dhṛtarāṣṭra makes more of an explicit attempt to stop the dicing match. By advising his son to follow *dharma* and seek peace, he acts more like a wise king than an overly permissive father. Moreover, when he does support his son, he has been given better reasons to do so. Dhṛtarāṣṭra not only hears his son draw on his education and background to make arguments based on *dharma*, but he also hears of the ways that the Pāṇḍavas humiliate his son. Another distinctive feature of the second version is that Śakuni's role in bringing about the game is significantly reduced. As we saw in the first version, Śakuni orchestrates the conversation between Duryodhana and Dhṛtarāṣṭra, while in the second there are no details about what led to their conversation. Instead, the second version portrays Duryodhana – not Śakuni –making the most significant arguments about the match: not only in telling Dhṛtarāṣṭra about Śakuni's skill at dice, but also in defending the game as an honourable pastime.

Returning to Janamejaya's question, we can see that these two versions of the Duryodhana/Dhṛtarāṣṭra dialogue give different accounts of the circumstances these characters and their interlocutors experience and the decisions they make. While in the first we might summarise the main causes as Duryodhana's self-pity, Dhṛtarāṣṭra's blind loyalty to his son, and Śakuni's cunning, the second version offers a more sympathetic portrayal of both Duryodhana and Dhṛtarāṣṭra, while also downplaying Śakuni's contribution. Meanwhile, the second version highlights the role of the Pāṇḍavas in triggering Duryodhana's despondency. By including the two versions side by side, the *Mahābhārata* invites us to understand the lead-up to the dicing match both as a combination of all the details in the two versions and as two distinct explanations for how events unfold.

Duryodhana and Dhṛtarāṣṭra: version 3: (12.124)

Another version of the exchange between Duryodhana and Dhṛtarāṣṭra appears in the *Śānti Parvan* during Bhīṣma's post-war instruction to

Yudhiṣṭhira. Towards the end of the *Rāja-dharma* section of the *parvan*, Yudhiṣṭhira asks Bhīṣma how to cultivate the practice of *dharma* (12.124.1–3). Bhīṣma replies with his own account of the encounter between Dhṛtarāṣṭra and Duryodhana, saying to Yudhiṣṭhira that 'Duryodhana was upset at having seen the fortune (*śrī*) that had come to you and your brothers at Indraprastha, great king, and because of the ridicule of him in your assembly hall' (12.124.4–6). Appearing in the *Śānti Parvan*, long after the events leading up to the way, this version is exactly the type of episode that, as we discussed in the Introduction, has troubled Western scholars. Not only does it appear in the *Śānti Parvan*, a section of the text consisting mainly of the so-called 'didactic' material, but it also blatantly contradicts events as recounted in the main story. Previous scholars might have been tempted to discard this episode as a later interpolation resulting from 'sloppy editing'. If we read the *Mahābhārata* as a contestatory debate, however, then the questions of originality and consistency are misplaced. Instead, our main questions should be about how this version characterises this vital episode and how its characterisation here relates to its portrayal in other versions. It is important, then, that Bhīṣma explicitly makes the connection between his instruction here and the main story by contextualising this exchange at exactly the same place in the narrative where our other versions appear, connecting Duryodhana's sorrow both to Yudhiṣṭhira's *rājasūya* and to his humiliation in the palace afterwards.[13]

As with the previous versions, Dhṛtarāṣṭra speaks first, asking his son why he is 'grieving' (*śoka*) when he has status, wealth, and fine food. In response, Duryodhana explains that he is upset because he saw the opulence of Yudhiṣṭhira's *rājasūya* (12.124.11–13). As with our two other versions, Duryodhana describes some of the specific guests and their gifts, but he goes into far less detail. He also neglects to include some of the arguments that he mentions in other versions, such as the killing of Śiśupāla (which he mentions to Śakuni in version one), or his role as receiving the gifts and his humiliation in the palace after the ritual (which he mentions to Dhṛtarāṣṭra in the second version). Here his feelings of resentment and sorrow are much more concentrated on the fortune itself, rather than on his humiliation or the power and prestige that he associates with the *rājasūya*. Indeed, this version puts far less emphasis on Duryodhana generally – his emotional plea to his father only lasts three verses (12.124.11–13) – and instead Dhṛtarāṣṭra's teaching is the focus of the dialogue.

Rather than tell his son not to seek revenge, Dhṛtarāṣṭra advises Duryodhana that he can attain fortune (*śrī*) equal or greater to that of Yudhiṣṭhira by becoming a person of good character (*śilavat*) (12.124.14). To illustrate this point, he tells Duryodhana the story of the rivalry between Indra and Prahrāda. When Prahrāda gains control of the three worlds, Indra seeks advice from Bṛhaspati, who tells him that 'knowledge' (*jñāna*) is the 'highest and most excellent thing' (12.124.21). Subsequently, Indra takes on the disguise of a brahmin to learn from Prahrāda, who at one point teaches him: 'abiding by *dharma* (*dharmātman*), my anger under control, I am restrained and I have restrained my senses' (12.124.35). When Prahrāda grants him a boon, Indra chooses Prahrāda's own virtuous disposition (*śīla*). Subsequently, Prahrāda's virtue (*śīla*) leaves him to go to Indra, as does *dharma*, truth (*satya*), good conduct (*vṛtta*), and strength (*bala*). When these five qualities leave him, then fortune (*śrī*) leaves him as well.

It is notable that this tale about Indra and one of his enemies has a very different message than the one Duryodhana invokes in the second version of the dialogue. Then, Duryodhana cited Indra's betrayal of Namuci as a justification for taking revenge on the Pāṇḍavas. Here, Dhṛtarāṣṭra recounts a different myth about Indra, one suggesting that Duryodhana can overcome his rivals through self-cultivation rather than armed conflict. After hearing this story, Duryodhana asks his father how to acquire virtue, with Dhṛtarāṣṭra telling him to practise kindness towards all creatures in thought, speech, and action: 'One should never do a deliberate deed for himself that is not beneficial to others, or that he would be ashamed of. One should do those deeds for which one would be praised in public' (12.124.65). Bhīṣma concludes: 'Dhṛtarāṣṭra told this to his son, king. Do this yourself, son of Kuntī, and then you will get its fruit' (12.124.69).

Like in the second version, Dhṛtarāṣṭra appeals to Duryodhana to act virtuously. But here he goes into more detail about how to cultivate dharmic behaviour.[14] Rather than an argument against Duryodhana hosting the match, this version portrays Dhṛtarāṣṭra as delivering a teaching on how Duryodhana can overcome his feelings of grief and sorrow by becoming a virtuous person. Also, unlike the other versions, both of which end with Dhṛtarāṣṭra sending Vidura to invite Yudhiṣṭhira to the match, this version is a self-contained episode without any explicit connection to what happens next in the narrative. Nonetheless, there are indirect allusions to the dicing match, as Dhṛtarāṣṭra tells his son that any king lacking in virtue will not be able to hold on to fortune (*śrī*) for long, even if they acquire her. For Duryodhana listening to this advice within the dialogue, this could be seen as a warning for what is to come during the match; for Yudhiṣṭhira listening to this dialogue after the war, this offers an explanation for what has already happened. Moreover, Dhṛtarāṣṭra's teaching about *śrī* leaving the body of Prahrāda when the five virtues depart can be seen as an allegory for the five Pāṇḍavas and Draupadī.

Although the third version does not directly address the question of how the dicing match came about, it nonetheless characterises the dynamic between fate and human agency differently. Whereas in the two other versions, Dhṛtarāṣṭra speaks of his circumstances in terms of determinism, here he does not mention either *daiva* or Dhātṛ, but rather focuses completely on how to cultivate virtuous conduct. Tapping into discussions about *karma-yoga*, Dhṛtarāṣṭra indicates that Duryodhana can take control over his circumstances through self-cultivation. By implication, Dhṛtarāṣṭra instructs his son that, despite his desires and intentions to seek revenge, he has the choice to act otherwise – that through virtuous behaviour, he can exert control over his circumstances.

Reflections on the Duryodhana/Dhṛtarāṣṭra dialogue

When looking at the three version of the Duryodhana/Dhṛtarāṣṭra dialogue together, we can see that, despite sharing some of the same details, the moral responsibility of each character is portrayed differently from one version to the next. In the first, Duryodhana is completely overcome by misery and resentment, so much so that he barely engages in a discussion and threatens to kill himself if he does not get his way. In the second version, his emotional state does not prevent him from making reasoned arguments about why he should take revenge. Indeed, he claims that his emotional response is perfectly aligned with his *dharma*. By sharing the details of how the Pāṇḍavas treated him at the *rājasūya*, Duryodhana makes the case that he was provoked, and that therefore the moral responsibility for his vengeful actions lies with the Pāṇḍavas. In the third version, his emotional state is the starting point for Dhṛtarāṣṭra's teaching about how to cultivate virtuous behaviour. Dhṛtarāṣṭra's instruction offers a different type of agency, one in which Duryodhana can take control of his circumstances through self-cultivation. Although Duryodhana does not follow his father's advice, Dhṛtarāṣṭra's instruction raises the possibility that Duryodhana could have acted radically differently.

The three versions explore Dhṛtarāṣṭra's culpability differently as well. In the first version, he is depicted as an overly permissive father who offers no resistance to what he knows to be a disastrous plan, despite the fact that his son offers no good reason to support it except for his histrionics. In the second version, Dhṛtarāṣṭra attempts to persuade him not to host the match. Moreover, by appealing to Duryodhana's education and background, we might even see Dhṛtarāṣṭra as eliciting his son's more rational side. He ultimately gives in to his son's arguments, but here Dhṛtarāṣṭra is presented with good reasons to support Duryodhana. In other words, the second version suggests that Dhṛtarāṣṭra agrees to the match because of more than merely his permissiveness. In the third version, he is portrayed as a wise king who instructs his son to cultivate good character, rather than seek revenge on the Pāṇḍavas. One of the extraordinary aspects of this version is that Dhṛtarāṣṭra is depicted as a teacher of self-restraint and self-cultivation – virtues that he seems nowhere else to exhibit.

In addition to highlighting both Duryodhana's and Dhṛtarāṣṭra's roles in bringing about the match, these three versions of the Duryodhana/Dhṛtarāṣṭra dialogue also offer different perspectives from which to account for Yudhiṣṭhira's part in the unfolding of events. In the first version, Duryodhana and Dhṛtarāṣṭra are almost entirely to blame, with the focus on Duryodhana's extreme response and Dhṛtarāṣṭra's permissiveness.

In the second version, however, Duryodhana reveals Yudhiṣṭhira's insults, both in asking him to receive the gifts and tauntingly referring to him as his elder. Additionally, he mentions the humiliation of Draupadī laughing at him. Duryodhana's more detailed portrayal of the external factors provoking his emotional state, combined with him reacting more rationally, makes the causes for the match far more complex, as both Duryodhana and Yudhiṣṭhira seem to have contributed to the devastating events unfolding before them. In the third version, Yudhiṣṭhira's role is explored through him as the listener to this dialogue. Bhīṣma specifically mentions the *rājasūya* and the humiliation Duryodhana suffers there. Although this version does not specifically mention receiving the gifts, the mocking remark, or Draupadī's laughter, we can imagine what Yudhiṣṭhira might have been thinking when he was reminded that Duryodhana was ridiculed, perhaps hearing for the first time of the emotional response that his own actions had triggered. We might wonder if Bhīṣma – who includes this dialogue as part of his long post-war instruction in the *Śānti Parvan* – is suggesting that an important part of Yudhiṣṭhira's education to become a *dharma*-king is reflecting back on his own experiences, particularly his own ill-advised actions and their contribution to the 'destruction of the world'.

Reading the Duryodhana/Dhṛtarāṣṭra dialogues together in this way offers a potential insight into how the dialectic between fate and human agency plays out in the *Mahābhārata*. Although each version accepts the inevitability of the match, each one also offers a different account of how characters respond to their situations. No matter how much the dicing match might be inevitable from a narrative perspective, our understanding of the moral responsibilities of the different characters depends on how they face up to their circumstances and what reasons they offer to explain and justify their actions. In each version, characters treat each other with reactive attitudes, through praise and blame, as well as through their attempts to influence each other's actions and decisions. Despite sometimes interpreting human actions as instruments of cosmic forces, characters nevertheless treat each other as morally responsible agents.

Yudhiṣṭhira's decision

Hill describes Yudhiṣṭhira's decision to play dice as one of the more 'inexplicable events in the *Mahābhārata*' (2001: 302):

> Of all the characters to appear in the *Mahābhārata*, it is the name of Yudhiṣṭhira that is most readily associated with dharma … given this almost excess of virtue Yudhiṣṭhira's gambling lapse takes on monumental proportions, and it is a problem the Epic bards could scarcely ignore. The result is one of the Epic's more subtle and considered views on the relative importance of fate and human action'
>
> (2001: 302)

The question of why Yudhiṣṭhira would agree to play dice has been eloquently articulated by van Buitenen:

> Why, when everything has been achieved, must it now be gambled away by the hero, in all of whose previous life there has not been so much as a hint of a compulsion to gamble, all of whose life has in fact been of exemplary rectitude and prudence? It is this disturbing contradiction in the character of Yudhiṣṭhira that demands the question whether this was indeed a contradiction, or whether the events in his life may not have been modelled on a preexisting structure.
>
> (1975: 5)

We will return to van Buitenen's own attempt to answer this question at the end of this chapter, but for now I would like to explore the several explanations Yudhiṣṭhira gives for accepting the invitation to play dice. As we will see, in a series of dialogues he has with Vidura, Draupadī, and Śakuni, Yudhiṣṭhira provides multiple justifications. In the process, he sets up a tension between understanding his decision as beyond his control and as his moral impetus to act virtuously in the face of his circumstances.

Yudhiṣṭhira and Vidura: (2.52.1–16)

When Vidura approaches Yudhiṣṭhira to invite him and his brothers to play dice, his precise words (2.52.7–8) are not exactly what Dhṛtarāṣṭra had instructed him to say (2.51.21). Both he and Dhṛtarāṣṭra mention the hall, the invitation to come play, and describe the game as 'friendly' (*suhṛd*).[15] Here we see that Vidura repeats Dhṛtarāṣṭra's mischaracterisation of the game, despite knowing its dangers. Crucially, Vidura adds an extra detail, describing the newly constructed Kaurava *sabhā* as 'comparable' (*tulya*) to the Pāṇḍava assembly hall (2.52.7–8). Considering the opulent descriptions of Yudhiṣṭhira's hall earlier in the *parvan* and its symbolic significance as representing his newfound power, Vidura's comparison of the two halls is a controversial statement. It seems unlikely that Vidura is intending to provoke, but by adding this remark he possibly nudges Yudhiṣṭhira towards accepting the invitation.

Yudhiṣṭhira immediately senses the danger, but asks for Vidura's advice and promises to follow it (2.52.10). In contrast with Dhṛtarāṣṭra, who avoided seeking his counsel on this issue, Yudhiṣṭhira asks for Vidura's advice straight away. But again there is a distinction between what Vidura says to Dhṛtarāṣṭra, who has already ignored him, and to Yudhiṣṭhira, who seems quite ready to act upon his instruction. Rather than advising him, Vidura responds by saying that he knows the game will bring disaster, that he has already tried to prevent it, that Dhṛtarāṣṭra has sent him to deliver the message, and that it is now up to Yudhiṣṭhira to do what is best (*śreyas*) (2.52.11). We might wonder why Vidura does not do more to prevent the game at this point. Does he think it is not his place to be an advisor for

Yudhiṣṭhira? Does he agree with the reasons that Yudhiṣṭhira subsequently gives for accepting the invitation? Or perhaps he thinks that by telling him to do what's 'best', Yudhiṣṭhira will not accept the challenge? Although these questions remain unanswered, it is notable that Vidura, who is quite willing to advise Dhṛtarāṣṭra to stop the game, is not nearly as assertive in his rhetoric when speaking to Yudhiṣṭhira. Despite objecting to the game, this exchange with Yudhiṣṭhira raises the question of whether Vidura could have done more to prevent the match.

When Yudhiṣṭhira then asks for more information, wondering who will be playing, he seems to be acting as a good king should: seeking counsel from a wise advisor before making any decisions and asking for further information when advice is not forthcoming. After hearing who will be there, Yudhiṣṭhira describes them as 'dangerous dice players' (*mahābhayāḥa kitava*), who will use deceiving 'tricks' (*māyā*) (2.52.14). This is the first explicit suggestion that the match will not be played fairly and indicates that Yudhiṣṭhira has an understanding of exactly what type of a contest this will be, despite Dhṛtarāṣṭra and Vidura suggesting otherwise. Aware of the dangers, Yudhiṣṭhira nevertheless accepts the challenge, saying that he is 'not unwilling to play Śakuni' (2.52.16).

The first reason Yudhiṣṭhira gives is because 'this world obeys Dhātṛ's design (*diṣṭa*)' (2.52.14). As we have seen, while sending Vidura to deliver the invitation to Yudhiṣṭhira, Dhṛtarāṣṭra also talks of the dicing game as Dhātṛ's design (2.51.25). It is interesting that both Dhṛtarāṣṭra and Yudhiṣṭhira characterise the game in this way. Despite seemingly sharing the same fatalistic outlook, however, these two kings respond to their circumstances very differently. Unlike Dhṛtarāṣṭra, who invokes *daiva* and Dhātṛ to avoid moral responsibility, Yudhiṣṭhira offers two further justifications for accepting the invitation: (1) a son must respect his father, and (2) a previous vow (*vrata*) not to refuse a challenge. Although Yudhiṣṭhira does not use the word *dharma* here, these reasons are related to the notions of *kula-dharma* and *kṣatriya-dharma*. It is noteworthy that *kula-dharma* and *kṣatriya-dharma* are often in tension with one another, but in this context they reinforce each other as two of the pillars of Yudhiṣṭhira's justification.

Yudhiṣṭhira's appeal to *kula-dharma* is interesting because it invokes parental authority, which is a recurring consideration in many of the central moral problems of the *Mahābhārata*. As we have seen in Chapter 1, Bhīṣma ignores his 'mother' Satyavatī's instructions, while in Chapter 2, Yudhiṣṭhira considers his mother's words binding when he defends the polyandrous marriage. In this case, Yudhiṣṭhira treats his uncle as a father, but Dhṛtarāṣṭra does not treat him as a true son. When Vidura warns Dhṛtarāṣṭra against a division (*bheda*) between his 'sons', the king assures him: 'my sons will not quarrel with my sons' (2.45.53). Although both Vidura and Dhṛtarāṣṭra use the word *putra*, the fact that Dhṛtarāṣṭra uses this word twice shows that he speaks as if he has two sets of sons, rather than speaking of all his sons together. Indeed, in other sections of the text,

Dhṛtarāṣṭra reveals his partiality towards his own sons. In his dialogue with Saṃjaya that features as one of Ugraśravas' summaries in the *Ādi Parvan*, for example, Dhṛtarāṣṭra says he felt doomed when he learned that the Pāṇḍavas were still united after being defeated by Śakuni in the dicing match (1.1.105). As Sibaji Bandyopadhyay suggests, such statements indicate that Dhṛtarāṣṭra's claims of impartiality are made in 'bad faith' (2014: 12). It is ironic, then, that one of Yudhiṣṭhira's reasons for accepting the invitation is to respect the wishes of his father, when Dhṛtarāṣṭra does not reciprocate with parental responsibility.

The other reason Yudhiṣṭhira gives is that he has sworn an 'eternal vow' (*śāśvata vrata*) not to refuse a challenge (2.52.16). We should recall here that this is exactly what Śakuni said he would do in the first version of the Duryodhana/Dhṛtarāṣṭra dialogue. Of the three reasons he gives to Vidura, we see an interesting tension between Yudhiṣṭhira portraying the game as destined to happen and his need to explain his acceptance of the invitation with good reasons. His appeal to Dhātṛ implies that he has no choice, but by citing his obligations to abide by his father and to fulfil an eternal vow, he indicates that he is making a conscious decision to do what he considers to be the virtuous deed. Although both of these reasons might make him feel further compelled to play, we know that other characters sometimes ignore the advice of their parents or even break their vows. In other words, these reasons indicate that he is making a decision to play, rather than merely following what he feels destined to do. But whether or not Yudhiṣṭhira is free to choose, it is nevertheless significant that he offers different explanations. As we have seen in the cases of Bhīṣma's vows and Draupadī's marriage, there is a recurring tendency for characters to give multiple justifications for their actions. Rather than this being a contradiction, this is consistent with Yudhiṣṭhira's own method of moral reasoning.

It is important to examine the process of Yudhiṣṭhira's moral reasoning because he has sometimes been interpreted as making an irrational decision to play dice. Amita Chatterjee, for example, has interpreted Yudhiṣṭhira's acceptance of the invitation as a conflict between reason and impulse:

> All things considered, Yudhiṣṭhira should never have participated in the game in which Śakuni was his opponent. But he ignored this judgment and, contrary to his best reason, acted in accordance with his preference ... his weakness overrode all other considerations when he received an invitation to play a game of dice. It is not that he was unaware of his weakness, yet he succumbed to it.
>
> (2018: 50)

What is problematic about this interpretation is that this is not how Yudhiṣṭhira's decision is portrayed in his dialogue with Vidura. As we have seen, the only character to declare Yudhiṣṭhira's fondness for dice before the match is Śakuni. Unlike his other claim that Yudhiṣṭhira is compelled to play by a previous vow, Śakuni's assertion about a pre-existing fondness for playing dice is never corroborated either by Yudhiṣṭhira or by any other character. In other words, it remains unclear whether a fondness for dice is a factor in Yudhiṣṭhira's decision.

Moreover, when we follow the justifications Yudhiṣṭhira offers Vidura, we see that he does not ignore his judgement, but rather offers three compelling reasons why he should accept the invitation. Additionally, Yudhiṣṭhira asks Vidura for advice and gathers information about the dicing match before accepting the invitation. We might still think, along with Chatterjee, that Yudhiṣṭhira makes the wrong choice, but when we take his dialogue with Vidura into account, it is not quite accurate to say that he acted contrary to reason. Indeed, we might say that he decided to play dice for exactly the right reasons, but was let down by the people around him. He adheres to his *kula-dharma* by following the advice of his 'father', but his uncle betrays him by not treating him as a son. He abides by his *kṣatriya-dharma* by upholding his vow never to refuse a fair challenge, but the challenge itself is not fair. As Norbert Klaes explains: 'Śakuni violated the varṇa-dharma of the Kṣatriyas by challenging somebody who was inexperienced in dicing and who, if challenged, was obliged to accept the invitation' (1975: 42), With all of these factors in mind, if Yudhiṣṭhira made the wrong decision, then it is not because he did not have good reasons to play, but rather because he naively follows his responsibilities towards others without recognising that others are not acting responsibly towards him.

Compared to some of the conversations leading up to Draupadī's marriage, it is noteworthy how relatively short his dialogue with Vidura is. In this sense, there is indeed an impulsiveness to Yudhiṣṭhira's decision. It is not that he does not offer good reasons for accepting the invitation, but rather that he makes his decision too quickly and with no substantial consultation. Considering how many decisions the Pāṇḍavas mull over as a group, it is noteworthy that in his most consequential decision, Yudhiṣṭhira never discusses it with his brothers, Draupadī, or his mother, until after he has already made up his mind. Nevertheless, it is a question that he will revisit throughout the text, sometimes adding further information that complicates what he says to Vidura.

Yudhiṣṭhira and Draupadī (2.52.17–19)

After his dialogue with Vidura, when he is surrounded 'by his relatives, attendants, and the women of the household led by Draupadī', Yudhiṣṭhira makes a remark that sheds further light on his decision:

> Fate (*daiva*) takes our reason (*prajñā*) away
> As glare blinds the eye.
> Man bound as with nooses (*pāśa*)
> Obeys Dhātṛ's sway (*vaśa*)
>
> (2.52.18)

Here, Yudhiṣṭhira returns to describing the dicing match in terms of Dhātṛ's power or control (*vaśa*), but now equates Dhātṛ with fate (*daiva*), vividly describing how he is compelled to act as if bound by a cord or rope (*pāśa*). As Hill has pointed out, the rope imagery is regularly associated with Dhātṛ, where 'Man is reduced to a powerless marionette with the course of events entirely predetermined by a power beyond his control. In this view, predestination is a theory about puppets and strings' (2001: 167).

In addition to attributing the match to Dhātṛ, Yudhiṣṭhira also reveals that he is not thinking clearly, that he has been robbed of his 'reason' (*prajñā*). It is noteworthy that although he is in the company of many people, Draupadī is the only person specifically named as being present when he says this. It is not clear to what extent he is speaking to everyone present, or to her in particular, but what he says here seems to have particular relevance to Draupadī. As we will see in Chapter 4, a crucial aspect of Draupadī's argument after the dicing match is that Yudhiṣṭhira was not in control of his senses (2.60.5).[16] Here we see that even before the usher reports this to her after the match, Draupadī had already heard Yudhiṣṭhira speak of himself in this way. Although this is not presented as a private conversation between Yudhiṣṭhira and Draupadī, it is nevertheless interesting that when Draupadī is present, he brings up his loss of reason for the first time. In contrast with his dialogue with Vidura – where he seems to accept some moral responsibility – here he offers none at all. Not only is the game out of his control, but he has lost control of himself.

Yudhiṣṭhira and Śakuni (2.53.1–16)

Yudhiṣṭhira's brief exchange with Śakuni just before they start playing adds a further dimension to his decision to play dice: that he has been tricked. As we have seen, there is already deceit involved in the invitation itself, with Dhṛtarāṣṭra misrepresenting the match as 'friendly' and Vidura contributing to the set-up by using the same term. Moreover, the possibility of deception is repeated on several occasions during the match itself and is reflected upon by a number of characters later on in the narrative. We might remember that Yudhiṣṭhira is immediately alerted to the possibility of cheating when he learns who will be playing (2.52.14). Yudhiṣṭhira again suspects underhandedness when discussing the rules of the game with Śakuni, saying that deceitful play is 'evil' (*pāpaṃ*) and imploring Śakuni not to use tricks (2.53.2).

When Yudhiṣṭhira accuses him of cheating, however, Śakuni calls his bluff, saying that if Yudhiṣṭhira is concerned about dishonesty, then he does not have to play (2.53.5). According to Śakuni, if Yudhiṣṭhira does not think it is a fair game, then his obligation to accept the challenge is not binding. Śakuni then tells Yudhiṣṭhira that he only says the game is time (*kāla*) because he fears losing (2.53.5). Notably, Yudhiṣṭhira has not used the term *kāla* to explain his acceptance of the invitation, nor had

Śakuni been within earshot when he spoke of the match in terms of *daiva* or Dhātṛ. Although he has not heard Yudhiṣṭhira characterise the game in this way, Śakuni's counterargument here nevertheless guesses correctly that Yudhiṣṭhira has taken a determinist position. Moreover, Śakuni's quip challenges Yudhiṣṭhira's motivations for portraying the dicing match as pre-determined. Similar to Draupadī's criticisms of Yudhiṣṭhira's appeal to Dhātṛ in the *Āraṇyaka Parvan* (3.31.21–42), Śakuni accuses Yudhiṣṭhira of not taking account of his actions. In the process, Śakuni offers a different way of understanding the relationship between fate and human agency, indicating that dicing is a game of skill and that the result rewards those who take matters into their own hands.

In response, Yudhiṣṭhira quotes Asita Devala, who contrasts playing dice with fighting a war, arguing that battles are won fairly: 'To game with gamblers who play tricks is an evil, but victory in battle according to *dharma* is a good game and superior to it' (2.53.7). In citing this quotation, Yudhiṣṭhira characterises dicing as violating *dharma*, an argument that several characters will make after the match when arguing that the result should not be binding. Yudhiṣṭhira then declares that he will not cheat and that there is no honour in gambling. Following this logic, Yudhiṣṭhira might well have been within the terms and conditions of his vow had he refused this challenge. Instead, this argument will become a tragic irony, when Yudhiṣṭhira ends up winning the war through tricks and deception.

But rather than deny using tricks himself, Śakuni defends the use of deception, arguing that the educated surpass the ignorant through trickery. However, in this case – he argues – it is not called a trick. By implication, Śakuni portrays his ploys as only a better knowledge and understanding of the game. That dicing was a game of skill as much as, or more than, a game of chance is suggested by J.C. Heesterman, who has argued that ancient Indian dice playing relied on advanced counting techniques. 'All seems to depend on the skill of the player in computing at a glance the number of the dice to be separated, taking at the same time into account the number of dice left for his adversaries' (1957: 145–146). Paul Bowlby (1991: 14) points out that this is similar to the counting skills that Ṛtuparṇa teaches Nala (3.70.23) in the story of Nala and Damayantī, which Yudhiṣṭhira hears in the *Āraṇyaka Parvan*. Vaiśaṃpāyana does not describe such counting expertise in his depiction of the dicing match between Yudhiṣṭhira and Śakuni, but knowing that they were part of the culture of playing dice adds credence to Śakuni's claim that what others call cheating might really be skilful tactics.

At this point, Śakuni again offers Yudhiṣṭhira the chance to opt out of the game (2.53.12), but for Yudhiṣṭhira, the proverbial die has already been cast. He explains to Śakuni that it is too late for him to withdraw now because he has already vowed to play. In this brief exchange with Śakuni, then, Yudhiṣṭhira once again portrays his decision to play in terms of a vow, but this time, rather than claim it was a previous vow not to refuse a challenge, here he refers to his acceptance of the invitation as a vow. In the process of restating his commitment to play, he also casts doubt on the fairness of the game.

Once they begin playing, the notion of cheating comes up several more times, with Yudhiṣṭhira accusing Śakuni of a trick (*kaitava*) after the very first throw (2.54.1). Moreover, before sixteen of his twenty throws, Vaiśampāyana says that Śakuni 'deceived' (*nikṛta*), as he rolled the dice (2.54–58). Insinuations that the game has been rigged continue throughout much of the remainder of the narrative, particularly in the *Udyoga Parvan*.[17] But while some characters indicate that Śakuni cheated, Duryodhana (5.2.1) and Balarāma (5.2.9–11) argue that Yudhiṣṭhira is to be blamed for agreeing to play. Draupadī also holds Yudhiṣṭhira responsible for gambling on a number of occasions. In the *Virāṭa Parvan*, when Yudhiṣṭhira is dicing in the hall and sends her back to the women's quarters, Draupadī explicitly calls him a 'gambler' (*akṣadhūrta*) and censures him for her needing to take up her disguise as a chambermaid (4.19.1). There is a sense that Draupadī never completely trusts him after the dicing match. As tensions remain throughout the story, we are repeatedly reminded of the varied and sometimes conflicting explanations Yudhiṣṭhira gives for agreeing to play dice in the lead-up to the match.

Yudhiṣṭhira: retrospective reflections

As we will see in the following chapter, Yudhiṣṭhira loses everything in the dicing match, including his brothers and himself. But controversy erupts over whether Draupadī has been lost as well. After Draupadī convinces Dhṛtarāṣṭra to nullify the result of the game, the Kauravas invite Yudhiṣṭhira back for one more throw of the dice. When invited for a second time, Yudhiṣṭhira again invokes Dhātṛ and again says that he cannot disobey his uncle (2.67.3). After losing the second match, however, he offers additional reasons for playing the game, indicating that he takes on more responsibility as he reflects on his decisions and actions retrospectively. In the *Āraṇyaka Parvan*, for example, Yudhiṣṭhira tells Bhīmasena that he decided to play dice 'to take Duryodhana's kingship and kingdom away' (3.35.2). Here he explains that when he agreed to participate, he thought he would be playing against Duryodhana, but learned he would be facing Śakuni only when he entered the hall. This account indicates that he was in control of his senses after all and had made the calculation that he could defeat Duryodhana. Yudhiṣṭhira then says the match was 'fated' (*bhavitavya*) (3.35.5), once again describing events as beyond his control. On another occasion, Yudhiṣṭhira gives us a glimpse of what he was thinking during the dicing match itself. In the *Udyoga Parvan*, when arguing that the Pāṇḍavas should not go to war, he describes his insight while he was gambling: that the Kauravas faced destruction as long as they neglected the advice of Vidura (5.26.15). By referring to his thoughts during the dicing match itself,

Yudhiṣṭhira indicates that, rather than losing control of his reason, he was reflecting on his situation as it was unfolding and already viewing the Kauravas with some degree of compassion.

With these retrospective reflections, Yudhiṣṭhira offers additional explanations for why he agreed to play dice, while also remaining conflicted about the degree of his own responsibility. By referring to Śakuni's tricks and the inevitability of the match, Yudhiṣṭhira once again characterises circumstances as beyond his control. Nevertheless, by claiming he agreed to the dicing match in order to take Duryodhana's half of the kingdom, he also introduces his imperial ambitions as an additional reason for agreeing to play. Meanwhile, by recalling what he was thinking during the game, Yudhiṣṭhira casts doubt on the claims that he lost himself during the match. Although some might view these later reflections as textual inconsistencies,[18] there is a narrative logic to Yudhiṣṭhira's remarks as examples of him trying to make sense of his past actions, perhaps remembering different details in response to different events taking shape. As with the case of Bhīṣma's vows, we see that a morally problematic episode is revisited several times in the narrative and understood in different ways as situations change.

Taking together what Yudhiṣṭhira says before, during, and after the match, we can break down his decision to accept the invitation to play dice into six distinct factors: (1) *daiva* /Dhātṛ's design; (2) responsibility to follow the words of his father/uncle; (3) responsibility to uphold his vow; (4) losing his reason; (5) wanting to win Duryodhana's kingdom; and (6) tricked into playing. Within this range of explanations, there exists a tension between portraying the game as pre-determined and as the consequences of his own decisions and actions. By specifically mentioning *daiva* and Dhātṛ, Yudhiṣṭhira portrays himself as powerless not to accept the invitation. According to this lens of interpretation, Yudhiṣṭhira has no decision to make, because events have already been decided in advance and he is merely playing out his prescribed roles.

Despite this fatalistic understanding, Yudhiṣṭhira nevertheless feels the need to justify his decision, invoking his obligations towards Dhṛtarāṣṭra and his vow, while also saying that he lost his reason and later claiming that he had imperial ambitions. Amidst his conflicting explanations, Yudhiṣṭhira indicates that freedom is not necessarily measured in terms of choosing between actions, but rather in deciding how he understands his circumstances. Tapping into wider discussions about of *karma-yoga* throughout the text, Yudhiṣṭhira offers an understanding of moral action in which true freedom is not acting however he wants, but acting according to his duties and obligations, regardless of the consequences. His own responsibility for his actions, however, remains unclear. Despite acting in accordance with his dharmic commitments, Draupadī and other characters will continue to blame him for the dicing match long after it is over. He might have decided to play for the right reasons, but he still has to live with the consequences of his actions for the remainder of his life.

Conclusion

One of the most widely accepted explanations among scholars for the dicing match is one that does not appear in the reconstituted text nor in any manuscript tradition. Rather, it has been put forth by J.A.B. van Buitenen, who argued that the *Sabhā Parvan* as a whole was structured according to the *rājasūya*:

> In my view it cannot be coincidental the Royal Consecration and the Unction in the *Mahābhārata* are followed by a gambling match and that dicing is prescribed as mandatory *after* the Unction (*abhiṣeka*) in the *rājasūya* ritual ... *The Assembly Hall* is structurally an epic dramatization of the Vedic ritual.
>
> (1975: 5–6)

While van Buitenen's argument might shed light on a structural feature of the *parvan* – thus adding depth to our understanding of the richly textured composition of the *Mahābhārata* – it nevertheless fails to answer his own question about Yudhiṣṭhira's motives for agreeing to risk everything at the very moment he has achieved universal sovereignty. As we have seen, not only does Yudhiṣṭhira give several reasons for agreeing to play dice, but there are a range of arguments and justifications regarding the match given by Duryodhana, Dhṛtarāṣṭra, Śakuni, and Vidura, not to mention other characters later in the narrative. In addition to devoting several dialogues to this question, the *Mahābhạrata* also brings attention to the controversial status of the entire dicing episode through textual anomalies and disjunctures, such as Ugraśravas' rare and unexpected intervention and the inclusion of three versions of the same exchange between Duryodhana and Dhṛtarāṣṭra. As with the other moral questions we are exploring in this book, the text treats the dicing match as a controversial episode that demands further philosophical reflection. Some of the crucial and recurring aspects of such moral cases in the *Mahābhārata* are that there are no easy answers, that there are multiple perspectives, and that multiple explanations can remain in creative tension with each other. While the composers might have modelled the *Sabhā Parvan* on the structure of the *rājsūya*, the organisational features of the text do not answer the question why Yudhiṣṭhira agreed to play, or Janamejaya's more general question about how such a morally problematic episode could have taken place. The dialogues about the dicing match demonstrate that there is no final answer to these questions, but nevertheless these are precisely the questions that the *Mahābhārata* invites us to ask and reflect upon.

In this chapter, we have seen that for Yudhiṣṭhira, Duryodhana, and Dhṛtarāṣṭra, an important part of the moral problems they face is not only what they decide to do, but how they understand their choices, how they explain their actions to others, and how they revisit and revise their explanations in different contexts as events unfold. Despite the many appeals to fate and predetermination, not to mention the doctrines of the divine plan and Kṛṣṇa's divinity, the characters in the *Mahābhārata* place an extraordinary amount of emphasis on their moral decision-making. In addition to articulating and reflecting upon their own choices, the characters in the *Mahābhārata* cannot help having reactive attitudes towards each other, expressing resentment and praise in response to each other's actions and behaviours. In other words, characters treat each other as moral agents who hold responsibility over their actions. But if this is one compatibilist solution, then another is the way that characters confront the limitations of human agency. The question for many characters is not whether or not they have the power to decide on their own actions, but rather how to act morally despite the fact that they might have limited control over their circumstances. While neither the characters in the narrative nor those of us who read about them are in complete control of our own destinies, the *Mahābhārata* suggests that external circumstances are not an excuse to avoid personal responsibility.

Notes

1 For further discussion on *pravṛtti* and *nivṛtti*, see Sutton (2000: 9–14) and Dhand (2008: 55–126).

2 Hill points out two rare examples of characters offering generous rationalisations of the actions of others. One example appears in the *Āśramavāsika Parvan*, when Yudhiṣṭhira claims not to blame Duryodhana for everything he had done because he was 'destined' (*bhavitavyaṃ*) to do what he did (15.6.10). Another example appears a bit further on in the same book (15.16.2–10), when a brahmin 'exonerates Dhṛtarāṣṭra, Duryodhana, and Karṇa from blame for the great destruction' (2001: 219).

3 One of the most famous examples is the so-called 'double introduction', which refers to two different conversations between Ugraśravas and the Naimiśa *ṛṣis* in the outer frame story. See Mehta (1973) and Adluri (2011).

4 I treat these four conversations as one version because they appear sequentially in the text and are clearly interlinked with each other. Although the second version of the Duryodhana/Dhṛtarāṣṭra dialogue appears to assume some of the details of these conversations, it does not seem to assume these exact accounts or this exact sequence.

5 There is no indication before the match that Yudhiṣṭhira had any association with playing dice. But on several occasions after the game, characters strongly associate him with gambling. In the *Karṇa Parvan* –perhaps with the death of his son in mind – Arjuna accuses his older brother of being addicted to the vice of dicing, calling him a gambler and blaming him for losing the kingdom (8.49.85–87). In the *Śalya Parvan*, Kṛṣṇa compares Yudhiṣṭhira's bad decision during the war to his decision to accept the invitation to play dice (9.32.7).

6 In this instance, *kali* probably refers generally to the terrible conflict the dicing match will cause. Wilmot, however, takes this as a reference to the four *yuga*s, which have names that correspond with the four throws of dice: Kali is

> the name of the last and worst of the four *yuga*s (aeons), the present age, the age of vice. There is possibly a pun here, for *kali* also refers to the side of the die marked with one dot, the losing die.
>
> (2006: 539)

7 Edgerton speculates that there must have been a version of the encounter between Vidura and Bhīṣma that got left out when the first version of the Duryodhana/ Dhṛtarāṣṭra dialogue got connected with the second (1944: xxxii).
8 The only other occasions in the Critical Edition are the *Āśramavāsika Parvan* when Vyāsa allows Dhṛtarāṣṭra to see the dead warriors (15.43.6) and at the very end of the text (18.5.6). Most manuscript traditions, however, also include three occasions when the narrative zooms out to the Ugraśravas frame in the *Nārāyaṇīya* section of the *Śānti Parvan*. Hiltebeitel (2006) has argued that these occasions should have been included in the Critical Edition.
9 We might conclude that Duryodhana's ability to recall in such detail all the gifts presented to Yudhiṣṭhira and exactly who gave them is because he was the one registering them at the ritual.
10 He does allude to this episode to Śakuni, but here suggests that he was humiliated by the guards, without mentioning the personal insults he received from the Pāṇḍavas, Kṛṣṇa, and Draupadī (2.43.35).
11 Additionally, rather than referring to the twins, as Vaiśaṃpāyana does, Duryodhana singles out Sahadeva.
12 As we will see in his exchange with Śakuni before the match, Yudhiṣṭhira also compares dicing to war, arguing that war is more honourable than gambling. Inversely, on several occasions, characters portray war as a form of dicing. In his dialogue with Saṃjaya leading up to *Bhagavad Gītā*, Dhṛtarāṣṭra compares the impending war to a dicing match (6.15.66–71).
13 As John Smith comments: 'The occasion referred to is described at 2.45, though that chapter contains little hint of the kind of advice that Dhṛtarāṣṭra is here said to have given his son' (2009: 619, no. 1).
14 Interestingly, Śakuni does not appear at all in this version, with Bhīṣma instead recounting that Duryodhana was with Karṇa (12.124.7).
15 I am following Smith and Wilmot, both of whom render *suhṛd* as 'friendly', and Bandyopadhyay, who – presumably with this word in mind – describes the match as 'pleasant, amiable' (2014: 16). It is worth noting, however, that van Buitenen's translation as 'family' does not quite have the positive connotations as the other renderings, but nevertheless still seems to describe the game as unthreatening, thus also implying a mischaracterisation of the type of match it will be.
16 Other characters who suggest that Yudhiṣṭhira has lost control of his senses are Vidura (2.55.5), the usher (2.60.4), and Vikarṇa (2.61.22). But none of them are present here, when Yudhiṣṭhira says so himself.
17 See, for example: Arjuna (5.47.85; 5.76.14), Kṛṣṇa (5.29.39; 5.126.4–7), Bhīṣma (5.138–148), and Saṃjaya (5.53.10; 5.156.11), as well as even Dhṛtarāṣṭra (5.56.26).
18 See Mehendale (1995: 37).

4 Draupadī's questions

Introduction

As we have seen in Chapter 2, Draupadī is married to the five Pāṇḍava brothers, the protagonists of the central narrative. In addition to being the heroine of the *Mahābhārata*, Draupadī is one of the most complexly developed female characters in any of the world's ancient literature. Her most famous scene is where she argues for her own freedom after she has been staked and lost by her husband Yudhiṣṭhira in the fateful dicing match. The Kauravas, who win the match, claim that they now own Draupadī as a slave-girl. As she makes her argument defending her autonomy, she is verbally insulted and sexually harassed. In her final address to the royal assembly, Draupadī asks the following questions:

> What is worse than that I, a virtuous woman (*satī*) and beautiful woman, now must enter the middle of the hall (*sabhā*)? What is left of the *dharma* of the lords of the earth? Formerly, we have heard, *dharma*-abiding women were not brought into the hall (*sabhā*). This eternal (*sanātana*) *dharma* is lost among the Kauravas. How can I, wife of the Pāṇḍus, sister of Dhṛṣṭadyumna Pārṣata, and friend of Vāsudeva, enter the hall of kings? I am the wife of King Dharma and equal to him by birth. Tell me: am I a slave or not a slave?
>
> (2.62.8–11)

This chapter will explore these and other questions that Draupadī raises in the assembly hall in the aftermath of the game of dice. As we will see, her first questions are about the procedure and legality of the game itself, but as the debate unfolds, she interrogates the basis of her social status as a woman and brings attention to her own virtuous behaviour. Because of the importance of this scene within the narrative, Draupadi's questions raise issues relating to the intersection between *dharma* and gender at the centre of the *Mahābhārata*.

In addition to analysing Draupadī's arguments, this chapter will discuss the arguments of two other women who debate in royal assemblies.

The first is Śakuntalā, who urges King Duḥṣanta to abide by his previous promise to recognise their son as the rightful heir to the throne; the second is Sulabhā, who challenges King Janaka's claim to be enlightened without being a renouncer. It is significant that Draupadī, Śakuntalā, and Sulabhā all make their arguments in the *sabhā*, in front of the king's assembly. In the *Mahābhārata*, the *sabhā* is depicted as where the king receives an audience, where moral questions are discussed, and where important political decisions are made. Alf Hiltebeitel has described the court as 'the epic's ultimate setting for constructing, deconstructing, and rethinking authority' (2001b: 240). By making their cases in the *sabhā*, Draupadī, Śakuntalā, and Sulabhā are all depicted as overtly political agents. Their arguments contribute to wider reflections upon *dharma* and gender relations, thus having far-reaching social and political implications. By looking at the debates featuring Draupadī, Śakuntalā, and Sulabhā together, I will argue that their words, actions, and circumstances contribute to emerging polycentric understandings of *dharma*, while also offering counter-perspectives to the *Mahābhārata*'s more patriarchal doctrines. Rather than rejecting *dharma*, they show that challenging dharmic authorities and assumptions is part of upholding a more general moral order.

Women and dialogue in the *Mahābhārata*

Nancy Falk once observed that some of the most complex discussions about *dharma* in the *Mahābhārata* are between men and women: 'the epic frequently develops its representations of ambiguities in the *dharma* in the context of conflicts between males and females' (1977: 105). Building on Falk's insight, in this chapter I will argue that female characters – particularly Draupadī, Śakuntalā, and Sulabhā – contribute to discussions on its ambiguities by exposing patriarchal biases in *dharma* and negotiating the possibilities for female agency. In the process, they contribute to ongoing debates by offering female perspectives to a pluralistic understanding of *dharma*.

For some scholars, female characters such as Draupadī, Śakuntalā, Sulabhā, and others represent anomalies to the *Mahābhārata*'s otherwise misogynist views and totalising statements about women. As Stephanie Jamison observes:

> We have the spectacle of a culture that professes to believe women are weak and silly embracing fictional females whose control of legal niceties or strategic planning far surpasses that of the men who surround them.
>
> (1996: 17)

Jamison explains this apparent contradiction as an 'almost accidental by-product of … conflicting (male) religious goals' (1996: 15–16). Arti Dhand has made the stronger claim that, because of the presumed male authorship of the *Mahābhārata*, the voices of female characters, 'even bold and powerful ones, nevertheless represent *male* opinions' (2008: 14; italics original). As she concludes: 'At no time, therefore, should we harbor any illusions that we are hearing *women's* perspectives' (2008: 15; italics original). The problem I see with these interpretations is that they restrict themselves from engaging with what the voices claiming to represent female perspectives actually say about women and gender. As Chakravarthi Ram-Prasad has argued, dismissing what a text says about gender because it was composed by men 'begs the question of what the text could possibly say about gender in the first place' (2018: 64).

As we will see, the arguments of Draupadī, Śakuntalā, and Sulabhā – as well as other female characters – explicitly address issues related to their experiences as women in complexly constructed ways. The *Mahābhārata* offers a particularly rich resource for exploring the gendered implications of the arguments made by both female and male characters because they speak with 'polyphonic voices'. Laurie Patton has demonstrated how Draupadī's words 'are not the monochrome statements of a *pativratā* [perfect wife], but rather, various voices ... which alternate between fierceness and meekness, savvy and servitude, authority and submission' (2007: 104). Although we cannot naively assume that the speech of female characters consists of the actual words of historical women, when we see them as complexly constructed 'dialogical selves', then we have much to learn from what Draupadī, Śakuntalā, and Sulabhā say about their experiences as women and about the female perspectives they offer to debates on *dharma*.

As I will argue, female characters such as Draupadī, Śakuntalā, and Sulabhā are not accidental by-products of male religious goals, but rather active participants in a sustained examination of *dharma* that prevails throughout the *Mahābhārata*. We can better understand the wider implications of their views when we try to make sense of their arguments from their unique perspectives within their debates. As we have seen in the Introduction, many characters argue that a true understanding of *dharma* necessitates an understanding of its various meanings and how they relate to each other in any given situation. Among the many meanings of *dharma* is *strī-dharma*, which is usually understood in term of the rules and roles that govern the totality of a woman's social interactions. As we will see in this chapter, rather than defining the *dharma* of women merely in terms of their prescribed responsibilities as wives and mothers, Draupadī, Śakuntalā, and Sulabhā offer female accounts of *strī-dharma* and its relationship with other *dharma*s. As they make arguments in the *sabhā* from their own unique circumstances and points of view, they invite their mostly male audiences to see *dharma* from their gendered perspectives. In the process, they add to the subtlety of *dharma* by showing that a female vantage point is an indispensable part of understanding *dharma*'s varieties and complexities. Taken together, their arguments strongly suggest that if part of *dharma* is engaging in a multi-perspectival moral reasoning, then a female perspective is integral to that moral reasoning.

Despite some sections of the text making totalising remarks about women, the dialogues featuring Draupadī, Śakuntalā, and Sulabhā complicate such views by highlighting the obstacles they face and the injustices they suffer as women. If we see the dialogical structure of the text as setting up 'contestatory' relationships, then, rather than contradictions or even paradoxes, Draupadī, Śakuntalā, and Sulabhā offer counter-perspectives towards the text's misogynist views. As I hope to demonstrate, when we listen to their arguments together, we can hear them not as lone voices of opposition, but as contributions towards a sustained criticism of the gender biases embedded within traditional understandings of *dharma*.

At the same time, Draupadī, Śakuntalā, and Sulabhā each have their own unique arguments to make. They share similarly gendered situations and make some overlapping points, but they do not say exactly the same things and do not speak from the same position. As Patton rightly observes: 'The *Mahābhārata* does not speak with a single voice when it comes to "women" or even "gender ideology"' (2007: 104). Draupadī, Śakuntalā, and Sulabhā each make arguments unique to their situations, emphasising different aspects of *dharma* and offering different types of female viewpoints in the process. By including the arguments and experiences of these three female characters, as well as others, the *Mahābhārata* offers a wide range of female perspectives, without reducing the experiences of women to one voice.

At the end of this chapter, we will review the arguments and experiences of Draupadī, Śakuntalā, and Sulabhā in relation to recent scholarly discussions about whether they can or should be considered feminists. As I will argue, the relationship between the views of women of the *Mahābhārata* and the views of feminist thinkers can be a fruitful discussion to have, but not for the sake of reifying feminism. Draupadī, Śakuntalā, and Sulabhā, as well as other female characters, have much to say in conversation with feminism – as well as conversations about gender in other contexts – but they make their most impactful contributions to these conversations when we evaluate their arguments from their own unique circumstances. In other words, we need to look at their arguments holistically, not only recognising their shared concerns with feminist issues, but also appreciating the ways that their outlooks remain unique to their own situations.

Draupadī in the *sabhā* (2.59–63)

Draupadī debates in front of the Kaurava royal assembly immediately after the dicing match. The Kauravas claim that they have won her as Yudhiṣṭhira's final stake, but Draupadī makes a compelling case for her own freedom. While articulating her arguments, she is dragged by her hair, insulted, almost stripped, groped, and sexually harassed. Falk has described this combination of slander and molestation as 'a sequence of the most intense insults to be found anywhere in the literature of the world' (1977: 99). Despite the extremity of the circumstances, Draupadī argues eloquently and tactically in front of a predominantly male audience, ultimately securing her own freedom and saving her husbands from servitude. This dramatic episode has received considerable scholarly attention and I will not describe it in all its details here. My focus is specifically on Draupadī's arguments, drawing attention to the different questions she poses and how they work together in making her overall case for her freedom. Before examining her arguments, however, let us briefly review the episode as a whole.

Draupadī's debate in the Kaurava court begins shortly after the infamous dicing match between her eldest husband, Yudhiṣṭhira, and her devious second-cousin-in-law, Śakuni. During the dicing match itself, Draupadī was in the women's quarters, because – as she will tell Duḥśāsana later – she was menstruating. Otherwise, she most likely would have been sitting with the Kuru women who are present in the *sabhā*. After Yudhiṣṭhira loses his final stake, Duryodhana orders an usher to bring Draupadī to the court to be the slave of the Kauravas. At this point, Vidura warns Duryodhana that his actions might come back to haunt him, pointing out that Yudhiṣṭhira 'was no longer his own master' when he made the stake (2.59.4). When the usher arrives in the woman's quarters, he tells Draupadī that Yudhiṣṭhira has been 'overcome by the intoxication of gambling' and that she has been won by Duryodhana (2.60.4). Draupadī's first questions about the implications of the match are directed towards the usher as she orders him to return to the hall to ask Yudhiṣṭhira about the order of the stakes.

When the usher announces Draupadī's question in front of the entire assembly, Yudhiṣṭhira remains silent, 'as though he had lost consciousness' (2.60.9). At this point, Duryodhana suggests that Draupadī should come to the hall to ask this question herself. When the usher arrives in the women's quarter to fetch her, Draupadī refuses to go. Finally, Duryodhana asks his brother Duḥśāsana to bring her before him. When Draupadī runs away, towards the Kuru women, Duḥśāsana chases after her, grabs her by her hair, and drags her across the assembly hall. Draupadī poses her second set of questions while being dragged by the hair by Duḥśāsana. As we will see, at this point she introduces new reasons to question the match, highlighting the subtlety of *dharma* and her own virtuous behaviour.

When she is brought before Duryodhana, Bhīṣma is the first to address her question. He reiterates her description of *dharma* as subtle, but he is unable to answer her question. Draupadī replies by expanding her criticism of how the game was played, now claiming that Yudhiṣṭhira was tricked. Finally, she reminds the assembly that her question needs to be answered (2.60.45). Draupadī's address here is the third time she articulates her objections to the stake.

At this point, Bhīmasena criticises Yudhiṣṭhira for staking Draupadī, threatening to burn his arms. Arjuna intervenes, saying that, by speaking such words to his elder brother, Bhīmasena has destroyed his respect for *dharma*. He then defends Yudhiṣṭhira's acceptance of the challenge as part of *kṣatriya-dharma* (2.61.9). After this squabble between the Pāṇḍava brothers, Vikarṇa – one of Duryodhana's younger brothers – speaks up to defend Draupadī, giving five reasons why he does not consider the outcome of the match legitimate: (1) the first is because gambling itself is abandoning *dharma* and therefore the actions of one who gambles should not be taken into account; (2) the second is because Yudhiṣṭhira was intoxicated by gambling; when making this argument, Vikarṇa also implies that Śakuni and Duryodhana did not play fairly; (3) his third is that Draupadī was not completely Yudhiṣṭhira's to stake, as she is also the wife of the four other Pāṇḍavas; (4) in his fourth point, Vikarṇa agrees with the argument already put forth by Vidura and Draupadī, that Yudhiṣṭhira had already gambled away his own freedom; and (5) his final point is that it was not Yudhiṣṭhira, but Śakuni, who suggested that Draupadī be staked. He concludes that she has not been won.

Karṇa completely dismisses Vikarṇa's case, but rather than offering any counterarguments to his points, he merely reiterates his position that she was won fairly. Still addressing Vikarṇa, but countering Draupadī's claim that it violates *dharma* for her to be dragged into the assembly hall, Karṇa argues that her marriage is undharmic in the first place. Karṇa then orders Duḥśāsana to strip the Pāṇḍavas and Draupadī. When the Pāṇḍavas take off their upper clothes, Duḥśāsana forcibly grabs Draupadī's garment. Duḥśāsana attempts to strip her by pulling at her sari, but her clothes miraculously replenish themselves.[1] Then Bhīmasena vows to tear open Duḥśāsana's chest and drink his blood. At this point, Vidura intervenes to tell the cautionary tale about the rivalry between Prahlāda and Kaśyapa. After narrating this story, Vidura urges those in the assembly to answer Draupadī's question. After this, Duḥśāsana drags Draupadī across the hall again. Crucially, Draupadī then poses her final set of questions. She continues to highlight her adherence to *dharma*, but here she adds another dimension to her overall argument by questioning the basis of her social identity.

Like before, Bhīṣma is the first to address her question; and again, he is unable to answer it. But here he praises Draupadī for acting according to *dharma*. Bhīṣma then defers to Yudhiṣṭhira, saying that he is the authority on her question. As Yudhiṣṭhira remains silent, Duryodhana addresses Draupadī, suggesting that one of her other husbands should speak on her behalf instead. Duryodhana then invites Yudhiṣṭhira to speak, but Yudhiṣṭhira again remains silent. At this point, Bhīmasena threatens to take revenge on the Kauravas, prompting three of the Kaurava elders – Bhīṣma, Droṇa, and Vidura – to tell him to control himself. Karṇa then enters the fray again, arguing that if Draupadī is the wife of a slave, then she herself must also be a slave. He instructs her to take another husband, accusing Yudhiṣṭhira of not valuing Draupadī. Then Duryodhana again invites Yudhiṣṭhira to speak. When Yudhiṣṭhira again remains silent,

Duryodhana looks at Draupadī and exposes his 'left thigh' (2.63.11).[2] In response, Bhīmasena announces that he will smash Duryodhana's left thigh with his club.

Again, Vidura intervenes, accusing the Kauravas of going too far and warning them that they are putting themselves in great danger. Vidura then restates his argument that the stake is invalid because it was made after Yudhiṣṭhira had already lost himself. Duryodhana declares that he will abide by what the Pāṇḍavas say, thus challenging the brothers to defy their brother Yudhiṣṭhira. Arjuna responds, saying that Yudhiṣṭhira 'lost himself' during the dicing match and was therefore no longer their master. At his point, the howl of a jackal – which is heard by a number of the Kauravas – prompts Vidura and Gāndhārī to warn King Dhṛtarāṣṭra that he is destroying his own household. Dhṛtarāṣṭra responds by granting Draupadī three boons. Draupadī chooses the freedom of Yudhiṣṭhira for her first wish, which she explains is for the sake of her children; and she chooses the freedom of her four other husbands for her second. Significantly, she declines a third wish. The fact that she does not take this opportunity to ask for her own freedom reinforces her conviction that she is already free.

Now that we have a sense of the debate as a whole, I will focus on three central aspects of Draupadī's overall case: (1) questioning the legitimacy of the stake; (2) interrogating the basis of her social status; and (3) highlighting her own adherence to *dharma*. As we will see, each aspect of her case offers a non-contingent reason to invalidate the Kauravas' claim to own her. Like Yudhiṣṭhira's defence of the polyandrous marriage, Draupadī uses a complex argument structure to challenge her interlocutors. At the same time, Draupadī grounds each of her arguments in *dharma*, yet in different ways. By following closely how Draupadī makes her arguments, we can get a better sense of their wider implications and how they resonate with the arguments of Śakuntalā and Sulabhā.

1) The legitimacy of the stake

As we have seen, Draupadī first learns about the result of the match when she is in the women's quarters and an usher brings her the news that Yudhiṣṭhira lost her because he was 'crazed by the dicing game' (2.60.4). Draupadī responds by amplifying the usher's characterisation of Yudhiṣṭhira's mental state, describing him as 'foolish' (*mūḍha*), in addition to being 'crazed by the game' (2.60.5). Perhaps she is thinking back to Yudhiṣṭhira's earlier admission that he had lost his reason. But with only limited information from the usher here, she already finds a potential loophole that might disqualify the match. She then solicits further details, asking whether there was nothing else left for him to stake. As it turns out, this was precisely the question to ask. When the usher responds, she learns that Yudhiṣṭhira lost himself first. Perhaps sensing that this might be enough to overturn the Kauravas' claim, she instructs the usher to return to the court to ask

Yudhiṣṭhira to confirm the order of his two final stakes: 'whom did you lose first, yourself or me' (2.60.7).

As Uma Chakravarti points out, Draupadī's question is rhetorical because the usher had already explained to her that Yudhiṣṭhira had lost his brothers and himself before losing her:

> She frames it thus even though she *knows* quite well what came first: clearly this rhetorical question is meant to raise the legality of the stake and get Yudhiṣṭhira to think about the 'lawfulness' of his act – the dharmik-ness of it – now that the momentary madness which gripped him seems to be over.
>
> (2014: 137)

In other words, by sending the usher back to the assembly hall, Draupadī extends her question about the stake to one about *dharma* more generally. As Hiltebeitel describes it, Draupadī 'definitely wants the question raised "in the sabhā," where she can expect it to be treated "in court" as a case of "law," dharma' (2001b: 242).

Draupadī further challenges the legitimacy of the stake in her exchange with Bhīṣma, just after she is dragged into the hall. As we have seen, when Bhīṣma is the first to respond to her question, he cannot offer a solution, citing the subtlety of *dharma*. He agrees with Draupadī that a man without property cannot stake property, but he also asserts that 'a woman is always subservient to her husband' (2.60.40). Bhīṣma concludes: 'therefore I cannot address your question (*praśna*)' (2.60.42).

Draupadī replies to Bhīṣma's equivocation by expanding her criticism of the procedural elements of the game, now claiming that Yudhiṣṭhira was tricked. As she describes, he was challenged by 'skilled gamblers' who are 'wicked, dishonest, and dishonourable' (2.60.43). Yudhiṣṭhira only went along with the game, she explains, because he was naive and inexperienced. Finally, she urges those assembled in the hall to answer her question (*praśna*) (2.60.45).

By indicating that Yudhiṣṭhira was tricked into playing and that Śakuni and the Kauravas cheated, Draupadī introduces further reasons for doubting the legality of the dicing match. By implication, she argues the result of this game should not be binding. Although Karna will insist that the rules of the game were followed (2.61.31–33), Draupadī's suspicions about the game are never fully addressed in this discussion. Indeed, all of her claims about the illegitimacy of the match have a basis in Vaiśaṃpāyana's narrative. After the very first throw, Yudhiṣṭhira accuses Śakuni of cheating (2.54.1), while Vaiśaṃpāyana describes Śakuni as 'resorting to trickery' almost every time he rolls the dice.[3] In subsequent sections of the text, in the *Udyoga Parvan* in particular, characters continue to voice suspicions that Śakuni cheated.[4] In other words, Draupadī's argument that the result of the game should not be binding is never countered, with doubts about the legitimacy of the game continuing to be voiced by other characters. Although Draupadī's other arguments will move away from procedural questions about the game, I interpret these legal considerations as giving her the opening to ask more far-reaching questions about *dharma*. As we will see, legal and procedural claims will also be important components of the arguments made by Śakuntalā and Sulabhā.

2) Social status

The second component of Draupadī's case is to interrogate the basis of her social status as a woman. Draupadī raises this issue in the series of questions she poses after Duḥśāsana's failed attempt to strip her:

> How can I, wife of the Pāṇḍus, sister of Dhṛṣṭadyumna Pārṣata, and friend of Vāsudeva, enter the hall of kings? I am the wife of King Dharma and equal to him by birth. Tell me: am I a slave or not a slave? (2.62.10–11)

Here, Draupadī brings attention to the complex web of social relations through which she has status. She begins with her social identity most relevant to the issue at hand – wife of the Pāṇḍavas. But by mentioning both her brother (Dhṛṣṭadyumna) and her friendship with Kṛṣṇa (Vāsudeva), she indicates that these men also contribute to her social identity.[5] We have already heard Bhīṣma's view that women are subservient to their husbands. Later in this debate, Karṇa will argue that Draupadī, as a woman, is by nature 'dependent' (*asvatantra*) (2.63.1). In using this term, Karṇa taps into more general views that women are dependent on their male relatives. For example, the *Mānava Dharmaśāstra* famously states that a woman is ruled over by men at each stage of her life – a father guards her in girlhood, a husband in her youth, and her sons in her old age (5.148; 9.3).[6] However, some characters seem to challenge this view. Duḥṣanta, as we will see, when he wants to seduce Śakuntalā, will argue that she rules over her own actions; and Sulabhā, in her argument with King Janaka, will claim that it is the king who is dependent, not her, as he has not become truly free from his worldly obligations. Another example, specifically related to the term that Karṇa uses here, is when Sūrya calls Kuntī *svatantrān* (3.291.13), which Hiltebeitel translates as 'free-female' (2011: 387–388), when he wants to have sex with her. In is notable that in the few examples we see here, when men want to have sex with women who desire them, then they are quite happy to acknowledge their independence, but when Draupadī is resisting servitude – which would include sexual servitude – the Kaurava men claim that she has no independence.

Although the very fact that she argues for her own freedom shows a resistance to Karṇa's claim that she is dependent, we should note that Draupadī never professes to be independent. By naming her brother and Kṛṣṇa,

Draupadī brings attention to her complex social identity. Here I take her references to the other men who contribute to defining her role within society as countering the Kauravas' claim that she would automatically become a slave just because her husbands have lost their freedom. In other words, I think we should see Draupadī's argument not about independence, but about inter-dependence – that there are a number of societal roles available for her without her husbands. In doing so, she also urges the Kuru elders in the hall – many of whom are her relatives – to act on their own responsibility towards her.

In the way she frames her final question, Draupadī equates her birth status with Yudhiṣṭhira's. Here, Draupadī implies that because she has had her social status since birth – and thus not through her marriage – then Yudhiṣṭhira losing his status should not equate to her losing hers. Chakravarti has argued that by invoking her birth identity, Draupadī reinscribes the hierarchy between royalty and slave:

> It is her own refusal to be a *dāśī* (slave) that leads her to ask the question in the way she does, framing it in a narrowly bounded way that works fully within a framework that accepts the master's right of lordship over his *dāśīs*, to do as they please. She never for a moment erases the difference between *Kṣatriya* princesses and *dāśīs*; she never once says: "you cannot do what you are doing, this violation of a woman's personhood, to any woman!" Her question is not *the* woman's question, it is the *Kṣatriyānī*'s question.
>
> (Chakravarti 2014: 150)

Chakravarti is right to highlight the unequal social dynamics that pervade this entire episode. Chakravarti also acutely observes that Draupadī is not making an argument for gender equality, but rather articulates her entire case within the specificity of her own situation. And, I agree with Chakravarti that Draupadī does not ask 'the women's question'. However, I think Chakravarti goes too far in suggesting that Draupadī's arguments do not reach beyond her own caste identity.

First, we need to keep in mind that this is not an abstract discussion about the *dharma* of women. Draupadī makes her entire case while she is verbally insulted and physically harassed. Considering the extreme circumstances she faces, we should appreciate that, rather than trying to make a case applicable to all women, she focuses all her attention on the issues that most directly relate to her own circumstances and makes the arguments that are tactically most likely to be successful. Moreover, although Draupadī clearly speaks from a position of privilege, I do not think her question reinscribes the differences between *kṣatriya* woman and slave as sharply as Chakravarti portrays it. In equating her own birth status with Yudhiṣṭhira's, Draupadī is not arguing that she cannot be a slave because she is a *kṣatriya*. Rather, her argument is that her social status is not derived from her husbands'. Seen from this perspective, although not an argument on behalf of all women, it is an argument based on her experiences as a woman and one that might resonate with other women, regardless of class differences.

3) Adherence to dharma

The third aspect to Draupadī's case is her emphasis on her own virtuous conduct. Draupadī begins this line of argument when she is being dragged by the hair by Duḥśāsana, informing him that she is menstruating and only wearing a single garment. Her point is to warn Duḥśāsana that it is a breach of *dharma* for her to be in the hall when menstruating.[7] By refusing to go to the court in this condition, Draupadī demonstrates her own adherence to established social norms, however restrictive they might be.[8]

When Duḥśāsana retorts that she has been won at gambling and is now the slave of the Kauravas, Draupadī then switches attention from her own moral conduct to *dharma* more generally, referring to Yudhiṣṭhira as the Son of Dharma and emphasising his adherence to *dharma*. She then says that '*dharma* is subtle (*sūkṣma*)' (2.60.31). As we have seen, this phrase is repeated throughout the *Mahābhārata*, but can have different connotations depending on the speaker and the context. Here, Draupadī is warning Duḥśāsana that there is a higher understanding of *dharma* than merely following the outcome of the game. She implicitly accuses Duḥśāsana and his brothers of not knowing this higher understanding of *dharma*. By referring to Yudhiṣṭhira as the Son of Dharma and repeating a phrase that he used when making his case for polyandry, Draupadī seems to expect him to intercede now as an authority on *dharma*. Instead, her words more closely match her brother's use of this phrase in that same discussion about her marriage – that because *dharma* is subtle, it is ambiguous and can become paralysing. Draupadī's questions will prove to be so subtle that the acute minds among the Kurus are unable to answer them. But by introducing a more general discussion about the nature of *dharma*, Draupadī shifts the focus from the result of the match to her actions and those of the Kauravas.

Draupadī explicitly points out that the elders in the hall are witnessing a savage breach of *dharma* (2.60.34). Here, she makes her case to the audience at large, juxtaposing her own blameless conduct with the Kauravas' blatant violation of *dharma*. In addition to pointing out the brutal behaviour of Duryodhana, Duḥśāsana, and Karṇa, she also accuses Bhīṣma, Droṇa, and Dhṛtarāṣṭra of lacking the resolve to intervene when they witness the *dharma* being destroyed (2.60.34). By referring to the *dharma* of the Bharatas, the *kṣatriya* way, and the limits of Kuru *dharma*, she points to the wider implications of their discussion. Implicitly, she argues that the Kauravas' behaviour demonstrates that they should not be the custodians of *dharma* – which is effectively what they would be if they were to get away with this result. By accusing the Kauravas of violating *dharma*, her argument shifts once again, this time to the restoration and preservation of moral order.

Karṇa's response is to cast doubt on her virtue. He reminds Draupadī and the assembly of the ambiguities surrounding her polyandrous marriage, claiming that it was undharmic:

> The Gods have laid down that a woman shall have one husband, scion of Kuru. She submits to many men and assuredly is a whore! (*bandhakī*). Thus there is, I think, nothing strange about taking her into the hall, or to have her in one piece of clothing, or for that matter naked!'.
>
> (2.61.35–36)

By mentioning the polyandrous marriage, Karṇa insinuates that Draupadī is not in a position to appeal to her own virtuous behaviour and, consequently, to speak for *dharma*. In addition to noting Karṇa's sexist insult, we should keep in mind that the discussions about Draupadī's marriage that we explored in Chapter 2 remain unresolved. Vyāsa and Yudhiṣṭhira may have persuaded Drupada to go along with the marriage, but their endorsements have not prevented others from viewing the marriage as a scandalous violation of *dharma*.

Returning to Draupadī's arguments, her final address to the assembly comes soon after Duḥśāsana's failed attempt to disrobe her. At this point, she cleverly apologises for not having paid her proper respects to her elders when she first entered the court:

> I have a *dharma* more pressing, which I could not perform before, confused as I was by this strong man who dragged me about forcibly. I must greet my betters in the assembly of the Kurus! Let it not be my fault, if I did not do this before!
>
> (2.62.1–2)

She then describes herself as a dutiful wife who has been confined to her home, not seen by either wind or sun since her marriage. By juxtaposing images of being dragged into the assembly hall, with how she has behaved throughout her life, as well as how she is conducting herself during this debate, Draupadī makes another strong contrast between her own impeccable behaviour and the unconscionable actions of the Kauravas. She also brings attention to her adherence to the ideal of the *pativratā* (devoted wife) – as confined to the home and not seen by any men in public. As Dhand explains, this ideal is particularly restrictive: 'The central tenet of the *pativratā dharma* is that a woman should hold her husband to be no less than God' (2008: 161). Here, we are reminded that despite any feminist implications of her arguments, her primary objective is to convince the Kuru elders that she is not a slave. She is not making an argument for gender equality, nor is she trying to challenge traditional gender roles.

Rather, her own adherence to the ideal of the *pativratā* is integral to establishing her virtuous conduct. But we should also keep in mind that when Draupadī invokes the ideal of the *pativratā*, her own understanding of this role is perhaps more complex than we might usually think. As we will see below, Patton, in her analysis of Draupadī's later dialogue with Satyabhāmā (Kṛṣṇa's wife), demonstrates that Draupadī, by adhering to the submissive aspects of her role as a *pativratā*, also gains supervision over her husbands and mastery over the palace treasury. Patton concludes that we learn from Draupadī 'something that most feminist analysis might not suggest: being a *pativratā* is a two-way street' (2007: 104).

Returning to Draupadī's debate in the *sabhā*, Bhīṣma is again unable to answer her questions. This time he says that *dharma* is merely the interests of the stronger: 'What a powerful man views as *dharma* in the world, that do others call *dharma* at a time when *dharma* is in question' (2.62.15). Although Bhīṣma appears to be saying something similar to Thrasymachus' argument about justice in Plato's *Republic* (338c), one difference is that Bhīṣma qualifies his position by suggesting that the stronger only impose *dharma* when it is in question. It is uncertain whether Bhīṣma has *āpad-dharma* in mind or more mundane disagreements about *dharma*. In any case, his comment highlights what is at stake in this discussion. If the Kauravas get their way, then they will be the custodians of *dharma*. Despite acknowledging the dire implications of what unfolds before him, Bhīṣma is once again unable to answer Draupadī's question. Although he equivocates, nevertheless he reinforces Draupadī's emphasis on her own virtuous behaviour by praising her actions: 'Your conduct is proper and appropriate, princess of the Pāñcālas; although you have come to grief, you still adhere to *dharma*' (2.62.20). Here we see that Draupadī might just be getting through to her royal audience.

Indeed, Dhṛtarāṣṭra implicitly refers to two of her arguments when he finally intervenes to settle the dispute by offering her a boon, saying that Draupadī is the most distinguished of his daughters-in-law and is intent on *dharma* (2.63.27). By referring to Draupadī as his daughter-in-law, he supports her claim that slavery is not necessarily the default position for her if her husbands lose their freedom. And by referring to her commitment to *dharma*, he affirms Draupadī's own arguments about her virtuous conduct. Dhṛtarāṣṭra reiterates these points when offering her a third boon, again referring to her as the most excellent of his daughters-in-law and a practitioner of *dharma* (2.63.33). As we have seen, Draupadī declines a third wish, explaining that greed destroys *dharma* (2.63.34). Considering the importance she places on her own adherence to *dharma* throughout her case, I think we can interpret Draupadī's abstention from a third wish as the final part of her argument that she is already free. Moreover, although Dhṛtarāṣṭra's intervention is initially prompted by the cry of the jackal, his comments indicate that Draupadī's arguments have made a direct impact on how he intervenes.

By constructing an argument around her own adherence to *dharma*, Draupadī taps into wider discussions in the *Mahābhārata* about *karma-yoga*. These arguments, as Dhand has argued, are potentially subversive because they are a 'reflection of the *Mahābhārata*'s larger extension of religious franchise to embrace all people, to dislocate piety and virtue from being the exclusive preserve of the priestly class' (2018: 102). But while these arguments have socially liberating potential, they can also be used to defend some of the most oppressive aspects of *dharma*. As we have seen, Draupadī demonstrates her virtuous behaviour by citing some of the most restrictive aspects of her role as a wife (*pativratā*). Dhand cites a similarly 'unsettling' episode from the *Āraṇyaka Parvan*, where a *pativratā* 'celebrates her subordinate status, claiming her subservience as the hallmark of virtue and deeming wicked any attempt at self-expression' (2018: 103). Dhand describes the *pativratā* as exemplifying

> a specific brand of *karmayoga*, that is *strī-dharma*, or the prescribed duties of women. In its directives, it is quintessential *karmayoga*: do your "duty" without desire or aversion, no matter how distasteful or debased ... do your duty even where it meets with indifference, neglect, or abuse.
> (2018: 100)

Clearly there are 'unsettling' aspects of *strī-dharma* in Draupadī's argument in the *sabhā*. But, as we have seen, Draupadī's own understanding of her role as a *pativratā* has empowering aspects as well. Moreover, unlike the *pativratā* of the *Āraṇyaka Parvan*, Draupadī's invocation of her subservient responsibilities as a wife does not prevent her from public self-expression. Rather, it is Draupadī's adherence to *dharma* that allows her to speak and compels Dhṛtarāṣṭra to intervene on her behalf. Although *dharma* can be oppressive and restricting, Draupadī, as well as Śakuntalā and Sulabhā, demonstrates that adherence to *dharma* gives her the authority to challenge dharmic authorities in the public arena of the *sabhā*.

Analysis of Draupadī's arguments

Despite the scholarly attention that this scene has received, many analyses have dwelled too heavily on Draupadī's first question, while missing out on how her argument evolves throughout this scene. B. K. Matilal, for example, characterised Draupadī's argument as a procedural one: 'the question that Draupadī asks was more concerned with the rights or legality of her husband's action than with the morality of the situation' (Matilal 1989: 2). Indeed, Matilal suggests that the *Mahābhārata* does not fully address the gender implications of Draupadī's question:

> Society still did not allow the wife any freedom or autonomy as an independent person. It regarded wives as "properties" of husbands, and

> hence can be staked in a gambling match. The incident seems to have a deep significance. If Draupadī's questions were properly answered, it would have required a "paradigm shift" in India's social thought.
>
> (Matilal 1989: 3)

Matilal is correct to characterise Draupadī's initial line of argument as about the 'legalities' of the stake, but he does not take into account how her case becomes increasingly about the intersection between *dharma* and gender as the scene unfolds. Indeed, when we follow the different components of her overall case more closely, as well as the different arguments made by other women in the text, then perhaps the *Mahābhārata* does give voice to a different paradigm in Indian social thought – not a different paradigm that eclipses a previous one, but one that remains in tension with it.

In contrast to Matilal, Hiltebeitel appreciates the more subversive potential of Draupadī's questions. In particular, he argues that Draupadī's point about Yudhiṣṭhira losing his state of mind might have wider philosophical implications about the self (*ātman*). In the previous chapter, we saw Yudhiṣṭhira tell Draupadī before the match that the he had lost his reason. As we have seen here, Vidura raises a similar concern before Draupadī enters the hall; and when the usher announces the result of the game, Draupadī's very first response is to echo his characterisation of Yudhiṣṭhira as 'crazed by the game'. Meanwhile, Vidura raises this issue once again, while both Vikarṇa and Arjuna refer to it as well. Hiltebeitel sees the discussion about Yudhiṣṭhira's loss of self as having philosophical implications: 'It is clear that in all this talk about betting oneself, Draupadī's question is a philosophical one about the nature of Self ... Yudhiṣṭhira's loss of self *appears* – it is only described so by others – to be a loss of consciousness. Is it the higher Self that is ultimately at stake in Draupadī's question?' (2000: 116–117). In bringing attention to the philosophical implications of Draupadī's question, Hiltebeitel notes the multi-dialogical reverberations that her verbal encounter has with dialogues in the Upaniṣads. By implication, Hiltebeitel suggests that Draupadī's debate with her male interlocutors is similar to the types of dialogues we see in the Upaniṣads that explore the nature of the self.

Although I would agree that there are important intertextual connections between the *Mahābhārata* and the Upaniṣads, I am not convinced that Draupadī's question is 'ultimately' about an ontological understanding of self. Rather, when Yudhiṣṭhira tells Draupadī that he has lost his reason (*prajñā*), his main point seems to be to avoid any culpability for bringing about the game – thus raising issues related to moral responsibility that we discussed in the previous chapter. Meanwhile, when Draupadī raises doubts about whether Yudhiṣṭhira has lost consciousness, her main objective is to offer another reason to challenge his final stake. She is not making an ontological point about *ātman*, but is questioning the legitimacy of the stake. It is worth clarifying what exactly Draupadī says about the self and what part it plays in her overall argument, because other women will talk about an ontological understanding of *ātman* much more explicitly. As we will see in our third dialogue, Sulabhā draws on an Upaniṣadic conception of the universality of the self to argue against gender discrimination. Here, however, Draupadī does not ground any of her arguments in such an understanding.

Like Matilal, Hiltebeitel focuses most of his attention on Draupadī's first line of questioning, without following up on her other questions as the discussion unfolds. As we have seen, we can gain a greater appreciation of Draupadī's overall case when we consider the different sets of questions she raises during the course of this debate. As her questions change, so does her argument, with her overall case for freedom resting on the fact that she offers a number of distinct reasons for doubting the Kauravas' claim to her. Each of her arguments exemplifies something different about *dharma*: (1) in questioning whether the rules of game have been followed, Draupadī taps into a legalistic, procedural understanding of *dharma;* (2) in invoking her birth status, she raises the question about which aspects of her social identity have priority over others; (3) in drawing attention to her own conduct, she invokes an understanding of *dharma* in terms of virtuous conduct. In combining these arguments, Draupadī offers three non-contingent reasons to support her case for freedom. At the same time, by demanding that her audience confront the abuses she suffers, she compels them to see the situation from her perspective, thus vividly exposing how, by following one set of dharmic criteria, the men in her family neglect to uphold other aspects of *dharma* – in particular, their duty to protect her and their responsibility to uphold a more general moral order.

Throughout the debate, Draupadī's arguments are presented in sharp contrast with the silences and equivocations of the male authorities on *dharma* assembled in the hall. As Emily Hudson describes it, the silence of the elders in this scene 'is one of the most hauntingly disturbing passages in the epic' (2013: 102). As we have seen, Bhīṣma – who is described as an authority on *dharma* and gives the text's most thoroughgoing teachings on *rāja-dharma*, *āpad-dharma*, *mokṣa-dharma*, and *dāna-dharma* in his long discourse to Yudhiṣṭhira in the *Śānti* and *Anuśāsana Parvan*s – twice addresses Draupadī without answering her questions. On the first occasion, Bhīṣma cites *dharma*'s subtlety to explain that he sees both sides of the issue. Although the subtlety of *dharma* is often characterised in terms of understanding a variety of perspectives, Vidura is absolutely clear that an understanding of *dharma* should not lead to silence. As he reminds the assembly: silence is not an option when *dharma* is being violated:

> If you do not resolve [Draupadī's question], men in this hall, *dharma* will be offended ... If a person sits in the hall and fails to answer a question, although he sees *dharma*, he incurs half the guilt that accrues if the answer is false.
>
> (2.61.52–57)

Vidura's warning, then, not only contrasts sharply with Bhīṣma's indecision, but even more so with the silence of Yudhiṣṭhira, who remains mute throughout this entire episode, even though he is repeatedly invited to speak, not only by Draupadī (2.60.7), but also by Bhīṣma (2.62.2) and Duryodhana (2.62.26). Although his silence can be explained in terms of him accepting the result of the match and resigning himself to the role of a slave,[9] I think we should also see his silence as a reflection on the limitations of his position as an authority on *dharma*. In other words, perhaps he is not merely acquiescing to the outcome of the game, but rather he has lost his position as an authority on *dharma* once his social status has been stripped away. Seen in this way, I would disagree with Hudson, who explains Yudhiṣṭhira's silence as 'a rupture, or gap in meaning, with the respect to the category of *dharma*' (2013: 102). Rather than a criticism of the category of *dharma* itself, this scene is an indictment of those who understand *dharma*, but who do not uphold it. Indeed, Draupadī's success in maintaining her own autonomy and recovering the freedom of her husbands demonstrates that it is not authority, but rather virtuous behaviour that upholds *dharma*. In contrast to Yudhiṣṭhira, Draupadī does not need an authoritative position to speak for *dharma*, but rather relies on her actions, as well as a more de-centred understanding of her social position. In other words, because her arguments do not explicitly rely on her status, she can speak for *dharma* even when her social position is put into question, while Yudhiṣṭhira cannot.

Throughout this scene, Draupadī argues eloquently and tactically in front of a predominantly male audience, maintaining her composure despite being insulted and molested on many occasions. Considering that by the end of the subsequent scene she is reduced to an exile who must wander in the forest and sleep on the ground for twelve years, any victory she achieves is both tainted and incomplete. Moreover, the long-term outcome of this entire discussion is that nobody wins. Armed conflict was only a vague possibility before the dicing game, but by the end of the post-match debate, war becomes almost inevitable. Not only does the breach widen between the Pāṇḍavas and Kauravas, but during the debate, members of both sides make specific vows to kill each other in battle. Nevertheless, considering that when she is initially dragged into the assembly hall the Kauravas claim that she and her husbands are their slaves, the fact that she is able to free her husbands and maintain her own autonomy shows that she emerges victorious. Ultimately, her arguments and demeanour convince King Dhṛtarāṣṭra to let her decide the outcome. At the end of the scene, even Karṇa – her most outspoken opponent – recognises her victory, saying: 'Draupadī has become the salvation of the Pāṇḍavas' (2.64.2).

Draupadī after the *sabhā*

Before turning our attention to Śakuntalā and Sulabhā, let us briefly survey some of Draupadī's most dialogical episodes after her argument in the *sabhā*.[10] What I want to emphasise is that she continues to support and resist traditional understandings of *dharma*. This complexity of her character is vividly articulated in Vaiśaṃpāyana's description of her as both a *pativratā* and a *paṇḍitā* (scholar) when introducing a dialogue she has with Yudhiṣṭhira in the forest about a year after the humiliating confrontation in the *sabhā* (3.28.2). As we have seen, Draupadī's enactment of her role as a *pativratā* is both restrictive and empowering. Meanwhile, Vaiśaṃpāyana's description of her as a *paṇḍitā* indicates that her views are considered to be philosophically significant.

During Draupadī's dialogue with Yudhiṣṭhira in the forest, the wounds of the dicing match and its damaging aftermath are still raw; it is striking, although not surprising, that neither of them mention anything that happened in the *sabhā*. In this scene, which has been discussed on numerous occasions,[11] Draupadī blames Yudhiṣṭhira for losing their kingdom, accusing him of being too passive. Rather than living out the twelve years in the forest, as they had agreed, Draupadī argues for taking revenge on the Kauravas immediately. At one point during their confrontation, she directly criticises the gods:

> I blame Dhātṛ ... If an act that has been done pursues its doer and no one else, then surely God is tainted by the evil he has done. Or if the evil that has been done does not pursue its doer, then mere power is the cause of everything, and I bemoan powerless folk'.
>
> (3.31.39–42)

Yudhiṣṭhira responds by accusing Draupadī of heresy (*nāstikya*) and then by advising her not to ask such questions, even for the sake of argument: 'Do not doubt *dharma*, either from arguing too much or from excitement. For the man who doubts *dharma* ends up an animal' (3.32.6). In addition to this rebuke from Yudhiṣṭhira, modern scholars have criticised Draupadī for showing this degree of scepticism. Angelika Malinar sees her *nāstikya* argument as 'crossing the line' (2007a: 88), while, more generally, Sally Sutherland characterises her as 'outspoken and aggressive' (1989: 63, 72). Meanwhile, Hiltebeitel has suggested that her heretical views might represent a version of ancient Indian materialism (2011: 506–516).

It is not clear to me, however, that what Draupadī says here really should be taken as heretical, especially in a text that represents such a wide range of views and encourages questioning and doubt. Considering his disastrous decision to play dice and his complete silence when the Kauravas were sexually harassing Draupadī in public, I do not think we should be too quick to take Yudhiṣṭhira's words as representing *dharma* here. Draupadī's adherence to and eloquence in *dharma* has just saved him and his brothers from servitude. His extreme criticism of Draupadī on this occasion not only seems like an overreaction, but also an offence, keeping in mind their still recent ordeal. Moreover, Draupadī's victory in the *sabhā* has just illustrated that authorities sometimes need to be questioned and challenged for *dharma* to be upheld. Despite everything that has happened to her and despite Vaiśaṃpāyana describing her as babbling from grief (3.33.2), Draupadī is still portrayed throughout the scene as presenting a carefully constructed and reasoned discourse, basing her points on traditionally accepted sources. In the same breath of accusing her of heresy, Yudhiṣṭhira praises her words as 'beautiful' (*valgu*), 'well-phrased' (*citrapada*), and 'polished' (*ślakṣṇa*) (3.32.1).

Moreover, the arguments she makes here are in line with authoritative views expressed in other sections of the text. When she declares that it is better to fail by acting than not to act at all (3.33.46–52), her argument follows Vidura's reminder in the *sabhā* that silence, or inaction, is not an option when *dharma* needs to be protected. Additionally, this view is similar to the one expressed in the *Bhagavad Gītā* by Kṛṣṇa to convince Arjuna to fight. A major difference between their arguments is, of course, that Draupadī's call for action is motivated by revenge, whereas Kṛṣṇa teaches that one must act without being attached to the consequences of one's actions. Nonetheless, the similarities in their points indicate that much of Draupadī's argument here is not particularly radical. Although she does not convince Yudhiṣṭhira, Vyāsa's later intervention in this discussion – as Malinar points out – suggests that 'both of their positions are partially accepted' (2007a: 81).

One of Draupadī's central points on this occasion – indeed, the final one she makes – is that there is not one course of action that is appropriate for all circumstances, but rather that actions are situational and conditional: 'the actual ways to success are declared to be various, as they depend on various times and conditions' (3.33.55). This view seems to coincide with her understanding of the subtlety of *dharma* that she expressed in the *sabhā* – that preserving *dharma* cannot be accomplished by adhering to a universal formula, but rather by adjusting to each particular situation. Rather than taking Yudhiṣṭhira's critique of her *nāstikya* argument as representing the authoritative point of view, I think we should see Draupadī as continuing to adjust to her circumstances. In the *sabhā*, her argument was firmly focused on maintaining her freedom. But now that she has saved herself and her husbands from servitude, she indicates that Yudhiṣṭhira should take responsibility for what has happened. Rather than offer any apologies or explanations for his inaction, however, Yudhiṣṭhira tells Draupadī that she is offending the gods. Instead of seeing Draupadī as crossing a line, I think we should see her as a *paṇḍitā* who continues to challenge authority for the sake of preserving *dharma*. As Falk observes, Draupadī 'persistently and perceptively lays bare the inconsistencies in Yudhiṣṭhira's supposedly righteous behavior' (1977: 96).

In addition to her disputes with male characters, she also participates in two of the *Mahābhārata*'s only prolonged dialogues between women – with Satyabhāmā (3.222–223) and with Queen Sudeṣṇā (4.8). In her conversation with Satyabhāmā (her cousin-in-law and Kṛṣṇa's wife), Draupadī outlines the ideal of the *pativratā* – the wife who is religiously devoted to her husband: 'My Law rests on my husband, as, I think, it eternally does with women. He is the God, he is the path, nothing else' (3.222.35). Yet she also explains how she manages the household and keeps track of the king's treasury. Moreover, twice she mentions her husbands' obedience to her (3.222.37, 56). As Patton argues, Draupadī not only conveys 'the classic *pativratā* devotion', but she also shows her 'awareness of the basic power dynamics between men and women, as well as her sense of her own powers and agency within a given situation' (2007: 100–101). Patton concludes that in this dialogue, as well as in her conversation with Sudeṣṇā, Draupadī has 'a polyphonic voice and a set of multifaceted roles which make it impossible to think of a single woman's voice embracing a single gender ideology' (2007: 104).

In addition to these dialogues where she takes on an active speaking role, Draupadī is present as a listener during some of the most important teachings and discussions in the *Mahābhārata*, including the many discourses and tales the Pāṇḍavas hear during their sojourn in the forest, as well as Bhīṣma's post-war instruction in the *Śānti* and *Anuśāsana Parvan*s – which includes, as we will see, the dialogue between Sulabhā and Janaka.[12] Draupadī's role as a listener not only establishes her as a well-educated and knowledgeable princess and queen (Black 2007b), but it also develops her character indirectly, as she hears stories about female characters in situations that mirror hers, such as Damayantī (whose husband loses his kingdom in a dicing match), Sitā (who is abducted while accompanying her husband on a forest exile), and Sāvitrī (who saves her husband through her tactical eloquence).[13]

By briefly surveying these dialogical episodes, we can see that Draupadī continues to be portrayed as both a *pativratā* and a *paṇḍitā*. Rather than revealing inconsistencies in her character or an anomaly in the text's otherwise patriarchal views, Draupadī continues to be an exemplar of virtuous conduct and to offer a critical perspective on traditional understandings of *dharma*. As we will see in the following two sections, Śakuntalā and Sulabhā face some of the same gender biases as Draupadī, while both make their own contributions to offering female perspectives on the subtlety of *dharma*.

Śakuntalā in the *sabhā* (1.62–69)

Another female character to make an argument in a royal assembly is Śakuntalā, who appears in the first book of the *Mahābhārata* (1.62–69). Śakuntalā lives in an ashram in the forest with her father Kaṇva, a renowned ascetic and scholar of *dharma*. One day, King Duḥṣanta, while out on a deer hunt, comes across the ashram and decides to pay his respects to the sage. With her father away, Śakuntalā offers the king a seat, water to wash his feet, and a guest gift, while asking about his health and well-being. Struck by her manner of speaking, Duḥṣanta asks her to be his wife by the rite of the *gandharva*s – which basically means by mutual consent. At first, Śakuntalā suggests waiting for her father to return, but the king assures her that she can give herself away: 'Oneself (*ātman*) is one's own best friend, oneself (*ātman*) is one's only recourse. You yourself can make the gift of yourself dharmically' (1.67.7).

Here, Duḥṣanta, when trying to persuade Śakuntalā to have sex with him, makes a case for her independence. He insists that she does not need her father's consent, but can speak on behalf of herself.[14] By using the term *ātman*, Duḥṣanta invokes an understanding of a universal self that is as much the ultimate identity of women as it is of men. As we have seen, this is the type of argument that Draupadī does not make. Intriguingly, Duḥṣanta seems to have a much different view of women's agency than the Kauravas do when they tell Draupadī that she cannot be independent. If we were to follow the logic of Karṇa's arguments from the previous dialogue, then Duḥṣanta should not be able to make this claim, as Śakuntalā could never be independent. But by citing the *gandharva* type of marriage, Duḥṣanta defends Śakuntalā's autonomy in terms of a widely accepted practice. Here, we see a vivid example of the type of ambiguities in dharmic authority that both Draupadī and Śakuntalā expose. Duḥṣanta is more than happy to acknowledge that Śakuntalā can speak for herself when her words can lead to the satisfaction of his own desires, but later in the royal assembly he will say that women cannot be trusted.

Śakuntalā gives a conditional reply to Duḥṣanta's marriage proposal:

> If this is the path of *dharma*, and if I am my own lord, then, chief of the Pauravas, this is my condition in giving myself in marriage. Give your own true promise to the secret covenant I make between us: the son that may be born from me shall be Young King to succeed you, great king, declare this to me as the truth.
>
> (1.67.15–16)

The king affirms that he will be true. Then, after they have sex, he announces that he will send for her and any child she might have. Notably, Vaiśaṃpāyana describes Duḥṣanta's words as a promise (*pratijñā*) (1.68.1), using the same term that he used to describe Bhīṣma's vows of renouncing the kingdom and practising celibacy (see Chapter 1). Several years later, when Duḥṣanta has betrayed his word by not sending for her or their son, Śakuntalā goes to his court to ask him to remember his former promise.[15] By beginning her case from the king's promise, Śakuntalā exposes another patriarchal bias in *dharma* – that promises made between men tend to be considered more binding than those a man makes to a woman. Crucially, the way that Vaiśaṃpāyana tells this story makes it clear that Duḥṣanta does indeed remember her. When she first arrives at Duḥṣanta's court, she is 'recognised' (*vidita*) and 'admitted' (*praveśita*) (1.68.14). Meanwhile, Vaiśaṃpāyana says that Duḥṣanta 'remembered very well' (*smara api*)

(1.68.18). But despite acknowledging Śakuntalā in private, in public he denies knowing her. Indeed, he even insults her, calling her an 'evil ascetic' (*duṣṭatāpasi*) and telling her to leave (1.68.18).

Although Śakuntalā is 'overcome with shame' and 'stunned with grief' (1.68.20), Vaiśaṃpāyana describes her as maintaining self-discipline: 'Yet, although driven by her fury, she checked her expression and controlled the heat (*tapas*) that had been accumulated by her austerities (*tejas*)' (1.68.22). Here, Vaiśaṃpāyana's narration brings attention to the way that Śakuntalā' conducts herself. Indeed, more explicitly than in the case of Draupadī, Vaiśaṃpāyana describes Śakuntalā's conduct in ascetic terms, referring to the self-control she has developed through her practice of austerities.

Śakuntalā proceeds with her argument, pointing out that Duḥṣanta is lying not only to her, but to himself, to the gods, and to the entire assembly. She then discusses the duties of a wife (1.68.36–52) and the importance of sons (1.69.53–65). Here, like Draupadī, Śakuntalā refers to a number of subservient aspects of the expectations of a *pativratā*: looking after the house, bearing children, and treating her husband as a lord. Like Draupadī, Śakuntalā is not attempting to redefine gender roles, but is grounding her arguments in her own adherence to her *dharma* as a wife. But at the same time, she characterises their relationship in terms of interdependence, describing a wife as half the man and the root of *dharma*. By implication, she suggests that Duḥṣanta is not fully himself without her and, therefore, cannot speak on behalf of *dharma* without her.

Despite her arguments, the king continues to deny knowing her, while blatantly accusing her of lying: 'I do not know that this is my son you have born, Śakuntalā. Women are liars – who will trust your word?' (1.68.72). Duḥṣanta also delivers more insults, condemning her for speaking like a 'whore' (*puṃścalī*) (1.68.75), while again calling her an 'evil ascetic' (1.68.76). The king then describes Śakuntalā's birth status as 'very humble', again calling her 'whore' (1.68.79). Here we see that, like Draupadī, Śakuntalā has to endure blatantly sexist insults from her male interlocutor.

Śakuntalā retorts that she has a higher birth status than Duḥṣanta, before proclaiming truth as the highest *dharma* and urging the king one more time not to forget their agreement (*samaya*) (1.69.24–25). Finally, she declares that even without Duḥṣanta's acquiescence, her son will rule the earth. She then dramatically walks out of the assembly hall. Upon leaving, a heavenly voice announces that Śakuntalā has spoken the truth and instructs Duḥṣanta not to reject her. Yet, even upon hearing this divine endorsement of Śakuntalā's words, the king does not immediately accept her, first making sure that his chaplain and councillors had heard the voice as well. At this point, Duḥṣanta admits that he knew Śakuntalā was speaking the truth all along, but explains that if he had taken her word, then his people would have remained suspicious (1.69.36).[16] In an irony seemingly lost on only the king himself, Duḥṣanta then forgives Śakuntalā for her harsh words, yet without offering any apologies for the insults he has directed at her. Nonetheless, the story ends in an upbeat fashion, with Vaiśaṃpāyana recounting that the son of Duḥṣanta and Śakuntalā subsequently became a great king named Bharata – the progenitor of the heroes of the *Mahābhārata*'s main story.

Like Draupadī, Śakuntalā bases much of her argument on her understanding of legal and traditional understandings of *dharma*. She first does this in the forest when she secures a promise from the king. Later, in the *sabhā*, she demonstrates her knowledge of traditional gender roles, drawing on this understanding of *dharma* when she cites the duties of a wife towards her husband. Throughout her argument, she also demonstrates her brahminical upbringing in the ashram of the famous sage Kaṇva by citing a number of traditional sources – such as the 'old poets' (1.68.36), Svayaṃbhū (1.68.38) 'the wise' (1.68.47), the Vedas (1.68.61), and Manu (1.69.18).

In another similarity with Draupadī, Śakuntalā grounds her arguments in terms of virtuous conduct. In addition to her self-control, her most vivid expression of following *dharma* is speaking the truth, which is sharply contrasted both with Duḥṣanta's explicit dishonesty and his accusation that Śakuntalā is lying. When Duḥṣanta publicly calls Śakuntalā a liar, his words tap into recurring prejudices in the *Mahābhārata*, as well as in the Dharma Śāstras, that women cannot be trusted. Duḥṣanta's actions suggest that he thinks it is more important to be perceived to be following *dharma* than to act in accordance with what he knows to be true. In other words, Duḥṣanta speaks in terms of *dharma*, but acts in ways that undermine his claims. That he is willing to lie publicly about the future of the lineage in front of the entire assembly to maintain his power reveals tensions between *rāja-dharma* and *kula-dharma* – between Duḥṣanta's responsibility to his kingdom and to his wife and son. These *dharmas* not only clash, but Duḥṣanta's treatment of Śakuntalā exposes the brutality of *rāja-dharma*, raising the question of how it can protect the kingdom when it cannot protect his wife and son. Duḥṣanta's behaviour also exposes blindspots within *rāja-dharma* itself, as he prioritises what he perceives to be his subjects' concerns in the short-term in place of the long-term dynasty. In publicly denying that Śakuntalā is telling the truth, Duḥṣanta risks the future of the lineage.

By exposing the king's lies and demonstrating her own truthfulness, Śakuntalā offers a counter-perspective, not only to Duḥṣanta's accusations, but also to the *Mahābhārata*'s misogynist claims about women. Like Draupadī, Śakuntalā uses the public dimension of the king's court to bring attention to the veracity of her arguments, pointing out that Duḥṣanta should speak truthfully because the gods and the assembly are listening to his words. She suggests that the king should be his own witness (*sākṣin*) (1.68.25), and she even points out that the king is not alone in himself, because he has an ancient seer inside him who observes all his evil deeds (1.68.27).[17] Śakuntalā's appeal to this multilayered audience does not convince Duḥṣanta, but her warning proves true in the end, as it is a divine witness, the heavenly voice, who ultimately determines the outcome of the story. Śakuntalā wins this debate, not because she is able to convince Duḥṣanta to speak the truth, but because she is more successful in convincing her wider audience.

At the end of the story, Śakuntalā is successful in securing the role of crown prince for her son and of queen for herself. However, her victory is compromised by the verbal insults she endures and the need for the intervention of a celestial voice to legitimise her words. As wife of the king, Śakuntalā is in the unique position of questioning *dharma;* she suffers the consequences of a king who neglects his duties to her because he is following what he perceives to be his royal responsibilities. In this way, she embodies the negative consequences for women when men follow a patriarchal understanding of *dharma* without reflecting on the consequences of their actions. In contrast to her husband, Śakuntalā demonstrates her adherence to *dharma* through the consistency between her speech and actions.

Taking into account the many resonances between these episodes, we might see Śakuntalā's confrontation with Duḥṣanta as foreshadowing Draupadī's ordeal after the dicing match. Indeed, as a princess well versed in traditional knowledge, we might expect Draupadī to know the story of Śakuntalā – the foremother of the family she has married into – and perhaps take inspiration from her when finding herself in an even more challenging situation.

Sulabhā in the *sabhā* (12.308)

Our third dialogue, from the *Mokṣadharma* section of the *Śānti Parvan*, features the female sage Sulabhā in a debate with King Janaka. This dialogue does not appear in the main story, but is told by Bhīṣma to Yudhiṣṭhira as part of his long instruction after the great war. Bhīṣma describes Sulabhā as a renunciate, who practises *yoga*, has wandered the earth on her own, and has attained *mokṣa* – characteristics that are extremely rare for a woman in brahminical literature. It is also important to keep in mind throughout our discussion of Sulabhā, that Draupadī is present during Bhīṣma's narration of this episode.

This episode begins with Sulabhā hearing reports from other renouncers that King Janaka has achieved *mokṣa* without giving up his kingdom. Doubtful of these claims, she uses her yogic powers to put on an immaculately beautiful body and travel to the court in the wink of an eye, to find out for herself about Janaka's claims to have attained enlightenment. When she arrives, after accepting the king's hospitality, she challenges him to an argument in front of the assembly. At this point, she uses her knowledge of *yoga* and enters into the king's being (*sattva*) with her being (12.308.16). One of the most intriguing aspects of this dialogue is that Sulabhā conducts her entire argument while dwelling within Janaka. As indicated by the *Yogasūtra* and other sources, the ability to inhabit another's body was widely accepted to be a power attained through the practise of *yoga*.[18] We can see, then, that an important implication of Sulabhā residing in Janaka's body is her demonstration of her yogic abilities.

Despite arguing within the same body, both Janaka and Sulabhā refer to the public dimension of their debate. After posing his first set of questions, Janaka asks Sulabhā to respond 'in this assembly of the good' (*satsamāgama*) (12.308.21); and before concluding, he accuses Sulabhā of plotting to take over his 'entire court' (12.308.66). Although it remains unclear, these references to the court imply that an audience can see Janaka and hear both voices emerging from him. If this is the case, then the audience in King Janaka's court would witness the rather humiliating situation of the king losing an argument that takes place inside his own body.

Janaka speaks first, posing a series of questions to Sulabhā about her social identity:

> Whose are you? And where are you from?... I cannot get a clear sense of your learning, of your age, or of the ethnic group you were born in, so please convey answers to these matters in this assembly of the good. (12.308.20–21)

Janaka returns to these questions throughout his argument, challenging Sulabhā's claim of achieving *mokṣa* by questioning her social identity in terms of class, family, and gender. Some of his accusations are explicitly discriminatory: at one point, he questions how she can be an ascetic when she is so young and beautiful (12.308.54); further on, he calls her 'wicked' (*duṣṭā*) (12.308.65), echoing the insult that Duḥṣanta directed towards Śakuntalā. As we can see, like Draupadī and Śakuntalā, Sulabhā not only encounters the gendered prejudices of her male interlocutor, but also endures his sexist insults.

In addition to challenging Sulabhā's ability to be enlightened, Janaka vehemently defends his own claims to have attained *mokṣa*. Grounding his position in *karmayoga*, he maintains he can achieve enlightenment without renouncing the world. He declares himself beyond *karma*, claiming that his knowledge keeps his actions from producing results, like a seed that has been roasted can no longer germinate (12.308.33). Janaka argues that *mokṣa* is not achieved by renouncing possessions, but rather through knowledge that releases one's bonds with the world. As we will see in the following chapter, this argument is similar to one of Kṛṣṇa's central teachings in the *Bhagavad Gītā*. It is interesting here, though, that Sulabhā rejects *karma-yoga*, making the case that one must live the life of a renouncer in order to achieve enlightenment. According to Nicholas Sutton:

> For Sulabhā, the compromise offered by Janaka and the *Gītā* is trite and specious, at best an attempt to serve two masters, at worst ... a sop

to the vanity of kings who wish to enjoy the delights of power and still claim superiority over members of the ascetic orders.

(1999: 61)

Sulabhā begins her response by outlining the characteristics of a proper argument. She describes five aspects of speech: subtlety (*saukṣmya*), deliberation (*saṁkhyā*), clear order (*krama*), a conclusion (*nirṇaya*), and purpose (*saprayojana*), in each case giving an example to illustrate her point. She then explains how she will articulate her speech, promising not to say too much or too little, not to say anything off-topic or untrue, adding that she will not be affected by emotions such as love, anger, fear, or greed. Here, she brings attention to her own philosophical training, while characterising Janaka's entire case as unsophisticated and confused. Arindam Chakrabarti, who describes Sulabhā discourse as 'a formal meta-discourse on the ethics of discourse' (2014: 262), draws some interesting parallels between the requisites of proper speech that she lists here and the rules of debate as outlined in the *Nyāya Sūtra* (2014: 264–265). We might also see Sulabhā as making a similar move to both Draupadī and Śakuntalā, who – as we have seen – highlight their understandings of proper procedural aspects of *dharma* and their own educational backgrounds.

Sulabhā then addresses Janaka's questions about her identity from a completely different perspective. Rather than speak of herself in terms of social roles, she talks about herself from a psycho-physical point of view. Using Sāṃkhyan terminology, she discusses twenty components that are responsible for the origination and passing away of beings, explaining that there is an unmanifest nature (*prakṛti*) that becomes manifest in these twenty components. Within this Sāṃkhyan scheme, there are physical differences between men and women, but they are not characterised as essential to one's overall identity (12.308.118). As Ram-Prasad explains: 'Sulabhā recognizes the morphological role of sex-properties that mark the developing human being, but gives it just one, contingent place in development' (2018: 83). More generally, Sulabhā argues that if Janaka were truly enlightened, he would not have been concerned about her social identity: that his question of who she is – from the point of view of an enlightened person – can only be discussed in terms of the combination of the twenty components in the context of which gender anatomical differences are just one component within a complex matrix that characterises a human being. She then summarises this discussion of the twenty components by making an analogy with fire: 'Just as fire comes to be from the combination of the sun, a crystal lens, and some twigs for tinder, so beings come to be from the combination of their components' (12.308.125).

At this point, Sulabhā poses a crucial question: 'Since you see yourself within yourself by means of yourself, why do you not, in exactly the same way, by means of yourself, see yourself in someone else?' (12.308.126). This question has generated considerable debate among scholars. Ruth Vanita interprets Sulabhā's question as making an argument for gender equality based on the universality of the self. According to Vanita, Sulabhā's point is that *ātman* 'is one and the same in all beings, regardless of the body's gender' (2003: 88). Fitzgerald, however, suggests that Sulabhā's words here neither match any of Janaka's earlier claims nor seem to fit with her own position (2002a: 674). As he points out, 'Sulabhā's later statement of the "singleness and separateness" of the soul (*jña*) at 308.176' contradicts her question here, which he understands as 'an expression of monistic soteriology' (2002a: 674). Taking Fitzgerald's suggestion into consideration, Ram-Prasad interprets Sulabhā's question as pointing out the inconsistency between Janaka's claim to enlightened status and the way that he treats others. In other words, Ram-Prasad takes Sulabhā's words as highlighting a contradiction between the king's words and actions, but not as representing her own commitment to an ontology of the self. As he explains, Sulabhā's 'interest is not in the metaphysics, but in the psychological consequences that would result from a freedom that treated everyone as the same' (2018: 85). Ram-Prasad further asserts that Sulabhā is 'altogether rejecting the doctrine that absolute freedom consists of the realization that one is fundamentally a neutral self (*ātman*)' (2018: 87).

Although this is an intriguing reading – and one that resonates with the arguments of feminist philosophers who reject claims to neutrality – I think this interpretation goes too far in disassociating Sulabhā's question here from her overall position. Ram-Prasad justifies his reading by claiming that Sulabhā otherwise does not seem to posit a notion of a universal self. He argues that 'at no point does she seem to think that there is a pure collection of selfhood behind the compositionally detailed ecologically embedded, bodily person' (2018: 87). It seems to me, however, that Sulabhā's use of the fire metaphor leading up to her question does imply some sense of an *ātman* behind the 'ecologically embedded, bodily person'. A few passages before asking Janaka this question, Sulabhā asks rhetorically: 'What is the connection between beings and the components that make them up?' (12.308.124). Then, in the fire analogy that immediately precedes her question, Sulabhā – as Fitzgerald points out – emphasises 'the theme of unifying a plurality (*samudaya*)' (2002a: 674). With this in mind, it would make sense if she sees the twenty components as unified in the *ātman* in the same way that she sees the sun, a crystal lens, and twigs for tinder as unified in fire. Additionally, the fact that, as Fitzgerald points out, Sulabhā talks about the self here in a way that is not specific to Janaka's own arguments could indicate that this view is more representative of her outlook than his. Meanwhile, I do not think that Sulabhā's later statement about the 'singleness and separateness' of the soul (*jña*) precludes her from conceptualising an individuated self that is beyond gender and operates the same way in all beings. Although questions remain about what precisely Sulabhā's ontological position is, I do not think we should take her question as a 'dismissal of the plausibility of such a concept in the first place' but rather as an assertion that from an enlightened perspective the universal self is beyond gender.

Throughout, a major theme in this dialogue is the gender difference between Janaka and Sulabhā, particularly in relation to the curious circumstances of both characters inhabiting the same body during their discussion. Janaka accuses Sulabhā of joining herself inappropriately with a man from a different social order, claiming that she has crossed distinctions of both caste and clan. Furthermore, Janaka argues that one who is unenlightened should not be joined with one who is enlightened, and that Sulabhā should not give herself to another man if she already has a husband (12.308.62). In all of these accusations, Janaka suggests that there is a physical dimension to her inhabiting his body. Further on, he alludes to a sexual dynamic of their interaction, arguing that one who is a renouncer should not still love and comparing their encounter to a man and a woman who desire each other (12.308.69). At the very end of his diatribe, he instructs Sulabhā that the power (*bala*) women have is their beauty, youth, and charm – insinuating that it is not possible for a woman to be an enlightened renunciate. As Chakrabarti nicely describes it, Janaka 'refused to recognize that it was he who had been smitten by Sulabhā and not the other way around' (2014: 260).

In her rebuttal, Sulabhā maintains that her yogic powers afford her the ability to dwell inside him without touching him, and, consequently, that there is no actual mixing or merging going on. Furthermore, she challenges Janaka's arguments about her social identity: she claims she is not a brahmin, but a *kṣatriya*; she is not unfaithful because she has no husband; she is the one who is enlightened and if he were enlightened she would not be able to inhabit his body; and, finally, if Janaka were truly enlightened, these class distinctions would not matter anyway. Sulabhā's inhabitation of Janaka's body, then, actively demonstrates her philosophical point – despite bodily appearances and social constructs, there is no ontological distinction between them. Through both her arguments and her actions, Sulabhā represents a model for enlightenment that is beyond the dualities of gender distinction and therefore as available for women as for men.

As an ascetic who lives on her own and who has achieved *mokṣa*, Sulabhā provides another response to Draupadī's question about whether independence is possible for her as a woman. Sulabhā has achieved *mokṣa* by herself, while living 'all alone' and 'according to the hermit (*muni*) way of life' (12.308.184). Although Sulabhā grounds her argument in her claim to have an enlightened perspective, here she also emphasises her adherence to the social conventions of a renouncer (*mokṣa-dharma*). Not only does she abide by the hermit way of live, but also claims: 'I hold firm to the practices of my own *dharma* (*sva-dharma*). I do not waiver in my promises; I do not speak without careful examination' (12.308.185–186). In making these points, Sulabhā brings attention to the social practices that contribute towards living the life of a renouncer.

In addition to demonstrating her independence, Sulabhā also argues that King Janaka cannot be free because of the many ways he, as king, is necessarily immersed in social relations. At one point she asks: 'How could the king be independent (*svatantra*)' (12.308.138). Here, Sulabhā seems to provide a direct rebuke to Karṇa, who – as we have seen – maintains that because she is a woman, Draupadī cannot be independent (*svatantra*). While the Kauravas object to the possibility that a woman can be free, Sulabhā makes it clear that a woman can achieve absolute freedom. Although Sulabhā, whose dialogue takes place in a former age, could not deliberately use the same word as Karṇa did, Bhīṣma – who is narrating this encounter – very well could have, perhaps with a glance at Draupadī at this point in his account. Indeed, in telling this story with Draupadī present, we might see Bhīṣma's narration of this episode – after failing to provide an answer in the *sabhā* – as finally responding to Draupadī's question. In any case, we might wonder what Draupadī herself is thinking, hearing Sulabhā's words while perhaps reflecting back on her own debate in the royal assembly.

Conclusion

We began this chapter with Nancy Falk's observation about dialogues between women and men exploring ambiguities in *dharma*. As we have seen, Draupadī, Śakuntalā, and Sulabhā not only explore ambiguities in *dharma*, but ambiguities that are specifically related to their experiences as women. None of them are literary characters who just happen to be female, as if what they experience, what they say, and how they act have nothing to do with their gender. Rather, each of them, from the very beginning of their encounters, confronts the gendered prejudices, words, and behaviours of their male interlocutors. Because they make their arguments from a distinctly female perspective and explicitly interrogate traditional gender biases, many scholars have discussed whether Draupadī, Śakuntalā, and Sulabhā can be seen as feminists. Hiltebeitel calls Draupadī an 'ambivalent feminist', saying that 'she speaks about, and publicly for *women as a class*, and challenges the men to consider a question that questions their lordship over and "ownership" of women in contexts of patriarchy' (2000: 116). Hiltebeitel rightly highlights lordship as a question 'that an interculturally sensitive feminism might find interesting, and one that Indian feminists sometimes find it worth writing and thinking about' (2000: 118). As much as I agree with Hiltebeitel that Draupadī asks 'a woman's question', however, I think he goes too far in suggesting that she asks '*the* women's question' (2000: 125; italics original). Indeed, Chakravarti rejects the label of feminist for Draupadī precisely because 'her question is not *the* woman's question', but 'the *Kṣatriyānī*'s question' (2014: 150; italics original). We might add that neither Śakuntalā nor Sulabhā set out to ask questions on behalf of all women either.

Although I agree with Chakravarti that Draupadī does not ask a question on behalf of all women, I think Draupadī's arguments have broad appeal beyond both her caste and gender. As with many characters in the *Mahābhārata,* she makes arguments rooted in a multi-perspectival understanding of *dharma* within the context of her own experiences. Draupadī does not ask '*the* woman's question' to be sure, but the specificity of her subject position does not limit the relevance of her arguments only to women who share her social standing. Arguably, her multi-tiered reasons grounded in her own unique – but specifically gendered – circumstances make her arguments more versatile for other women, as well as for men, than if she had attempted to speak for all women. Moreover, Draupadī, despite facing similar obstacles and making overlapping arguments, makes different arguments from those of Śakuntalā and Sulabhā. The distinctive voices of these three female characters, along with other others, demonstrate that the *Mahābhārata* does not represent women as one monolithic category, but rather as diverse dialogical selves.

Ram-Prasad warns against what he calls 'the empty task of deciding whether an ancient text is feminist, and if not, whether it then ceases to have all possibility of being read through today's feminist insights' (2018: 64). In his analysis of the Sulabhā-Janaka debate, he avoids this task by offering a critical engagement between the arguments of Sulabhā and a number of feminist thinkers. As he shows, this is a more productive engagement when we highlight the differences between feminism and the women of the *Mahābhārata*, rather than try to evaluate their arguments through feminist lenses. Throughout this chapter, I have attempted to follow this approach by reflecting on how Draupadī, Śakuntalā, and Sulabhā construct their overall arguments, rather than only on the claims they make with possible feminist concerns.

One clear way that these women from the *Mahābhārata* differ from most modern feminist thinkers is that they do not set out to make arguments in favour of gender equality. Draupadī and Śakuntalā, in particular, make arguments that many feminists would find too supportive of patriarchal structures. Draupadī does not challenge the traditional roles expected of her as a women, including those that are most restrictive. Similarly, Śakuntalā's main objective is to retain the birthright of her son, as well to hold Duḥṣanta accountable to his marriage vows to her. Despite the king's appalling behaviour towards her throughout the entire episode, Śakuntalā takes him back without question at the end. Meanwhile, Sulabhā's initial reason for challenging Janaka seems to be for defending the superiority of the renunciate path, rather than anything having to do with gender.

Despite their initial intentions, however, Draupadī, Śakuntalā, and Sulabhā respond to the explicitly gendered abuse they endure by making arguments that are compatible with feminist concerns. They are well aware of the asymmetrical power dynamics they face in their verbal encounters with their male interlocutors. Although their cultural milieu is different from modern societies – in India and elsewhere – the gendered nature of the challenges they confront still have deep resonances with discriminations experienced by women around the world today. Draupadī poses compelling questions about which relationships with males form the basis of women's social status, while also offering ways of enacting *dharma* that could empower other women in comparable situations. Śakuntalā challenges traditional gender roles by claiming to be a source of *dharma* for her husband and threatening to raise their son to be king on her own. Of the three, Sulabhā offers the most radical alternative to traditional gender roles. Not only does she refuse to be defined in terms of her relations to any man, but she demonstrates that she can achieve ultimate freedom completely on her own. Speaking from an enlightened perspective, Sulabhā proclaims that distinctions based on gender are merely indications of an unenlightened point of view.

In addition to offering a critical perspective on traditional gender roles, Draupadī, Śakuntalā, and Sulabhā make arguments in the *sabhā* with political implications. In particular, they each expose the limits of the king's ability to uphold *dharma*. Draupadī's argument in the *sabhā* contrasts sharply with Yudhiṣṭhira's silence on issues of her autonomy; Śakuntalā shows that Duḥṣanta is more concerned about public opinion than about speaking the truth; Sulabhā reveals the gender biases that prevent Janaka from cultivating an enlightened perspective. With kings portrayed as indecisive, duplicitous, and arrogant, these dialogues question the king's ability to uphold *dharma*, especially regarding issues of gender. Indeed, all three offer harsh criticisms of royal authority and highlight the blatant sexism in accepted dharmic practices. Despite transgressing the more restrictive expectations of *strī-dharma* by speaking out in the assembly, each of these women is depicted positively, and their arguments are portrayed as effective; in each case, the narrative voice shows sympathy with their positions. In this sense, Draupadī, Śakuntalā, and Sulabhā demonstrate that royal authority needs to be challenged for the sake of preserving and developing a higher understanding of *dharma*. This does not mean that authority should be challenged arbitrarily, but rather that when *adharma* prevails, silence is not an option. Not only do Draupadī, Śakuntalā, and Sulabhā speak out in situations where they clearly experience injustice, but they also have earned the credentials to make the arguments that they do – each of them demonstrates both their erudition in traditional sources of *dharma* and their virtuosity in performing their dharmic roles and responsibilities.

While the arguments of Draupadī, Śakuntalā, and Sulabhā might appear to be three lone voices in a text dominated by the speech of men, their voices are given a certain authority because of the *Mahābhārata*'s multi-vocal, polycentric character. Moreover, when we understand the subtlety of *dharma* in terms of both its range of understandings and the tensions between those understandings, then *strī-dharma* is not merely the rules women must follow and the roles they must perform, but it is also a vital perspective from which to assess any morally ambiguous situation. In this way, the stories of Draupadī, Śakuntalā, and Sulabhā are not only about virtuous women who encounter sexist discrimination, but they also offer female perspectives from which to view discriminatory doctrines and practices in other circumstances. In the context of understanding their words as part of more general conversations taking place throughout the *Mahābhārata*, Draupadī, Śakuntalā, and Sulabhā challenge the more androcentric and misogynist aspects of *dharma*, with even their most subversive claims supported and enhanced by other voices in the text. Rather than reducing the characters of Draupadī, Śakuntalā, and Sulabhā to unintentional by-products of an otherwise patriarchal agenda, we can engage with their actions and arguments as vital contributions towards a deeper understanding of *dharma* that insists upon female perspectives. Despite the abuses they suffer, nevertheless they persist – becoming exemplars, not only for the power of truth, but also for speaking truth to power.

Notes

1 The Critical Edition depicts Draupadī's remaining clothes as 'an unexplained wonder', but Kṛṣṇa is responsible for replenishing her saris in most popular versions of the story.

2 Van Buitenen argues that although this might seem like a euphemism for 'more private parts', it is not necessary to take it in this way. He explains Duryodhana's exposure of his left thigh as an invitation to sit on it as his wife (1975: 817, note 10). Because Vaiśaṃpāyana describes the left thigh suggestively as 'long like a plantain-stem' and 'firm as an elephant's trunk' (tr. Smith), I am not entirely convinced. In any case, this is clearly another sexualised insult to Draupadī.

3 Vaiśaṃpāyana says that Śakuni resorts to trickery a total of fourteen times (2.54.7; 15; 18; 23; 27; 29; 2.58.4; 6; 8; 10; 15; 21; 25; 28).

4 In a discussion at the beginning of the *Udyoga Parvan*, for example, Kṛṣṇa says that Yudhiṣṭhira was defeated with tricks (5.1.10), while Balarāma counters that Śakuni is not to blame because Yudhiṣṭhira had agreed to play dice with him (5.2.1). Later, Kṛṣṇa refers to 'the lawless dicing match with that crook' (5.126.7). Meanwhile, Arjuna calls Śakuni a cheater (5.76.14). Saṃjaya tells Dhṛtarāṣṭra: the Pandavas were 'cheated at the dicing' (5.156.11).

5 Indeed, Draupadī speaks about her social identity in the same way when she reflects back on this episode in a conversation with Kṛṣṇa in the *Udyoga Parvan*, referring to herself as the daughter of Drupada, sister of Dhṛṣṭadyumna, and friend of Kṛṣṇa (5.80.21–23). Interestingly, she also describes herself to Kṛṣṇa as the daughter-in-law of both Bhīṣma and Dhṛtarāṣṭra (5.80.30).

6 An almost identical passage appears in the *Anuśāsana Parvan* (13.21.19). In this context, it is the sage Aṣṭāvakra who argues that women are dependent, but the female ascetic Diśā objects, demonstrating that she is her own mistress.

7 For further discussion about the dramatic impact that Draupadī's menstruation has on this scene, see Falk (1977). See also Sutherland (1989: 65 n. 10); Jamison (1996: 14–15).

8 As Jamison points out, the *Mānava Dharmaśāstra* (4.57) states that men should not carry on a conversation with a menstruating woman (1996: 14).

9 Another possible explanation, as implied by an episode that appears in the Vulgate but not in the Critical Edition, is that his silence is the fulfilment of a vow not to utter any harsh words (See the Critical Edition, *Sabhā Parvan*, Appendix 1, No. 30, or Vulgate 2.46.27–29).

10 For further discussion of the characterisation of Draupadī, including her divine identity as Śri, see Black (2013).
11 See Hill (2001: 168–176), Bailey (2005: 68–73), Malinar (2007a), Hiltebeitel (2011: 506–516).
12 For Draupadī's presence during Bhīṣma's instruction to Yudhiṣṭhira, see Hiltebeitel (2005: 490).
13 For further discussion on how these stories add depth to the characters who listen to them, see Biardeau (1984, 1985); Shulman (1994); and Hiltebeitel (2001b: 216).
14 As Jamison points out, by giving herself away, Śakuntalā implicitly has a legal authority that is denied in the *Mānava Dharmaśāstra*. For a detailed discussion concerning marriage and the significance of exchange, see Jamison 1996: 207–250.
15 Here, Śakuntalā uses the term *samaya* (1.68.16), the same word that Satyavatī's father used when asking Śaṃtanu to promise to make any offspring with his daughter heir to the throne (1.94.48). It is also the term that Yudhiṣṭhira uses when referring to a previous agreement with his brothers as one of the justification for the polyandrous marriage (1.187.24).
16 This is the same argument that Rāma makes when he asks Sītā to perform the trial by fire in Valmiki's *Rāmāyaṇa* (7.86–88).
17 The *Mānava Dharmaśāstra* mentions a sage within the heart who observes good and evil deeds (8.90–91). For further discussion, see Hiltebeitel (2011: 213).
18 'By loosening the cause of bondage, and by knowledge of the passageways of the mind, the mind can enter into the bodies of others' (3.38, translation Bryant). As White points out, many medieval texts also describe the technique for entering into a foreign body, including the *Yogavasiṣṭha*, *Hemacandra*, and *Yogaśāstra* (White 2009: 164).

5 Kṛṣṇa's conversations

Introduction

The *Bhagavad Gītā* takes place on the battlefield of Kurukṣetra, just as the great war of the Bhāratas – which all major events in the *Mahābhārata* have been leading up to – is about to begin. At this moment, Arjuna throws down his Gāṇḍīva bow and declares to Kṛṣṇa that he will not fight. In order to convince him to join the battle, Kṛṣṇa delivers his most famous teaching and eventually reveals his divine form. When confronted with this terrifying vision, Arjuna asks Kṛṣṇa to explain his true nature:

> Tell me who you are in your terrible form. May you be honoured, chosen of the Gods. Show compassion! I want to know you, Primal One; I do not understand your activity.
>
> (BG 11.31)[1]

Arjuna's question is essentially a theological one, wanting to know the nature of the divine and how it reveals itself. This is not only one of the central questions in the *Bhagavad Gītā* itself, but it also lingers throughout the *Mahābhārata*, as Kṛṣṇa's divinity comes in and out of focus from one encounter to another. In this chapter, we will explore how the question of Kṛṣṇa's divinity is addressed through dialogue. We will not only analyse Kṛṣṇa's interaction with Arjuna in the *Bhagavad Gītā* itself, but also examine how he engages with other interlocutors in other verbal encounters during and after the war. As we will see, different dialogues characterise Kṛṣṇa differently, with some highlighting his divine nature, but with others emphasising his teachings and actions. Reading them together gives us insights into how dialogue develops theological understandings of Kṛṣṇa, yet also offers critical reflections on and challenges to his claim to divine status.

We will begin our exploration into the theological implications of dialogue with the *Bhagavad Gītā*, paying particular attention to Arjuna's contributions to the conversation, both in how he frames the encounter through the lens of his moral problem and in how his subsequent questions continue to direct the course of their exchange. In addition to Arjuna's questions, we will also explore the rhetorical dimensions of Kṛṣṇa's responses, examining how dialogue conveys his sometimes abstract theological teachings as rooted within a specific situation. Recalling some of the dialectical features of dialogue we explored in Chapter 1, we will follow the conversation between Kṛṣṇa and Arjuna as proceeding 'in terms of opposites', like the way Dmitri Nikulin describes the relationship between dialogue and dialectic. As Nikulin explains: 'Moving in and through opposites constantly opens up the possibility for contradiction, refutation ..., opposition, and disagreement' (2010: 5–6). Similarly, dialogue in the *Bhagavad Gītā* opens up oppositions and disagreements between a number of central religious and philosophical ideas. While these ideas are harmonised through the figure of Kṛṣṇa, the dialogue form leaves many questions unanswered and tensions unresolved.

After looking at its dialectical features, we will then consider the *Bhagavad Gītā* in relation to five subsequent dialogues with Kṛṣṇa: (1) Kṛṣṇa and Arjuna, during the war; (2) Kṛṣṇa and Arjuna, after the war, in an episode known as the *Anu Gītā*; (3) Kṛṣṇa and Balarāma, at the very end of the war; (4) Kṛṣṇa and Gāndhārī, on the battlefield, immediately after the war; and (5) Kṛṣṇa and Uttaṅka, just after the *Anu Gītā*. With the participation of Arjuna, Balarāma, Gāndhārī, and Uttaṅka, these five dialogues offer a variety of perspectives from which to view Kṛṣṇa's teachings and divine nature. Taken together, they invite a dialogical reading of the *Bhagavad Gītā*, in which his teachings before the war continue to be reiterated, expanded, and contested in numerous ways. Because they come after the *Bhagavad Gītā* within the narrative and explore some of the same themes, we can take these later conversations with Kṛṣṇa as the *Mahābhārata*'s own internal reflections on the *Bhagavad Gītā* – reflections that offer a critical perspective on its advocacy for war, on its teaching of *karma-yoga*, on its role and significance within the *Mahābhārata* as a whole, and on Kṛṣṇa's divinity. As I will suggest, these dialogues characterise Kṛṣṇa's instruction before the war as both relational and contextual. Although it is often portrayed as the epic's most authoritative teaching, when we examine the *Bhagavad Gītā* as a dialogue in an intra-textual relationship with other dialogues in the *Mahābhārata*, it becomes apparent that Kṛṣṇa's pre-war instruction is a position that can be contested, criticised, and even rejected. Indeed, this is particularly the case if we keep in mind the challenges to Kṛṣṇa's divinity made by Śiśupāla, which we examined in Chapter 1. As important as the *Bhagavad Gītā* is, the repeated challenges to Kṛṣṇa's teachings, as well as the range of views Kṛṣṇa himself espouses on different occasions, characterise his pre-war instruction as one authoritative view among others in a complex web of interacting conversations. Whatever truths Kṛṣṇa imparts to Arjuna as the war is about to begin are truths articulated in that moment. When that moments changes – as we will see – some aspects of his teachings are challenged, while new ones emerge.

If we understand theology as an enquiry into the nature of the divine, then we can see that dialogue plays a crucial role in characterising Kṛṣṇa's divinity throughout the *Mahābhārata*. In the *Bhagavad Gītā*, Kṛṣṇa gives his most detailed description and most explicit enactment of his status as the all-powerful creator and destroyer of the universe. The five subsequent dialogues with Kṛṣṇa also tend to acknowledge him as God, but develop his divine nature in different ways. In addition to presenting different possibilities for conceptualising his divinity, these dialogues offer several models of how to enter into dialogue with Kṛṣṇa. While it is through dialogue that Kṛṣṇa is given the occasion to reveal his divinity, it is also through dialogue that he is characterised as a deity who can be questioned, challenged, ridiculed, and even cursed. Read together, these verbal encounters suggest a theological understanding of Kṛṣṇa in which the interrogation of his divine status creates the possibility for his divinity to be revealed, but at the same time leaves room for questioning and doubt.

Kṛṣṇa in the *Mahābhārata*

As we have seen in the Introduction, there has been considerable debate about the history of the *Mahābhārata*'s composition. Crucially, arguments about the historical development of the text often characterise the different stages of composition in terms of different depictions of Kṛṣṇa.[2] E.W. Hopkins, who proposed several different historical stages of the text's development, postulated that in the oldest strata, Kṛṣṇa is 'just a demigod', while only at a later stage is he depicted 'as all-god' [1901: 398]. More recently, Keven McGrath has claimed to identify a 'pre-Hindu', 'mortal' Kṛṣṇa, who was 'principally and originally heroic' (2013: 2–3). According to such interpretations, any seeming inconsistencies in his character can be explained away as belonging to different layers of the text's history. John Brockington, for example, finds 'little connection between the passages where he appears as a prince and those where he appears as a god', pointing out that 'after his self-revelation in the *Bhagavadgītā*, he continues to be treated as a human ally rather than a deity' (1998: 259).

Other scholars, such as Madeleine Biardeau and Alf Hiltebeitel, have argued that the *Mahābhārata* displays a much greater unity than was assumed previously.[3] Indeed, much of the unity they and others have highlighted pertains directly to the characterisation of Kṛṣṇa. Hiltebeitel, for example, rejects McGrath's 'whole isolation of a Bronze Age "heroic Kṛṣṇa" who was not yet "divinized"'. Rather, according to Hiltebeitel, 'Kṛṣṇa *bhakti*' is subtly present throughout 'a heterogenous *Mahābhārata*' (2015b: 156). In other words, according to Hiltebeitel, there is no 'layer' of the text where Kṛṣṇa is somehow less divine than others. It is not as if in some particular sections Kṛṣṇa is human, but in other sections is divine. As Nicholas Sutton points out: 'references to his being the Supreme Deity and also to his apparent limitation are found in close proximity', thus undermining 'the theory of early scholars that passages in which Kṛṣṇa is portrayed with limitations are early and those in which he is divine follow a brahminical revision of the text' (2000: 177).

In approaching the text dialogically, my assumption is that ambiguities about Kṛṣṇa's divinity are not some accidental by-product of the text's growth over time, but at least partly a deliberate portrayal of the mysteriousness of his divine nature. As we will see, the different voices represented through dialogue offer different ways of approaching Kṛṣṇa and different ways for Kṛṣṇa to respond. Each interlocutor offers a distinctive perspective from which to engage with Kṛṣṇa, from devotee to sceptic. At the same time, as he speaks to each interlocutor in their unique situations, Kṛṣṇa assumes a variety of roles, from friend to ally, from teacher to God. As we have seen, in the Introduction and in Chapter 4, the dialogue form depicts individual characters as dialogical selves that are internally plural, who speak with different voices depending on their interlocutors and their circumstances. Similarly, through its portrayal of his conversations with his interlocutors, the text depicts Kṛṣṇa as a dialogical deity in the sense that he has multifaceted roles and speaks with a polyphonic voice.

In addition to contributing to a theological understanding of Kṛṣṇa, each dialogue also contains unresolved elements, some of which question, or even challenge, his claim to be the supreme deity. In paying attention to these tensions, I am not suggesting that there was ever a version or layer of the text in which Kṛṣṇa's divinity was not an indelible part, but I am bringing attention to the fact that the dialogues addressing the question of Kṛṣṇa's divine status are sometimes contestatory in relation to each other – that even if there is no historical layer of the text in which Kṛṣṇa is not divine, the *Mahābhārata* does not speak with one voice about his divinity. As we will see, the dialogical nature of the *Mahābhārata* offers both theological understandings of Kṛṣṇa and critical responses to those understandings. Of course, these critical responses can be understood as absorbed by a theology of Kṛṣṇa, but they also can be seen as the inclusion of sceptical voices within the *Mahābhārata*'s often contestatory conversations.

Kṛṣṇa and Arjuna (the *Bhagavad Gītā*)

The *Bhagavad Gītā* is the most well-known and most reflected upon section of the *Mahābhārata*, and I do not intend to offer a full examination of its teachings here. What I would like to suggest, however, is that we can gain a fuller understanding of Kṛṣṇa's teachings and divine nature, as well as the *Bhagavad Gītā*'s relationship with other sections of the *Mahābhārata*, if we examine closely its form as a dialogue. Not only is the *Bhagavad Gītā* a conversation between Kṛṣṇa and Arjuna, but it is part of a larger conversation, in which Saṃjaya describes all the action on the battlefield to the blind king Dhṛtarāṣṭra. We should also keep in mind that Saṃjaya's narration is embedded within the two dialogues that frame the entire *Mahābhārata*.

Although the *Bhagavad Gītā* might seem at times to be more monological than dialogical because Kṛṣṇa does most of the speaking, in this section I want to highlight the crucial role played by Arjuna in how the dialogue unfolds. Arjuna does not offer a sustained counterargument to Kṛṣṇa's positions, but his questions direct the course of the conversation and overtly challenge Kṛṣṇa on some occasions. As we will see, Arjuna's questions and doubts are key to developing an understanding of Kṛṣṇa's divinity because they provide the occasion for Kṛṣṇa to reveal his divine nature. In the *Bhagavad Gītā*, as well as in subsequent dialogues with Kṛṣṇa, an important dimension of Kṛṣṇa's divinity is that he offers teachings and reveals his divine form in face-to-face encounters to particular individuals in specific circumstances.

Dialectics of emotion

Arjuna shapes the conversation from the very beginning, when he articulates his reluctance to fight in terms of his strong feelings of compassion (*kṛpā*) and grief (*śoka*). Arjuna is overcome by these emotions when he sees his family members and teachers on the opposing side of the battlefield. His strong revulsion to facing his family members and teachers in battle prompts his mouth to dry, his body to shiver, and his hair to stand on end (1.29). Appropriately, then, Kṛṣṇa's initial reply is to appeal to Arjuna on an emotional level. But rather than accept Arjuna's own description of his feelings in terms of compassion, Kṛṣṇa portrays his emotional response as a 'weakness' (*kaśmala*) (2.2). Kṛṣṇa then questions Arjuna's manhood, telling him not to become 'impotent' (*klaibya*) (2.3). Here, Kṛṣṇa's response parallels Arjuna's initial articulation of his moral problem: in reply to Arjuna's first words about his feelings of compassion and suffering, Kṛṣṇa's first answer is an attempt to prompt a visceral reaction by insulting his manhood. Kṛṣṇa will continue to characterise his teaching as addressing Arjuna's emotional state all the way to the end of their conversation.[4]

As we have seen throughout this book, the *Mahābhārata* highlights the role of emotions in many of the most consequential moral dilemmas, whether it is Śaṃtanu's grief that prompts Bhīṣma to make his vows, the Pāṇḍava brothers' love for Draupadī that provokes Yudhiṣṭhira's decision for all five of them to marry her, or Duryodhana's deep sorrow and jealously after Yudhiṣṭhira's *rājasūya*.[5] On this occasion, Arjuna's strong feelings of compassion and grief provide the initial occasion for a moral deliberation. Crucially, Arjuna's strong feelings are provoked, not because of an objection to killing in principle, but because of his revulsion at the thought of killing his own kinsmen. Arjuna refers to his enemies as 'my people' (*svajana*) (1.31), and, like Saṃjaya, he lists the specific relationships he has with his opponents on the other side of the battlefield: teachers, fathers and sons and grandfathers, mother's brothers, fathers-in-law, grandsons, and brothers-in-law (1.34). Here, Arjuna adds poignancy by personalising his dilemma. At the same time, by using kinship terms, he also makes his dilemma more general, as anyone with a teacher, father, son, grandfather, and so forth can potentially relate to his reluctance to fight. Here we see an interesting tension between Arjuna's roles as a 'chosen one' who is uniquely suited to experience Kṛṣṇa's divine revelation and as an 'everyman' who acts as a conduit for a universal message.[6] As we will see, similar tensions are apparent in other dialogues as well, as Kṛṣṇa personally reveals himself to particular individuals in unique situations, but where each of his encounters is also relatable to others.

Dialectics of dharma

In addition to highlighting his emotional condition, Arjuna frames his reaction in terms of *kula-dharma* (1.40). Not only does he mention his obligation to his family, but he also argues that by fighting he would contribute to the decline of *varṇa-dharma* with the mixing of castes (1.43). Just as Arjuna moves from describing his emotions to justifying them in terms of *dharma*, Kṛṣṇa shifts from insults and provocations to offering substantive reasons for why Arjuna should fight. In the same passage where he says that Arjuna has a 'weakness' (*kaśmala*), Kṛṣṇa also appeals to Arjuna's social status, saying that his hesitation is 'not suitable for a noble one' (*ārya*) (2.2). Kṛṣṇa explicitly invokes *kṣatriya-dharma* later when he argues that for a warrior 'there can be nothing greater than battle for the sake of *dharma*' (2.31). Additionally, Kṛṣṇa's many appeals to Arjuna to uphold his reputation are connected to what is expected of him as a warrior. For example, Kṛṣṇa argues that if Arjuna does not fight, then he will risk losing his 'good name' (2.33). He also warns Arjuna that he will be disgraced if he does not fight, as people will 'tell stories' about his 'eternal disgrace' (2.34–36); they will think that he didn't fight 'because of fear', and they will think of him as 'unworthy' (2.35). We can see all of these remarks – loosely based around *kṣatriya-dharma* – as responding to Arjuna's arguments based on *kula-dharma*, as well as his more general appeals to family loyalty.

Although this initial tension between *kula-dharma* and *kṣatriya-dharma* does not appear after Chapter 2, other notions of *dharma* are developed throughout Kṛṣṇa's teaching. In Chapter 3, for example, Kṛṣṇa delivers his famous line that it is better to perform one's own *dharma* (*sva-dharma*) ineffectively than another person's *dharma* well (3.35). Arjuna does not challenge Kṛṣṇa directly here, but his questions elsewhere raise the issue of which *dharma* is one's 'own' (3.35). Throughout most of the *Bhagavad Gītā*, Kṛṣṇa's arguments about following *dharma* are clearly based on *varṇa-dharma*. In Chapter 18, for example, Kṛṣṇa explicitly says that *varṇa-dharma* is one's 'true nature' (*svabhāva*) rooted in the *guṇas* (18.41). He then repeats his claim that it is better to follow one's *sva-dharma* badly, than to perform another's well (18.47). Despite Kṛṣṇa's strong association between *kṣatriya-dharma* and *sva-dharma*, in other contexts – as Bruce

Sullivan points out – they 'are not necessarily synonymous' (2019: 197).[7] According to Hiltebeitel, in the Dharmasūtras, the main meaning of *sva-dharma* pertains to the *varṇas* and *āśrama*s, 'especially the Kṣatriya' (2011: 520). But in the *Bhagavad Gītā*, the term has overlapping connotations with *svakarma* and *svabhāva*. In this context, as Hiltebeitel explains: 'doing one's duty and occupation properly springs ultimately from one's "intrinsic", "innate", and "inherent nature"' (2011: 540). Despite making the association between *kṣatriya-dharma* and *sva-dharma* in the *Bhagavad Gītā*, Kṛṣṇa's claim elsewhere – that *dharma* is subtle – tends to reject the assumption that one *dharma* can be considered more fundamental than another. As we will see in the *Karṇa Parvan*, Kṛṣṇa will offer a more nuanced understanding of *dharma* which complicates his assumption here, as he associates *sva-dharma* more with virtuous action than with class responsibility.

Dialectics of karma

Another reason Arjuna gives for not fighting is karmic retribution. Early on in his argument, he claims that 'evil' would cling to him and his brothers if they were to kill the sons of Dhṛtarāṣṭra (1.36). He also evokes *karma* when talking about how he would not be able to enjoy victory if he were to win by killing his family members. Further on, Arjuna again argues that there is no use in gaining the kingship, or even living, if one cannot enjoy it (1.32). He repeats this concern several stanzas later, asking how he could 'take pleasure' afterwards if he killed them (1.37). Arjuna restates these sentiments again when he claims that killing family members is not worth the reward 'of pleasure and a kingdom' (1.45). Here he also voices his concern that by breaking *dharma*, he 'will live forever in hell' (1.44). Then again, in Chapter 2, Arjuna anticipates the emotional consequences of killing his teachers and family members: 'Even after we've killed them we would not want to live' (2.6).

Kṛṣṇa initially confronts Arjuna's apprehension by appealing to the rewards that he will gain in heaven and earth if he wins the war (2.37). Here Kṛṣṇa does not argue that Arjuna's acts will not have consequences, but rather he maintains that the karmic outcome of his actions will be positive, not negative. In addition to what we might see as an Upaniṣadic notion of *karma* (2.12–30), Kṛṣṇa also develops the doctrine of *karma-yoga*, arguing that if Arjuna acts disinterestedly, he will not have to suffer any karmic consequence. He encourages Arjuna to act without thinking of the consequences. 'Your authority is in action alone, and never in its fruits; motive should never be in the fruits of action, nor should you cling to inaction' (2.47). Again, we see the rhetorical dimension of Kṛṣṇa's teaching: in response to Arjuna's arguments based on *karma*, Kṛṣṇa first responds with a counterargument, but then offers a different understanding of *karma* altogether – an understanding that specifically addresses Arjuna's emotional repulsion towards fighting.

Arjuna's questions

Throughout these exchanges, Arjuna's questions direct the flow of Kṛṣṇa's teaching. Everything that Kṛṣṇa teaches can, in one way or another, be traced back to Arjuna's emotional response and initial arguments not to fight. In addition to prompting Kṛṣṇa to make the case for fighting, Arjuna's questions also lead Kṛṣṇa towards disclosing his divinity. Crucially, Arjuna's questions do this by challenging Kṛṣṇa to address the potential inconsistencies or underdeveloped aspects of his own teachings. At the beginning of Chapter 3, for example, Arjuna asks Kṛṣṇa why he 'enjoins' him 'to such terrible action' if 'insight is stronger than action' (3.1). Arjuna further reflects that Kṛṣṇa's words seem 'contradictory' (*vyāmiśra*) (3.2). As we will see, both Saṃjaya and Balarāma will question the consistency of Kṛṣṇa's arguments in subsequent dialogues.

In addition to challenging the consistency of his arguments, Arjuna expresses doubts about Kṛṣṇa's divine powers. When Kṛṣṇa declares that he was the first teacher in a genealogy of *yoga* going back to Vivasvat, Arjuna's response is to question how he could be the originator of this teaching in the distant past when he is alive today: 'But your birth was later, and the birth of Vivasvat was earlier; how should I understand that you spoke it in the beginning?' (4.4). As Madhav Deshpande points out: 'This is the first time when Kṛṣṇa has directly brought in a notion that he represents the eternal godhead and that he is more than and beyond the limitations of his particular moral appearance' (1991: 345). Although Arjuna will fully accept Kṛṣṇa as God later in their dialogue, here he receives this news with 'an air of disbelief' (1991: 345).

On another occasion, Arjuna challenges Kṛṣṇa's teaching on *yoga*. Towards the end of Chapter 6, he asks whether controlling the mind is really possible:

> I don't see the stable foundation of this *yoga*, declared by you with such balance. Kṛṣṇa, the mind is ever straying, troubling, strong and unyielding; I think holding it back is as hard to bring about as holding back the wind.
>
> (6.33–34)

A few stanzas later, Arjuna proclaims that he still has doubts (6.39). Here he is particularly concerned that the *karma-yoga* advocated by Kṛṣṇa seems extremely difficult, and he wants to know what opportunities there are for people who cannot practice such self-control, but approach Kṛṣṇa with trust instead (6.37). At the end of this chapter, prompted by Arjuna's question, Kṛṣṇa answers him that those who trust and love him are the ones 'most closely joined in *yoga*' (6.47). At the beginning of Chapter 7, Kṛṣṇa then shifts his focus from *karma-yoga* to *bhakti-yoga*, giving his first detailed explanation about his divine nature (7.4–30). Here, Kṛṣṇa's declaration that he is 'the highest being, the highest god, the highest sacrifice', follows directly from Arjuna's challenging question about how to practice *yoga* (7.30). From the beginning, Kṛṣṇa is trying to convince Arjuna to fight, and, despite developing his arguments in a number of different directions, he never loses sight of this objective.[8]

As we can see throughout these exchanges, Arjuna's questions direct Kṛṣṇa's teaching and lead him towards disclosing his divinity. The way that Arjuna's questions provoke Kṛṣṇa towards his revelation is similar to the way that students elicit teachings in the Upaniṣads.[9] In the Upaniṣads, teachers show a reluctance to teach and often test pupils as a pedagogical exercise. Teachers only reveal their insights when students demonstrate their receptivity to a higher understanding through the questions they ask and how they ask them. Similarly, not only is Kṛṣṇa's disclosure dependent on the questions Arjuna asks, but Arjuna's questions also demonstrate that he is a worthy recipient of Kṛṣṇa's teachings and revelation. When he challenges Kṛṣṇa's apparent inconsistencies and doubts his initial claims to be divine, Arjuna is not treated as a heretic, but rather rewarded for proving his credentials to receive Kṛṣṇa's revelation.

Kṛṣṇa's divinity

More than any of his doctrinal arguments, however, it is the revelation of his divine form that most seems to convince Arjuna to fight. Kṛṣṇa's theophany in Chapter 11 marks a shift in the dynamics between the interlocutors, with Arjuna asking fewer and less provocative questions for the remainder of their conversation. Already by Chapter 10, he tells Kṛṣṇa, 'I believe all that you say to me is true' (10.14); and after seeing Kṛṣṇa's divine form in Chapter 11, Arjuna never challenges him again. His final words in the *Bhagavad Gītā* are: 'Through your grace I have gained wise memory and lost delusion. I stand here with my doubt gone. I will do what you say' (18.73).

Returning to Arjuna's emotional condition at the beginning of their dialogue, it is crucial to note that Kṛṣṇa's revelation addresses Arjuna on a visceral level. As Saṃjaya describes it, when Arjuna was confronted with Kṛṣṇa's divine form, he was 'seized by awe' and 'his hair stood on end' (11.14). Arjuna then says that he trembles at the sight and finds neither courage nor calm (11.23–24). He later says that his mind is 'shaken with fear' (11.43). Here, we see intriguing parallels between Arjuna's response to seeing Kṛṣṇa's divine form and his reaction to facing his family in battle. In both instances, he trembles and his hair bristles; he is so stunned that he is uncertain of what to do; and he asks Kṛṣṇa to help him. If we take Kṛṣṇa's theophany as the main factor in convincing Arjuna to fight, then what ultimately makes Arjuna overcome his initial grief at the sight of his kinsmen in the opposing army is a sight even more harrowing. Indeed, part of this harrowing sight is the vision of the deaths of the very kinsmen that Arjuna is so aggrieved to be facing in battle:

> All in a rush, they enter your terrible mouths, gaping with tusks. Some appear with heads crushed, clinging between your teeth. The heroes of the mortal world enter your flaming mouths, as so many currents of water in a river might run towards the ocean.
>
> (11.28)

Arjuna's response to seeing Kṛṣṇa's divine form is to plead with him to resort to his human form. As we saw at the beginning of this chapter, Arjuna is horrified by Kṛṣṇa's 'terrible' form and urges him to explain his 'activity' (11.31). This moment of their conversation, I suggest, tells us something fundamentally important about the relationship between dialogue and theology. As we have seen, Arjuna's questions direct the course of the conversation, thus providing the occasion for Kṛṣṇa to reveal his true form. In this sense, dialogue makes the revelation of Kṛṣṇa's divinity possible. But, crucially, once God reveals himself, the dialogue ceases. Kṛṣṇa must return to his human form for Arjuna to continue to be in conversation with him.

Admittedly, Kṛṣṇa does speak three verses while in his divine form – making his famous pronouncement that he is time (*kāla*), who has come forth to destroy the worlds, and reiterating his command to Arjuna to join the battle and kill his enemies (11.32–34). However, Kṛṣṇa is silent for most of the theophany, with the description of his divine form articulated by Saṃjaya (11.9–14) and Arjuna (11.15–31). So, while dialogue can lead to an encounter with God, revelation itself seems to transcend words. This is an important point, because it suggests that divinity cannot be articulated through argument. Here I have in mind an observation that Chakravarthi Ram-Prasad makes when discussing a dialogue between Rāma and Vālin from the *Rāmāyaṇa*: 'Talking with God is ultimately not about argument but surrender' (2019: 232). Similarly, at the end of the *Bhagavad Gītā*, Arjuna 'surrenders' to Kṛṣṇa by saying he will do exactly what he says (18.73). Nevertheless, even if Kṛṣṇa ultimately convinces Arjuna of his divine identity when he grants him divine sight (11.8), he does declare his divine identity on several occasions, both before and after his theophany. Moreover, it is important to keep in mind that Kṛṣṇa's theophany itself is made in support of his wider argument for Arjuna to fight. In other words, as he will do with Uttaṅka later, Kṛṣṇa reveals his divine form in situations where he wants to persuade his interlocutors.

Bhagavad Gītā: dialogue as dialectic

As we have seen, the depiction of Kṛṣṇa in dialogue contributes to the text's theological inquiry into his divine nature. Arjuna's questions direct the course of the conversation, providing its initial context and shaping what

Kṛṣṇa teaches. There is also a narrative arc to their dialogue, from Arjuna's initial articulation of his moral problem, to his inquisitive early participation in the conversation, to his experience of Kṛṣṇa's divine form, and to his final declaration to follow Kṛṣṇa's instructions. The narrative dimension of their dialogue not only explores their interpersonal relationship, but also highlights the different ways that Arjuna responds to Kṛṣṇa's teaching, ranging from perplexed and slightly sceptical, to completely convinced and devoted. In addition to exemplifying the ideal devotee, Arjuna's different responses offer models of critical engagement that can question and criticise Kṛṣṇa's teaching.

By paying closer attention to the *Bhagavad Gītā* as a dialogue, we can also see that Arjuna's arguments and Kṛṣṇa's counterarguments have a certain degree of symmetry. In response to Arjuna's feelings of grief, Kṛṣṇa appeals to him on an emotional level. In response to Arjuna's arguments based on *kula-dharma*, Kṛṣṇa counters with appeals to *kṣatriya-dharma*. In response to Arjuna's concern about the karmic consequences of his actions, Kṛṣṇa first tries to assure him that he will enjoy rewards on earth and in heaven and then makes arguments based on *karma-yoga*. In response to the harrowing sight of Arjuna's family on the other side of the battlefield, Kṛṣṇa gives Arjuna the divine sight to see the terrifying vision of Kṛṣṇa's true nature.

Seen in this way, the verbal encounter between Arjuna and Kṛṣṇa proceeds 'in terms of opposites', just like Nikulin's description of the relationship between dialogue and dialectic (2010: 5–6). We have looked at different understandings of *karma* and *dharma* in dialectical relationships with each other, but one could also examine the tensions between other doctrines, such as between Upaniṣadic monism and a theism based on Kṛṣṇa, or between *sāṃkhya* and *yoga*. Kenneth Dorter is one of the few scholars to have approached the *Bhagavad Gītā* as a dialectic (2012). According to Dorter, a characteristic feature of dialectic is that 'opposing points of view ... progressively come to agreement' (2012: 308). As Dorter argues, the *Bhagavad Gītā* uses a dialectical rather than an analytical method, because it 'requires a change of perspective' (2012: 308). Dorter sees dialectic in the *Bhagavad Gītā* as moving towards a resolution, with Arjuna's initial dilemma resolved through *yoga*. It seems to me, however, that if the opposing views are resolved, then they are more resolved through Kṛṣṇa's theophany than through any of his teachings. Indeed, one of the ways that Saṃjaya describes Kṛṣṇa's divine form is in terms of bringing together unity and diversity: 'There, Arjuna, the son of Paṇḍu, saw in the body of the God of gods the whole world, standing as one, and yet divided up in many ways' (11.13).

But in addition to resolving some contradictions, the *Bhagavad Gītā* also allows tensions to remain. As we will see in the remainder of this chapter, despite Arjuna's last words in the *Bhagavad Gītā*, his questions, as well as the tensions between opposing ideas, continue to be debated long after their pre-war conversation. In particular, the *Bhāgavad Gītā* contributes to the ongoing dialectic between fate and human agency by characterising Arjuna as both compelled to fight and free to choose otherwise. Kṛṣṇa implies an inevitability about Arjuna's actions in the war when he argues that he should not grieve for the deaths of his family members (2.27). More specifically, in Chapter 11, Kṛṣṇa argues – while he is demonstrating his divine form – that he himself is time (*kāla*) and that he determines the time of death of all creatures:

> Even without you, these warriors facing off against each other will no longer exist. So stand up, and gain honour! After conquering enemies, enjoy an abundant reign. I've already destroyed them. You who sling arrows from the left and the right, be an instrument, and nothing more. (11.32–33)

Here, Kṛṣṇa characterises Arjuna as a mere instrument in his own divine actions. These arguments resonate with Vaiśaṃpāyana's depiction of the divine plan, in which royal seers, such as Arjuna, are born for the sake of saving the earth from being over-run by demons.

Despite portraying Arjuna's actions as predetermined, Kṛṣṇa nevertheless goes to great lengths to convince him to fight.[10] The very fact that he makes such complex and sustained arguments indicates that Kṛṣṇa approaches the dialogue as if Arjuna has a real choice to make. As we have explored in Chapter 3, despite the strong emphasis on fate and determinism throughout the narrative, characters display reactive attitudes towards each other. This is exactly how Kṛṣṇa seems to behave towards Arjuna: despite claiming that Arjuna's actions are merely the instruments if his own divine activity, Kṛṣṇa engages with him as a moral agent who can make his own decisions. One of the last things he says to Arjuna in the *Bhagavad Gītā* is that he is free to choose: 'So this wisdom told to you by me is more hidden than the hidden; and when you have pondered this completely, then do as you like' (18.63).

Like other moral dilemmas in the *Mahābhārata*, Arjuna's situation is characterised both as inevitable and as requiring him to make a choice. We are left to wonder, however, how exactly these explanations relate to each other. One of the implications of Kṛṣṇa's teaching of *karma-yoga* is that the issue of moral responsibility is addressed, not through the consequences of whichever actions Arjuna performs, but through cultivating the correct mental attitude towards his actions. By instructing Arjuna to act without considering the fruits of his actions, Kṛṣṇa offers an understanding of moral action in which true freedom is not acting however one wants, but acting according to one's duties and responsibilities, regardless of the consequences.

Nevertheless, because some of Arjuna's questions remain unanswered, we are left to wonder if choosing to fight was the only moral option he had. As we have seen, it is not clear why his class obligations should eclipse his family obligations, especially in a textual context in which rule-based and role-based understandings of *dharma* are repeatedly questioned. We should keep in mind that Kṛṣṇa never responds to Arjuna's question about why, if 'insight is stronger than action' (3.1), it is so necessary on this occasion for him to act in this precise way, especially considering all the suffering it will cause. As Douglas Berger points out, Arjuna has 'legitimate moral concerns' about the prospect of facing his kin in battle, but Kṛṣṇa addresses his emotional condition more than this ethical questions (2015: 629). As we will see, some of the unanswered questions raised by Arjuna and unresolved tensions within Kṛṣṇa's teachings are addressed in subsequent dialogues with Kṛṣṇa.

The *Bhagavad Gītā* in dialogue with the *Mahābhārata*

Scholars continue to debate the textual history of the *Bhagavad Gītā* and its relationship with the *Mahābhārata*. As discussed in the Introduction, my approach to the *Mahābhārata*, which includes the *Bhagavad Gītā*, is to read the text holistically and synchronically. But in doing so, I also approach the *Mahābhārata* dialogically, as a heterogeneous text that contains different voices that sometimes have a contestatory relationship with each other. In the remainder of this chapter, we will continue our enquiry in the intra-textual dimensions of dialogue by examining the relationship between the *Bhagavad Gītā* and other dialogues with Kṛṣṇa in the *Mahābhārata*.

Even scholars who have speculated that the *Bhagavad Gītā* might have been an interpolation have seen it as well integrated into the *Mahābhārata* as a whole. Van Buitenen, for example, shows how the complex web of relationships between Arjuna and Kṛṣṇa as established in other sections of the narrative – as friends, cousins, brothers-in-law, Nara and Nārāyaṇa, and Indra and Viṣṇu – adds further layers of meaning to Kṛṣṇa's teaching, as well as to the place of the *Bhagavad Gītā* within the *Mahābhārata*. As van Buitenen concludes: 'Among the many ways of looking at the *Gītā* is as a creation of the *Mahābhārata* itself' (1981: 3).[11]

Indeed, several other scholars have drawn attention to the intra-textual relationship between the *Bhagavad Gītā* and other sections of the *Mahābhārata*. Arvind Sharma has suggested that the *Anu Gītā* could be seen as the first commentary on the *Bhagavad Gītā* (1986: 2). Similarly, Bruce Sullivan (2019) takes a dialogue featuring Hanūmān and Bhīmasena in the *Āraṇyaka Parvan* (3.146–153) as a 'comment' on the *Bhagavad Gītā* (2019: 207).[12] In the remainder of this chapter, we will look at five dialogues in the *Mahābhārata* that appear after the *Bhagavad Gītā*. These dialogues indicate, I will argue, that Arjuna's questions have not been completely answered and that uncertainties remain about the meaning of Kṛṣṇa's teachings and the nature of his divine status. Taken together, these dialogues offer a dialectical reading of the *Bhagavad Gītā*.

Kṛṣṇa and Arjuna in the *Karṇa Parvan* (8.49)

Our first dialogue takes place in the *Karṇa Parvan*, before the climactic episodes of that book, when both Duḥśāsana and Karṇa are killed. This dialogue is an extended exchange between Kṛṣṇa, Arjuna, and Yudhiṣṭhira, during which Yudhiṣṭhira criticises Arjuna for returning from the battlefield and not staying to fight alongside Bhīmasena, when Karṇa had not yet been killed. Yudhiṣṭhira rashly calls Arjuna a coward, adding that Kuntī should have aborted him. He subsequently tells Arjuna to give up his Gāṇḍīva bow. At this point, Arjuna discloses a secret vow he had taken to kill anyone who asked him to give up his bow. Declaring that he will uphold his vow, he asks Kṛṣṇa what he should do: 'What do you think is the right thing to do now that this situation's happened? Dear friend, you know everything about the past and future of this world. I will do whatever you tell me' (8.49.13).[13]

Although Arjuna will later forget Kṛṣṇa's *Bhagavad Gītā* sermon, here he seems at least to remember the main message, referring to Kṛṣṇa's knowledge of the past and future of the world. Unlike the *Bhagavad Gītā*, however, Kṛṣṇa does not make any self-proclamations about his divinity. Indeed, this is the only explicit reference in this dialogue. But despite not emphasising Kṛṣṇa's divine status, this dialogue has strong similarities with the *Bhagavad Gītā* in other ways. Just like in the *Bhagavad Gītā*, Arjuna is confronted with a dilemma, he asks Kṛṣṇa for advice, Kṛṣṇa offers instruction, and Arjuna agrees to follow it. Despite the similarity in structure, however, Kṛṣṇa's teachings are very different: whereas in the *Bhagavad Gītā*, Kṛṣṇa urges Arjuna to fight, here he persuades him to refrain from violence.

First, Kṛṣṇa accuses Arjuna of not understanding the nuances of *dharma*, explaining that 'it isn't at all easy to know what should or shouldn't be done' (8.49.19). Kṛṣṇa argues that *dharma* can be understood through *śruti*, but that Arjuna does not have the proper knowledge of tradition. As a consequence, Arjuna does not understand *dharma* and does not know when and when not to kill people. Here, Kṛṣṇa extols the virtues of non-violence, saying that it is 'infinitely better not to destroy life ... One can speak false words, but one should never kill in any way at all' (8.49.20). While the argument not to kill makes perfect sense in this conflict between Arjuna and Yudhiṣṭhira, it is surprising that Kṛṣṇa makes the more general case for non-violence, especially when the war he himself supports is still raging around him and he by no means is suggesting that Arjuna should stop fighting in it.

Then Kṛṣṇa asks Arjuna how he could attack his older brother without considering the subtle (*sūkṣma*) and unfathomable (*duranvaya*) way (*gati*) of *dharma* (8.49.24). Kṛṣṇa offers a fuller understanding of this subtle and unfathomable way by revealing to Arjuna the 'secret teaching of *dharma*' (*dharma-rahasya*). He begins by declaring that the one who speaks truth is 'virtuous' (*sadhu*) and that 'there is nothing higher than truth' (8.49.27). The difficulty, as Kṛṣṇa explains, is that the 'truth is certainly difficult in practice ... falsehood is truth and truth is falsehood' (8.49.28–29). To illustrate this point, Kṛṣṇa recounts two short parables, one of Balāka the hunter and the other of the sage Kauśika. As we have seen in Chapter 1, Bhīṣma will later refer to these two stories when instructing Yudhiṣṭhira in the *Śānti Parvan* (12.110).[14] We noted too that, unlike Kṛṣṇa, Bhīṣma does not give the longer accounts of either Balāka or Kauśika. It is also worth mentioning that Bhīṣma does not use these stories to demonstrate the subtlety of *dharma*, as Kṛṣṇa does here.

According to Kṛṣṇa, Balāka is a reluctant hunter, who does not take pleasure from killing, but does so to support his family, including his blind parents. Kṛṣṇa describes Balāka as following his own *dharma* (*sva-dharma*), always speaking the truth (*satya*), and never spiteful (*anasūyaka*) (8.49.35). In contrast to his teaching in the *Bhagavad Gītā*, on this occasion Kṛṣṇa associates *sva-dharma* more with virtuous behaviour than with *varṇa* identity. One day Balāka kills a wild creature who turns out to be an ascetic in disguise, intent on killing all living beings. Although Balāka is unaware of this, he goes straight to heaven after slaying the creature. Matilal explains this fortuitous and rather surprising outcome in terms of 'moral luck' (2002: 29). Indeed, Kṛṣṇa concludes from this story that *dharma* is 'very difficult to understand' (*sudurvida*) (8.49.40).

Kṛṣṇa then tells the story of Kauśika, a sage who had taken a vow always to tell the truth, but who was unlearned in *śruti*. On one occasion, he sees some people running away from bandits. Because of his vow always to tell the truth, when asked by the bandits, he tells them where the innocent people are, causing them to be killed. In this case, Kauśika, who might seemingly be virtuous – both because he has kept his vow and because he always tells the truth – ends up falling into a terrible hell. Kṛṣṇa explains this outcome by once again invoking the description of *dharma* as *sūkṣma*, saying that Kauśika did not understand its subtle way (8.49.46). Considering Bhīṣma's omissions when referring to Kauśika, it is interesting that when Kṛṣṇa tells this story, he directly relates an understanding of the subtlety of *dharma* with knowing when to break a vow. Interestingly, Kṛṣṇa adds that Kauśika did not 'question his elders about his doubts' (8.49.46). As we saw in Chapter 4, Draupadī, Śakuntalā, and Sulabhā all demonstrate how *dharma* can sometimes be upheld when questioning authority. Here, it seems that Kṛṣṇa is taking a similar position, associating critical questioning with an understanding of the subtlety of *dharma*.

Kṛṣṇa further instructs Arjuna that it is not enough to be truthful, but one must also be able to determine the best way to act in a particular situation: 'In this case this most profound and complex knowledge is determined through reason (*tarka*)' (8.49.48). As Hiltebeitel points out, *tarka* is mainly a technical and philosophical term in the *Mahābhārata* that is used rarely (2011: 25). By referring to *tarka*, Kṛṣṇa seems to be making a point about using reason to navigate the subtlety of *dharma*, rather than completely relying on traditional obligations and scripture. Hiltebeitel interprets Kṛṣṇa's point here as instructing Arjuna that 'where there is no rule, such cases call for reason if *dharma* is to flourish' (2011: 25). But, as Hiltebeitel notes, the term *tarka* often has negative connotations in the *Mahābhārata*. Bhīṣma sometimes speaks of *tarka* as 'to be shunned as a useless science' (2011: 25). Indeed, the one occasion where Bhīṣma uses this term positively is when he refers to the stories of Balāka and Kauśika. Returning to the *Karṇa Parvan*, Arjuna responds, saying that he accepts Kṛṣṇa's argument not to kill Yudhiṣṭhira, but needs advice on how he can nevertheless maintain his vow. Kṛṣṇa instructs Arjuna to kill Yudhiṣṭhira metaphorically, by addressing him in familiar language (8.49.67). At the end of their exchange, Kṛṣṇa tells Arjuna that he has to decide for himself what to do.

As we can see, this dialogue in the *Karṇa Parvan* revisits Kṛṣṇa's teaching in the *Bhagavad Gītā* in a number of ways, including offering some interesting reflections on his attitude towards scripture. In the *Bhagavad Gītā*, Kṛṣṇa both criticises and seeks authority in *śruti*, making some claims that dismiss the Vedas altogether (BG 2.46), but on other occasions he argues that scripture is an important means for understanding his own divine status (BG 15.15). In the *Karṇa Parvan*, Kṛṣṇa seems to take a more positive stand on scripture, but yet one that emphasises its limitations. We might also see this brief segue into scripture as contributing to a theology of Kṛṣṇa. In contrast to the *Bhagavad Gītā*, here Kṛṣṇa does not reveal his divine form, but he does indicate ways to access his teachings through scripture.[15]

His main point in referring to *śruti* is to emphasise that a good grounding in tradition is necessary for understanding the subtleties of *dharma*. Indeed, Kṛṣṇa's instructions in the *Karṇa Parvan* complicate his earlier teachings on *dharma*. Whereas in the *Bhagavad Gītā* Kṛṣṇa characterises *dharma* primarily in terms of *kṣatriya-dharma*, here he teaches a more elusive understanding according to which he advocates behaviour that would explicitly violate *dharma* based on caste duty. As Matilal has described it:

> The same Kṛṣṇa who advised Arjuna to fight the bloody war and kill his great grandfather for it was his duty as a *kṣatriya*, prevented Arjuna on another occasion from killing his elder, Yudhiṣṭhira, although that involved breaking the same code of conduct of a *kṣatriya*: truth-keeping.
> (2002: 47)

Kṛṣṇa's use of the Balāka and Kauśika stories to illustrate *dharma* as *sūkṣma* points to an understanding where *dharma* is not what it seems, where doing the opposite of a conventional understanding is the way to uphold *dharma* in some circumstances. But it also invites a critical reflection on his far more conservative and rigid teaching on *dharma* in the *Bhagavad Gītā*.

Additionally, this dialogue refines Kṛṣṇa's earlier teaching on violence. In the *Bhagavad Gītā*, Kṛṣṇa invokes the Upaniṣadic doctrine of the universal self (*ātman*), arguing that Arjuna need not be concerned about killing his kinsmen, because the universal self can never be killed (BG 2.12–30). Echoing the *Kaṭha Upaniṣad* (KU 2.18–19), Kṛṣṇa teaches that the self does not die when the body dies (BG 2.20). He reiterates later: 'the embodied self which exists in the body of everyone is eternally free from harm; so you should not grieve for any living beings' (BG 2.30). In a shocking reversal of teachings in the Upaniṣads and other sections of the *Mahābhārata* – which sometimes associate teachings of the self with the practice of *ahiṃsā* – Kṛṣṇa uses the *ātman* doctrine as a justification for killing.

In contrast, Kṛṣṇa's discourse in the *Karṇa Parvan* – as well as in the *Anu Gītā*, as we will see – modifies his earlier stance on violence, suggesting that fighting and killing cannot be justified in all circumstances. Here, Kṛṣṇa stipulates a number of situations in war when killing is not appropriate. At one point, he also explicitly endorses the teaching of non-violence. And finally, he offers Arjuna a substitute for violence in this particular situation. Kṛṣṇa further contextualises violence in how he describes violent acts in the parables he tells Arjuna. In the Balāka story, he brings attention to the fact that despite being a hunter, Balāka only kills to provide for his family. In the Kauśika story, Kṛṣṇa characterises the deaths of innocent people in the forest as evidence that Kauśika's actions led to an evil outcome. Kṛṣṇa's identification of violence to the innocent as the negative consequence of Kauśika's vow provides an interesting contrast to his argument in the *Bhagavad Gītā*, where he rationalises that the dead should not be mourned because the immortal self does not die.

In this dialogue, the same man and the same god face some of the same questions regarding duty, violence, and moral decision-making, but in different circumstances, the answers to those questions are considerably different. As contributing to a theology of Kṛṣṇa, this dialogue suggests that God's divine teachings are relational and contextual, while also indicating that Kṛṣṇa does not always rely on his divinity to back up his teachings. We might glean from this dialogue that scripture and reason are ways to access his divine message.

Kṛṣṇa and Arjuna in the *Anu Gītā* (14.16–50)

Our next dialogue is another conversation between Kṛṣṇa and Arjuna. Known as the *Anu Gītā*, this dialogue – which appears in the *Aśvamedhika Parvan* – takes place soon after the Pāṇḍava and the Kaurava elders have had their baths in the Ganges after Bhīṣma's cremation and before Yudhiṣṭhira performs his *aśvamedha* to relieve his grief after the war. This is the last conversation between Arjuna and Kṛṣṇa in the *Mahābhārata*, with Kṛṣṇa returning to Dvārakā soon afterwards. Their dialogue begins with Arjuna referring back to Kṛṣṇa's revelation of his divine form (*rūpa aiśvarya*) in the *Bhagavad Gītā* and asking to hear his teaching all over again, admitting that he had forgotten much of what Kṛṣṇa had taught. Kṛṣṇa says it is 'disagreeable' (*apriya*) that Arjuna has not remembered his 'secret' (*guhya*) teaching (14.16.9–10), but admits that he can no longer recall his earlier teachings either![16] This initial exchange, where both interlocutors involved in the *Mahābhārata*'s most famous dialogue forget its teachings, takes a humorous and irreverent stance towards the *Bhagavad Gītā*.

The *Anu Gītā* consists of three separate parts, each of which is in the form of a dialogue: the first is between a *siddha* and his student (14.16–19), the second between a brahmin and his wife (14.20–34), and the third between the god Brahmā and a group of *ṛṣis* (14.35–50). Notably, the second and third sections contain further embedded dialogues, with the *Anu Gītā* containing some of the most deeply embedded dialogues in the entire *Mahābhārata* – going up to six dialogues deep. The multiple layers of dialogue in the *Anu Gītā* help integrate the text and its teachings with other sections of the *Mahābhārata*, as it includes a number of characters (such as Janaka and Rāma Jāmadagnya) and dialogical situations (such as a conversation between a teacher and student, and between a husband and wife) that appear elsewhere. In comparison with the *Bhagavad Gītā*, which has no embedded dialogues, the multiple levels of dialogue in the *Anu Gītā* also suggest that this teaching is less of Kṛṣṇa's direct revelation and more of his engagement with authoritative teachings within renunciate traditions. In terms of its theological implications, the many layers of dialogue perhaps give Kṛṣṇa more of a licence to deliver a discourse that at times overtly challenges his earlier teaching, without blatantly contradicting himself. In this way, it allows for Kṛṣṇa to be the mouthpiece for a wide range of views.

Indeed, what is remarkable about the *Anu Gītā* is that Kṛṣṇa frames his discourse as a recapitulation of what he taught in the *Bhagavad Gītā*, but then goes on to deliver a very different message. According to Herman Tieken, the main message of the *Anu Gītā* is that the path of knowledge (*jñāna*) is the way to final liberation – a teaching that is 'completely opposite to the one found in the *Bhagavadgītā*' (2009: 212). Crucially, as Arvind Sharma has pointed out, the *Anu Gītā* does not contain the devotional elements of the *Bhagavad Gītā* (1986: 5). Arjuna mentions Kṛṣṇa's divine form at the very beginning of their conversation, (14.16.5), but it is not referred to again. As Sharma remarks: 'What is conspicuous by its absence is any glorification of Kṛṣṇa' (1986: 5).

Another notable feature is that it puts forth a strong case for non-violence and renunciation, thus positioning its teachings in contrast with the doctrine of *karma-yoga*. In the first section, the *siddha* presents the ideal religious life as that of the *yogin*, who controls his mind and body, and retires alone to the forest (14.19.34). In the second section, the brahmin tells his wife stories of Rāma Jāmadagnya and Alarka (14.29.20–14.30.31) who are instructed to give up violence and perform austerities. In the third section, the god Brahmā teaches that non-harm (*ahiṃsā*) is the greatest *dharma* and that violence is the essence of *adharma* (14.43.19).[17] And in the final chapter of the text – in what Tieken suggests (2009: 216) is an overt rejection of the teachings of the *Bhagavad Gītā* – Brahmā says that 'some dull persons praise *karma*' (14.50.30).

While Kṛṣṇa's discourse in the *Bhagavad Gītā* was delivered in response to Arjuna's strong feelings of grief and compassion before the war, in the *Anu Gītā* he offers his teaching within the context of Arjuna's remorse afterwards. Kṛṣṇa teaches Arjuna that the only way to overcome all his sins (*pāpa*) and attain the ultimate peace of *mokṣa* is through non-violence (4.50.47).[18] Perhaps the change of context explains any apparent contradictions in Kṛṣṇa's arguments, but we should also remember that the remorse Arjuna is feeling after the war is almost exactly as he had predicted in the second chapter of the *Bhagavad Gītā* (2.6–8). Keeping this in mind, as well as what he says to Arjuna in the *Karṇa Parvan*, the *Anu Gītā* offers a counter-perspective to Kṛṣṇa's pre-war endorsement of violence.

As we can see, the *Anu Gītā* is in dialogue with the *Bhagavad Gītā*, making both explicit and implicit references to it, developing some of its ideas, challenging others, and mimicking some of its passages. Compared to the *Bhagavad Gītā*, the *Anu Gītā* features far less interaction between the two interlocutors, with Kṛṣṇa recounting the teachings of others and Arjuna rarely asking questions. However, their brief interactions link the two dialogues. In addition to their opening exchange that pokes fun at the *Bhagavad Gītā*, at one point Kṛṣṇa checks to make sure that Arjuna is paying attention, saying that he covered the same topics when they were on the chariot (14.19.50).[19] But while claiming to restate the *Bhagavad Gītā*'s message, the *Anu Gītā* goes on to offer quite different teachings, emphasising non-violence and renunciation, while sometimes overtly criticising the teaching of *karma-yoga*.

Kṛṣṇa and Balarāma in the *Śalya Parvan* (9.59.1–30)

Now we will consider three dialogues featuring Kṛṣṇa with interlocutors other than Arjuna: one with Balarāma, one with Gāndhārī, and one with Uttaṅka. The first of these appears in the *Śalya Parvan*, towards the very bitter end of the war. In a final showdown, Bhīmasena is about to face Duryodhana, one of the last Kaurava warriors still standing, in a mace fight. But just before the battle begins, Balarāma arrives. Balarāma, Kṛṣṇa's older brother, has been absent during the war, on a vast pilgrimage of sacred sites. When he witnesses Bhīmasena strike Duryodhana below the naval, Balarāma becomes very angry, threatening to curse him and then rushing towards him with a plough – his signature weapon, which he had brought with him on his pilgrimage. Kṛṣṇa restrains him, before urging his brother to act out of loyalty to the Pāṇḍavas and not to give in to his anger. He also argues that the method of killing is justified because Bhīmasena had vowed to strike Duryodhana in this way and that Bhīmasena's actions are fulfilling a curse that Maitreya put on Duryodhana (see 2.63.14; 3.11). Balarāma, however, replies that *dharma* should be practised properly, explaining that

Bhīmasena has been misled by *kāma* and *artha*, when they need to be in harmony with *dharma*.

Balarāma finishes his point by claiming that Kṛṣṇa is merely saying 'what he likes' (9.59.19), implying that he is not making proper arguments. This sentiment is echoed by Saṃjaya – the narrator of this episode – who describes Kṛṣṇa's arguments as 'fallacious' (*viśa*) (9.59.22). Keeping in mind that Saṃjaya is a self-proclaimed devotee of Kṛṣṇa (5.67), it is notable that he still recognises inconsistencies in his arguments. We might also recall that at one point in the *Bhagavad Gītā*, Arjuna calls Kṛṣṇa's words 'contradictory' (*vyāmiśra*) (3.2). Returning to Saṃjaya's remark, the specific argument he describes as fallacious is that Bhīmasena's vow justifies his non-dharmic fighting tactics. This offers an interesting contrast to how Kṛṣṇa treats Arjuna's vow in the dialogue we discussed from the *Karṇa Parvan*, where he offered a clever way to circumvent it. As both Balarāma and Saṃjaya imply, Kṛṣṇa seems to be making whatever argument he can to favour his case, even if it contradicts arguments he has made on previous occasions.

Balarāma then proclaims that Bhīmasena will be known as a 'crooked warrior' (*jihmayodhin*), contrasting him to Duryodhana, who he describes as 'virtuous' (*dharma-ātman*) (9.59.23). As we have seen in the Introduction, dharmic instruction is often instigated by inversions and paradoxes. Here, Balarāma questions Kṛṣṇa's adherence to *dharma* when he clearly supports behaviour that violates it. Finally, Balarāma gets on his chariot and goes off to Dvārakā, with the dialogue ending inconclusively. Balarāma gets in the last word, leaving without being convinced by any of Kṛṣṇa's arguments, but without convincing Kṛṣṇa either.

This short exchange is not about the war itself, but about Bhīmasena's underhanded tactics in this episode. At no point does Balarāma accuse Kṛṣṇa of collaborating in such tactics with Bhīmasena, or with the other Pāṇḍavas on other occasions, nor does he overtly oppose Kṛṣṇa's overall support of the war. It makes sense that Balarāma just focuses on what he sees, particularly because he has been absent since before the war began and we cannot assume that he knows about these other details. Nonetheless, Balarāma addresses Kṛṣṇa, not Bhīmasena, throughout this exchange, and his anger about the unjust way Duryodhana is slain would be equally applicable to the situations surrounding the deaths of the other major Kaurava warriors, in all of whose cases Kṛṣṇa participated in their undharmic demise.[20] In other words, we might see Balarāma's intervention here as an invitation to reflect on Kṛṣṇa's role in the deaths of the Kaurava generals.

There is also an interesting contrast, as pointed out by B.K. Matilal, between 'two different sets of arguments to justify Bhīma's unlawful killing of Duryodhana' (1991: 411). When speaking to the Pāṇḍavas before Balarāma arrives, Kṛṣṇa's defence is that Bhīmasena would not have been able to defeat Duryodhana without using underhanded tactics. Kṛṣṇa further justifies 'this breach in ethical conduct' by suggesting that Indra defeated Vairocana in a 'similar manner' (1991: 411). When speaking to his brother, however, Kṛṣṇa seems to anticipate that Balarāma will not accept this justification for breaking the codes of war. Instead of highlighting Duryodhana's superior fighting skills, Kṛṣṇa refers to Bhīmasena's vow 'of breaking Duryodhana's thigh during the fatal and deceitful gambling match' (1991: 411). Here, in addition to highlighting the ethical ambiguities of Kṛṣṇa's methods, this encounter portrays Kṛṣṇa as giving different answers to different audiences. For Balarāma, this might be further evidence of Kṛṣṇa's inconsistency, but we might also see this as an example of Kṛṣṇa's dharmic reasoning – in which he makes distinct arguments for each interlocutor and in every unique context.

Balarāma's critical perspective is particularly important when considering that he is depicted as an impartial observer. When asking Saṃjaya to narrate the episode, Dhṛtarāṣṭra remarks that Balarāma was an expert in mace fighting and acquainted with all its rules (9.59.2). Moreover, as Justin Meiland points out, the pilgrimage Balarāma takes during the war establishes him 'as a man of religious virtue and devotion, thus giving heightened significance to his outrage at the dishonorable way in which the Kaurava king is slain' (2007: 25). Indeed, his neutrality is established when he first arrives on the battlefield, with Balarāma referring to both Duryodhana and Bhīmasena as his pupils (9.33.5)[21]; and with Janamejaya reminding Vaiśaṃpāyana that Balarāma had departed on his pilgrimage declaring that he would aid neither the sons of Dhṛtarāṣṭra nor the sons of Pandu (9.34.2). In contrast to Gāndhārī, who – as we will see – criticises Kṛṣṇa after having lost one hundred sons on the battlefield, Balarāma does not have a vested interest in who wins the war. As such, Balarāma acts as a sort of judge or arbitrator, as his is the closest one can get to an objective view about the events on Kurukṣetra. By siding with Duryodhana, he sanctions the Kaurava perspective and calls into question how the final battle was won. In this way, Balarāma's criticisms of Kṛṣṇa's involvement here have reverberations concerning his brother's contributions toward the deaths of all the major Kaurava warriors, as well as his arguments justifying for the war itself.

Kṛṣṇa and Gāndhārī in the *Strī Parvan* (11.16–25)

The dialogue between Kṛṣṇa and Gāndhārī (11.16–25) takes place in the immediate aftermath of the apocalyptic war between the Pāṇḍavas and the Kauravas.[22] Gāndhārī, wife of Dhṛtarāṣṭra, has worn a blindfold since the day of her marriage because of her devotion to her blind husband. Although she rarely speaks, she is present for many of the *Mahābhārata*'s most central episodes, such as the dicing match, Draupadī's appeal against its result, some of the negotiations for peace in the Kaurava court, and the entire recitation of the war, including the *Bhagavad Gītā*. As the mother of a hundreds sons who were killed in battle fighting for the losing side, Gāndhārī suffers as much as anyone from the tragic consequences of the war. Addressing Kṛṣṇa, Gāndhārī – still wearing her blindfold, but aided by the divine eye (*divya cakṣus*) granted to her by Vyāsa – describes in vivid detail the dismembered bodies that are strewn across the blood-soaked battlefield. As she mourns the deaths of her sons, she speaks of the losses suffered by the Kuru women and makes several statements denouncing the war. Gāndhārī addresses her entire account to Kṛṣṇa, whom she repeatedly urges to see for himself the harrowing scenes of decaying corpses and wailing widows.

Of the dialogues with Kṛṣṇa we are looking at in this chapter, this is one of three in which Kṛṣṇa's interlocutor has divine sight at some point during their verbal encounter.[23] As we have seen, Kṛṣṇa grants Arjuna this special vision in order for him to observe his divine form. Similarly, as we will see in the next section, Uttaṅka receives the divine vision from Kṛṣṇa for the same purpose. In contrast, Gāndhārī receives it from Vyāsa and it enables her to see the battlefield from afar, as well as to perceive the thoughts of all those she describes. It is interesting, then, that even with divine sight, she does not see Kṛṣṇa's divine form. This is explained, of course, by the fact that she receives the divine eye from Vyāsa for a different purpose, but – as we will see – there might be other factors as well.

Despite not perceiving his divine form first-hand, she addresses Kṛṣṇa as God and is very much aware of his divinity. Not only was she in attendance when Saṃjaya first tells Dhṛtarāṣṭra about Kṛṣṇa's divine status (5.66–68), but she was also present in the Kaurava court when Kṛṣṇa revealed his divine form (5.129.4–11), even though she was not given the divine sight to see it. We also know that, because of her attendance alongside Dhṛtarāṣṭra for Saṃjaya's account of the *Bhīṣma Parvan*, she has heard the *Bhagavad Gītā*, so is aware to Kṛṣṇa's revelation to Arjuna, not to mention his teachings. That Gāndhārī knows the full extent of Kṛṣṇa's divine status is significant because much of her narration in the *Strī Parvan* is delivered as a diatribe against him, whom she holds responsible for the war's tragic outcome.

Throughout her lament, Gāndhārī reflects upon her own actions and inactions that have contributed to this tragic outcome. Blaming herself, she thinks back to what she said to Duryodhana before the war (11.17.5) and to what she said to him after the dicing scene, when she warned him to keep his distance from Śakuni (11.18.25). On two occasions she muses that she must have done something terrible in a past life to bring about her present suffering (11.16.55; 11.18.10). By addressing Kṛṣṇa throughout her lament, there is a strong sense that all these vivid descriptions of suffering are leading up to her concluding remarks, when Gāndhārī blames Kṛṣṇa directly for not preventing the war. She finally asks Kṛṣṇa why he did not do anything when he had the power to stop the war. She then accuses him of not preventing the war because he wanted it to happen (11.25.36–38).

At this point, Gāndhārī uses her ascetic powers – which she has acquired because of obedience to her husband – to curse Kṛṣṇa. Because he was unable to prevent the Kauravas and Pāṇḍavas from killing each other, she proclaims that he will slay his own family and suffer a shameful death (11.25.36–42). Kṛṣṇa responds that only he can bring about his own death and his family's destruction, and he criticises Gāndhārī for blaming him, saying that because she could not control her son, she should hold herself accountable instead. He then harshly holds her responsible for the deaths of her own sons:

> The Kurus have gone to their end because of your mistakes (11.26.1) ... You judged his [Duryodhana's] wicked deeds to be fine ... Why do you want to pin the blame on me for something you did yourself?
> (11.26.3)[24]

Unlike any of the other dialogues we are exploring in this chapter, this one exposes a cruel side to Kṛṣṇa. Considering that Kṛṣṇa made his own failed attempt to prevent the war and that he – arguably – wanted the war to happen to fulfil the divine plan, it seems extremely harsh for him to lay the blame on Gāndhārī here.[25] Moreover, Kṛṣṇa completely misrepresents her actions before the war. Gāndhārī has just reminded Kṛṣṇa of the various warnings she gave to Duryodhana, clearly demonstrating that she did not ignore her son's ruthless behaviour. Indeed, she has done perhaps more than any other character to prevent the war, attempting to persuade her son Duryodhana not to fight on several occasions. (5.67.9–10; 5.127.19–53; 5.146.28–35). On one occasion, in the *Udyoga Parvan*, Gāndhārī criticises Dhṛtarāṣṭra for not standing up to their son (5.127.10–15) and then strongly urges Duryodhana to make peace. Here, she instructs her son that he is led astray by greed and anger, advising him to control his emotions and abide by *dharma* (5.127.19–53). She also tells him to seek the help of Kṛṣṇa. Crucially, Kṛṣṇa is present when Gāndhārī reproaches her son and criticises her husband – as a first-hand witness, he is clearly aware of what she has done to prevent the war. Accordingly, Prabal Kumar Sen describes the charge levelled by Kṛṣṇa as 'totally baseless and unjustified' (2014: 190). Indeed, with the dialogues from the previous chapter in mind – particularly Duḥṣanta's harsh words to Śakuntalā when he knew she was speaking the truth – Kṛṣṇa's words here come across as cruel and misogynistic.

Like the exchange between Kṛṣṇa and Balarāma, this dialogue ends ambiguously. Kṛṣṇa has the last word; Gāndhārī remains silent, but is hardly convinced; and we are left wondering what to make of her curse. Because she describes exactly what eventually happens to Kṛṣṇa and his family, as reported subsequently in the *Mausāla Parvan* (16.4–5), we might take her curse as causing Kṛṣṇa's death, even though Kṛṣṇa denies her agency. If we were to interpret events in this way, then it would suggest that despite Kṛṣṇa being the creator and destroyer of the universe, his actions are bound by the laws of *karma*. Kṛṣṇa refutes this by saying that only he has the power to bring about his own death, yet he also engages in the logic of *karma* by claiming that it was Gāndhārī's actions, not his, that contributed to the death of her son. Peter Hill has suggested that there is a 'clear implication' that 'Kṛṣṇa has the power to override the curse but chose not to. The power of Gāndhārī's *tapas* was effective, but only because the great God allowed it to be so' (2001: 286). Although I would agree that this passage could be read in this way, it seems to me that the causes of Kṛṣṇa's death remain much more ambiguous.

Indeed, Vaiśaṃpāyana's narration in the *Mausāla Parvan* implies that Kṛṣṇa's death comes about by a combination of Gāndhārī's curse and Kṛṣṇa allowing it to happen. Vaiśaṃpāyana recounts how – thirty-six years after the war – Kṛṣṇa anticipates that Gāndhārī's curse is about to come to pass (16.3.19). Yet, Vaiśaṃpāyana also tells his listeners that Kṛṣṇa resolved to make these events happen, suggesting that ultimately he has the agency to do so (16.3.21). The *Mausāla Parvan* gives two further explanations, one where Vaiśaṃpāyana attributes the destruction of Kṛṣṇa's family to time (*kāla*) (16.2.2), and another where he explains it in terms of a curse by the *ṛṣis* Viśvāmitra, Kaṇva, and Nārada.

Kṛṣṇa's death, then, is another case where there are multiple explanations for the same event. We have seen the *Mahābhārata*'s tendency to offer a surplus of reasons to explain controversial or morally problematic episodes, such as Bhīṣma's death, Draupadī's marriage, and the dicing match. Similarly, the multiple reasons offered for Kṛṣṇa's demise portray the death of God as another moral question that remains unresolved. Although no character explicitly asks how Kṛṣṇa could possibly die, the many explanations indicate a range of understandings. As such, the death of Kṛṣṇa is presented an enigmatic question that we are invited to ask about, but for which there are no clear answers.

Nonetheless, the fact that Gāndhārī could play a seemingly necessary, if not sufficient, role in his death gives her a considerable amount of agency. What is even more remarkable is that she has gained her powers as a mere mortal living a virtuous life. She is not divine like Kṛṣṇa, nor is she an immortal sage like Viśvāmitra, Kaṇva, or Nārada. Her role in Kṛṣṇa's death, as well as her harsh criticism of him, brings attention to possible limitations on his divine powers and sense of justice. The fact that Gāndhārī does address Kṛṣṇa as God, however, raises the question as to why he does not disclose his divine form to her, or even attempt to persuade her. As we will see with Uttaṅka, Kṛṣṇa does engage with those who threaten to curse him, so it hardly seems likely that she has been too critical. The fact that she is not a devotee most likely explains why Kṛṣṇa does not reveal his divine form to her, but we still might wonder why he does not engage with her in further dialogue. We know that there is much more that Kṛṣṇa could tell Gāndhārī about why the war has taken place or about his own divine nature. We are left to wonder why, then, he would blame her without giving her a chance to understand his reasons. While Kṛṣṇa's dialogues with Arjuna and Uttaṅka reveal his divine identity, his encounter with Gāndhārī seems to expose a cruel misogyny.

Kṛṣṇa and Uttaṅka in the *Aśvamedhika Parvan* (14.53–55)

Our final dialogue with Kṛṣṇa appears in the *Aśvamedhika Parvan*, soon after the *Anu Gītā* and just after Kṛṣṇa has bid farewell to Arjuna to return to Dvārakā. As he is crossing a desert that is suffering a drought, Kṛṣṇa encounters the renowned ascetic Uttaṅka. Like Balarāma, Uttaṅka is presented as a complete outsider in regards to the events that have taken place at Kurukṣetra.[26] He remembers that Kṛṣṇa had gone to the Kaurava court to negotiate a peace settlement, but he knows nothing about the war or its outcome. He thus asks if Kṛṣṇa has been successful at brokering peace between the Pāṇḍavas and Kauravas. Unlike Arjuna at the beginning of the *Bhagavad Gītā,* Uttaṅka approaches Kṛṣṇa as an all-powerful deity, fully expecting him to have used his divine powers to have stopped the war.

Kṛṣṇa replies that he had tried his best, but that all the Kauravas were killed because he could not prevent destiny (*diṣṭa*). Here, Kṛṣṇa claims that destiny limits his own divine powers. Uttaṅka becomes very angry, accusing Kṛṣṇa of not protecting the Pāṇḍavas and Kauravas even though he was capable of doing so. He then threatens to put a curse on him for acting deceitfully and not preventing the war (14.52.19–22). But before he can act on this, Kṛṣṇa persuades the brahmin to hear him out and then launches into a short theological teaching, during which he proclaims himself the creator (*prabhava*) and destroyer (*apyaya*) of all things (14.53.14). Here, we see Kṛṣṇa returning to the theme of his own divine status, describing himself in similar ways to how he does in the *Bhagavad Gītā* (7.6). This is the first time Kṛṣṇa has made such claims about himself since the *Bhagavad Gītā*.

Kṛṣṇa then addresses the question of why he did not prevent the war. As he explains, he takes births in different wombs to uphold *dharma*; because he currently inhabits a human body, he is restricted to the capacities of a human (14.53.17–19). After hearing Kṛṣṇa's explanation, Uttaṅka is satisfied, declaring himself a devotee and asking to see his divine form. Kṛṣṇa obliges, before granting Uttaṅka the boon of always finding water when he is thirsty. This episode then segues into two intriguing stories about ways in which Uttaṅka is tested by Kṛṣṇa.[27]

In comparison with the *Anu Gītā,* Uttaṅka does not question Kṛṣṇa's philosophy, nor does he accuse him of acting undharmically, as Balarāma does. Rather, his criticism, like Gāndhārī's, is more of a theological one: if he is God, why did he not prevent this horrible war from taking place. Kṛṣṇa responds to this criticism by offering a theological explanation about the limits of his divine powers. Matilal sees Kṛṣṇa's response here as evidence that 'omnipotence is not an important concept in Indian philosophy of religion' (1991: 410). As he explains: 'Kṛṣṇa's own admission that he did not have any power to stop the battle or devastation either of the Kauravas or of the Yādavas (his own people) is an important evidence to show that the Hindu conception of God does not always include the attribute of Omnipotence' (1991: 410). Despite Kṛṣṇa's answer here, however, clearly both Gāndhārī and Uttaṅka expected him to have the power to stop the war. Obviously, neither of them fully understands the nature of his divinity, but their behaviour towards Kṛṣṇa as God includes an expectation that he is omnipotent. With this in mind, it is difficult to agree with Matilal, when he argues that 'the concept of Kṛṣṇa as God does not include omnipotence' (1991: 410–411). Rather, it seems that some conceptions of Kṛṣṇa as God do include omnipotence and that this is a theological question that is addressed in a number of instances. As we have seen in the *Bhagavad Gītā*, on some occasions, Kṛṣṇa makes proclamations suggesting that he is omnipotent (11.32–34), while his response to Uttaṅka portrays his divine power as restricted. As Emily Hudson concludes: 'the question of the extent of Kṛṣṇa's power is rendered by the text's strategies as one more issue or "knot" that joins the ranks of the epic's many riddle-questions' (2013: 202). In other words, rather than dismissing the question of omnipotence, the *Mahābhārata* seems to invite it. The text's ambiguous response to this question further contributes to the overall characterisation of Kṛṣṇa as – in Matilal's own words – 'an enigma ... a riddle, a paradox' (1991: 401).

In addition to the question about the extent of his divine powers, we are also left to wonder about the dialogical situations in which he discusses his divine powers. When explaining the limitations on his actions, Kṛṣṇa not only answers Uttaṅka's question, but Gāndhārī's as well. Indeed, there are a number of parallels between the two of them as both Gāndhārī and Uttaṅka blame Kṛṣṇa for the war and both either curse or threaten to curse him. Given that Kṛṣṇa's explanation to Uttaṅka prevents the sage from cursing him, we might wonder why Kṛṣṇa did not attempt to explain himself to Gāndhārī. As we have seen in the *Bhagavad Gītā*, Arjuna elicits Kṛṣṇa's teachings and revelation through the questions he asks. In this case, however, Gāndhārī and Uttaṅka raise the same question about Kṛṣṇa's divine powers; for Uttaṅka, this leads to revelation, but for Gāndhārī, this leads to be being blamed for the war.

Conclusion

Throughout this chapter we have returned to the question of how dialogue contributes to a theological understanding of Kṛṣṇa. In the dialogues we have examined, Kṛṣṇa's interlocutors tend to recognise him as God, but their interactions with him exhibit his divine status in different ways. In his dialogue with Arjuna in the *Bhagavad Gītā*, Kṛṣṇa offers his most detailed description and most explicit enactment of his divinity. In his dialogue with Arjuna in the *Karṇa Parvan*, he does not proclaim any divine attributes, but expresses his authority through his wisdom about the subtleties of *dharma*. At the end of the war, in the *Śalya Parvan*, Balarāma does not doubt his brother's divinity, but questions the ethics of his actions. Gāndhārī confronts Kṛṣṇa as God, holding him responsible for the war and all the suffering it had caused. Although she never questions his divine status, her curse perhaps points to limitations on his powers and judgement. In the *Anu Gītā*, Kṛṣṇa acts more like a teacher than a divine figure. Despite engaging with a number of teachings and narrative features from the *Bhagavad Gītā*, the *Anu Gītā* does not discuss the divinity of Kṛṣṇa. Only in his dialogue with Uttaṅka, his final teaching in the *Mahābhārata*, does Kṛṣṇa reveal his divine form again and make further self-proclamations about his divine nature. Kṛṣṇa eventually dies in the *Mausāla Parvan* (16.5), and at the end of the text, he is almost completely forgotten about by most characters: when the Pāṇḍavas go to heaven, only Arjuna continues to be a devotee.

In looking at the different ways that Kṛṣṇa's divine status is portrayed, I am not arguing about historical layers of the text, but rather suggesting that the *Mahābhārata* offers a range of understandings of Kṛṣṇa as he responds to his interlocutors in different ways. Indeed, Kṛṣṇa's participation in dialogue is crucial to how he is characterised as God. As we have seen, he does not enter into dialogue as God, but engages with his interlocutors in his human form. Only as a dialogue unfolds does he articulate and demonstrate the nature of his divine status, yet he only does this with some interlocutors on some occasions. It is through the questions of interlocutors such as Arjuna and Uttaṅka that Kṛṣṇa reveals his divine nature, while his dialogue with Gāndhārī shows that he withholds his cosmic form from some of his interlocutors. Considering that Gāndhārī is no more critical of Kṛṣṇa than other characters and acts virtuously throughout the text, we are left to question why he does not attempt to engage with her further in dialogue and why he blames her for the war when he knows it is not her fault. Just as Draupadī offered a critique of *dharma* from a female perspective, we might see Gāndhārī's arguments as presenting a critical view of Kṛṣṇa's divinity from a female perspective.

In addition to offering different portrayals of his divine nature, the dialogues featuring Kṛṣṇa depict his interlocutors engaging with him in different ways. He is praised as the creator and destroyer of the universe, but he is also criticised for his undharmic behaviour and his contradictory teachings. Through the questions and criticisms of his interlocutors, we hear the sorts of theological issues they are concerned about. Gāndhārī's and Uttaṅka's questions share a concern about his divine powers and responsibility to act. Meanwhile, his mid-war conversation with Arjuna, as well as his dialogues with Balarāma and Gāndhārī, raise questions about his adherence to *dharma*. In highlighting these issues, I am not assuming that all conceptions of God need to be ethical or consistent. Rather, I am highlighting the fact that Kṛṣṇa's own interlocutors seem to have these expectations of him. While the *Mahābhārata* ultimately seems comfortable with these ambiguities, it nevertheless raises these questions.

As Kṛṣṇa engages with each of his interlocutors uniquely, he offers different instructions for each specific situation. As we have seen, many teachings put forth in the *Bhagavad Gītā* are modified or even contradicted in subsequent dialogues. If the *Bhagavad Gītā* is Kṛṣṇa's most emphatic revelation of his divine nature, then the five subsequent dialogues with Kṛṣṇa are various elaborations on, responses to, and reflections on his divinity. In the *Karṇa Parvan*, for example, Kṛṣṇa emphasises *dharma*'s complexity and elusiveness, rather than taking the position that one type of *dharma* eclipses another. Here, he also qualifies his earlier position on violence, detailing the rules of combat and explaining that generally violence should be avoided altogether. Similarly, in the *Anu Gītā*, Kṛṣṇa gives counter-perspectives to the *Bhagavad Gītā*'s positions on both violence and renunciation. Kṛṣṇa does not attempt to articulate a formulaic message that would be true to all his interlocutors in all circumstances. Rather he addresses his teachings to specific individuals in their respective contexts. Although some of his interlocutors accuse him of being inconsistent, Kṛṣṇa's ability to hold several views simultaneously is also part of a dialogical theology in which he personifies the text's tendency to explore tensions and contradictions. As Matilal has suggested, the figure of Kṛṣṇa represents the elusive and ambiguous nature of *dharma*: 'If the *Mahābhārata* imparts a moral lesson, it emphazises again and again, the ever-elusive character, the unresolved ambiguity of the concept of dharma. Kṛṣṇa's role was not to resolve the ambiguity but to heighten the mystery' (1991: 404).

In personifying the unresolved ambiguity of *dharma*, Kṛṣṇa does not put an end to dialogue, but rather promotes it. In other words, the type of theology about Kṛṣṇa that emerges through dialogue is one that invites us to ask difficult questions about his divine nature and allows for disagreement. As we have seen, Kṛṣṇa is questioned, challenged, ridiculed, and even cursed. If his interlocutors model different ways through which one can encounter God, then they encourage his devotees to approach Kṛṣṇa with a healthy scepticism. As readers of dialogues with Kṛṣṇa, we are shown by his interlocutors how to pay attention to inconsistencies, how to ask difficult questions, and even how to doubt his divinity. It is only when his interlocutors look for contradictions in his arguments or inconsistencies in his actions that he delivers his deepest teachings or reveals his divine form. The dialogues we have looked at in this chapter suggest that devotees get closer to Kṛṣṇa by engaging with ambiguity and plurality. Because each of us, as readers in dialogue with the *Mahābhārata*, comes from our own unique starting point, we are left to ponder – as we try to make sense of Kṛṣṇa's teachings – which ones would apply to us, in the specificity of who we are and in the uniqueness of our own situations.

Notes

1 Translation of the *Bhagavad Gītā* loosely follow Patton (2007).
2 For an excellent overview of 19th and early 20th century scholarship on the *Mahābhārata*, see Sukthankar [1957] (2016: 1–31). For more recent overviews, see Brockington (1998: 129–158), Adluri (2011) and Hiltebeitel (2012).
3 Dahlmann, of course, was an early proponent of a synchronic approach, but for most of the 20th century, the analytic view represented the scholarly consensus.

For a discussion of Dahlmann's view, see Sukthankar [1957] (2016: 19–25) and Brockington (1998: 46–47).

4 After the first two chapters, Kṛṣṇa specifically addresses Arjuna's emotional state in the following places: 4.35; 4.42; 16.5; 18.66; 18.72.

5 For comparable episodes, see Vidura's and Sanatsujāta's teachings to Dhṛtarāṣṭra in the *Udyoga Parvan* (5.33–45) and Bhīṣma's instruction to Yudhiṣṭhira's after the war (Books 12–13).

6 See Ruth Katz for a discussion of the tension in Arjuna's character between divine hero and 'everyman' (1989: 6, ff.).

7 See also Fitzgerald (2004b: 679).

8 See, for example, the following instances: 2.18; 2.37; 3.43; 18.59.

9 See Black (2007a: 41–46).

10 Similarly, as we have seen in Chapter 2, Vyāsa tells Drupada that his daughter's wedding is inevitable, while also putting pressure on him to agree to it.

11 Similarly, Deshpande, who concludes that 'there was a version of *Mahābhārata* which did not contain a notion Kṛṣṇa as a divinity', argues that the epic context is crucial to understanding the *Bhagavad Gītā* (1991: 347). See also, Malinar, who writes: 'The *Bhagavad Gītā* was not composed independently of the epic tradition, but in relation to the epic and even for it' (2007b: 5).

12 See also Hegarty (2019), who has indicated an intra-textual relationship between the *Bhagavad Gītā* and the dialogue between Dhṛtarāṣṭra and Sanatsujāta in the *Udyoga Parvan* (5.42–45).

13 Translations from the *Karṇa Parvan* loosely follow Bowles (2007).

14 For further discussion of the parables of Balāka and Kauśika, see Matilal (1989, 2002: 26–35), Ganeri (2007: 89–92), and Hiltebeitel (2011: 21–25).

15 The importance of understanding Kṛṣṇa's divinity through scripture is noted by other characters as well. In the *Udyoga Parvan*, for example, Saṃjaya – a self-professed devotee – tells Dhṛtarāṣṭra that he knows Kṛṣṇa from scripture (*śāstra*; 5.67.5).

16 Kṛṣṇa explains that he was in a state of *yoga* when he delivered the *Bhagavad Gītā*, but cannot recall those teachings now because he is no longer in that state (14.16.12)

17 See also 14.49.4.

18 In addition to addressing Arjuna's remorse, we might also see Kṛṣṇa's teaching here as indirectly addressing Yudhiṣṭhira's grief. The *Aśvamedhika Parvan* begins with Yudhiṣṭhira collapsing in grief (*śoka*) on the banks of the Gaṅgā (14.1–5). Then, just before the *Anu Gītā*, there is a short dialogue in which Kṛṣṇa tries to soothe Yudhiṣṭhira, who is described as 'bereft' (*dīnamanasa*) because of the relatives he has lost in battle (14.11.2). Kṛṣṇa advises Yudhiṣṭhira that the real battle takes place inside himself, which he must fight before he becomes king. Kṛṣṇa then suggests that Yudhiṣṭhira perform an *aśvamedha*. The metaphor of the body as a battlefield, with the real war against one's senses and emotions – which is mentioned in the *Bhagavad Gītā* – is a recurring theme in the *Anu Gītā*.

19 Sharma points out that this line is nearly identical to what Kṛṣṇa says to Arjuna at the end of the *Bhagavad Gītā* (18.72) (1986: 4).

20 See also Duryodhana's list of ways that Kṛṣṇa acts undharmically during the war (9.60.27–38). For a discussion of Kṛṣṇa's endorsement of underhanded tactics during the war, see Matilal (1991).

21 See also 5.154; and Smith's note (2009: 542).

22 For further discussion of Gāndhārī and this dialogue with Kṛṣṇa, see Black (2007b: 62–65).

23 Gāndhārī's divine sight consists of much more than being able to see the battlefield despite wearing a blindfold. It also lets her listen in on all of the conversations and know the thoughts of those on the battlefield. Similarly, Saṃjaya's divine eye gives him a universal perspective that allows him to know the thoughts, and even the dreams, of the warriors of Kurukṣetra. As Belvalkar comments: 'There are minor miracles without end that Saṃjaya is able to perform as a consequence of Vyāsa's boon' (1946: 317). For more discussion about Saṃjaya and the powers of the divine eye, see Belvalkar (1947) and Hiltebeitel (2001b: 32–91).

24 Translation of the *Strī Parvan* loosely follow Fitzgerald (2004b).

25 Although Kṛṣṇa attempts to negotiate a peaceful settlement, many of arguments and actions suggest that he wants the war to take place. According to Deshpande: 'Kṛṣṇa is the one character that is consistently advocating war with the Kauravas' (1991: 341). We might also recall Gāndhārī's charge that Kṛṣṇa did not prevent the war because he wanted the destruction of the Kauravas (11.25.35).

26 Indeed, Adluri, who compares this episode featuring Uttaṅka with his appearance in the *Ādi Parvan*, argues that he 'maintains a distance from the narrative'. In comparison with Vyāsa, who authors and directly shapes the narrative through his participation, Uttaṅka is characterised – according to Adluri – as an 'interpreter' who reappears towards the end of the text to interpret its meaning (2013a: 9, note 28).

27 For an excellent discussion of these two stories, see Reich (1998: 358–370).

Conclusion

The subtlety of *dharma*

We began this book by taking the *Mahābhārata*'s self-description as an *upaniṣad* as an important lens through which to understand the philosophical implications of dialogue. As we noted, a number of ways that dialogue operates in the *Mahābhārata* seem to develop out of the Upaniṣads. Most fundamentally, like the Upaniṣads, the *Mahābhārata* includes narrative depictions of characters in verbal encounters with each other debating about religious and philosophical issues. In this way, the dialogue form roots otherwise abstract philosophical doctrines as arguments of specific individuals in concrete circumstances.

One Upaniṣadic trope in particular that is further developed by the *Mahābhārata* is the rhetoric of subtlety. As we noted in the Introduction, the *Mahābhārata* expands upon the Upaniṣadic tendency to portray its most central ideas as elusive and unfathomable. In the *Mahābhārata,* the most significant example of this tendency is the often repeated description of *dharma* as *sūkṣma*. As we have seen, A.K. Ramanujan has suggested that 'not *dharma*', but '*dharmasūkṣmatā* or the subtle nature of *dharma* ... is the central theme of the *Mahābhārata*' (1999: 23). Now that we have examined a number of dialogues where characters use this phrase, we can build on Ramanujan's observation by noting that *dharma* is described as subtle by different characters for different reasons. By looking at the rhetorical implications of *dharma-sūkṣmatā* across the specific contexts we have discussed in this book, we can gain a deeper appreciation of some of its different connotations.

In Chapter 1 we saw that Śiśupāla describes *dharma* as subtle when insinuating to Yudhiṣṭhira that, if he really understood *dharma*, then he would not follow the advice of Bhīṣma to install Kṛṣṇa as successor to the position of universal sovereign. We noted that Śiśupāla says this not only to Yudhiṣṭhira, but also to Bhīṣma and Kṛṣṇa, both of whom are present and who are the main targets of his criticisms throughout the remainder of this encounter. It is interesting, then, that Śiśupāla invokes the subtlety of *dharma* when he is arguing against three of the text's most authoritative speakers about *dharma*, all of whom describe *dharma* as *sūkṣma* at one point or another. Crucially, Śiśupāla seems to use this phrase differently from his interlocutors. As we have seen, Yudhiṣṭhira describes *dharma* as subtle when bringing together a range of different arguments based on different understandings of *dharma.* Alternatively, both Bhīṣma and Kṛṣṇa speak of *dharma*'s subtlety when defending actions that seemingly violate accepted practices. In comparison, Śiśupāla uses this phrase to describe a more conventional understanding of *dharma.* We do not have enough information to reconstruct Śiśupāla's exact meaning here, but his main point is that Yudhiṣṭhira is not following the proper procedure of the ritual when installing Kṛṣṇa as his successor. While many other characters also make procedural or rule-based arguments, this is the only time that someone portrays *sūkṣma dharma* in this way. We might wonder if Śiśupāla really means to characterise *dharma* as elusive here, or rather if his primary aim is to appropriate a way of speaking about *dharma* often associated with his interlocutors. Although *dharma*'s subtlety is not mentioned in any of the other dialogues we explored in Chapter 1, when Bhīṣma tells Yudhiṣṭhira the parables of Balāka and Kauśika, it is notable that he does not describe *dharma* in this way. As we have seen, Kṛṣṇa also tells the stories of Balāka and Kauśika, not only offering more narrative details, but also using these stories explicitly to illustrate the subtlety of *dharma.* Although Bhīṣma describes *dharma* as *sūkṣma* on other occasions, he does not associate this understanding with these stories. Moreover, he never invokes the subtlety of *dharma* to defend his vows.

We saw in Chapter 2 that both Yudhiṣṭhira and Dhṛṣṭadyumna describe *dharma* as *sūkṣma.* Yudhiṣṭhira says this as he shifts his argument from procedural and traditional points to talking about *dharma* in terms of his own actions and his authority to speak on its behalf. Meanwhile, Dhṛṣṭadyumna portrays *dharma* as subtle to claim that it is impossible to know whether his sister's polyandrous marriage can be defended in terms of *dharma.* Dhṛṣṭadyumna seems to be arguing that as long as he can cast doubt on the dharmic status of the marriage, then he can prevent it from taking place. Rather than arguing that the practice of polyandry for women is definitely a violation of *dharma* – like his father argues – Dhṛṣṭadyumna merely raises doubts over whether it is possible to determine, thus putting the burden of proof on Yudhiṣṭhira. Thus, in opposition to Yudhiṣṭhira, who describes *dharma* as subtle when asserting his own authority to speak on its behalf, Dhṛṣṭadyumna's invocation of *sūkṣma dharma* challenges Yudhiṣṭhira's claim to be able to determine *dharma* in this situation.

None of the dialogues we examined in Chapter 3 feature anyone describing *dharma* as subtle. Although Yudhiṣṭhira talks about *dharma*'s subtlety on other occasions, he does not say this in any of the discussions about his decision to play dice. Perhaps unsurprisingly, Duryodhana does not claim to have such an understanding at any point in the *Mahābhārata.* Meanwhile, Dhṛtarāṣṭra does describe *dharma* as subtle on two occasions:

once when speaking to Yudhiṣṭhira immediately after the first dicing match (2.65.4) and on another occasion when in conversation with Vidura during the *Āraṇyaka Parvan* (3.5.2). On neither occasion does Dhṛtarāṣṭra claim to have such an understanding himself, but rather he uses this description to praise the text's two most explicit personifications of *dharma* for their depth of knowledge.

In Chapter 4, we saw that both Draupadī and Bhīṣma describe *dharma* as *sūkṣma*. Draupadī says this while being dragged across the hall by her hair. Although addressing Duḥśāsana, she seems to be directing her words towards everyone present in the *sabhā*, particularly the Kuru elders, such as Bhīṣma, Droṇa, and Dhṛtarāṣṭra. It is not entirely clear what Draupadī means here, but in the context of her argument as a whole, she seems to be pointing to an understanding of *dharma* as a moral order. Her invocation of this phrase serves as a warning to Duḥśāsana and the Kauravas that, despite abiding by rules and procedures within the narrow confines of the game itself, they are violating *dharma* in the way they are treating her. Not only do her words imply that Duḥśāsana and his brothers have not achieved a higher understanding of *dharma*, but also, by referring to Yudhiṣṭhira as the Son of Dharma and repeating a phrase that he used when making his case for polyandry, Draupadī seems to expect him to intercede. The fact that Yudhiṣṭhira does not respond to this invitation – indeed, the fact that he remains silent during this entire episode – contributes to characterising *dharma* as elusive. His silence remains a mystery, and we are left to wonder whether it is a sign of him following *dharma* or violating it, of whether his silence reveals a deeper insight or exposes a lack of understanding. In contrast, Draupadī's successful navigation of her precarious situation indicates that she has achieved the type of understanding of *dharma* she accuses the Kauravas of not attaining. Indeed, if part of *sūkṣma dharma* is grasping *dharma*'s plurality, then the way that she makes her arguments and conducts herself throughout this debate could be seen as a demonstration of this understanding. In contrast to Draupadī, Bhīṣma's acknowledgement of *dharma* as subtle paralyses him. As he hides behind its ambiguity to avoid addressing Draupadī's questions, we might wonder if Bhīṣma truly does understand *dharma*'s subtle nature. Or perhaps his inability to act – as well as Yudhiṣṭhira's inability to speak – tells us something important about *sūkṣma dharma*; that because *dharma* is so elusive, it eludes even its greatest authorities on some occasions.

In Chapter 5, we saw that, despite embodying *dharma*'s complexities and contradictions, the only occasions where Kṛṣṇa describes *dharma* as subtle are when he introduces and concludes the Balāka and Kauśika episodes. Although Kṛṣṇa instructs Arjuna that the subtle nature of *dharma* can be determined through reason (*tarka*) (8.49.48), these stories seem to demonstrate *dharma*'s subtlety through its surprising paradoxes. Indeed, the consequences of Balāka's and Kauśika's actions are in direct opposition to traditional understandings of *dharma*. Balāka goes straight to heaven even though he impulsively kills another living being, whereas Kauśika goes to hell even though he upholds his vow always to tell the truth. Both cases illustrate that the dharmic quality of an action cannot be determined by a general formula – that whether an action upholds *dharma* depends on the specificity of the circumstances.

Although this is the only dialogue we discussed where Kṛṣṇa explicitly describes *dharma* as *sūkṣma*, he behaves according to this understanding in his heated exchange with Balarāma, who accuses him of violating *dharma*. As we noted, it is unclear why Kṛṣṇa does not do more in this encounter to explain his actions. We might also wonder why, considering his appreciation of *dharma*'s ambiguities in other contexts, Kṛṣṇa is so strict about maintaining a very narrow understanding of *dharma* when speaking to Arjuna in the *Bhagavad Gītā*. When it comes to his various pronouncements on *dharma*, perhaps Saṃjaya and Balarāma are correct to accuse Kṛṣṇa of making any argument that suits him. In any case, the inconsistencies in his arguments contribute to characterising *dharma* as difficult to understand.

Before moving on to the different understandings of dialogue we explored throughout this book, let us briefly reflect on what these verbal encounters tell us about the *sūkṣma dharma*. What I want to highlight is that, despite often evoking a higher, more esoteric understanding, the portrayal of *dharma* as *sūkṣma* has quite different connotations depending on the speaker and the circumstance. Kṛṣṇa's use of the Balāka and Kauśika stories as an illustration of its subtlety points to an understanding where *dharma* is not what it seems, where doing the opposite of a conventional understanding is the way to uphold *dharma* in some circumstances. While this characterises *dharma* as paradoxical, on other occasions, *sūkṣma* conveys more of a sense of its pluralistic complexity. As we have seen, both Yudhiṣṭhira and Draupadī seem to understand *dharma* in this way when they make multi-tiered arguments in which they bring together a range of its meanings. In contrast, both Dhṛṣṭadyumna and Bhīṣma appeal to its ambiguity. For Dhṛṣṭadyumna, its lack of clarity means that Yudhiṣṭhira cannot claim to speak on its behalf, while for Bhīṣma, its uncertainty means that he does not know what to say.

Dialogue as verbal encounter

In this book we have understood the term 'dialogue' in three main ways: (1) as verbal encounter, (2) as intra-textuality, and (3) as hermeneutics. In the context of dialogue as verbal encounter, we noted that philosophical dialogue is a genre of philosophy found in traditions around the world. One of the ways that the dialogues in the *Mahābhārata* are comparable to philosophical dialogue in other contexts is in how the form contains embedded practices of philosophy. In each chapter, we highlighted a particular aspect of how dialogue portrays ways of doing philosophy.

In Chapter 1, we focused on dialectic, looking at how dialogues between characters juxtapose arguments in different ways. Whereas the verbal encounter between Bhīṣma and Satyavatī can be understood in terms of providing a synthesis, or at least a compromise, between two opposing views, the debate between Bhīṣma and Śiśupāla is an irreconcilable confrontation that concludes with Śiśupāla losing his head. In addition to examining different types of oppositional relationships between arguments within dialogues, we have also traced how dialectic operates across the *Mahābhārata*, as the same issue can be explored differently in contrasting contexts as circumstances change. By tracing the ongoing deliberations on Bhīṣma's vows along with the unfolding of the narrative, we have seen that the changing vantage points of Bhīṣma and his interlocutors demonstrate the temporal contingency of moral decisions. Although Bhīṣma's vows provided a particularly vivid illustration of the dialectical aspects of the dialogue form, we have explored comparable dialectical relationship in every chapter.

In Chapter 2, we focused on dharmic reasoning and dialogue itself as a dharmic practice. By closely examining Yudhiṣṭhira's arguments, we observed that he exhibits a pluralistic understanding of *dharma*. Additionally, the ways Vyāsa, Yudhiṣṭhira, and Drupada conduct themselves throughout this discussion indicate shared practices of interactive decision-making. Perhaps we could say that by following such practices together, and not letting the conversation descend into the type of confrontation we see on other occasions, the interlocutors not only abide by shared practices of group debate, but also contribute to the dharmic status of their collective decision.

In Chapter 3, we looked at the dialectic between fate and human agency. Despite the emphasis on destiny in some contexts, we noted that in verbal encounters with others, characters reflect on their own situations and treat each other with a considerable degree of agency. Although there are many occasions where characters explain their own actions or inactions as compelled by fate, rarely do they treat others as if they do not have moral responsibility for their actions. Rather than offering a metaphysical solution to the dialectic between freedom/determinism debate, the *Mahābhārata* explores their relationship through the arguments that characters make when in dialogue with others. Despite sometimes expressing a deterministic outlook, characters praise and blame their interlocutors, while also engaging in deep and ongoing reflections on their own decisions and actions.

Although we highlighted the dialectic between fate and human agency in Chapter 3, this is a tension that we have explored, in one way or another, in each chapter. In Chapter 1, we saw that despite his destiny not to have offspring, Bhīṣma's vows are a topic of intense and continuing debate as the narrative unfolds. In Chapter 2, we observed that despite presenting Draupadī's polyandrous marriage as determined by her previous life, as well as ordained by the actions of the gods, Vyāsa goes to great lengths to convince Drupada and calls attention to his agency in choosing whether or not to agree to the marriage. In Chapter 4, neither Draupadī nor Śakuntalā accepts what they could have considered to be a miserable fate, as both challenge the decisions of their royal interlocutors to achieve a different outcome from the one they are confronted with at the beginning of their dialogues. Finally, in Chapter 5, we saw that despite telling Arjuna that his actions are merely the instruments of his divine agency, Kṛṣṇa, nevertheless, at the end of the *Bhagavad Gīta*, instructs him that it is up to him to decide what to do. By looking at these instances together, we see that the tension between fate and human agency plays out across the entire *Mahābhārata*. In each case, despite the mythological scope of the narrative and the divine identities of individual characters, these dialogues take the pivotal events of the story as opportunities for ongoing moral reflection.

In Chapter 4, we returned to the issue of dharmic reasoning, examining the arguments of Draupadī. Like Yudhiṣṭhira, Draupadī makes a complex argument that incorporates different understandings of *dharma*. Her overall case for freedom rests on the fact that she offers three distinct, but overlapping, reasons for doubting the Kauravas' claim to her. By looking at her arguments alongside those of Śakuntalā and Sulabhā, we saw that they offer vital female perspectives to wider discussions about the nature of *dharma*. As we have seen, by including the arguments and experiences of these three female characters, as well as others, the *Mahābhārata* offers a wide range of female perspectives, without reducing the experiences of women to one voice.

In Chapter 5, we returned to the issue of dialectic, while looking at the dialogue between Arjuna and Kṛṣṇa in the *Bhagavad Gītā*. As we saw, their contrasting arguments set up a series of oppositional relationships between central religious and philosophical ideas. While these ideas are harmonised through the figure of Kṛṣṇa, the dialogue form leaves questions unanswered and tensions unresolved. When we then compared the *Bhagavad Gītā* with five subsequent dialogues with Kṛṣṇa, we further explored the temporal nature of dialogue, observing that a number of issues raised in the *Bhagavad Gītā* play out differently as his interlocutors and contexts change.

In addition to exhibiting a range of methods for discussing philosophy, each dialogue portrays ethical discussions as dynamic encounters in dramatic circumstances. From attempts to persuade Bhīṣma to relinquish his vows (Chapter 1), to discussions about the legitimacy of Draupadī's marriage (Chapter 2); from the contrasting accounts of how Duryodhana justifies his envy of his cousin's power and the multiple justifications Yudhiṣṭhira gives for his decision to play dice (Chapter 3), to the problems posed by Draupadī's questions in the *sabhā* after the dicing match (Chapter 4), and to Arjuna's despair over whether or not to fight in the *Bhagavad Gītā* (Chapter 5) – these five discussions address some of the most consequential episodes in the main narrative. In these cases, philosophical dialogue in the *Mahābhārata* takes place in urgent circumstances, where every decision and action has enormous consequences. By placing discussions about *dharma*, *karma*, fate, agency, and other central doctrines in the context of these specific and momentous situations, the *Mahābhārata* emphasises the context-sensitive nature of moral decisions.

We have also noted that the *Mahābhārata* explores the perspectival dimension of dialogue. Now that we can reflect back on the dialogues we have discussed in this book, we can see that through its range of characters and the different arguments they make, the *Mahābhārata* offers a variety of different perspectives that are accentuated through their contrasts with each other. In Chapter 2, for example, we saw that the brahmin Vyāsa and the king Yudhiṣṭhira offered different understandings of *dharma*, while in Chapter 5, we explored a number of encounters between humans and the divine, as different interlocutors approached their encounters with Kṛṣṇa with their own unique questions and expectations, while eliciting varying manifestations of his divinity.

In particular, different perspectives are represented through the gender distinctions between characters. As we saw in Chapter 4, characters such as Draupadī, Śakuntalā, and Sulabhā offer female perspectives on some of the text's central issues. Whereas both Draupadī and Śakuntalā expose some of the male biases in traditional understandings of *dharma*, Sulabhā provides a gendered twist to the ongoing debates between householders and renunciates. By looking at them together, we saw that Draupadī, Śakuntalā, and Sulabhā each make arguments unique to their situations, emphasising different aspects of *dharma* and offering a range of female viewpoints in the process.

Although we paid particular attention to the gender implications of dialogue in Chapter 4, this is a theme we have traced throughout this book. In Chapter 1, we saw how some of the most significant challenges to Bhīṣma's vows are from female characters. Satyavatī presents a stark choice for Bhīṣma between personal integrity and saving the lineage. Despite portraying Saytavatī as making solid arguments and as having a genuine concern about the future of the lineage, Vaiśaṃpāyana adds some rather patronising comments when narrating this episode, describing her as wretched and begging for grandchildren. Considering that Vaiśaṃpāyana has only recently recounted the story of Śakuntalā, in which his own narration offers a corrective to Duḥṣanta's sexist remarks and accusations, we might wonder whether Vaiśaṃpāyana could be more self-reflective about his own narration here. In any case, his account of the Śakuntalā episode offers us a more gender-conscious frame through which to interpret his misogynistic description of Satyavatī. Another critical perspective on Bhīṣma's vows comes from Ambā, who suffers their consequences as much as anyone. As we have seen, Bhīṣma's portrayal of Ambā's circumstances after the *rākṣasa* marriage offers a vivid account of the harm his vows cause others. It also points to larger injustices suffered by women when men neglect to consider the negative effects of their actions.

In Chapter 2, we saw that Kuntī's words have considerable weight in the arguments that attempt to justify Draupadī's marriage. Nevertheless, we also explored the recurring double standard attributed to women's speech – that their words are less likely to be trusted or treated with authority, but can at the same time be considered more binding than the words of men. Whereas male characters can get out of their vows and even the most ardent truth-tellers can lie on some occasions, female characters are somehow expected to speak the truth in a completely literal and consistent way, even in situations where they are wilfully misinterpreted or flippantly misled. Clearly Kuntī feels the burden of the weight of her words, perhaps sensing that the escape clauses available to men are not options for her. Despite her predicament, however, Kuntī shows considerable agency in making absolutely sure that her words are taken into account. Neither Yudhiṣṭhira nor Vyāsa abides by her words merely because she said them – as they might a vow or an oath. Rather, both of them emphasise the authority of her words because she convinces them to do so.

In the dialogues we have looked at in Chapter 3, there are no female voices and only one encounter where women are explicitly present. As we noted, when Yudhiṣṭhira explains his decision when Draupadī is in attendance, he brings up his loss of reason for the first time. In contrast with his dialogue with Vidura – where he seems to accept some moral responsibility – here he offers none at all. Moreover, by saying that he lost his reason, he informs Draupadī of what will be her first argument to challenge the legitimacy of his final stake after the match. It is noteworthy, though, that as the one who most suffers for this disastrous decision, Draupadī continues to blame Yudhiṣṭhira for the dicing match long after it is over. In this way, Draupadī offers an ongoing counter-perspective to Yudhiṣṭhira's views on *dharma*.

In Chapter 5, we saw that Gāndhārī offers perhaps the greatest challenge to Kṛṣṇa's teachings and divine powers. Throughout the narrative, Gāndhārī does as much as any other character to prevent the war. Nevertheless, when she holds Kṛṣṇa accountable for his actions, he, in turn, condemns Gāndhārī – rather than accepting any responsibility or offering any divine or cosmic explanations. Keeping in mind the double standards that Draupadī, Śakuntalā, and Sulabhā all blatantly confront, Gāndhārī seems to be facing some of the same gender biases here. But if this dialogue reveals a misogynistic side to Kṛṣṇa, then it also offers the possibility of understanding his demise as karmic retribution for his harsh treatment of Gāndhārī. In comparison, Gāndhārī does not suffer any karmic consequences for a curse that contributes to the death of Kṛṣṇa.

In addition to the different perspectives of different interlocutors, we have also seen that the same character can offer a range of perspectives depending on their situations. Bhīṣma defends his vows differently as circumstances change and Yudhiṣṭhira explains his decision to play dice in a variety of ways. Rather than treating the diversity of explanations as inconsistencies, we have seen them as examples of characters reinterpreting their own actions in the presence of different interlocutors in evolving contexts. Meanwhile, with the alternative versions of the Duryodhana/Dhṛtarāṣṭra dialogue, we have seen that the arguments of the same characters in the same situation can be represented in contrasting ways. In these examples and others, the *Mahābhārata* invites a multi-perspectival exploration into philosophical questions, particularly questions about *dharma*, by portraying characters disagreeing with each other, responding to each other's arguments, and revising their own arguments as circumstances change.

As noted in the Introduction, multiple perspectives remain in tension because many of the *Mahābhārata*'s most consequential dialogues remain unresolved. Such non-closure, however, is conveyed in different ways. In Chapter 1, uncertainties about Bhīṣma's vows are maintained by each critical perspective, as well the cumulative weight between them. In the discussions about Draupadī's marriage, uncertainties remain because Drupada is not convinced by the arguments of Yudhiṣṭhira and Vyāsa. Although Yudhiṣṭhira and Vyāsa make strong cases for why this particular instance of polyandry can be justified, the fact that Draupadī is sexually harassed on three occasions after her marriage indicates that Drupada's fears were well founded and raises doubts about whether the marriage really abides by *dharma* after all.

Three versions of the Duryodhana/Dhṛtarāṣṭra dialogue convey a different sense of uncertainty – in all three instances of this encounter the outcome is the same, but the way the dialogue unfolds is portrayed differently, with each version offering a unique account of how moral responsibility for the dicing match is shared by Duryodhana, Dhṛtarāṣṭra, and Yudhiṣṭhira. Meanwhile, in the same chapter, we saw that we never really know why Yudhiṣṭhira decides to play dice, not only because his interlocutors ascribe to him varying motivations, but also because his own understanding shifts as he talks to different people and reflects back on his decision from changing vantage points.

In comparison with our other dialogues, the debates in the *sabhā* featuring Draupadī, Śakuntalā, and Sulabhā are perhaps the least ambiguous, because all three women emerge successful in their encounters. Despite their short-term victories, however, perhaps what remains uncertain is whether their voices are heard beyond their own specific circumstances.

In Chapter 5, we explored how dialogue contributes to conveying Kṛṣṇa's divine nature. Only as a dialogue unfolds does Kṛṣṇa articulate and demonstrate his divine identity, yet he only does this with some interlocutors on some occasions. Although some of his interlocutors accuse him of being inconsistent, Kṛṣṇa's ability to hold several views simultaneously is also part of a dialogical theology in which he personifies the text's tendency to explore tensions and contradictions. The type of theology of Kṛṣṇa that emerges through dialogue is one that invites difficult questions about his divine nature and allows for disagreement. It is only when his interlocutors look for contradictions in his arguments or inconsistencies in his actions that he delivers his deepest teachings or reveals his divine form.

Dialogue as intra-textuality

In addition to exploring a number of different dialogues that address moral questions, much of this book has examined the relationship between different dialogues within the text. From a series of conversations that take place over an entire lifetime (Bhīṣma's vows), to four interlinked discussions over a short period of time (Draupadī's marriage), to three different accounts of the same verbal encounter (Duryodhana's despair), to the intra-textual resonances between similar dialogues (Draupadī's questions), and to another series of dialogues featuring the same character, but within different situations and with different interlocutors (Kṛṣṇa's conversations) – these sets of discussions demonstrate some of the multiple ways that dialogues relate to each other across the text.

In Chapter 1, we treated a series of dialogues about Bhīṣma's vows as an ongoing dialectic. In Chapter 2, we looked at how different arguments defending Draupadī's marriage are distinct from each other, but nevertheless can work together towards the same goal of trying to convince Drupada. In Chapter 3, we interpreted versions of the dialogue between Duryodhana and Dhṛtarāṣṭra as three different lenses examining how this pivotal exchange unfolds. In Chapter 4, we saw how the different arguments of Draupadī, Śakuntalā, and Sulabhā reinforce and amplify each other. While in Chapter 5, we saw how dialogues with Kṛṣṇa after the *Bhagavad Gītā* offer a range of perspectives on his pre-war teaching and divine revelation. Now that we can reflect back on our five dialogical case studies, we can see that one of the ways that the *Mahābhārata*'s dharmic instruction emerges is by inviting intra-textual readings.

In reading the *Mahābhārata* dialogically, we have also confronted what could be considered inconsistencies or contradictions. Rather than explain these occasions as textual flaws, however, we have approached them in terms of the *Mahābhārata*'s multi-vocality. In Chapter 1, for example, we saw how different narrators sometimes depict the same events in different ways. In this case, Bhīṣma's two accounts of his own past differ distinctly from Vaiśaṃpāyana's narration in the *Ādi Parvan*. Rather than take Bhīṣma's accounts as interpolations that do not fit into the main narrative, we interpreted these occasions as offering psychological depth to Bhīṣma's character, portraying him as reflecting back on how own his actions led to the breach in his family as he attempts to persuade Duryodhana to save the family from even more catastrophic division. Moreover, Bhīṣma's account of the Kauśika story takes place in a section of the *Mahābhārata* that most early Western scholars would have considered didactic and, therefore, superfluous to the main story. We have seen, however, that Bhīṣma's teachings of the *Śānti* and *Anuśāsana Parvan*s offer alternative perspectives on his actions that lead to the war. In some ways, the stories of Bhīṣma's vows and Kauśika's vows have a contestatory relationship with each other – with opposing understandings of the practice of vow-taking – but the fact that it is Bhīṣma who tells the Kauśika story offers further complexity to his character, perhaps indicating that he is modifying his own views on taking vows as he prepares himself for death.

In Chapter 2, we saw several examples of what some scholars have referred to as 'overdetermination'. Not only does the text include two versions of Vyāsa's narration of the story of Draupadī's previous birth and the juxtaposition of this story with the story of the five Indras, but also Yudhiṣṭhira offers at least six different dharmic explanations to defend the polyandrous marriage. Rather than see this as a surplus of justifications or as a case of textual growth, we have explored the discussions about Draupadī's marriage as demonstrating a method of moral reasoning that takes into consideration a range of factors, without reducing arguments to one criterion.

In Chapter 3, we saw another example of what might be considered a repetition or inconsistency – the inclusion of three versions of the dialogue between Duryodhana and Dhṛtarāṣṭra. Rather than taking any one of them as more original or integral to the text, we examined how each one characterises this episode differently – not only offering a different perspective on how the dialogue unfolds, but also providing alternative portrayals of how each of the main contributors are morally responsible for bringing about 'the destruction of the world'.

In Chapter 4, we looked at three episodes featuring women arguing in the *sabhā*. Rather than taking their arguments as somehow accidental or marginal to the text's otherwise patriarchal agenda, we interpreted them as offering valuable female perspectives that contribute to the text's ongoing deliberation about *dharma*. Meanwhile, in Chapter 5, we approached a number of Kṛṣṇa's dialogues during and after the war as commentaries on his pre-war teaching in the *Bhagavad Gītā*. Rather than assume that the sections proclaiming Kṛṣṇa's divinity are later additions to the text, we have seen that each of his dialogical episodes assumes his divine status in one way or another, even if only some interlocutors affirm his divine identity, while others remain sceptical. In each chapter, then, we have taken contradictions and inconsistencies as vital contributions to ongoing debates across the text.

Dialogue as hermeneutics

The third understanding of dialogue that we have explored throughout this book is the dialogue between the *Mahābhārata* and its audiences. Building on the insights of Vrinda Dalmiya and Gangeya Mukherji, we have observed how the dialogue form contributes to conveying the text's dharmic instructions. In each chapter, we have seen how the medium of dialogue is integral to provoking ongoing dialogues with others, as well as with ourselves.

The *Mahābhārata* compels us into dialogue with others by vividly portraying the ways that characters engage in discussions with each other. Despite the wide range of views expressed and the variety of ways that moral discussions unfold, one recurring feature of dialogue is that it is portrayed as an integral aspect of living dharmically. Many of the dialogues we have examined express the sense that abiding by *dharma* is not merely following family and class obligations as rules or commandments, but it also requires a moral commitment and context sensitivity to all interactions that one has with others. Part of *dharma*, then, is entering into dialogue with the uniqueness of each person and the specificity of every situation.

The ethical questions posed by the *Mahābhārata* not only indicate that the text's own social context was complex and diverse, but that its approach to moral reasoning might be relevant in pluralistic contexts today. As Matilal has suggested, the demand for complex methods of moral reasoning is all the more crucial in pluralistic contexts (2002: 68). In other words, in situations where there is greater diversity and less moral certainty, the models of debate and discussion that address the plurality of viewpoints are particularly important. In relating these lessons to contemporary moral debates, I suggest that what the *Mahābhārata* brings to conversations today is not a particular doctrine or viewpoint, but rather its capacity to represent multiple perspectives and its vivid portrayals of the vicissitudes of verbal encounters with others. The dialogues in the *Mahābhārata* do not unfold formulaically, but nevertheless they contain implicit methods for navigating diversity and plurality. Through the ways that characters such as Yudhiṣṭhira, Draupadī, and Kṛṣṇa argue, the *Mahābhārata* conveys what could be considered a dharmic way of reasoning, which takes into account a variety of perspectives and the specificity of each unique moral quandary. According to this understanding, one's own capacity to uphold *dharma* is always developing and never perfected, as each new encounter with others presents new challenges and offers the potential to confound us.

The *Mahābhārata* compels us into dialogue with ourselves by conveying unresolved tensions in *dharma* that require further deliberation. As we have seen, the text repeatedly juxtaposes a number of contrasting religious or philosophical ideas, such as fate and human agency, *karma-yoga* and renunciation, violence and non-violence, *pravṛtti* and *nivṛtti*, as well as a range of understandings of *dharma*. Such ideas are in tension from one dialogue to the next, but their relationship plays out differently in each case, as different characters offer contrasting arguments in changing narrative contexts. None of the central religious or philosophical ideas in the *Mahābhārata* eclipse all others in advance and in all circumstances. Moreover, the moral status of each of the text's central episodes remains unresolved. We are left to contemplate whether Bhīṣma should have given up his vows, whether Drupada might have done more to prevent his daughter from marrying five men, whether Dhṛtarāṣṭra could have forestalled the dicing match, whether Yudhiṣṭhira could have replied to Draupadī's questions, or whether Arjuna might have refused to fight. While the cosmic context of the story and the retrospective quality of the narrative perhaps make the deliberations of the characters seem futile, the *Mahābhārata* nevertheless urges us to engage with its characters' searching questions about how to live a moral life in volatile times.

Through dialogue, the *Mahābhārata* poses ethical questions without closing off interpretations, offers a range of perspectives without endorsing a singular authoritative view, and includes competing worldviews without reducing all to the same. Through the verbal encounters between characters and the intra-textual relationship between them, the *Mahābhārata* conveys multi-perspectival and open-ended ways of thinking about moral questions. Its poly-vocal dharmic instruction does not tell us what to do, but rather invites us to reflect upon our own choices in our own circumstances.

Characters

- Ambā: princess of Kāśi; she is abducted by Bhīṣma to marry Vicitravīrya; when she returns to her fiancée Śālva, he rejects her; she then becomes a wandering ascetic and vows to kill Bhīṣma in her next life; she is reborn as Śikhaṇḍin.
- Ambālikā: one of the three princesses that Bhīṣma abducts to marry Vicitravīrya; she is the mother of Paṇḍu and sister of Ambā and Ambikā
- Ambikā: one of the three princesses that Bhīṣma abducts to marry Vicitravīrya; she is the mother of Dhṛtarāṣṭra and sister of Ambā and Ambālikā
- Arjuna: third eldest of the Pāṇḍava brothers; his divine father is Indra; he is also the great-grandfather of Janamejaya, the primary listener of the *Mahābhārata* in the inner frame dialogue; Arjuna is Kṛṣṇa's interlocutor in the *Bhagavad Gītā*
- Asita Devala: a divine seer
- Asuras: the cosmic rivals of the main Vedic gods, especially Indra
- Balāka: a reluctant hunter who goes to heaven for killing a wild creature; his story is told by both Bhīṣma and Kṛṣṇa
- Balarāma: older brother of Kṛṣṇa; he remains neutral during the war
- Bharata: son of Śakuntalā and Duḥṣanta; he is the progenitor of the Bharata family
- Bhīmasena: also known as Bhīma, he is the second eldest of the Pāṇḍava brothers; his divine father is Vāyu, the god of the Wind
- Bhīṣma: son of King Śaṃtanu and the goddess Gaṅgā; his divine identity is Dyaus, the eighth of a group of deities known as the Vasus; often referred to as grandfather, he is the great-uncle of the Pāṇḍavas and Kauravas; before he is mortally wounded, he is the general of the Kaurava army; he is the teacher of Yudhiṣṭhira after the war; he is also known as Devavrata (he whose vows are of the gods)
- Brahmā: the creator god
- Bṛhaspati: household priest of the gods
- Citrāṅgada: elder son of Satyavatī and Śaṃtanu; he dies before producing an heir
- Damayantī: wife of Nala

- Dhātṛ: the Ordainer; the deity associated with fate and destiny
- Dhṛṣṭadyumna: brother of Draupadī
- Dhṛtarāṣṭra: father of the Kauravas, husband of Gāndhārī, older brother of Paṇḍu; he would have been the heir to the throne, but was disqualified because he was born blind; nevertheless, he acts as regent king after Paṇḍu dies and before the Pāṇḍavas and Kauravas come of age; he is the son of Ambikā and Vyāsa
- Draupadī: wife of the five Pāṇḍavas; she is an incarnation of the goddess Śrī
- Droṇa: teacher of the Kauravas and Pāṇḍavas; he is the general of the Kaurava army after Bhīṣma is mortally wounded
- Drupada: father of Draupadī; king of Pāñcāla; also father of Dhṛṣṭadyumna and Śikhaṇḍin
- Duḥṣanta: husband of Śakuntalā; father of Bharata
- Duḥśāsana: second-eldest son of Dhṛtarāṣṭra; brother of Duryodhana; he drags Draupadī by the hair and tries to strip her after the dicing match
- Duryodhana: eldest of the Kauravas; he is the main rival of the Pāṇḍavas
- Gāndhārī: wife of Dhṛtarāṣṭra and mother of the Kauravas
- Gaṅgā: goddess of the Ganges river; mother of Bhīṣma
- Hāstinapura: capital of the Kuru kingdom; capital of the Kauravas after the kingdom is divided
- Indraprastha: capital of the Pāṇḍava kingdom after the Kuru kingdom is divided
- Indra: king of the gods in the Vedic pantheon; in the *Mahābhārata* he features in several stories about his rivalry with *asura* kings such as Vairocana, Namuci, and Prahlāda/Prahrāda
- Janaka: name of a king who appears in the Upaniṣads and is closely associated with renunciation in later Brahminical, as well as Buddhist and Jain, literature; in the *Mahābhārata*, he appears in a number of dialogues in the *Śānti Parvan*; one of which is with the female sage Sulabhā, who questions his enlightened status on the basis that he lives as a householder, not as a renouncer
- Janamejaya: he is the primary listener to the *Mahābhārata* in the inner frame-dialogue; he is the great-grandson of Arjuna
- Karṇa: Kuntī's premarital son with the sun god Sūrya; he is a loyal ally of Duryodhana; he only learns on the eve of the war that he is the older brother of the Pāṇḍavas
- Kauravas: literally means 'descendants of the Kurus'; refers to Duryodhana and his ninety-nine brothers, and their allies
- Kauśika: a sage whose vow always to tell the truth leads to the death of innocent people; his story is told by both Kṛṣṇa and Bhīṣma
- Kṛṣṇa: son of Vasudeva, he is a cousin of the Pāṇḍavas; he is also Arjuna's brother-in-law (Arjuna marries his sister Subhadrā); his divine identity is equated with Viṣṇu and Nārāyaṇa

- Kuntī: first wife of Pāṇḍu and mother of the three eldest Pāṇḍavas (Yudhiṣṭhira, Bhīmasena, and Arjuna); she is also Kṛṣṇa's aunt (her brother is Vasudeva, Kṛṣṇa's father)
- Naimiṣa: name of the forest where Ugraśravas narrates the *Mahābhārata* to Śaunaka and a group of divine *ṛṣi*s
- Nala: a king who gambles away his kingdom in a dicing match; he appears in a story in the *Āraṇyaka Parvan* that Yudhiṣṭhira and Draupadī hear when in exile after the dicing match
- Namuci: an *asura* king with an ongoing rivalry with Indra
- Nārada: a divine *ṛṣi*; he is the messenger between gods and humans
- Nārāyaṇa: supreme god; another name for Viṣṇu
- Pāṇḍavas: the sons of Paṇḍu and their allies
- Paṇḍu: father of the Pāṇḍavas; younger brother of Dhṛtarāṣṭra and older brother of Vidura; husband of Kuntī; he dies when his children are very young; he is the son of Ambālikā and Vyāsa
- Prahlāda/Prahrāda: *asura* king with an ongoing rivalry with Indra
- Rāma Jāmadagnya: a warrior brahmin known for killing off the *kṣatriya*s twenty-one times; he is the *guru* of both Bhīṣma and Karṇa
- Sahadeva: fourth eldest of the Pāṇḍavas, he and Nakula are twins; their mother is Madrī, Pandu's second wife
- Śakuni: brother of Gāndhārī; Duryodhana's uncle; known as an expert at playing dice
- Śakuntalā: mother of Bharata; adopted daughter of the sage Kaṇva
- Śālva: fiancée of Ambā before she was abducted by Bhīṣma
- Saṃjaya: personal assistant to Dhṛtarāṣṭra, he received the divine eye from Vyāsa to report the war to the blind king; he is also a self-proclaimed devotee of Kṛṣṇa
- Śaṃtanu: father of Bhīṣma, whom he had with the goddess Gaṅgā; after she returns to heaven, Śaṃtanu marries Satyavatī
- Satyabhāmā: Kṛṣṇa's wife
- Satyavatī: wife of Śaṃtanu, with whom she has two sons: Citrāṅgada and Vicitravīrya; she is also the mother of Vyāsa, who she had before she married Śaṃtanu
- Śaunaka: the primary listener to Ugraśravas' narration in the text's outer frame dialogue; characters with the name Śaunaka appear on several occasions in the Upaniṣads
- Śikhaṇḍin: son of Drupada; brother of Draupadī and Dhṛṣṭadyumna; he was Ambā in a previous life; he is an ally of the Pāṇḍavas and plays a crucial role in the slaying of Bhīṣma
- Śiśupāla: king of Cedi who is killed by Kṛṣṇa; longtime rival of Kṛṣṇa
- Śiva: one of the major deities of Hinduism; he plays a crucial role in the dialogues about Draupadī's marriage
- Śrī: goddess of fortune; wife of Viṣṇu
- Sudeṣṇā: a princess in the kingdom where the Pāṇḍavas hide in the thirteenth year of their exile after the dicing match

- Śukra: household priests of the *asuras*
- Sulabhā: female renunciate who defeats King Janaka in a debate
- Ugraśravas: a professional storyteller; he recites the *Mahābhārata* to Śaunaka and the *ṛṣis* in the Naimiṣa forest
- Uttaṅka: a sage and devotee of Kṛṣṇa
- Vairocana: an *asura* king with an ongoing rivalry with Indra
- Vaiśaṃpāyana: one of Vyāsa's students who has learned the *Mahābhārata* from him; he recites the entire story to Janamejaya at his snake sacrifice
- Vicitravīrya: younger son of Śaṃtanu; his wives Ambikā and Ambālikā have sons (Dhṛtarāṣṭhra and Paṇḍu) with Vyāsa after he dies
- Vidura: the younger brother of Dhṛtarāṣṭra and Paṇḍu; he is the son of Ambikā's maidservant and Vyāsa; the incarnation of the god Dharma
- Vikarṇa: one of the sons of Dhṛtarāṣṭra; he takes Draupadī's side in the argument after the dicing match
- Vyāsa: the composer of the *Mahābhārata*, as well as surrogate father to Dhṛtarāṣṭra, Paṇḍu, and Vidura; Vyāsa is a brahmin renunciate, who is known for dividing the Vedas
- Yudhiṣṭhira: eldest of the Pāṇḍava brothers; son of Dharma; repeatedly referred to as the Dharma King.

Parvans

1 *Ādi Parvan (Book of the Beginning)*: This book begins with the two frame dialogues featuring (1) Ugraśravas and Śaunaka with the Naimiṣa *ṛṣis* and (2) Vaiśaṃpāyana and Janamejaya. In addition to containing accounts of the ancestors of the Kurus and the beginnings of the Bharata family, the *Ādi Parvan* features a number of the dialogues discussed in this book, including the exchange between Śakuntalā and Duḥṣana (Chapter 4), the account of Bhīṣma's vows and Satyavatī's attempt to persuade him to give them up (Chapter 1), and the discussions about Draupadī's polyandrous marriage (Chapter 2).

2 *Sabhā Parvan (Book of the Assembly Hall)*: In this book, Yudhiṣṭhira builds a magnificent *sabhā* and then hosts a *rājasūya* ritual, which asserts his universal sovereignty. It is during this ritual that Śiśupāla offers a scathing criticism of Bhīṣma and his vows, as well as of Kṛṣṇa and his claims of a divine status (Chapter 1). After the ritual, the pivotal dialogues between Duryodhana and Dhṛtarāṣṭra take place, in which the eldest Kaurava – feeling deeply jealous of his cousin Yudhiṣṭhira – convinces his father to approve of a dicing match (Chapter 3). During the match, Yudhiṣṭhira loses everything, staking Draupadī with his final throw. After the match, Draupadī successfully challenges the outcome in her contentious debate with the Kauravas in their assembly hall (Chapter 4). Despite Draupadī saving her husbands from servitude, Yudhiṣṭhira accepts the invitation to another game. After losing this game, Yudhiṣṭhira, his brothers, and Draupadī must live in exile for twelve years, plus a thirteenth year in disguise.

3 *Āraṇyaka Parvan (Book of the Forest)*: This book chronicles the first twelve years of their exile, in which the Pāṇḍavas and Draupadi meet numerous brahmins, seers, and storytellers, who they learn from while reflecting upon their plight. The *Āraṇyaka Parvan* contains a difficult conversation between Yudhiṣṭhira and Draupadī (Chapter 4), as well as a number of stories that mirror the Pāṇḍavas' own situation, in one way or another.

4 *Virāṭa Parvan (Book of Virāṭa)*: The Pāṇḍavas spend a year in hiding in the kingdom of Virata to fulfil the stakes of the dicing match.

5 *Udyoga Parvan (Book of Preparations)*: After thirteen years in exile, the Pāṇḍavas return and attempt to negotiate a settlement with the Kauravas. After three diplomatic missions fail, both the Pāṇḍavas and Kauravas prepare for war. This book contains two dialogues between Bhīṣma and Duryodhana, one where he reflects back on his vows and the other where he tells the story of Ambā (Chapter 1).

6 *Bhīṣma Parvan (Book of Bhīṣma)*: This book recounts the first ten days of the eighteen-day war, when Bhīṣma is the general of the Kaurava army. At the beginning of this book, just as the war is about the begin, Kṛṣṇa offers his famous teaching of the *Bhagavad Gītā* (Chapter 5). This book ends when Bhīṣma is mortally wounded.

7 *Droṇa Parvan (Book of Droṇa)*: After Bhīṣma is incapacitated, Droṇa becomes the general of the Kaurava army. During this book, Arjuna's son Abhimanyu is killed. At the end of this book, Droṇa is killed

8 *Karṇa Parvan (Book of Karṇa)*: After the death of Droṇa, Karṇa becomes the general of the Kaurava army. In this book, Yudhiṣṭhira criticises Arjuna for returning from the battlefield and not staying to fight alongside Bhīma, when Karṇa had not yet been killed. Subsequently, Yudhiṣṭhira offends Arjuna's bow, only to learn that Arjuna had previously taken a vow to kill anyone who offended his bow. Kṛṣṇa persuades Arjuna to spare Yudhiṣṭhira's life by offering a discourse on *dharma*, during which he tells the stories of Balāka and Kauśika (Chapter 5). At the end of this *parvan*, Arjuna kills Karṇa.

9 *Śalya Parvan (Book of Śalya)*: Śalya becomes the fourth general of the Kaurava army and is killed by Yudhiṣṭhira. At the end of this book, there is a final confrontation between Duryodhana and Bhīmasena. At this point, Balarāma, Kṛṣṇa's brother, arrives and criticises Kṛṣṇa for the underhanded tactics of the Pāṇḍavas (Chapter 5). At the end of the book, Duryodhana, as he lays dying, reminds the Pāṇḍavas of their many adharmic actions during the war.

10 *Sauptika Parvan (Book of the Night Attack)*: The remaining Kauravas attack the Pāṇḍava camp during the night when the entire army is asleep.

11 *Strī Parvan (Book of Women)*: After the war, the Kuru women grieve for their husbands and sons who died on the battlefield. Gāndhārī, who lost one-hundred sons, offers a moving lament during which she blames Kṛṣṇa for the war (Chapter 5).

12 *Śānti Parvan (Book of Peace)*: As Yudhiṣṭhira feels remorse after the war, he, his brothers, and Draupadī seek out the advice of Bhīṣma who lies, mortally wounded, on a bed of arrows. Bhīṣma's long instruction includes sections on *rāja-dharma*, *āpad-dharma*, and *mokṣa-dharma*. Included among Bhīṣma's instruction to Yudhiṣṭhira are three dialogues we have looked at: his account of the pre-dicing dialogue between Duryodhana and Dhṛtarāṣṭra (Chapter 2), his versions of the Balāka and Kauśika episodes (Chapter 1), and the debate between Sulabhā and Janaka (Chapter 4).

13 *Anuśāsana* Parvan *(Book of Instruction)*: Bhīṣma continues his post-war instruction to Yudhiṣṭhira, with this book focusing on giving to brahmins. The book ends with the death of Bhīṣma.

14 *Aśvamedhika Parvan (Book of the Horse Sacrifice)*: In this book, Yudhiṣṭhira is persuaded to host an *aśvamedha* ritual to expiate his sins for the war. Before this ritual, Kṛṣṇa and Arjuna have one final dialogue, in which Kṛṣṇa praises the virtues of renunciation: this dialogue is called the *Anu Gītā* (Chapter 5). At the end of the *Aśvamedhika Parvan*, Kṛṣṇa encounters the sage Uttaṅka, to whom he discloses a teaching and reveals his divine form one last time (Chapter 5).

15 *Āśramavāsika Parvan (Book of the Hermitage)*: Dhṛtarāṣṭra, Gāndhārī, Kuntī, and Vidura all retire the forest. After being visited by the younger generation, Dhṛtarāṣṭra, Gāndhārī, and Kuntī die in a forest fire.

16 *Mausāla Parvan (Book of the Clubs)*: This book recounts the death of Kṛṣṇa and the demise of his entire family in a drunken brawl.

17 *Mahāprasthānika Parvan (Book of the Great Departure)*: After installing Arjuna's son Parkiṣit on the throne, the Pāṇḍavas and Draupadī embark on a pilgrimage of the major holy sites around India. As they ascend the Himalayas, one by one, Draupadī, Nakula, Sahadeva, Arjuna, and Bhīmasena die, leaving Yudhiṣṭhira all alone, accompanied by a dog.

18 *Svargārohaṇa Parvan (Book of the Ascent to Heaven)*: Yudhiṣṭhira ascends to heaven, only to find that the Kauravas are in heaven, while his brothers and Draupadī have been confined to hell. Yudhiṣṭhira chooses to reside in hell with his brothers and Draupadī. Indra reveals that this has only been an illusion, Yudhiṣṭhira's final test. He and his family then go to heaven. The narration then returns to the Vaiśaṃpāyana frame dialogue, before closing with the Ugraśravas frame dialogue

Bibliography

Texts and translations

The Bhagavad Gītā. Trans. Laurie L. Patton. London: Penguin Books, 2008.

The Mahābhārata. Abridged and trans. John D. Smith, Harmondsworth: Penguin, 2009.

The Mahābhārata (e-text). Ed. John Smith. Pune: Bhandarkar Oriental Research Institute, 1999, http://bombay.indology.info/mahabharata/statement.html

The Mahābhārata for the First Time Critically Edited. 19 Volumes. Eds. V. S. Sukthankar et al. Poona: Bhandarkar Oriental Research Institute, 1933–1966.

The Mahābhārata of Krishna-Dwaipayana Vyasa Translated into English Prose from the Original Sanskrit Text, 12 vols. Trans. K. M. Ganguli. New Delhi: Munshiram Manoharlal, 1993 [1883–1896].

The Mahābhārata: 1. The Book of the Beginning. Trans. J.A.B. van Buitenen. Chicago: The University of Chicago Press, 1973.

The Mahābhārata: 2. The Book of the Assembly Hall; 3 The Book of the Forest. Trans. J. A. B. van Buitenen. Chicago: The University of Chicago Press, 1975.

The Mahābhārata Book Two: The Great Hall. Trans. Paul Wilmot. New York: New York University Press / John and Jennifer Clay Foundation, 2006.

The Mahābhārata: 4. The Book of Virāṭa; 5. The Book of the Effort. Trans. J. A. B. van Buitenen. Chicago: The University of Chicago Press, 1978.

Mahābhārata Book Six: Bhīṣma, Volume One. Trans. Alex Cherniak. New York: New York University Press / John and Jennifer Clay Foundation, 2008.

Mahābhārata Book Six: Bhīṣma, Volume Two. Trans. Alex Cherniak. New York: New York University Press / John and Jennifer Clay Foundation, 2009.

Mahābhārata Book Seven: Droṇa, Volume One. Trans. Vaughan Pilikan. New York: New York University Press / John and Jennifer Clay Foundation, 2006.

Mahābhārata Book Seven: Droṇa, Volume One. Trans. Vaughan Pilikan. New York: New York University Press / John and Jennifer Clay Foundation, 2009.

Mahābhārata Book Eight: Karṇa, Volume One. Trans. Adam Bowles. New York: New York University Press / John and Jennifer Clay Foundation, 2007.

Mahābhārata Book Eight: Karṇa, Volume Two. Trans. Adam Bowles. New York: New York University Press / John and Jennifer Clay Foundation, 2008.

Mahābhārata Book Nine: Shalya, Volume One. Trans. Justin Meiland. New York: New York University Press / John and Jennifer Clay Foundation, 2005.

Mahābhārata Book Nine: Shalya, Volume Two. Trans. Justin Meiland. New York: New York University Press / John and Jennifer Clay Foundation, 2007.

The Mahābhārata Books 11 The Book of Women; Book 12 The Book of Peace, Part One. Trans James L. Fitzgerald. Chicago: Chicago University Press, 2004.

Mahābhārata 12.308: 'Nun Befuddles King, Shows Karmayoga Does Not Work: Sulabhā's Refutation of King Janaka at *MBh* 12.308'. Trans. James L. Fitzgerald. *Journal of Indian Philosophy*, Vol. 30, No. 6: pp. 641–677, 2002.

[Mānava Dharmaśāstra] Law Code of Manu. Trans. Patrick Olivelle. New York: Oxford University Press, 2004.

The Rāmāyaṇa of Válmíki: An Epic of Ancient India, Volume VII: Uttarakāṇḍa. Trans. Robert Goldman and Sally Sutherland Goldman. Princeton: Princeton University Press, 2017.

The Republic, Plato. Trans. G. M. A Grube, revised by C.D.C. Reeve. Indianapolis: Hackett Publishing Company, 1992.

[*Upaniṣads*] *The Early Upaniṣads: Annotated Text and Translation*. Ed. and trans. Patrick Olivelle. New York: Oxford University Press, 1998.

The Yoga Sūtras of Patañjali, Trans. Edwin F. Bryant. New York: North Point Press. 2009.

Works cited

Adluri, Vishwa. 2011. 'Frame Narratives and Forked Beginnings: Or, How to Read the Ādiparvan'. *Journal of Vaishnava Studies*, Vol. 19, No. 2: pp. 143–210.

Adluri, Vishwa. 2013a. 'Hermeneutics and Narrative Architecture in the *Mahābhārata*'. In *Ways and Reasons for Thinking about the Mahābhārata as a Whole*, edited by Vishwa Adluri, pp. 1–27. Pune: Bhandarkar Oriental Research Institute.

Adluri, Vishwa. 2013b. 'Introduction'. In *Ways and Reasons for Thinking about the Mahābhārata as a Whole*, edited by Vishwa Adluri, pp. viii–xxxii. Pune: Bhandarkar Oriental Research Institute.

Adluri, Vishwa. 2017. 'Hindu Studies in a Christian, Secular Academy'. *International Journal of Dharma Studies*, Vol. 5, No. 6: pp. 1–31.

Adluri, Vishwa and Bagchee, Joydeep. 2018. *Philology and Criticism: A Guide to Mahābhārata Textual Criticism*. London: Anthem Press.

Appleton, Naomi. 2014. *Narrating Karma and Rebirth: Buddhist and Jain Multi-Life Stories*. Cambridge: Cambridge University Press.

Bailey, Gregory M. 1983. 'Suffering in the *Mahābhārata*: Draupadī and Yudhiṣṭhira'. *Puruṣārtha*, Vol. 7: pp. 109–129.

Bailey, Gregory M. 1999. 'Intertextuality and the Purāṇas: A Neglected Element in the Study of Sanskrit Literature'. In *Composing a Tradition: Concepts, Techniques and Relationships*, edited by Mary Brockington and Peter Schreiner, pp. 178–198. Zagreb: Croatian Academy of Arts and Sciences.

Bailey, Gregory M. 2005. 'The *Mahābhārata*'s Simultaneous Affirmation and Critique of the Universal Validity of *Dharma*'. In *The Mahābhārata: What Is Not Here Is Nowhere Else (Yannehāsti na Tadkvacit)*, edited by T. S. Rukmani, pp. 63–77. Delhi: Munshiram Manoharlal.

Bandlamudi, Lakshmi. 2011. *Dialogics of Self, the Mahabharata and Culture: The History of Understanding and Understanding of History*. London: Anthem Press.

Bandlamudi, Lakshmi. 2018. 'Answerability between Lived Life and Living Texts: Chronotopicity in Finding Agency in the *Mahābhārata*'. In *Exploring Agency in the Mahābhārata: Ethical and Political Dimensions of Dharma*, edited by Sibesh

Chandra Bhattacharya, Vrinda Dalmiya and Gangeya Mukherji, pp. 214–231. Abingdon: Routledge.

Bandyopadhyay, Sibaji. 2014. 'Of Gambling: A Few Lessons from the *Mahābhārata*'. In *Mahābhārata Now: Narration, Aesthetics, Ethics*, edited by Arindam Chakrabarti and Sibaji Bandyopadhyay, pp. 3–28. New Delhi: Routledge.

Belvalkar, S. K. 1946. 'Saṃjaya's "Eye Divine"'. *Annals of the Bhandarkar Oriental Research Institute*, Vol. 27: pp. 329–338.

Berger, Douglas. 2015. 'Review of *Divine Self, Human Self: The Philosophy of Being in Two Gītā Commentaries* by Chakravarthi Ram-Prasad'. *Philosophy East and West*, Vol. 65, No. 2: pp. 626–630.

Bhattacharya, Pradip. 2004. 'Part IV: Five Holy Virgins, Five Sacred Myths: She Who Must Be Obeyed: Draupadi: The Ill-Fated One.' *Manushi*, Vol. 144: pp. 19–30.

Biardeau, Madeleine. 1984. 'Nala et Damayant́: héros épiques' (Part 1). *Indo-Iranian Journal*, Vol. 27, No. 4: pp. 247–274.

Biardeau, Madeleine. 1985. 'Nala et Damayant́: héros épiques' (Part 2). *Indo-Iranian Journal*, Vol. 28, No. 1: pp. 1–34.

Black, Brian. 2007a. *The Character of the Self in Ancient India: Priests, Kings, and Women in the Early Upaniṣads*. Albany: State University of New York Press.

Black, Brian. 2007b 'Eavesdropping on the Epic: Female Listeners in the *Mahābhārata*'. In *Gender and Narrative in the* Mahābhārata, edited by Simon Brodbeck and Brian Black, pp. 53–78. London: Routledge.

Black, Brian. 2011. 'The Rhetoric of Secrecy in the Upaniṣads'. In *Religion and Identity in South Asia and Beyond: Essays in Honor of Patrick Olivelle*, edited by Steven Lindquist, pp. 101–125. London: Anthem Press.

Black, Brian. 2013. 'Draupadī in the *Mahābhārata*'. *Religion Compass*, Vol. 7/5: pp. 169–178.

Black, Brian. 2015a. 'Dialogue and Difference: Encountering the Other in Indian Religious and Philosophical Sources'. In *Dialogue in Early South Asian Religions: Hindu, Buddhist, and Jain Traditions*, edited by Brian Black and Laurie Patton, pp. 243–257. Farnham: Ashgate.

Black, Brian. 2015b. 'Upaniṣads', *The Internet Encyclopedia of Philosophy*, ISSN 2161–0002, http://www.iep.utm.edu/.

Black, Brian. 2017. The Upaniṣads and the *Mahābhārata*. In *The Upaniṣads: A Complete Guide*, edited by Signe Cohen, pp. 186–199. New York: Routledge.

Black, Brian. 2019. 'Sources of Indian Secularism? Dialogues on Politics and Religion in Hindu and Buddhist Traditions'. In *In Dialogue with Classical Indian Traditions: Encounter, Transformation and Interpretation*, edited by Brian Black and Chakravarthi Ram-Prasad, pp. 23–35. London: Routledge.

Black, Brian and Geen, Jonathan. 2011. 'The Character of "Character" in Early South Asian Religious Narratives'. *Journal of the American Academy of Religion*, Vol. 79, No. 1: pp. 6–32.

Black, Brian and Patton, Laurie, eds. 2015. *Dialogue in Early South Asian Religions: Hindu, Buddhist, and Jain Traditions*. Farnham: Ashgate.

Black, Brian and Ram-Prasad, Chakravarthi, eds. 2019. *In Dialogue with Classical Indian Traditions: Encounter, Transformation and Interpretation*. London: Routledge.

Bowlby, Paul. 1991. 'Kings without Authority: The Obligation of the Ruler to Gamble in the *Mahābhārata*'. *Studies in Religion / Sciences Religieuses*, Vol. 20: pp. 3–17.

Bowles, Adam. 2007. *Dharma, Disorder and the Political in Ancient India: The Āpaddharmaparvan of the Mahābhārata.* Leiden: Brill.

Brereton, Joel. 2004. '*Dhárman* in the *Ṛgveda*'. *Journal of Indian Philosophy*, Vol. 32, No. 5: pp. 449–489.

Brockington, John. 1998. *The Sanskrit Epics.* Leiden: Brill.

Brodbeck, Simon. 2009. *The Mahābhārata Patriline: Gender, Culture and the Royal Hereditary.* Farnham: Ashgate.

Chakrabarti, Arindam. 2014. 'Just Words: An Ethics of Conversation in the *Mahābhārata*'. In *Mahābhārata Now: Narration, Aesthetics, Ethics*, edited by Arindam Chakrabarti and Sibaji Bandyopadhyay, pp. 244–283. New Delhi: Routledge.

Chakrabarti, Arindam and Bandyopadhyay, Sibaji. 2014. 'Introduction'. In *Mahābhārata Now: Narration, Aesthetics, Ethics*, edited by Arindam Chakrabarti and Sibaji Bandyopadhyay, pp. xvii–xxviii. New Delhi: Routledge.

Chakravarti, Uma. 2014. 'Who Speaks for Whom? The Queen, the *Dāsī* and Sexual Politics in the *Sabhāparvan*'. In *Mahābhārata Now: Narration, Aesthetics, Ethics*, edited by Arindam Chakrabarti and Sibaji Bandyopadhyay, pp. 132–152. New Delhi: Routledge.

Chatterjee, Amita. 2018. 'In Search of Genuine Agency: A Review of Action, Freedom and *Karma* in the *Mahābhārata*. In *Exploring Agency in the* Mahābhārata: *Ethical and Political Dimensions of* Dharma, edited by Sibesh Chandra Bhattacharya, Vrinda Dalmiya, and Gangeya Mukherji, pp. 45–61. Abingdon: Routledge.

Dalmiya, Vrinda and Mukherji, Gangeya. 2018. 'Introduction: To Do'. In *Exploring Agency in the* Mahābhārata: *Ethical and Political Dimensions of* Dharma, edited by Sibesh Chandra Bhattacharya, Vrinda Dalmiya, and Gangeya Mukherji, pp.1–27. Abingdon: Routledge.

Deshpande, Madhav M. 1991. 'The Epic Context of the *Bhagavad Gītā*'. In *Essays on the Mahābhārata*, edited by Arvind Sharma., pp. 334–348. Leiden: Brill.

Dhand, Arti. 2004. 'The Subversive Nature of Virtue in the *Mahābhārata*: A Tale about Women, Smelly Ascetics, and God'. *Journal of the American Academy of Religion*, Vol. 72, No. 1: pp. 33–58.

Dhand, Arti. 2008. *Woman as Fire, Woman as Sage: Sexual Ideology in the Mahābhārata.* Albany: State University of New York Press.

Dhand, Arti. 2018. '*Karmayoga* and the Vexed Moral Agent'. In *Exploring Agency in the* Mahābhārata: *Ethical and Political Dimensions of* Dharma, edited by Sibesh Chandra Bhattacharya, Vrinda Dalmiya and Gangeya Mukherji, pp. 81–106. Abingdon: Routledge.

Dorter, Kenneth. 2012. 'A Dialectical Reading of the *Bhagavadgita*'. *Asian Philosophy*, Vol. 22, No. 4: pp. 307–326.

Earl, James. 2011. *Beginning the Mahābhārata: A Reader's Guide to the Frame Stories.* Woodland Hills: South Asian Studies Association Press.

Edgerton, Franklin, 1944. 'Introduction: The Critical Apparatus'. In *The Sabhāparvan: Being the Second Book of the Mahābhārata, The Great Epic of India*, edited by Franklin Edgerton. Poona: Bhandarkar Oriental Research Institute, pp. ix–l.

Falk, Nancy. 1977. 'Draupadī and the Dharma'. In *Beyond Androcentrism: New Essays on Women and Religion*, edited by Rita M. Gross, pp. 89–114. Missoula: Scholars Press.

Fitzgerald, James L. 2002a. 'Nun Befuddles King, Shows *Karmayoga* Does Not Work: Sulabhā's Refutation of King Janaka at MBh 12.308'. *Journal of Indian Philosophy*, Vol. 30, No. 6: pp. 641–677.

Fitzgerald, James L. 2002b. 'The Rāma Jāmadagnya Thread of the *Mahābhārata*: A New Survey of Rāma Jāmadagnya in the Pune Text'. In *Stages and Transitions: Temporal and Historical Frameworks in Epic and Purāṇic Literature*, Proceedings of the Second Dubrovnik International Conference on the Sanskrit Epics and Purāṇas, August 1999, edited by Mary Brockington, pp. 89–132. Zagreb: Croatian Academy of Sciences and Arts.

Fitzgerald, James L. 2004a. 'Mahābhārata'. In *The Hindu World*, edited by Sushil Mittal and Gene R. Thursby, pp. 52–74. London: Routledge.

Fitzgerald, James L. 2004b. Trans. *The Mahābhārata Books 11 The Book of Women; Book 12 The Book of Peace, Part One*. Chicago: Chicago University Press.

Fitzgerald, James L. 2009. '*Dharma* and Its Translation in the *Mahābhārata*'. In *Dharma: Studies in Its Semantic, Cultural and Religious History*, edited by Patrick Olivelle, pp. 249–263. Delhi: Motilal Banarsidass.

Framarin, Christopher. 2018. 'The Theory of *Karma* in the *Mahābhārata*. In *Exploring Agency in the* Mahābhārata: *Ethical and Political Dimensions of* Dharma, edited by Sibesh Chandra Bhattacharya, Vrinda Dalmiya and Gangeya Mukherji, pp. 62–80. Abingdon: Routledge.

Gadamer, Hans-Georg. 1975. *Truth and Method*. Trans. revised by Joel Weinsheimer and Donald G. Marshall. London: Bloomsbury.

Gadamer, Hans-Georg. 1980. *Dialogue and Dialectic: Eight Hermeneutical Studies on Plato*. Trans. with an Introduction by P. Christopher Smith. New Haven: Yale University Press.

Gadamer, Hans-Georg. 1985. *Philosophical Apprenticeships*. Cambridge: MIT Press.

Ganeri, Jonardon. 2007. *The Concealed Art of the Soul: Theories of Self and Practices of Truth in Indian Ethics and Epistemology*. Oxford: Oxford University Press.

Geen, Jonathan. 2005. 'The Evolution of Draupadī's Marriage in the Jaina Tradition'. *Asiatische Studien / Études Asiatiques*, Vol. 59, No. 2: pp. 443–497.

Geen, Jonathan. 2006. 'Jaina Origins for the Mahābhārata's Story of Draupadī's Past Life'. *Asiatische Studien / Études Asiatiques*, Vol. 60, No. 3: pp. 575–606.

González-Reimann, Luis. 2010. *The Mahābhārata and the Yugas: India's Great Epic Poem and the Hindu System of World Ages*. Delhi: Motilal Banarsidass.

Halbfass, Wilhelm. 1988. *India and Europe: An Essay in Understanding*. Albany: State University of New York Press.

Hara, Minoru. 1997. 'A Note on *Dharmasya Sūkṣmā Gatiḥ*'. In *Beyond Orientalism: The Work of Wilhelm Halbfass and Its Impact on Indian and Cross Cultural Studies*, edited by Eli Franco and Karin Preisendanz, pp. 515–532. Amsterdam, Atlanta: Rodopi.

Heesterman, Jan C. 1957. *The Ancient Indian Royal Consecration*. The Hague: Mouton & Co.

Hegarty, James. 2012. *Religion, Narrative and Public Imagination in South Asia: Past and Place in the Sanskrit Mahābhārata*. London: Routledge.

Hegarty, James. 2019. 'Models of Royal Piety in the *Mahābhārata*: The Case of Vidura, Sanatsujāta and Vidurā'. In *In Dialogue with Classical Indian Traditions: Encounter, Transformation and Interpretation*, edited by Brian Black and Chakravarthi Ram-Prasad, pp. 211–227. London: Routledge.

Hill, Peter. 2001. *Fate, Predestination and Human Action in the Mahābhārata: A Study in the History of Ideas*. New Delhi: Munshiram Manoharlal.

Hiltebeitel, Alf. 1976. *The Ritual of Battle: Krishna in the Mahābhārata*. Ithaca: Cornell University Press.

Hiltebeitel, Alf. 2000. 'Draupadī's Question'. In *Is the Goddess a Feminist? The Politics of South Asian Goddesses*, edited by Alf Hiltebeitel and Kathleen Erndl, pp. 113–122. New York: New York University Press.

Hiltebeitel, Alf. 2001a. 'Bhīṣma's Sources'. In *Vidyārṇavavandanam: Essays in Honour of Asko Parpola*, edited by Klaus Karttunen and Petteri Koskikallio. *Studia Orientalia*, Vol. 94: pp. 261–278.

Hiltebeitel, Alf. 2001b. *Rethinking the Mahābhārata: A Reader's Guide to the Education of the Dharma King*. Chicago: University of Chicago Press.

Hiltebeitel, Alf. 2005. 'Not without Subtales: Telling Laws and Truths in the Sanskrit Epics'. *Journal of Indian Philosophy*, Vol. 33, No. 4: 455–511.

Hiltebeitel, Alf. 2006. 'The *Nārāyaṇīya* and the Early Reading Communities of the *Mahābhārata*'. In *Between the Empires: Society in India 300 BCE to 400 CE*, edited by Patrick Olivelle, pp. 227–255. New York: Oxford University Press.

Hiltebeitel, Alf. 2011. *Dharma: Its Early History in Law, Religion, and Narrative*. New York: Oxford University Press.

Hiltebeitel, Alf. 2012. 'The *Mahābhārata* and the Stories Some People Tell about It – Part 1'. *Exemplar: The Journal of South Asian Studies*, Vol. V1, No. 2: pp. 2–26.

Hiltebeitel, Alf. 2015a. 'Dialogue and Apostrophe: A Move by Vālmīki?' In *Dialogue in Early South Asian Religions: Hindu, Buddhist, and Jain Traditions*, edited by Brian Black and Laurie Patton, pp. 243–257. Farnham: Ashgate.

Hiltebeitel, Alf. 2015b. 'Introducing the *Mahābbhārata*'. *Religious Studies Review*, Vol. 41, No. 4: pp. 153–174.

Hopkins, E. Washburn. 1898. 'The Bhārata and the Great Bhārata'. *American Journal of Philology*, Vol. 19, No. 1: pp. 1–24.

Hopkins, E. Washburn. [1901] (1993). *The Great Epic of India: Character and Origin of the Mahabharata*. Delhi: Motilal Banarsidass.

Höslc, Vittorio. 2012. *The Philosophical Dialogue: A Poetics and Hermeneutics*. Trans. Steven Rendall. Notre Dame: University of Notre Dame Press.

Hudson, Emily. (2013). *Disorienting Dharma: Ethics and the Aesthetics of Suffering in the Mahābhārata*. New York: Oxford University Press.

Jaini, A. N. 1989. 'The Socio-Moral Implications of Draupadī's Marriage to Five Husbands'. In *Moral Dilemmas in the Mahābhārata*, edited by Bimal Krishna Matilal, pp. 69–76. Delhi: Motilal Banarsidass.

Jamison, Stephanie. 1996. *Sacrificed Wife, Sacrificer's Wife: Women, Ritual, and Hospitality in Ancient India*. Oxford: Oxford University Press.

Katz, Ruth Cecily. 1989. *Arjuna in the Mahabharata: Where Krishna Is, There Is Victory*. Columbia: University of South Carolina Press.

Klaes, Norbert. 1975. *Conscience and Consciousness: Ethical Problems of the* Mahābhārata. Bangalore: Dharmaram College.

Kristeva, Julia. 1980. *Desire in Language: A Semiotic Approach to Literature and Art*. Oxford: Blackwell.

Malinar, Angelika. 2007a. 'Arguments of a Queen: Draupadī's View on Kingship'. In *Gender and Narrative in the* Mahābhārata, edited by Simon Brodbeck and Brian Black, pp. 79–96. London: Routledge.

Malinar, Angelika. 2007b. *The Bhagavadgītā: Doctrines and Contexts*. Cambridge: Cambridge University Press.

Manzo, Lawrence. 2010–2012. *The Mahabharata Podcast*. https://mahabharatapodcast.blogspot.com/search?updated-max=2011-09-26T20:53:00-07:00&max-results=15&start=15&by-date=false.

Matilal, Bimal Krishna. 1989. 'Moral Dilemmas: Insights from Indian Epics'. In *Moral Dilemmas in the Mahābhārata*, edited by Bimal Krishna Matilal, pp. 1–19. Delhi: Motilal Banarsidass.

Matilal, Bimal Krishna. 1991. 'Kṛṣṇa: In Defence of a Devious Divinity'. In *Essays on the Mahābhārata*, edited by Arvind Sharma, pp. 401–418. Leiden: Brill.

Matilal, Bimal Krishna. 2002. '*Dharma* and Rationality'. In *Ethics and Epics: Philosophy, Culture, and Religion. The Collected Essays of Bimal Krishna Matilal, Volume 2*, edited by Jonardon Ganeri, pp. 49–71. New Delhi: Oxford University Press.

McGrath, Kevin. 2013. *Heroic Kṛṣṇa: Friendship in the Epic Mahābhārata*. Boston: Ilex Foundation.

Mehendale, M. A. 1995. 'Is There Only One Version of the Game of Dice in the Mahābhārata?' In *Modern Evaluation of the Mahābhārata: Prof. R.K. Sharma Felicitation Volume*, edited by Satya Pal Narang, pp. 33–39. Delhi: Nag Publishers.

Mehendale, M. A. 2009. 'The Critical Edition of the Mahābhārata: Its Constitution, Achievements, and Limitations'. In *Text and Variation of the Mahābhārata*, edited by Kalyan Kumar Chakravarty, pp. 3–23. New Delhi: Munshiram Manoharlal Publishers.

Mehta, Maheshi. 1973. 'The Problem of the Double Introduction to the *Mahābhārata*'. *Journal of the American Oriental Society*, Vol. 93, No. 4: pp. 547–550.

Meiland, Justin, trans. 2007. *Mahābhārata Book Nine: Shalya, Volume Two*. New York: New York University Press / John and Jennifer Clay Foundation.

Minkowski, Christopher Z. 1989. 'Janamejaya's Sattra and Ritual Structure'. *Journal of the American Oriental Society*, Vol. 109, No. 3: pp. 401–420.

Narasimhan, C.V. 1996. *The Mahābhārata: An English Version Based on Selected Verses*. Delhi: Oxford University Press.

Nikulin, Dmitri. 2010. *Dialectic and Dialogue*. Stanford: Stanford University Press.

O'Flaherty, Wendy Donger and Derrett, J. Duncan M. 1978. 'Introduction'. In *The Concept of Duty in South Asia*, edited by Wendy Doniger O'Flaherty and J. Duncan M. Derrett, pp. xiii–xix. London: South Asia Books.

Olivelle, Patrick. 2004. 'The Semantic History of Dharma: The Middle and Late Vedic Periods'. *Journal of Indian Philosophy*, Vol. 32, No. 5: pp. 491–511.

Patton, Laurie L. 2007. 'How Do You Conduct Yourself? Gender and the Construction of a Dialogical Self in the *Mahābhārata*'. In *Gender and Narrative in the* Mahābhārata, edited by Simon Brodbeck and Brian Black, pp. 97–109. London: Routledge.

Patton, Laurie L. 2011. 'Traces of Śaunaka: A Literary Assessment'. *Journal of the American Academy of Religion*, Vol. 79, No. 1: pp. 113–135.

Ram-Prasad, Chakravarthi. 2018. *Human Being, Bodily Being: Phenomenology from Classical India*. Oxford: Oxford University Press.

Ram-Prasad, Chakravarthi. 2019. 'Dialogue in Extremis: Vālin in the Vālmīki *Rāmāyaṇa*'. In *In Dialogue with Classical Indian Traditions: Encounter, Transformation and Interpretation*, edited by Brian Black and Chakravarthi Ram-Prasad, pp. 228–243. London: Routledge.

Ramanujan, A. K. 1991. 'Repetition in the *Mahābhārata*'. In *Essays on the Mahābhārata*, edited by Arvind Sharma., pp. 419–443. Leiden: Brill.

Ramanujan, A. K. 1999. 'Where Mirrors Are Windows: Towards an Anthology of Reflections'. In *The Collected Essays of A.K. Ramanujan*, edited by Vinay Dharwadker, pp. 6–33. New Delhi: Oxford University Press.

Reich, Tamar. 1998. 'A Battleground of a Text: Inner Textual Interpretation in the Sanskrit Mahābhārata'. PhD dissertation, Chicago: University of Chicago.

Reich, Tamar. 2001. 'Sacrificial Violence and Textual Battles: Inner Textual Interpretations in the Sanskrit Mahābhārata'. *History of Religions*, Vol. 41, No. 2: pp. 142–169.

Sen, Prabal Kumar. 2014. 'Moral Doubts, Moral Dilemmas and Situational Ethics in the *Mahābhārata*'. In *Mahābhārata Now: Narration, Aesthetics, Ethics*, edited by Arindam Chakrabarti and Sibaji Bandyopadhyay, pp. 153–202. New Delhi: Routledge.

Sharma, Arvind. 1986. *The Hindu Gītā: Ancient and Classical Interpretations of the Bhagavad Gītā*. London: Duckworth.

Shulman, David. 1994. 'On Being Human in the Sanskrit Epic: The Riddle of Nala'. *Journal of Indian Philosophy*, Vol. 22: pp. 1–29.

Shulman, David. 1996. 'The Yakṣa's Questions'. In *Untying the Knot: On Riddles and Other Enigmatic Modes*, edited by Galit Hasan-Rokem and David Shulman, pp. 151–167. New York: Oxford University Press.

Smith, John D. tr. 2009. *The Mahābhārata*. Harmondsworth: Penguin.

Smith, P. Christopher. 1980. 'Translator's Introduction'. In P. Christopher Smith translation of Hans-Georg Gadamer's *Dialogue and Dialectic: Eight Hermeneutical Studies on Plato*, pp. ix–xv. New Haven: Yale University Press.

Strawson, P. F. 2008. *Freedom and Resentment and Other Essays*. London: Routledge.

Sukthankar, Vishnu S. 1933. 'Prolegomena'. In *The Ādiparvan: Being the First Book of the Mahābhārata, the Great Epic of India*, edited by Vishnu S. Sukthankar. Poona: Bhandarkar Oriental Research Institute, pp. i–cx.

Sukthankar, Vishnu S. [1957] (2016). *On the Meaning of the Mahābhārata*. Delhi: Motilal Banarsidass.

Sullivan, Bruce. 1999. *Seer of the Fifth Veda: Kṛṣṇa Dvaipāyana Vyāsa in the Mahābhārata*. Delhi: Motilal Banarsidass.

Sullivan, Bruce. 2016. 'An Overview of *Mahābhārata* Scholarship: A Perspective on the State of the Field'. *Religion Compass*, Vol. 10, No. 7: pp. 165–175.

Sullivan, Bruce. 2019. '*Mahābhārata* Dialogues on *Dharma* and Devotion with Kṛṣṇa and Hanumān'. In *In Dialogue with Classical Indian Traditions: Encounter, Transformation and Interpretation*, edited by Brian Black and Chakravarthi Ram-Prasad, pp. 197–210. London: Routledge.

Sutherland, Sally J. M. 1989. 'Sītā and Draupadī: Aggressive Behavior and Female Role-models in the Sanskrit Epics'. *Journal of the American Oriental Society*, Vol. 109, No. 1: pp. 63–79.

Sutton, Nicholas. 1999. 'An Exposition of Early Sāṃkhya, A Rejection of the *Bhagavad Gītā* and a Critique of the Role of Women in Hindu Society: The *Sulabhā-Janaka-Saṃvāda*'. *Annal of the Bhandarkar Oriental Research Institute*, Vol. 80: pp. 55–65.

Sutton, Nicholas. 2000. *Religious Doctrine in the Mahābhārata*. Delhi: Motilal Banarsidass.

Thomas, Lynn. 2007. 'Does the Age Make the King or the King Make the Age? Exploring the Relationship between the King and the *Yugas* in the *Mahābhārata*'. *Religions of South Asia*, Vol. 1, No. 2: pp. 183–201.

Thomas, Lynn. 2019. 'Being Human, Dialogically'. In *In Dialogue with Classical Indian Traditions: Encounter, Transformation and Interpretation*, edited by Brian Black and Chakravarthi Ram-Prasad, pp. 130–144. London: Routledge.

Thompson, George. 1988. 'On Truth-Acts in Vedic'. *The Indo-Iranian Journal*, Vol. 41: pp. 125–153.

Tieken, Herman. 2009. 'Kill and Be Killed: *The Bhagavadgītā* and *Anugītā* in the *Mahābhārata*'. *Journal of Hindu Studies*, Vol. 2, No. 2: pp. 209–228.

Tubb, Gary. 1991. '*Śāntarasa* in the *Mahābhārata*'. In *Essays on the Mahābhārata*, edited by Arvind Sharma, pp. 171–203. Leiden: Brill.

van Buitenen, J. A. B. trans. 1973. *The Mahābhārata: 1. The Book of the Beginning*. Chicago: The University of Chicago Press.

van Buitenen, J. A. B. 1975. *The Mahābhārata: 2. The Book of the Assembly Hall; 3 The Book of the Forest*. Chicago: The University of Chicago Press.

van Buitenen, J. A. B. 1978. *The Mahābhārata: 4. The Book of Virāṭa; 5. The Book of the Effort*. Chicago: The University of Chicago Press.

van Buitenen, J. A. B. 1981. *The Bhagavadgītā in the Mahābhārata*. Chicago: The University of Chicago Press.

Vanita, Ruth. 2003. 'The Self Is Not Gendered: Sulabha's Debate with King Janaka'. *National Women's Studies Association Journal*, Vol. 15, No. 2: pp. 76–93.

White, David Gordon. 2009. *Sinister Yogis*. Chicago: University of Chicago Press.

Wilmot, Paul. trans. 2006 *The Mahābhārata Book Two: The Great Hall*. New York: New York University Press / John and Jennifer Clay Foundation.

Woods, Julian F. 2001. *Destiny and Human Initiative in the Mahābhārata*. Albany: State University of New York Press.

Index

Note: Page numbers followed by "n" denote endnotes.

adharma 20, 59, 69, 71, 77, 97, 145, 165
Ādi Parvan 38, 39, 40, 42, 46, 50, 51, 55n12, 76, 177n26, 187, 195
Adluri, Vishwa 21n2, 21n4, 22n9, 113n3, 175n2, 177n26
ahiṃsā (non-violence) 3, 16, 26, 48, 161, 164, 165
Ambā 30, 36, 38, 40–46, 48–52, 62, 63, 87, 184, 194, 196
Ambā Upākhyāna 38, 40–46, 50, 53
Ambālikā 30, 31, 33, 41, 191, 193, 194
Ambikā 30, 31, 33, 41, 191, 192, 194
Anu Gītā 149, 164–166, 172, 174, 175, 176n18
Anuśāsana Parvan 46, 47, 49, 51, 53, 130, 134, 146, 187, 197
āpad-dharma (*dharma* of extenuating circumstance) 20, 31–33, 55n5, 127, 130, 196
Appleton, Naomi 63
Āraṇyaka Parvan 109, 110, 128, 160, 180, 192, 195
Arjuna 6, 55n8, 96, 113n5, 114n17, 146n4, 176n6, 191; in *Anu Gītā* 164–166, 172; in *Bhagavad Gītā* 8, 85, 133, 148, 149, 151–160, 167, 169, 173, 183, 189; and Bhīṣma's death 51–52; and Draupadī's questions 119, 121, 129; and Draupadī's wedding 57, 58, 61, 65, 68; in *Karṇa Parvan* 47–48, 80n5, 161–164, 167, 180; and Kuntī's words 66, 81n7
Asita Devala 109, 191
Āśramavāsika Parvan 113n2, 114n8, 198
Asuras 31, 191, 194
aśvamedha 37, 164, 176n18, 197
Aśvamedhika Parvan 164, 172, 176n18, 197
ātman 2, 3, 19, 129–130, 135, 141, 163–164

Bailey, Gregory 21n2, 22n14, 147n11
Bakhtin, Mikhail Mikhailovich 1, 15–16
Balāka 47–48, 162–164, 176n14, 179–181, 191, 196
Balarāma 149, 166–168, 172, 181, 191
Bandlamudi, Lakshmi 1
Bandyopadhyay, Sibaji 22n22, 106, 114n15
Belvalkar, S.K. 177n23
Berger, Douglas 160
Bhagavad Gītā 15, 148, 150, 196; and dialectic 33–34, 149, 157–160; as dialogue 8, 9, 151–160; Kṛṣṇa's teaching 85, 133, 139, 150, 181, 183; and *Mahābhārata* 17, 148, 160–169, 172–175, 176n11, 176n12, 187, 188
Bharata 137
Bhattacharya, Pradip 80n4
Bhīmasena 51, 65–66, 96, 110, 119–121, 161, 166–168, 191, 196
Bhīṣma 5, 11, 82, 92, 93, 191; and death 25, 30, 40, 43, 44, 45, 49–52, 62, 72, 171, 187; and *dharma* 21, 26, 29, 31–34, 35–36, 43, 47–49, 53, 100, 119–120, 130, 162, 179, 180, 181; and Draupadī's questions 119–120, 122, 125, 127, 131; and gender 42, 49, 56n19, 66, 123, 184; and Kṛṣṇa 35, 36, 37; as narrator 40,

46, 49, 53, 103, 138, 143, 162, 187; and post-war teachings 24, 32, 99–100, 134, 176n5; and vows 6, 8, 17, 23–55, 57, 65, 66, 80n5, 106, 111, 135, 152, 182, 183, 184, 185, 186, 189
Bhīṣma Parvan 40, 46, 50, 51, 169, 196
Biardeau, Madeleine 14, 75, 147n13, 150
Bowlby, Paul 109
Bowles, Adam 3, 13, 21n2, 22n9, 32, 176n13
Brahmā 74–75, 165–166, 191
brahman 2, 3, 19
brahmin/s 39, 58, 69, 74, 113n2, 165, 172; Dīrghatamas 32; as disguise 62, 65, 100
in the Naimiṣa forest 1, 2; Rāma Jāmadagnya 38, 42; Vyāsa 79, 184
Brereton, Joel 81n8
Bṛhaspati 30, 31, 97–98, 100, 191
Brockington, John 13, 22n15, 175n2, 175–176n3
Brodbeck, Simon 55n6

caste 20, 87, 124, 142, 144, 153, 163
Chakrabarti, Arindam 22n22, 142
Chakravarti, Uma 122, 124, 143
Chatterjee, Amita 106–107
Citrāṅgada 30, 191, 193
Critical Edition 13–15, 17, 22n19, 88, 114n8, 146n1

Dahlmann, Joseph 13–14, 175n3
Dalmiya, Vrinda 18–21, 85–86, 188
Damayantī 109, 134, 191
Derrett, J. Duncan M. 60
Deshpande, Madhav 155, 176n11, 177n25
Dhand, Arti 18, 22n23, 32, 55n6, 69, 113n1, 116–117, 126, 128
dharma 3, 4, 6, 11, 17, 19, 20–21, 27, 32–34, 49, 59–61, 67–73; ambiguities in 21, 143, 175, 181; and *adharma* 59, 77, 97, 165; adherence to 53, 69, 86, 120, 121, 125, 128, 132, 136, 138, 167, 174; *dharma-rāja* 70, 103; dharmic reasoning 6, 48, 60, 72, 79, 80, 168, 182, 183, 188, 189; and dialogue 19–21, 60–61, 80, 182, 188–189; different types of/understanding of 53, 57, 72–73, 79, 116, 118, 144, 183–184; elusive nature 3, 58, 70, 175, 179, 180; female perspectives 8, 17, 116–118, 134, 174, 183, 188; and gender 7, 41, 81n10, 115–118, 129, 134, 136–137, 145; highest *dharma* 136, 145; of householder 42; and *kāma* and *artha* 167; and *mokṣa* 16; patriarchal bias in 116, 135, 138, 146, 188; pluralistic understanding of 116, 181–182, 189; procedural understanding of 66, 68, 123, 128, 130, 140, 179; *sanātana dharma* 47, 71, 72, 115; secular and religious 68, 69, 81n8; son of Dharma 125, 180, 194; traditional understandings of 118, 132, 134, 137, 145, 179, 180; violating 6, 35, 36, 59, 65, 109, 120, 126, 130, 167, 180, 181; and women 116, 124, 146; *see also* *āpad-dharma* (*dharma* of extenuating circumstance); *kṣatriya-dharma*; *kula-dharma* (*dharma* of family obligations); *mokṣa-dharma* (*dharma* of renouncers); *rāja-dharma* (*dharma* of kings); *strī-dharma* (*dharma* of women); *sūkṣma dharma* (subtle *dharma*); *sva-dharma* (own *dharma*); *varṇāśrama-dharma* (*dharma* of caste and stage of life)
Dhātṛ (Ordainer) 24, 41, 84, 87, 98, 101, 105–111, 132, 192
Dhṛṣṭadyumna 51, 58–60, 70, 73, 116, 123, 179, 181, 192
Dhṛtarāṣṭra 8, 82, 104, 105, 106, 108, 111, 189, 192; and Draupadī 110, 121, 127–128, 131, 146n5; and Duryodhana 7, 17, 87, 88–103, 112, 113n4, 185, 186, 187, 188; and fate 36, 83, 86, 92–93, 98, 101, 105, 113n2; and Saṃjaya 40, 46, 50, 51, 61, 151, 168, 169; and *sūkṣma dharma* 179–180
dialectic 25–26, 54, 181, 183, 187; and *Bhagavad Gītā* 34, 157–160; and *dharma* 61, 153–154; and dialogue 20, 22 no. 13, 26–27, 149, 158, 182; and emotion 152–153; between fate and agency 7, 83, 85, 88, 103, 159; and *karma* 154; between *kula-dharma* and *kṣatriya dharma* 33
dialogical self/selves 117, 144, 151
dialogue 52, 54, 86, 87; and *Bhagavad Gītā* 8, 9, 148, 149, 151–160, 166; and *dharma* 19–21, 60–61, 80, 182,

188–189; and dialectic 25–27, 33–34, 149, 181–182; embedded dialogue 165; frame dialogues 6, 11, 61, 74, 75, 94; as hermeneutics 4, 17–21, 188–190; as intra-textuality 4, 12–17, 160, 186–188; and Kṛṣṇa's divinity 148, 150, 157, 173–175, 186; as literary form 1, 2, 5, 9, 57, 79, 151; non-closure 11, 34, 112, 183; and philosophy 9–11, 22n13, 25, 178, 181, 183; and Upaniṣads 3, 129, 178; as verbal encounter 4, 8–11, 181–186
dicing match 5, 6, 7, 8, 15, 17, 31, 49, 68, 101, 106, 107, 168, 171; allegory for fate and human agency 83, 86, 108–109; causes of 36, 76, 77, 82–114; discussion afterwards 8, 31, 49, 68, 115, 118, 119, 132, 138, 183; legality of 122, 146n4; and Nala 134; and war 98
Dīrghatamas 32
diṣṭa (fate) 77–78, 92, 98, 105, 172
divine eye (*divya cakṣus*) 46, 47, 49, 75, 169, 177n23
divine plan 7, 24, 73–75, 77–78, 84, 113, 159, 170
Dorter, Kenneth 33, 158
Draupadī 14, 81n12, 192; on *dharma* (and *sūkṣma dharma*) 21, 115–118, 119, 121, 122–123, 125–128, 129–132, 133, 136, 137, 140, 143, 145, 146, 174, 180–181, 183, 185, 189; and Dhṛtarāṣṭra's boons 93, 121, 127; disrobing 15, 120, 177, 146n1; and feminism 118, 127, 143–144; questions in the *sabhā* 31, 115–131, 142, 168; laughing at Duryodhana 96–97, 103, 114n10; as listener 46, 134, 143, 147n12; marriage 6, 57–81, 106, 171, 182, 184, 186, 187; and *pativratā* 117, 126–128, 132, 134, 136; previous birth 17, 61–64, 65, 71, 73, 74, 75–77, 78, 188; silence 58, 67, 75, 79; as Śrī 75, 101, 147n10; and Śukuntalā and Sulabhā 8, 116–118, 143–146, 162, 184; and Yudhiṣṭhira's decision to play dice 7, 83, 104, 107–108, 110, 111, 185; and Yudhiṣṭhira in forest 109, 132
Droṇa 120, 125, 180, 192, 196
Droṇa Parvan 51, 196
Drupada 6, 44, 51, 57–59, 61, 64, 66, 79, 87, 126, 182, 186–187, 189, 192; dialogue with Vyāsa 73–78; dialogue with Yudhiṣṭhira 67–73
duḥkha (sorrow, suffering) 28, 41, 44, 67, 95
Duḥṣanta 66, 116, 123, 134–138, 139, 144, 145, 170, 184, 192
Duḥśāsana 76, 119–120, 123, 125–126, 161, 180, 192
Dumézil, Georges 92
Duryodhana 5, 110, 111, 192; and Bhīṣma 24, 37–40, 41, 42, 46, 48, 49, 50, 53; criticism of Kṛṣṇa 176n20; despair after Yudhiṣṭhira's *rājasūya* 8, 87, 89, 90, 93, 95–97, 99, 100, 102–103, 114n9, 152, 183, 187; and *dharma* 97, 98, 99, 179; Dialogues with Dhṛtarāṣṭra 7, 17, 82–83, 88, 89–103, 112, 113n4, 185, 186, 187, 188; and Draupadī's question 119, 120, 125, 131; exposing his left thigh 121, 146n2; and fate 83, 87, 89, 93, 103, 113n2; fight with Bhīmasena 76, 166–168; and Gāndhārī 169–170; on Śiśuphāla 34

Earl, James 21n2
Edgerton, Franklin 88, 95, 114n7

Falk, Nancy 116, 118, 133, 143, 146n7
fate (*daiva*) 3, 24, 25, 26, 36, 77, 92–93, 94, 98, 107, 108, 112; and human agency 7, 83–88, 89, 101, 103, 109, 159, 182–183, 189
feminist/feminism 118, 127, 141, 143–144
Fisher King 27–29, 38, 52
Fitzgerald, James 21n3, 22n11, 55n14, 56n18, 59, 141, 176n7, 177n24
Framarin, Christopher 80n3

Gadamer, Hans-Georg 10, 17–19, 25
gambling 82, 103, 109, 110, 112, 113n5, 114n12, 119, 120, 125, 129, 168
Gāndhārī 8, 121; and divine eye 169, 177n23; and Kṛṣṇa 149, 166, 168–171, 172, 173, 174, 176n22, 185, 192
gandharva marriage 135
Gāṇḍīva bow 48, 148, 161
Ganeri, Jonardon 21n5, 56n16, 176n14
Gaṅgā (Bhīṣma's mother, river goddess) 23, 43, 51, 192

Gaṅgā (river) 74
Geen, Jonathan 21n7, 22n14, 63–65, 76, 80n4
gender 18, 24, 117, 142, 143, 144–145, 184, 185; and Ambā 44; anatomy 140; and *dharma* 7, 115, 116, 118; gender discrimination 130; gender equality 124, 126, 141, 144; gender hierarchies 56; gender ideology 118, 134; gender roles 136, 137, 139, 145; and *karma* 63; *Mahābhārata*'s views on 49; and marriage 81n10; and speech 64, 66, 79; and vows 42
González-Reimann, Luis 84

Halbfass, Wilhelm 19
Hara, Minoru 22n8, 60
Hāstinapura 27, 29, 30, 89, 192
Heesterman, Jan C. 109
Hegarty James 21n2, 176n12
Hegel 25, 33
hermeneutics 4, 17, 188
Hill, Peter 62, 77, 80n3, 84, 86, 103, 108, 113n2, 147n11, 171
Hiltebeitel, Alf 96, 123; on Balāka and Kauśika 56n16, 176n14; on Bhīṣma's sources 49, 56n55; on composition of the *Mahābhārata* 2, 14–15, 88, 150, 175n3; on divine eye 177n23; on Draupadī's forest dialogue with Yudhiṣṭhira 132, 147n11; on Draupadī's laughter 97; on Draupadī's questions 129–130, 143; on five Indra's 75; on frame stories 22n9, 114n8; on Kuntī's words 81n7; on the *sabhā* 116, 122; on *sva-dharma* 154; on *tarka* 162–163; on Vyāsa 47, 80n2
Hopkins, E. Washburn 12–13
Hösle, Vittorio 9
Hudson, Emily 22n10, 62, 80n3, 94, 130–131, 173
human agency (*puruṣakāra*) 3, 26, 63, 113; and divine agency 57, 58; and fate 7, 83–88, 89, 101, 103, 109, 159, 182–183, 189

Indra 43, 89, 99–101, 160, 167, 192; five Indras 61, 63, 73–77, 188
Indraprastha 100, 192
intra-textuality 4, 12, 27, 181, 186

Jaini, A.N. 71
Jamison, Stephanie 55n3, 80n1, 116, 146n7, 146n8, 147n14
Janaka 2, 116, 123, 134, 145, 165, 192, 196; dialogue with Sulabhā 138–143
Janamejaya 1, 6, 51, 67, 74, 82, 93, 95, 99, 112, 135, 168, 192, 195
Jarāsaṃdha 34, 55n8, 55n9
Jaṭilā 71, 72

kāla (time) 84, 87, 94, 108, 157, 159, 171
karma 2, 3, 61–64, 65, 73, 75, 81n11, 154, 158, 166, 170, 183
karma-yoga 26, 87, 101, 111, 128, 139, 154, 155, 158, 159, 165, 166
Karṇa 76, 77, 123, 125, 126, 131, 143, 192, 196
Karṇa Parvan 47, 48, 154, 175, 176n13, 196; Kṛṣṇa and Arjuna dialogue 80n5, 113n5, 161–164, 166, 167, 173
Katz, Ruch Cecily 176n6
Kauravas 1, 5, 7, 8, 38, 45, 76, 77, 82, 84, 96, 110, 115, 118–122, 124–126, 130–132, 135, 143, 169, 172, 180, 183
Kauśika 46–49, 53, 162–164, 179, 180–181, 187, 192, 196
Klaes, Norbert 107
Kristeva, Julia 22n14
Kṛṣṇa 11, 40, 51, 52, 74, 82, 123, 148–150; and *Anu Gītā* 164–166; and Balarāma 166–168; and *Bhagavad Gītā* 17, 85, 133, 139, 150, 151–160, 175; death of Kṛṣṇa 170–171, 185; and *dharma* 21, 59, 153–154, 158, 160, 161, 167, 175; and disrobing of Draupadī 146n1; and divine eye 47, 49; and divinity 7, 8, 17, 35, 36, 113, 148–150, 152, 155, 156–157, 161, 164, 169, 173–175, 176n11, 184, 188; and Gāndhārī 168–171, 185; as God 8, 150, 151, 155, 157, 164, 169, 171–175; in *Karṇa Parvan* 48, 80n5, 161–164; laughing at Duryodhana 96, 97, 114n10; and *Mahābhārata* 150–151; and Śiśupāla 34–37; and *sūkṣma dharma* (subtle *dharma*) 55n10, 161–163, 178–179, 180–181; and Uttaṅka 172–173
kṣatriya-dharma 24, 52, 61, 97–98, 99, 107, 120, 153, 163; and *kula-dharma* 26, 33–35, 105, 153, 158; and *sva-dharma* 153–154; and vows 29, 42–43
kula-dharma (*dharma* of family obligations) 20, 27, 73, 107; and

kṣatriya-dharma 26, 33–35, 105, 153, 158; and *rāja-dharma* 137
Kuntī 6, 57–59, 61, 64–67, 68, 70–74, 78, 79, 101, 123, 161, 184–185, 193, 197
Kurukṣetra 148, 168, 172

Malinar, Angelika 21n3, 132, 133, 147n11, 176n11
Mānava Dharmaśāstra 123, 146n8, 147n14
Manzo, Lawrence 22n11
Matilal, Bimal Krishna 4, 56n16, 58, 80, 128–130, 162, 163, 167, 172–173, 175, 176n14
Mausāla Parvan 170, 171, 174, 197
McGrath, Kevin 150
Mehta, Maheshi 113n3
Meiland, Justin 168
Minkowski, Chris 21n2
mokṣa 2, 3, 16, 18, 85, 139, 142, 166
Mokṣadharma 138
mokṣa-dharma (*dharma* of renunciation) 20, 26, 130, 142, 196
Mukherji, Gangeya 18–21, 85–86, 188

Naimiṣa Forest 1, 51, 74, 193
Naimiṣa *ṛṣis* 61, 94
Nala 83, 109, 193
Namuci 98, 101, 193
Nārada 35, 43, 82, 171, 193
Narasimhan, C.V. 22n11
Nārāyaṇa 35, 74, 75, 76, 160, 193
Nikāyas 26
Nikulin, Dmitri 9, 22n13, 25, 149, 158
nivṛtti 16, 28, 85–86, 113n1, 189
niyoga 32–33, 39, 55n6
Norther Recension 97

O'Flaherty, Wendy Doniger 60
Olivelle, Patrick 81n8

Pañcendra Upākhyāna 74–76
Pāṇḍavas 5, 24, 35, 39, 49, 79, 89, 91, 106, 107, 120, 121, 166, 167, 174; and Draupadī 6, 57, 58, 59, 61, 62, 67, 68, 69, 71, 73, 78, 82, 123, 131, 134; and Duryodhana 93, 95–99, 101, 102, 114n10; exile 38, 77; as five Indras 74–76; war with Kauravas 8, 46, 84, 90, 168, 169, 172
Paṇḍu 39, 193
pativratā 117, 126–128, 132, 134, 136
Patton, Laurie 21n1, 21n3, 22n12, 117–118, 127, 134, 175n1
philosophy 4, 13, 85, 172; and dialogue 9–10, 22n13, 181; *Mahābhārata* as philosophy 11
Plato 10–11, 19, 25, 127
polyandrous marriage 6, 17, 31, 55n10, 57–58, 60, 62, 64, 66, 68, 76, 77, 87, 105, 121, 126, 147n15, 179, 182, 188
Prahlāda/Prahrāda 100–101, 120, 193
praśna (question) 3, 122, 113n1, 189
pratijñā (promise) 29, 31, 33, 38, 39, 51, 69, 135; *see also* vow/s; *vrata*
pravṛtti 16, 26, 85–86

rāja-dharma (*dharma* of kings) 20, 130, 137, 196
Rāja-dharma Parvan 100
rājasūya 24, 34, 35, 37, 82, 89, 90–91, 95–96, 99, 100, 102, 103, 112, 152, 195
rākṣasa marriage 30, 40, 184
Rāma Jāmadagnya 38, 42–46, 69, 165, 193
Ramanujan, A.K. 3, 15, 20, 22n14, 88, 178
Ram-Prasad, Chakravarthi 21n1, 22n12, 56n19, 117, 140–141, 144, 157
reactive attitudes 78, 86–87, 103, 113, 159
rebirth 61–63, 65, 73, 75
Reich, Tamar 1, 12, 15–16, 37, 55n11, 177n27
Ṛgveda 59

sabhā 8, 104, 115, 118, 119, 127, 137, 143, 180, 183; and *dharma* 116, 122, 128, 145; and gender 117, 186, 188
Sabhā Parvan 37, 55n8, 88, 112, 146n9, 195
Sahadeva 96, 114n11, 193
Śakuni 7, 82, 83, 89–91, 93–95, 98–100, 104–112, 114, 119–120, 122, 169, 193
Śakuntalā 7–8, 17, 66, 116–118, 121, 123, 128, 131, 139, 140, 143–147, 162, 170, 182–187, 191, 193, 195; dialogue with Duḥṣanta 134–138
Śālva 41–42, 193
Śalya Parvan 113n5, 166, 173, 196
samaya (agreement) 23, 27, 69, 98, 136, 147n15
Saṃjaya 40, 46, 50–51, 61, 92, 106, 151, 152, 155–158, 167–169, 181, 193

sāṃkhya 140, 158
Śaṃtanu 5, 23, 27–31, 38, 69, 152, 193
Śānti Parvan 46, 47, 49, 53, 54, 55n5, 88, 99–100, 103, 114n8, 130, 134, 138, 162, 187, 196
satya (truth) 3, 28, 31, 47, 101, 162
Satyabhāmā 127, 133–134, 193
Satyavatī 5, 23, 24, 27–34, 37–39, 42, 46, 48, 49, 52–53, 66, 69, 105, 182, 184, 193, 195
Śaunaka 2, 21n7, 94, 194, 195
Sen, Prabal Kumar 170
Sharma, Arvind 160, 165, 176n19
Shulman, David 3, 83, 147n13
Śikhaṇḍin 40–41, 44–45, 50–52, 193
Śiśupāla 5, 24, 53, 149, 178–179, 182, 193, 195; dialogue with Bhīṣma 34–37; killing of 89, 91, 100
Śiva 44, 62–65, 74–77, 193
Smith, John 22n11, 74, 84, 94, 114n13, 146n2, 176n21
Smith, P. Christopher 10
śoka (sorrow) 91, 95, 100, 152, 176n18
Southern Recension 81n11, 96–97
Śrī 74, 75, 91, 100, 101, 193
śruti 30, 161–163
Strawson, Peter 86–87
strī-dharma (*dharma* of women) 21, 86, 117, 128, 145, 196
Strī Parvan 168, 169, 177n24
Sudeṣṇā 133–134, 193
Śukra 30–31, 194
sūkṣma dharma (subtle *dharma*) 3, 20, 22n8, 22n10, 34–35, 55n10, 60, 69–70, 72, 117, 119, 122, 125, 130, 133, 134, 145, 154, 161–163, 173, 178–181
Sukthankar, Vishnu S. 13–14, 20, 22n15, 22n17, 59, 81n11, 175n2, 176n3
Sulabhā 7–8, 17, 56n19, 116–118, 121, 123, 128, 130, 131, 134, 144–146, 162, 183, 184, 185, 186, 187, 194; dialogue with Janaka 138–143
Sullivan, Bruce 21n3, 22n15, 29, 36, 55n2, 62, 80n2, 154, 160
Sutherland, Sally 132, 146n7
Sutton, Nicholas 85–86, 113n1, 139, 150
sva-dharma (own *dharma*) 85–86, 142, 153–154, 162
svayaṃvara 57, 61, 64, 65, 67, 68, 75, 80n1

tapas 41, 43, 62, 136, 171
theology 150, 151, 163, 164, 175, 186
Thomas, Lynn 21n3, 39
Thompson, George 29
Tiekan, Herman 165
Tubb, Gary 22n23

Udyoga Parvan 37–38, 40, 51, 80n5, 110, 122, 146n4, 146n5, 170, 176n5, 196
Ugraśravas 1, 2, 51, 61, 75, 93–94, 106, 112, 194, 195, 197
Upaniṣads 2–3, 11, 19, 20, 26, 129, 156, 164, 178, 192, 193
Uttaṅka 8, 149, 157, 166, 169, 171, 174, 194, 197; and Kṛṣṇa 172–173

Vairocana 167, 194
Vaiśaṃpāyana 1, 6, 23, 27, 29–33, 35–40, 42, 49–53, 61, 67, 72, 74, 82, 91, 93–97, 109–110, 122, 132–133, 135–137, 159, 168, 171, 184, 187, 194, 195, 197
Van Buitenen 4, 22n11, 23, 34, 36, 84, 88, 94, 104, 112, 146n2, 160
Vanita, Ruth 140–141
varṇa-dharma 107, 153
varṇāśrama-dharma (*dharma* of caste and stage of life) 20, 86
Vasus 23, 191
Vicitravīrya 23, 30, 32, 38, 46, 194
Vidura 7, 83, 89, 91–93, 95, 98, 101, 108, 110, 112, 119–121, 129–131, 133, 180, 185, 194; dialogue with Yudhiṣṭhira 104–107
Vikarṇa 120, 129, 194
Virāṭa Parvan 110, 195
vow/s (*vrata*, *pratijña*) 29, 36, 69, 79, 87, 131; Ambā's vows 41, 44, 45, 62; Arjuna's vows 51–52, 80n5, 161, 163, 167; Bhīmasena's vow 120, 166, 167, 168; Bhīṣma's vows 5–6, 8, 17, 23–56, 57, 65, 66, 111, 135, 152, 179, 182, 183, 184, 185, 186, 187, 189; Duḥṣanta's vow 144; and gender 65–66, 79, 80n5, 185; Kauśika's vow 47, 48, 53, 162, 164, 180; Rāma Jāmadagnya's vows 42–43, 45, 80n5; Śikhaṇḍin's vow 51–52; Yudhiṣṭhira's vows 105–107, 109, 110, 111, 146n9; *see also pratijñā*; *vrata*
vrata (vow) 29, 41, 42, 43, 44, 45, 48, 51, 69, 105, 106; *see also pratijñā*; vow/s

Vyāsa 11, 80n2, 133, 194; and divine eye 46, 47, 114n8, 169, 177n23; and Draupadī's marriage 6, 57, 58, 59, 68, 70–72, 78, 79, 81n11, 126, 176n10, 182, 184, 185, 186; and Draupadī's previous birth 17, 61–64, 67, 75–77, 188; and five Indras 61, 73–75, 188; and *niyoga* 33

White, David Gordon 147n18
Wilmot, Paul 84, 113, 114n15
Winternitz, Moriz 12, 22n17
Woods, Julian 85, 87, 89, 92

yoga 2, 3, 138–139, 147n18, 155–156, 158

Yudhiṣṭhira 86, 88, 94, 102–103, 194; and argument with Arjuna 161, 163; and Bhīṣma 5, 24, 32, 46–49, 50, 53, 130, 162; decision to play dice 7, 8, 36, 82–83, 87, 90–91, 93, 98, 101, 104–111, 114n12; and *dharma* 11, 21, 31, 55, 59–60, 67–73, 79, 125, 131, 179, 181, 182, 184, 189; and Draupadī's marriage 6, 57–60, 64–73, 74, 77, 78, 87, 126, 186, 188; and forest dialogue with Draupadī 132–133; and Kṛṣṇa 40; and the *rājasūya* 7, 89, 95–96, 99–100, 152; and Śikhaṇḍin 51; and Śiśupāla 34, 37; and staking Draupadī 115, 119–121, 122, 129, 146n4, 185, 186